The Earl of Oxford
and the Making of
"Shakespeare"

The Earl of Oxford and the Making of "Shakespeare"

The Literary Life of Edward de Vere in Context

RICHARD MALIM

McFarland & Company, Inc., Publishers
Jefferson, North Carolina, and London

Acknowledgments The translation of Ronsard, owned by the estate of Peter Levi, 1988 is reproduced with permission of Johnson & Alcock Ltd. The Peacham Chronogram is reproduced with the permission of the Marquess of Bath, Longleat, Warminster, Wiltshire, United Kingdom. Detail from the Barberini Titian *Venus and Adonis* is reproduced with the permission of Soprintendenza Speciale per il Patrimonio Storico Artistico ed Etnoantropologico e per il Polo Museale della, Rome. Fresco of the Horse by Giulio Romano is reproduced with the permission of the Palazzo Te, Mantua. Fresco of *Achilles Avenging Patroclus* by Giulio Romano from the Palazzo Te by concession of the Ministero per I Beni e le Attività Culturali, Mantua. Alabaster tomb of the 13th Earl of Oxford is reproduced with the permission of the Vicar and Churchwardens of St. Nicholas Church, Castle Hedingham and Mr. Charles Bird. Portrait of the Duke of Urbino is reproduced with the permission of Soprintendenza Speciale per il Polo Museale, Florence. Portrait of Elizabeth Trentham, Lady Cockayne, by Sir Peter Lely is reproduced with the permission of the owner and courtesy of Mr. Jeremy Crick. Portrait of the 17th Earl of Oxford is reproduced by kind permission of Ms. Katherine Chiljan. Portrait of the 3rd Earl of Southampton is reproduced with the permission of the Bridgeman Art Library. The *Minerva Britanna* title page is reproduced with the permission of The National Library of Australia. Thomas Jenner's engraving of the Two Henrys is reproduced with the permission of the Syndics of The Fitzwilliam Museum, Cambridge, Great Britain. The 1623 Folio pages are reproduced with the permission of the State Reference Library, State Library of New South Wales (Call no. SAFE/AB/Y1/1). The six signatures of William Shakespeare are reproduced by courtesy of Ms. Diana Price.

LIBRARY OF CONGRESS CATALOGUING-IN-PUBLICATION DATA

Malim, Richard.
 The Earl of Oxford and the making of "Shakespeare" :
the literary life of Edward de Vere in context / Richard Malim.
  p. cm.
 Includes bibliographical references and index.

 ISBN 978-0-7864-6313-8
 softcover : acid free paper ∞

 1. Oxford, Edward De Vere, Earl of, 1550–1604. 2. Shakespeare, William, 1564–1616 — Authorship — Oxford theory. 3. Oxford, Edward De Vere, Earl of, 1550–1604 — Authorship. 4. Authors, English — Early modern, 1500–1700 — Biography. I. Title.
 PR2947.O9M37 2012
 821'.309 — dc23   2011046187

BRITISH LIBRARY CATALOGUING DATA ARE AVAILABLE

© 2012 Richard Malim. All rights reserved

No part of this book may be reproduced or transmitted in any form or by any means, electronic or mechanical, including photocopying or recording, or by any information storage and retrieval system, without permission in writing from the publisher.

On the cover: Edward de Vere, 1575 (unknown artist after lost original 1575); *inset* William Shakespeare, 1610 (the Chandos portrait, artist and authenticity unconfirmed)

Manufactured in the United States of America

McFarland & Company, Inc., Publishers
 Box 611, Jefferson, North Carolina 28640
 www.mcfarlandpub.com

To Jane: without whose love and support, much-taxed
patience and endless tolerance and forgiveness...

And to the memory of the unknown Scotsman,
who in 1576 recognized the pirates'
prisoner and saved his life;

And to the memory of Ben Jonson, who in 1623
recognized the writer's genius and saved his works.

Contents

Acknowledgments	ix
Introduction	1
ONE. English Literature 1530–1575	7
TWO. The Life 1550–1575	13
THREE. Oxford in Italy	46
FOUR. The Revolution in English Literature	61
FIVE. The Revolution in the Theater	69
SIX. The Life 1576–1590	76
SEVEN. The Life 1590–1604	164
EIGHT. Aftermath	197
Afterword	230
Appendix A—Tables of Literary References	232
Appendix B—William Shakespeare: The Irrelevant Life	235
Chapter Notes	265
Bibliography	297
Index	303

Acknowledgments

My profound thanks are offered to the following:

Mrs. Elizabeth Imlay: the value of her encouragement and professional rigor cannot be exaggerated.

The progenitors of the De Vere Society Playdating Project: A. M. Challinor, C. H. Dams, the late Philip Johnson, Mrs. Emma Jolly and Kevin Gilvary.

Those authors of anti–Stratfordian books — who freely acknowledge a debt to J. Looney, *Shakespeare Identified* (Cecil Palmer, 1923) and B. M. Ward: *The 17th Earl of Oxford from Contemporary Documents* (Murray, 1928) — namely: *Eva Turner Clark—The R. L. Miller Edition* (Kennikat, 1971) which contains substantial contributions from Ruth L. Miller, Admiral H. Holland, B. R. Saunders and C. W. Barrell; Charlton Ogburn, *The Mystery of William Shakespeare* (Clarendon edition 1988); Diana Price, *Shakespeare's Unorthodox Biography* (Greenwood 2001); and Mark Anderson, *Shakespeare by Another Name* (Gotham 2005).

Linda Proud, who read the original manuscript and proposed many of those improving changes which I have adopted, and to the Writers' Workshop of Bicester, Oxfordshire.

That marvelous and sainted scholar Nina Green and her website www.oxford-shakespeare.com.

The following members of the American and United Kingdom Oxfordian Societies, to whose originality, research and primary scholarship (and in some cases websites) add much to the force of the arguments I adduce: M. Alexander, P. Altrocchi, C. Beauclerk, Dorna Bewley, W. Boyle, D. Charlton, Katherine Chiljan, Bernice Cohen, Alice Crampin, J. Crick, F. Davis, M. Delahoyde, R. Desper, R. Detobel, P.W. Dickson, Barbara Flues, Fran Gidley, G. Goldstein, Rima Greenhill, J. Hamill, W. R. Hess, Donna B. Hamilton, R. Jimenez, Lynne Kositzky, Uwe Laugwitz, Lu Lewellen, Judge P. O'Brien, C. Paul, A, Pointon, Galina Popova, R. Prechter, J. Rollett, S. Saunders, E. Showerman, S. Smith, R, Stritmatter, A. Tarica, H. Wember, A. Werth, R. Whalen, C. M. Willis, D. Wright.

To the memory of those now deceased: Michael Brame, Robert Brazil,

Edward Holmes, Philip Johnson, K.C. Ligon, Peter Moore, N. Magri, Alan Robinson, Joseph Sobran.

And those other members and supporters whose assistance I have failed to acknowledge in this list, to whom I apologize now.

And the members generally of the two societies, whose friendship and interest has been a cushion of inspiration: the De Vere Society (The Courtyard, 45 Royal York Crescent, Bristol BS8 4JS, UK. www.deveresociety.co.uk); and the Shakespeare Oxford Society (P.O. Box 808, Yorktown Heights NY 10598, U.S.A. www.Shakepeare-Oxford.com).

And the staff and volunteers at the University of Bristol Theatre Collection; Lyme Regis Public Library, Dorset; Lymenet, Lyme Regis, Dorset.

Lastly I thank those polite and patient friends whose ears have been bent when the word Shakespeare comes up in conversation.

Introduction

The Aim of This Book

In April 1576, the twenty-six-year-old Edward de Vere, Earl of Oxford (1550–1604), returned from his journey to Italy, then the cultural center of Europe. His journey is the most important in terms of world literary development. This book investigates and establishes the basis for that claim, and reveals the link between his literary career and the changes in the forms and status of English literature and language. It shows him as the real writer[1] of the Shakespeare canon and much more.

The current "orthodox" view describes literature in English in the 1570s as "drab,"[2] this drabness being followed by a sudden flowering of talent across the board from the mid–1580s, led by Lyly, Spencer, Sidney and Marlowe, followed by William Shakespeare from 1590 on. "Sometimes, in speaking of English Literature, we are apt to forget that the first twenty five years of the queen's reign did not produce much of peculiar excellence. The great surge of poetry and prose which we associate with her was not truly prophesied until the eighties of the sixteenth century and did not reach its fulfillment until the nineties."[3] The weakness of the argument lies in the word "prophesied": as we shall see, contemporary critics did not prophesy, they recorded their opinions of events in literature.

In contrast, the new Elizabethan critics of the time, Richard Mulcaster (*The First Part of the Elementary*, 1582) and Stephen Gosson (for example, in his *Plays Confuted in Five Actions*, 1582) clearly indicate that by, say, 1580, that a flowering of talent — which may, because of the completeness and suddenness of its appearance, properly be called a revolution — had already happened. So in reality there is a gap in that period circa 1575/80, between the earlier "barbarous" period and the later cultural magnificence, for which the modern critic can provide no serious explanation, let alone an alternative to the claims of Oxford.

I am establishing or in some sense restoring the thesis that the primary leader of the English literary revolution was Oxford writing as "Shakespeare." The primacy of "Shakespeare," both in talent and in time, was in fact acknowledged by all critics up to, and to an extent including, the Irish scholar and barrister Edmund Malone, with his 1778 *An Attempt to Ascertain the Order in Which the Plays of Shakespeare Were Written*. Malone and his successors insist that "Shakespeare" must be the insufficiently educated and otherwise deficient William Shakespeare of Stratford-upon-Avon (1564–1616). Many of those earlier post–Restoration critics would have subscribed to that view, because the dates of Shakespeare were not uppermost in their minds when they wrote their critiques. Biography was a new discipline, and when applied to William Shakespeare (first by the playwright and critic Nicholas Rowe in 1709), produced the strange result that, if he were the primary revolutionary leader, he could only have been in his mid-teens by 1580, by which time, as contemporary critics tell us, the revolution was in full flood. For that reason alone (the appendix in particular investigates others) we can readily see that William Shakespeare cannot be "Shakespeare the revolutionary."

The quotations from later critics in this book are only a selection. They serve to point up in "orthodox" terms the arguments which merit further examination and criticism in the light of the revolution, and the logical extent in which their authors travel in rejection of that general misconception. Some of these opinions (whether the authors would like it or not) support my thesis.

This book traces that revolution both in the use of language in prose and poetry and in the theater as evidenced by contemporary critics; shows that the writers of the 1580s on, Lyly (who for a time was Oxford's secretary), Spenser, Sidney and Marlowe, are children of that revolution; outlines a literary life of Oxford; and assesses the attitude of his critics up to Malone. My intention is to illustrate the true and infinite extent of Oxford's triumph. In addition, I refute the "orthodox" objection to Oxford's claims, that some of the plays are dated (by them, as they are locked into Malone's dating scheme) to after his death.

The Failure of Modern Critical Perspective

> *The fact that an opinion is widely held is no evidence whatever that it is not utterly absurd.*—Bertrand Russell

William Shakespeare of Stratford-upon-Avon 1564–1616, will be considered and contrasted with the Earl of Oxford 1550–1604: poet, playwright, producer and actor; also athlete, diplomat, spymaster and pamphleteer.

Modern critics may agree: "In his own time, Shakespeare was one author among many," and "Shakespeare, once part of a group, has been reduced [sic] over time to pre-eminent singularity."[4] These opinions are totally out of line with the facts, and are the consequence of the distortion of literary history I have described above and the overlooking of Shakespeare juvenilia.[5] Modern critics are in a bind for another reason, because they are constrained by the dates of William Shakespeare, whom they find they have to place as subsequent to Marlowe (1564–1593), though they are aged the same. While they can point to the record of the plays and verse naming William Shakespeare as author with printing dates from 1593 on (*Venus and Adonis* and *The Rape of Lucrece*) and 1598 (those plays with Shakespeare's name on the title page[6]), they have to discount the clear references in the plays to much earlier dates of composition, and to earlier versions of them.

In effect, by forcing "Shakespeare's" works into a date span from as late as 1590 on, they devalue his primacy as Dryden's "Homer, or Father of our dramatic Poets," and reduce his towering contribution to the development of English as the primary world language power.

Lyly was experimenting with romantic comedy "as early as"[7] 1583, Marlowe's *Tamburlaine* came out in 1587, and 1589/90 saw Greene's *Friar Bacon and Friar Bungay* and Kidd's *The Spanish Tragedy*. All these appeared after the revolution.

By failing to examine the pre–1580 period properly without preconceptions, these critics inadvertently create a chasm, which in part by distortion they fill by placing Lyly, Marlowe and the others in front of "Shakespeare" as his exemplars. Edmund Malone's solution was apparently more radical in effect: he dismissed as contemptible all plays produced before 1592 — "the titles are scarcely known, except to antiquaries nor is there one of them that will bear a second perusal."[8] In this sweeping condemnation he relegates to that outer darkness where cultural nonentities are found, the quite reputable and competent authors of *The Arraignment of Paris* (Peele, c. 1582), *The Spanish Tragedy* (Kidd, c. 1587), *Friar Bacon and Friar Bungay* (Greene, c. 1590), and the entire Marlowe canon (written c. 1582–1592). This would be a critical bellyflop, caused by Malone's need for his dating system to reconcile the received truth of Shakespeare's priority in time, with William Shakespeare as chief artist in the revolution.

The critics give credit to the works of many of "Shakespeare's" successors as sources for him to use. Thomas Nashe, playwright, novelist, wit and satirist (as well as a firm admirer of Oxford) wrote in 1589: "If you will entreat him fair on a frosty morning, he will afford you whole Hamlets, I should say handfuls, of tragical speeches."[9] The critics then have to invent explanations for that reference (which wrecks their dating scheme by putting his most accomplished play to a year before they say he had written anything) by erecting them on a fictitious (but brilliant) play which some call ur–Hamlet.[10] This piece of fiction has to be by an otherwise un-evidenced playwright, good enough and well-reputed enough by that date to evoke the reference, yet otherwise totally unknown. They also ignore the cut at the successor-plagiarists of "Shakespeare."

In addition, these modern critics freely admit that they invent facts from which they draw their conclusions, logical and illogical. The absence of real facts forces them to do so: "No formal life of Shakespeare laying claim to serious regard can limit itself to facts and to logical deductions from the facts alone; the writing of literary biography after all requires the play of literary imagination."[11] Why should literary biography differ from any other kind? As if in answer to this question (and in direct contradiction of his later dictum quoted above), the same critic had already written rules for the examination of Elizabethan dramatic authorship: "Rule 7: Intuitions, convictions and subjective judgments generally, carry no weight as evidence. This is no matter how learned, respected or confident the authority."[12] A later critic growled, "Should have been Rule 1."[13]

Antonia Fraser[14] writes that, as a teenager, she read Lytton Strachey on Cardinal Manning, but when she looked into the facts via her school library, "a very different picture emerged" from that portrayed by Strachey. "Gradually as I pursued the topic, I became aware of Strachey's daring sallies into 'artistic truth' (as opposed to historical truth)," and later she wrote that "historical truth not Stracheyesque truth must be established"; to which I would add that, if historical truth cannot be established, the historian should say so.

Nevertheless, in writing of William Shakespeare one modern biographer, perhaps with honest self-deprecation, has to write, "I quite often risk conjecture, in the hope of putting some spectral, or speculative, flesh on those well guarded bones. I am aware that I am laying myself open both to challenge and, at times, to flat disbelief."[15] A second in more self-confident mood has "found that many assumptions about the dramatist had to be overturned and that others could be fleshed out to give a much stronger sense of the man's experience (i.e., he has to replace one lot of fictions with another)."[16] "To understand how Shakespeare used his imagination to transform his life into art," warns a third,[17] "it is *important* to use *our* imagination" (my italics).

The convoluted English of one summary, "Perhaps we should despair of ever bridging the vertiginous expanse between the sublimity of the subject and the mundane inconsequence of the documentary record,"[18] may disguise the subconscious perception that his life's dedication was misplaced. It is noticeable that Malone himself became hopelessly bogged down over 24 years[19] and failed to come anywhere near completing his biography.

Sometimes critics are careful with the facts, but from them produce a conclusion with no standing in logic. By way of example at this stage, another biographer has no intention of taking on board the whole of Ben Jonson's caricature[20] of Shakespeare as Sogliardo-cum-Sordido in *Every Man Out of His Humour*. We are allowed to mock the pretensions of the coat of arms, the motto, and the use of gold in the coat of arms in that play, and link *As You Like It*'s Malvolio's yellow cross gartering with them, because "It would come naturally to (William) Shakespeare[21]—to parody his pretensions to gentility at the same time as he pursued them with the utmost seriousness, to mock that which was most important to him." Where critics realize it, they have to agree with this suggestion if only to keep the show on the road: an earlier critic writes after referring to the opening lines of *The Merry Wives of Windsor*, "yet these very words..., so applicable to himself, suggest that he may have looked upon his own pretensions with a tolerant smile. His was no solemn-faced and aggressive claim to birth and a coat of arms."[22] Without a "solemn-faced and aggressive claim," he nevertheless made three, no doubt very expensive, applications in four years to Garter King of Arms (see appendix, pages 249ff).

This attitude now comes under severe attack principally from Professor Shapiro, who blames Malone for opening the floodgates to such autobiographical speculation, which he correctly assesses as valueless, and "even if Shakespeare occasionally drew in his poems and plays on personal experiences, and I don't doubt he did, I don't see how anyone can know with any confidence if or when or where he does so.... It is wiser to accept that these experiences can never be recovered."[23] Shapiro falls back on Shakespeare's imagination — full and rich though the author's was, there must have been life experiences on which to base the exercise of that imagination. That basis is found in the study of the life of Oxford, as this book demonstrates.

While such critics are quick to denounce all contrary evidence as "circumstantial,"[24] the propensity of some to find biographical or local allusions gives rise to the wisdom of this comment: "Yet the difficulty of establishing such allusions[25]—and the risk of looking silly in proposing them—tend to be disproportionate to the size of the interpretative claims that are made for them. The gap between artistic achievement and biographical explanation for it seems unbridgeable, sometimes embarrassingly so." Perhaps the critic had in mind the reference to the school wall in Stratford that needed constant repair in the 1570s, which is linked to Snout playing the part of the Wall in the rustics' playlet in *A Midsummer Night's Dream*.

Most critics do not wish to enter upon any academic debate or examination. They can point to the huge disparity in the quality of the outpourings of the anti–Stratford brigade, some of which ranges from the anti-scholastic to the frankly lunatic, and to avoid a serious debate on the shortcomings of their approach.

Here is an illustration of this facet of the current critical approach. While quoting an unrepresentative passage of anti–Stratfordian theory from a gentleman I had never heard of, the critic wishes to claim for herself "the standards of scholarly fair play."[26] When her application of two different standards was pointed out to her, she did not reply in detail.[27] Others rely on the mud of derision, rather than argument. Perhaps that kind of critic might learn from an earlier writer: "But always their [the nonbelievers'] fervent disloyalty to Stratford is based on an equally fervent loyalty to the author of the plays: the anti–Stratfordians are not denigrators of the poet: they see themselves as rescue parties allotting the glory where they believe it to be due. This must be saluted as an honorable exercise, whether you agree or disagree with the theories and attributions that are advanced."[28] To which I would add that it is perverse to disagree with the facts or the volume of circumstantial evidence, and an honorable exercise to allot the due amount of "glory."

In general, the modern "orthodox" critic will not read, let alone draw benefit from, this book. Others may take the chance to correct four centuries of error.

CHAPTER ONE

English Literature 1530–1575

"Seldom indeed has the spirit of an age changed so quickly as that which viewed the vernacular as inherently rude and uneloquent. The suddenness with which writers began to recognize the eloquent nature of the mother tongue enables us to date the turning point not earlier than 1575 nor later than 1580."[1]

The question is to what extent this large and confident claim in "the standard work[2] on attitudes to the language in the sixteenth and seventeenth centuries" is justified. First we must consider the position prior to that "turning point." Put another way, into what kind of cultural world in England was Edward de Vere born on April 12, 1550?

To give a flavor of the regard in which critics held English in the middle of the sixteenth century, the virulent nationalist Andrew Borde (writer of the first medical treatise in English, writing in 1549) in praise of all things English and in mockery of all things foreign baldly states (here and throughout I modernize the spelling, because it is tedious to sort the "i"s and "j"s, the "u"s and "v"s and repeat the vagaries of earlier spelling generally, and "improve" the punctuation): "The speech of England is a base speech to other noble speeches, as Italian, Castilian [Spanish] and French; howbeit the speech of late days is amended."

One of the earliest exponents of modern English prose is Sir Thomas Elyot who in 1531 writes in his book *The Governour* that poets who write in Latin "do express them [good ideas] incomparably with more grace and delectation to the reader than our English tongue may yet comprehend." Perhaps by "yet comprehend" he may mean "yet aspire to," for he writes in 1543 (in a translation of Isocrates) that he undertook the translation

> to the intent only that I would essay [try to find out] if our English tongue mought [might, ought to] receive the quick and proper sentences [ideas] pronounced by the Greeks. And in this experience I have found, if I be not much

deceived, that the form of speaking used by the Greeks, called in Greek and also in Latin phrasis, much nearer approacheth to that which at this day we use than the order of the Latin tongue: I mean in the sentences, and not in the words: which I doubt not will be affirmed by them, who sufficiently instructed in all the said three tongues, shall with a good judgement read this work.

In other words he is saying that the English language is perfectly capable of reproducing classic ideas, without making any claims culturally or in eloquence for it.

At this period there begins a great outpouring, particularly of Latin and Greek translations. In 1548, Robert Recorde in his *The First Boke of the Introduction of Knowledge* writes to the ten-year-old Edward VI, the handling that "this sentence in Cicero am I loath to translate into English, partly for that unto your Majesty it needeth no translation, but especially knowing how far the grace of Tully's [Cicero's] eloquence doth excel any Englishman's tongue and much more exceedeth the baseness of my Barbarous style."

About the same time the educational humanist Roger Ascham in the dedication of *Toxophilus* (1545) says, "And as for the Latin or Greek Tongue, every thing is so excellently done in them, that none can do better: in the English tongue contrary, every thing in a manner so meanly, both in the matter and no man can do worse," and later in *The Scholemaster* (1570), while recognizing the efficacy and versatility of English, "Yet, nevertheless, the rudeness of common and mother tongues, is no bar to wise speaking. For in the rudest country, and most barbarous mother language, many be found (who) can speak very wisely."

Yet there must have been some who recognized that there was still a problem, as the volume of translations published in the first decade of Elizabeth's reign multiplied fourfold.

Many writers of the period emphasize this cultural and eloquential deficiency (while sometimes indicating that it is these deficiencies which affect their translations in particular, and this sometimes with mock humility). In 1559 Jasper Heywood, translating Seneca's *Troas*, apologizes for his own limitations, adding, "And how far above my power to keep that grace and majesty of style that Seneca doth, when both so excellent a writer hath passed the reach of all imitation, and also that this our English tongue (as many think and here I find) is far unable to compare with the latin."

Likewise Alexander Neville translating Seneca's *Oedipus* in 1563 reveals his opinion: "When first ... I travailed of this present Tragedy, written by the most grave, virtuous and Christian Ethnic [i.e., neither Jew nor Christian] (for so doubteth not Erasmus to term him) Lucius Annaeus Seneca, I minded nothing less, that at any time thus rudely transformed he should come into the Printers' hands. For I to no other end removed him from his natural and lofty style to our own corrupt and base, as all men affirm it, but only to satisfy the instant requests of a few my familiar friends," and again, "I suffered this my base translated Tragedy to be published: from his word and Verse far transformed though in Sense little altered."

Oxford's maternal uncle Arthur Golding, whom we shall meet again, apologizes for his "rude and unpolished translation" from the Italian of Leonardo Aretine in 1563, admitting that "for the want of fine penning and eloquent inditing [rendering]" the writer's original has been "spoiled of his Roman Garment and turned into a plain English coat." The same metaphor occurs in his dedication to another translation[3]:

> In like manner as oftentimes beautiful and wellfavored persons, turned out of their gorgeous apparel and costly attire into simple raiment do like [please] the beholders as well as they did in their gayest garments: even in like wise (I trust) it may so come to pass that in this my rude translation, void of ornate terms and eloquent inditing, may (as it were) in his plain and homely English coat be as well accepted of the favorable reader as when it were richly clad in Roman vesture, considering that the value and estimation of the History is no more abased thereby than should the virtue of a precious stone by setting it brass and iron or by carrying it in a closure of leather.

Similar uses of this cloth metaphor may be found in the dedication of *An Italian Grammar* (1575) by Henry Granthan: "Now such as it is rudely attired with this English habit, I betake unto your favorable acceptance"; likewise, in a commentary to the Epistle of St. Paul to the Ephesians (1581), Abraham Fleming excuses "this my homely handled Expositor, a stranger born and newly arrayed with coarse English cloth." Even at the approach of the revolutionary half decade of 1575–80, Lyly — who at present receives some credit for the revolution in the appreciation of English — does not seem to share even his critics' confidence that he deserves that credit: "It is a world to see how English men desire to hear finer speech than the language will allow, to eat finer bread than is made of wheat, to wear finer cloth than is wrought of wool" (Introduction to *Euphues*, 1578).

Even Golding, who should glory in the English of "his" translation of Ovid[4] (the substance of which I will consider later — for the time being "his" is in quotation marks), in the dedication writes: "If this work were fully performed with like eloquence and cunning of endyting by me in English as it were written by the author thereof in his mother tongue, it might perchance delight your honor" (*Metamorphoses*, 1565).

As with Abraham Fleming, the revolution had yet to reach other academics by 1581. "B.R." (probably Barnaby Rich) tells his readers that the history of Herodotus "being most sweet in Greek, converted into English loseth a great part of his grace." Henry Savile can say of his translation of Tacitus as late as 1591 that it is presented "with much loss of their lustre, as being transported from their natural light of the Latin by an unskilful hand into a strange language, perchance not so fit to set out a piece drawn with so curious a pencil."

In its way the Reformation inculcated part of this denigratory attitude: The language was only to be shown as a vehicle to educate the non–Latined bulk of the population and as a weapon in the fight to establish Protestantism. The great gift of printing was also to be employed in these meritorious tasks; and the employment of printing in secular literature diverted effort from them. In effect there seems to have been a subconscious attitude that literature equals Rome, and so there was an uphill task for any writer of a different mind. Thus Sir William Cecil, whom I shall from now on refer to as Burghley, could advise his son: "And suffer not thy sons to pass the Alps, for they shall learn nothing there but pride, blasphemy and atheism. And if they travel they get a few broken languages, that shall profit them nothing more than to have one meat served in divers dishes."[5]

The Puritan (and former playwright) Stephen Gosson, evidencing that subconscious attitude, considers that the devil must have been much troubled by the inroads made by the Reformation in converting the English to right-thinking godliness, and therefore, "First he sent over many wanton Italian books, which, being translated into English, have poisoned the manners of our country with foreign delights" (*Plays Confuted in Five Actions*, 1582).[6]

In this he was only following Ascham:

> These be the enchantments of Circe's, brought out of Italy to mar men's manners in England: much by example of ill life, but more by precepts of fond books, of late [1570] translated out of Italian into English, sold in every shop in London.... There be more of these ungracious books set out in print within these few months than have been seen in England many score years before.... Then they have in more reverence the triumphs of Petrarch than the Genesis of Moses: they make more account of Tully's [Cicero's] offices than St. Paul's Epistles; of a tale in Boccaccio than a story in the Bible.[7]

The first Tudor critics were all "very set against Gallicisms and Italianisms and.... This was lucky because England had been overdosed with French influence for centuries, which their opposition to Italian did perhaps some good, and certainly little harm. But all were thoroughly possessed with the idea that English, adjusted to classical models as far as possible, but not denationalized or denaturalized, ought to be raised to sufficient medium of literary, as of familiar, communication for Englishmen."[8]

In contrast there was the Italianate style of poets of such promise as Wyatt and Surrey.[9] "Yet it must be remembered that Wyatt and Surrey themselves are, after all, poets of more promise than performance; that their promise looks much more promising to us, seeing as we do its fulfilment in Spenser and onward, than it need have done, or could do, to contemporaries."

While these are elements in the revolution, the important point at this stage is to establish the occurrence of that revolution, so that the results of it, which I illustrate by the quotations in chapters 4 and 5, can be compared to the preexisting cultural ambience illustrated above.

However, there must have been an irresistible attraction to the literary-minded even in this early period to Italian Renaissance literature, and the young Oxford might have been so influenced that his desire to experience the Italian ambience became a matter of supreme importance to him. Arthos wrote, "(Shakespeare) was to draw ... frequently upon Italian story writers — Boccaccio, Bandello, Cinthio, Masuccio di Salerno as the Italian playwrights themselves did, and for the same reasons. It was the nature and spirit of the *novella* as Boccaccio established it that more than any other single influence was to direct the imitation of classical drama into new ways."[10] The poet Petrarch introduced the Italian language into a literature readily understandable and appreciated by his countrymen, thus much influencing these story-writers following him, and the whole of European literature, including English.

An Italian critic[11] adds: "The fact that our comic writers saw in the great testament of ... Boccaccio not only an exemplary repository of intrigues and of comic characters, but, however indistinctly, they saw the forms and even the scenic attributes of theatrical representation; they found in his writing the kernel of a lay-profane theatre." Critics can point to a wealth of examples for that Italian ambience, and how it provided inspiration for "Shakespeare"[12]: the *Othello* of Cinthio; Machiavelli's *Mandragola*; Dovisi's *La Calandria*; Ariosto's *La Cassaria* and *Orlando Furioso*; *Gli Suppositi* (for *The Taming of the Shrew*); *Gl'Ingannati* (for *Twelfth Night*) and *Il Negromante*; Cecchi's *L'Ammalata* (for *The Comedy of Errors* and *Pericles*).[13]

However, as early as 1895 before there was any serious modern effort to investigate "Shakespeare's" authorship, the editor of *The Cambridge History of Literature* says it is clear that William Shakespeare was writing within a literary tradition in part hatched by that type of "Italianate Englishman, bitterly reproached by his contemporaries (who) brought back from Italy with his fantastic costume and new-fangled manners, a love of Italian Literature and Romance."[14] To this critic, this man appears to be a general type rather than a specific Englishman (exemplified by those travelers whom Sir Thomas Wilson had in mind as early as 1553): he provides inspiration for works by William Painter published in 1566-67 from whose example "Shakespeare" and the others draw benefit, whereas as we shall see the vital eloquential element of the revolution must be dated to ten years later. Yet even if only subconsciously, the writer seems to be recognizing, and is looking for the answer to, the critics' problem, but at the same time risking creating his own chronological distortion, if a particular Englishman is the source. We must however recognize the point well put by a theater academic referring to the period 1560–75: "To have no reading knowledge of either Greek or Latin at a time when the Italian *novella* and the literature out of which it was born was being imported into England from so many quarters would have been a crippling disadvantage to any aspiring artist, especially a poet. Yet to have acquired an authoritative mastery of either or both carried with it not only the risk of being branded a heretic, an atheist or a political revolutionary, but the certainty of isolation from the mainstream of popular attitudes and thought."[15] To avoid both these political and cultural dangers the best placed poet would have to be an aristocrat above such considerations.

While in London these attitudes would be dispersed by the opening of The Theatre in 1576 (see Chapter Five) and the need for translations for the repertoires, it is difficult to see how it would be mitigated in provincial Stratford-upon-Avon by the time William Shakespeare was of school age.[16]

CHAPTER TWO

The Life 1550–1575

> *Of all Shakespeare's plays, this is the most personal: a solution of the puzzle he has set here (and I had better say at once that I cannot provide it) would not only satisfy the most rabid detective ardor but illuminate Shakespeare's own early life and the conditions that shaped his career and his first plays, an essential background of which at present absolutely nothing is known.* — Richard David, Introduction to Arden 5th edition of *Love's Labour's Lost* (1951) p. xvi

Edward de Vere, 17th Earl of Oxford,[1] was born on April 12, 1550, probably at his ancestral home, Castle Hedingham in Suffolk. By the beginning of the revolution in, say, 1575, he was twenty-five years old.

Now a substantial life has been published, and I have pleasure in referring those who want every biographical detail to Mark Anderson's *Shakespeare by Another Name*.[2] It is a truly monumental book of scholarship: perhaps I hope some may think this effort of mine as in some sense complementary (as well as complimentary) to Anderson. For the consultation of original documents, one may need Professor Alan Nelson's book *Monstrous Adversary*.[3] Professor Nelson's commentary on the documents is met by Anderson, and should be approached with care — the very title, taken from a desperate libel by one of Oxford's opponents,[4] indicates where the professor is coming from: his views will receive further criticism in these pages.

We must never forget that when we record autobiographical or topical references we are looking at the trees (or even perhaps the dead twigs off trees), and not the limitless forest which constitute the works. These references are not the substance of the plots or the poetry. They are ornaments to them, and in some cases irrelevant, except to the writer who wished us to learn through them something which otherwise might be overlooked.

The first question is: If Oxford is Shakespeare, where does he come from to achieve the critical recognition I have already outlined? A first portion in his life might take him to the death in August 1562 of his father, the 16th earl. He was a man of some culture who kept a troop of players. Hedingham

Castle (now open to the public) has a rectangular Great Hall which has a gallery on one of the shorter sides: it requires nothing by way of imagination to visualize its resemblance to the backdrop of the restored Globe. I assume this is where the 16th earl's troop performed.

In 1920 Edward Gepp produced the *Essex Dialect Dictionary*[5] with references collated back to the Tudor period. From that work the indefatigable Oxfordian scholar Gary Goldstein found over one hundred Essex dialect words and expressions scattered over twenty-seven plays in the canon. The claims of the Warwickshire dialect are modest to the point of invisibility by comparison.

As a quite young child, Oxford was put into the household of Sir Thomas Smith, possibly as early as 1554: he may have remained with Sir Thomas and even accompanied him to France when Sir Thomas was appointed ambassador there in 1562. There is extant a letter in French by the thirteen-year-old earl, apparently written from France, which I set out and discuss below.

Sir Thomas was the foremost scholar of his generation, and possessor of probably the largest library in private hands.[6] He was very much attached to Oxford, writing as late as 1576 to Burghley asking him to pass on his good wishes, "for the love I bear him, because he was brought up in my house." This "house" appears to be Sir Thomas' residence at Ankerwicke, near Windsor, right on the Thames. Here, deep in the country, Oxford would at an early age begin his great appreciation of the countryside — books have been written on Shakespeare's knowledge of botany. Indeed, one authority claims that gardening metaphors rank at the top in Shakespeare's use of imagery, followed by those for rivers.

Because of the political situation in 1553, when Queen Mary restored the Roman Catholic politico-religious state, England was a dangerous place for those who had supported the government of Edward VI. Sir Thomas Smith had been in effect chief adviser to Protector Somerset and principal secretary to the king until Somerset fell from power in 1549. He was able to lie low in the countryside. His friend, Oxford's father, the 16th earl, was in a more perilous position because his status and local power in East Anglia meant that he needed to play a very careful game. No doubt to hedge his bets, he placed his son early in the reign with Sir Thomas.

Oxford may have been only five years old at this time. Nevertheless he would be introduced to a very full education. The reason for this was political: he was the heir to the senior earldom of England, and great riches and power would be his in the future. In addition, as Elyot put it in 1531, "That infelicity of our time and country compelleth us to encroach somewhat on the years of children, and especially of noblemen, that they may sooner attain wisdom and gravity."[8] If you add genius to an early start, who knows what the result might be: Montaigne was fluent in Latin at the age of six.

As well as the nation's leading scholar, Smith was an outstanding teacher. One contemporary compared him to Plato. His seventeenth-century biographer Strype writes, "Smith was reckoned the best scholar at [Cambridge] University, not only for rhetoric and the learned languages, but for mathematics, arithmetic, law, natural and moral philosophy." Oxford aged eight and a half spends five months at Queen's College, Cambridge, in 1558-59. At the same time a tutor was hired for him at Ankerwicke, near Windsor. Thomas Smith was, as we shall see (see page 61), an advocate of English as a literary language.

There are examples in literary history of very young talents producing publishable works: Jane Austen and the Brontë sisters come to mind. A work of 192 lines entitled *Ovid's Fable of Narcissus* was published in 1560[9] in iambics, a seven-foot line being followed by a six-foot line. This poem is usually assigned to a Thomas Howell, but the consensus is that the later works of Howell published between 1568 and 1581 are of (even) less quality than *Ovid's Fable*. While Howell's name appears on the title page of these later works, *Ovid's Fable* has the letters T.H. on the title page, which happen to be the same as the printer's, one Thomas Hachette. The 192 lines from Ovid put into verse would be a feat indeed for a ten-year-old and perhaps a trial run for his contribution to Golding's *Metamorphoses*; as was the custom the translation is followed by a piece of moralization on the story, with the following by way of autobiography:

> For neither I presume, by youthful years,
> To claim the skill that elder folks do want.

And

> I have declared, what I can conceive
> Full glad to learn, what wiser folk perceive ...

This work together with the next attributed to Oxford bear some comparisons with Golding and indeed later "Shakespeare" works. In 1562 comes *Romeus and Juliet*,[10] purportedly written by Arthur Brooke in the same iambic heptameters. While some believe this is an early Oxford work, Brooke's existence seems clear, as he appears to be the same person by that name who drowned shortly afterwards. He was a member of the Brooke-Cobham family, much the same age as Oxford, and Oxford may have had some influence.

Like the vast majority of children at the time, Oxford's formative years were spent in the country. The plays illustrate the deep love and sympathy he conceived for the countryside and nature, and in *The Merry Wives of Windsor* knowledge of the topography of Windsor.[11]

Monsieur treshonorable

Monsieur i'ay receu voz lettres, plaines d'humanité et courtoysie, & fort resemblantes a vostre grand amour et singuliere affeccion enuers moy. comme vrais enfans deuëment procreéz d'une telle mere. pour la quelle ie me treuue de iour en iour plus tenu a v.h. voz bons admonestemens pour l'obseruation du bon ordre selon voz appointemens, ie me delibere (dieu aidant) de garder en tout a l'agenue. comme chose que ie cognois et considere tendre especialement a mon propre bien et profit. vsant en cela l'aduis et authorité de ceux qui sont au pres de moy. la discretion desquels i'estime si grande (s'il me conuient parler quelque chose a leur aduanage) qui non seulement ilz se porteront selon qu'un tel temps le requiert, ains que plus est feront tant que ie me gouerne selon que vous aues ordonné et commandé. Quant a l'ordre de mon estude pour ce que il requiert vn long discours a l'expliquer par le menu, et le temps est court a ceste heure, ie vous prie affectueusement m'en excuser pour le present. vous asseurant que par le premier passant ie le vous feray scauoir bien au long. Cependant ie prie a dieu vous donner santé.

Edward Oxinford

Letter in French dated 1563 by Oxford, aged 13, to Lord Burghley.

In 1558 Mary died, but neither Oxford's father nor Smith receive the immediate favor of the new queen. In 1562 the 16th earl died and Smith was appointed ambassador to Paris. We do not know if Oxford went with Smith to Paris or if he were sent there at a later stage. However, he became a crown ward under the guardianship of Cecil, afterwards Lord Burghley, Elizabeth's chief minister. Burghley, too, was the owner of a very full library,[12] rivaling Sir Thomas Smith's, which he kept at Cecil House, on the western boundary of London. This property was also renowned for its garden.

The committal of Oxford as a crown ward to the guardianship of Burghley is recorded in *All's Well That Ends Well*, when in the first four lines of the first scene the widowed Countess of Rousillon and her son Bertram bewail their separation on Bertram, the new count, being taken away to be a crown ward in the same way as Oxford:

> COUNTESS: In delivering my son from me, I bury a second husband.
> BERTRAM: And I, in going, madam, weep o'er my father's death anew: but I must attend his majesty's command, to whom I am now in ward, evermore in subjection.[13]

Perhaps *EVERmore* draws attention to E. Ver(e), Edward de Vere Earl of Oxford.

As this is the first autobiographical quotation I take from the works of "Shakespeare," it is important to point out that the words in the works are just as much evidence as anything else. They cannot be ignored. Some seek to explain them away as poetic or dramatic imagination at work, but they are clear autobiographical pointers to the life of the author. They are not contemporary autobiographical references, and would not necessarily appear in the first version of the play, but might have only been inserted at some later rewrite. Equally instructive at this point is the attitude of current critics.[14]

His education was supervised by Burghley, and a rigorous program[15] installed. The following schedule survives:

    7.00–7.30 — Dancing
    7.30–8.00 — Breakfast
    8.00–9.00 — French
    9.00–10.00 — Latin
    10.00–10.30 — Writing and Drawing
    Common Prayers and so to Dinner
    1.00–2.00 — Cosmography [this would include history, astronomy, geography and many other disciplines]
    2.00–3.00 — Latin
    3.00–4.00 — French
    4.00–4.30 — Exercises with his pen

On holidays such studies were suspended to make time for Oxford to "read before dinner the Epistle and Gospel in his own tongue and in the other tongue after dinner." The "other tongue" is unlikely to have been Latin, as to read the Bible in Latin would have been too Romanist; it must have been Greek.

Burghley evidently took a keen interest in those of the crown wards reserved to his special care; apparently he would test the students by such questions as "Where is the thigh-bone of England?"[16] This is parodied in Act III of *Comedy of Errors*, where Antiochus of Syracuse quizzes his servant Dromio on the qualities of the body of his new love as compared to the world's geography:

> ANTIOCHUS: In what part of her body stands Ireland?
> DROMIO: Marry, sir, in her buttocks; I found it by the bogs [ii, ll. 114–15].

and so on for six more questions.

One of his early tutors was Lawrence Nowell (his cousin of the same name was the dean of Lichfield Cathedral), a cartographer and Anglo-Saxon scholar. However, after one year, in June 1563 he asked to be released from his post so that he could return to pure research, desiring to be entrusted with the making of a more accurate map of England. He wrote, "I can clearly see that my work for the Earl of Oxford cannot be much longer required."[17] Perhaps it was soon after this that Oxford might have been re-placed in the care of Sir Thomas Smith in Paris.

Abroad, English in 1550 had very little standing as a language of culture.[18] Very few foreigners learned or appreciated the language or its literature. An exception seems to be the young Ronsard, who spent nearly three years as a page in various diplomatic missions to Scotland and England from 1537 to 1540. In addition, therefore, to the contemporary "local" evidence for the revolution, we can take on board his reaction.

One critic[19] in his book expresses his opinion that certain verses of Ronsard's represent an "astonishing prophecy," and so one is put on inquiry. What part prophecy, as opposed to a reasoned approach to possible future developments, should play in scientific biography is a question I leave to others.

The verses in question were first published in 1565. At the time Ronsard was 41 years old, the court poet and leading poet of France and probably the world. The critic quotes from the *Bocage Royale* (*Elegies Mascarades et Bergerie*), the version published in 1584. First he quotes a passage on the virtues of English beer in French and then switches to a translation (which I have verified as the critic's own) to English for these verses:

Two—The Life 1550–1575

> Soon the proud Thames shall see
> A flock of white swans nesting on his grass,
> his holy guests, they mount to the heavens
> in circles over those delightful banks
> uttering song which is the certain sign
> that many a Poet, and the heavenly troop
> of sister Muses quitting Parnassus
> shall take it for their gracious dwelling place,
> and tell the famous praise of England's Kings
> unto the crowded nations of the world.

Suspicion is aroused that we are not being given what was written by the failure to supply the original French. This is totally unfounded. The 1584 version reads:

> Bien tost verra la Tamise superbe
> Maint Cygne blanc loger dessus son herbe,
> Hostes sacrez, puis eslevez aux cieux,
> Tout à l'entour des bords délicieux
> Jetter un chant, pour signe manifeste
> Que meint Poëte, & la troupe celeste
> Des Muses sœurs y feront quelque jour,
> Laissant Parnasse, un gracieux séjour,
> Pour envoyer aux nations estranges
> Des Roys Anglois les fameuses louanges [ll. 345–354].

Perhaps the original 1565 version is more relevant? No. Apart from the substitution in lines 2 and 3 above of "Meint Cygne blanc les hostes de son herbe,/En nombre espais," there is nothing of consequence.

Before discussing the 1587 posthumous version below, it might be helpful to consider how Ronsard came to write the original version in the first place.

In France, in 1562/3 there took place the first of the debilitating Civil Wars of Religion, when the Catholic party attempted to suppress the Protestant Huguenots. In her inexperience Elizabeth intervened (unofficially) on the side of the Protestants, and gave considerable help to them. Early in 1563, the Protestants made a peace treaty behind her back with the Catholics, and both factions then turned upon the English forces. Elizabeth attempted to negotiate the position by sending a special envoy, Nicholas Throckmorton, but the French refused to recognize his credentials and put him in prison. In a rage Elizabeth then imprisoned the French ambassador in London. The French followed suit and imprisoned the English ambassador, who was Sir Thomas Smith, who had earlier been the de facto guardian of the very young Oxford. Finally, the following year Elizabeth was forced to sign a rather humiliating peace treaty.

Ronsard the court poet, in an effort to mollify Elizabeth, and perhaps to keep her neutral in any future conflict involving the Protestants, then produced the long poem in praise of England in which the "astonishing prophecy" appears.

Sir Thomas Smith, with his access to the French Court, must have had some degree of acquaintance with him if only as the court poet: this could have been quite close, with Sir Thomas being one of the foremost English classical scholars and a man of deep cultural interests, as we have seen.

In 1585 Ronsard died. The 1584 edition of his works is quoted above. However, before he died he prepared another edition subsequently published in 1587. In it he substantially rewrote the lines in question:

> Bien tost verra la Tamise superbe
> Maint Cygne blanc les hostes de son herbe,
> Chantant en l'air d'un son melodieux
> Tourner ses bordes & rejouyr les cieux:
> Oiseaux sacrez à Phebus pour prédire
> Que les neufs Sœurs, & l'auteur de la Lyre,
> Changeant la Grèce, y feront quelque jour
> Comme en Parnasse un désiré séjour
> Pour envoyer aux nations estranges
> Des Rois Anglois les fameuses louanges [ll. 345–354].

In 1584 John Soothern, apparently a Frenchman, wrote in his dedication of his work *Pandora*[20]:

> I will de Vere push thy loanges
> To the ears of people estrange [Epode ll. 11,12].

This would seem to be an echo of Ronsard's last two lines and evidence of the poem's circulation.

This is a translation of the revised Ronsard version:

> Soon the proud Thames will see
> Many a white Swan guests on his grass
> Sing in the air with their melodious sound,
> Go by her banks, rejoice the skies:
> Birds sacred to Phoebus to foretell
> That the nine Sisters, and Poetry's progenitor,
> Displacing Greece, will make some day
> There as in Parnassus a desired stay
> To send to foreign nations
> The famous praises of the English Kings.

"Les neuf soeurs" are the nine Muses. The description "et l'auteur de la Lyre/ Changeant la Grèce" may well refer to an Englishman of very great literary attainment. "Orthodox" literary criticism would not be able to produce a candidate who would have arisen in the period 1564–1585, since the first version of the verses was published, but by the latter date as we shall see there had been in fact already written and in part produced about half of the "Shakespeare" oeuvre. In this context "Changeant" would mean "replacing" Greece. However "l'auteur de la Lyre" may well refer to Apollo rather than any Englishman, but then a strained interpretation of "Changeant" would produce "Changing his residence from Greece," which duplicates and distorts "les neuf soeurs, et l'auteur de la Lyre/... y feront quelque jour/Comme en Parnase, un gracieux séjour." Perhaps Ronsard was synthesizing the two ideas, like a classical author: Apollo/the author (or Apollo personified by the author) in displacing or replacing Greece as the fount of literature will make a stay on the banks of the Thames. "L'auteur de la Lyre" may specifically refer to Apollo, but whether "changeant la Grèce" refers only to removing his residence, and not something more fundamental, must be arguable.

If there had not been some radical development in English literature just before 1585, why rewrite the passage? Is Ronsard really putting Shakespeare on the same pedestal as Apollo? Note that "changeant" applies only to "l'auteur," and not to the muses. Even if the reference is really only to Apollo, it is quite revolutionary enough to support my thesis.

The problem for those who disagree is that, where there might be a literary compulsion, there was no political compulsion on Ronsard to alter his original version(s)—quite the reverse, as Ronsard was or would have been against both the Henry III moderates (with whom he had apparently fallen out) and the Navarre Protestant party, and in fact in simple terms a Catholic Guise supporter, and as such very anti–English. But then why so full of increased expectancy about English literature in 1585?

In any event it is significant that instead of merely repeating, or even deleting, the earlier version, Ronsard in 1584/5 is rewriting the verses in an even stronger form, plainly to make them more applicable to the current literary scene in England in 1584/5 rather than to any prospective literary renaissance in 1564. We may term the rewriting revolutionary in its implications. It provides further clear evidence that Shakespeare's revolution had already taken place by that later date.

The following year Oxford received a master of arts degree from Cambridge, and in September 1566, a similar degree from Oxford University. These were most likely honorary. However, the plays have some reference to Cambridge jargon[21] which might be evidence of at least some attendance at the University. Thus Titus Andronicus:

> Knock at his study, where they say he keeps
> To ruminate strange plots of dire revenge [V, ii, ll. 5, 6].

While "study" is a common word for the room now, it appears to have come from Cambridge in this use.

At Cambridge the words "act," "commence," and "proceed" were used as terms of art: "act" means partaking in a formal dispute leading to a degree; after graduating, one was said to "commence" in arts, and to "proceed" to a higher degree. Thus in 1 *Henry IV*, Falstaff says:

> So that skill weapons is nothing without sack [sherry], for that sets it a-work, and learning is a mere hoard of gold, till sack *commences* it and sets it in *act* and use [emphasis added] [IV, iii, ll. 126–27].

In *Timon of Athens*:

> Hadst thou like us, from our first swathe *proceeded*
> The sweet degree that this brief world affords ...
> Thy nature did *commence* in sufferance, time
> Hath made thee hard in't [emphasis added] [IV, iii, ll. 253–54, 269–70].

At Cambridge a "size" was a meal of a certain type, hence "sizar," still in use. "Scant" was a form of punishment for undergraduates. There are over a dozen uses of "scant" as a verb in the canon, including from *King Lear*: "'Tis not in thee to *scant* my *sizes*" (emphasis added) (II, iv, l. 348).

And Sonnet 97: "Accuse me thus: that I have *scanted* all/Wherein I should your great deserts repay." Involving real work would be his studies in law at Gray's Inn which he began in February 1567. He began to take part in court life and became an accomplished performer at the tilt.

In the following year, 1568, there was performed at Gray's Inn the play *Horestes*,[22] ostensibly by one John Pykeryng, about whom nothing more is known. A strong case for this play being a piece of Oxford's juvenilia has been produced: "Most scholars now accept that in John Pykeryng's *Horestes* Elizabeth I is being urged to execute Mary Queen of Scots (Clytemnestra) for her role in the murder of her husband, Darnley (Agamemnon), by the Earl of

Portrait of Edward de Vere, 17th Earl of Oxford (1581).

Bothwell (Aegisthus)." *Horestes* demonstrates authorial inventiveness with neologisms, rare words subsequently found in the canon and a large number of classical allusions: besides those from the Trojan War, there are examples from Socrates, Plato, Pythagoras, Nero, Ovid, Livy and Juvenal. In Aeschylus' *Oresteia* and in *Horestes*, Clytemnestra uses a net to trap and kill Agamemnon, while in every other version she does the deed while Agamemnon is in the bath. *Horestes* was apparently the first play in English to use soliloquy to tell the audience the characters' thoughts. The play is clearly the product of a young, irreverent, politically connected talent. It also has a strong musical content. The political content foreshadows the use which Oxford will make of this element in many of his plays in the next two decades.

Oxford's support for literature was becoming known to a wider circle, and a number of translations were dedicated to him, beginning at the age of fourteen with his uncle Arthur Golding's *Th' Abridgment of the Histories of Trogus Pompeius* (1564). Thomas Underdown (apparently Oxford and he had not met) dedicated in 1569 his *An Aethiopian History*, written in Greek by Heliodorus, in these terms:

> Now of all knowledge fit for a noble gentleman, I suppose the knowledge of histories is the most seeming. For furthering whereof I have engaged a passing fine and witty history written in Greek by Heliodorus, and for the right good cause consecrated the same to your honorable Lordship. For such virtues be in your honor's so haughty courage joined with great skill, such sufficiency in learning, so good nature and common sense [not always displayed] that in your honor, I think, expressed the right pattern of a noble gentleman.

He expresses the wish that "if opportunity shall seem hereafter, there shall greater things appear under your honour's name." Perhaps some discount should be made for flattery and hope of patronage, but nevertheless, even on the modest basis of no smoke without fire, Oxford's skills were manifesting themselves.

Sometime in 1569 Oxford was very ill indeed and convalesced at Windsor; but his expenses in the first quarter include the purchase of a Geneva Bible (now, with "Shakespearian" passages heavily underlined,[23] in the Folger Library), a Chaucer, Plutarch's works in French, two books in Italian,[24] and "other books and papers." After vast sums were spent on his illness he managed to persuade Burghley and the queen to let him join the Earl of Sussex, the commander of a force engaged in putting down a pro–Catholic rebellion in the North, and with it a punishment expedition into the borders of Scotland. Oxford arrived almost too late and probably saw only some trudging about in the mud: nevertheless he had some military experience. In particular he was scathing on the subject of soldiers' pay and welfare (which later on were spectacularly mismanaged by Leicester in the Netherlands — perhaps, although there is no record of performance, these well-polished lines were inserted later):

> He that for private base commodity
> Will starve his soldiers or keep back their pay
> He that to deck himself in gorgeous tire
> Will see his men go naked, die for cold
> Is a plain cutthroat to the commonwealth.
> A worthy captain seeing a tall soldier
> March barefoot, halting plucked off his own shoes
> And gave them to the soldier, saying, "Fellow
> When I want these shoes then give me these again."
> But captains nowadays
> Pluck off their soldiers' shoes, nay, sell their lives
> To make them rich and gallant to the eye.
> [*Edmund Ironside* I, iii, ll. 346–357].[25]

Perhaps the young soldier was Oxford himself. Then Burghley made arguably the worst decision of his life: he promoted the marriage of his beloved fifteen-year-old daughter Ann with Oxford just as Oxford was turning twenty-one and no longer subject to Cecil's guardianship. He persuaded the queen to ennoble him so that his daughter would be a peer's child, not a mere commoner's, and so fit for an earl. She was a retiring, studious, sedate, demure, and domestically accomplished girl, on the face of it quite the wrong choice for the sophisticated yet inexperienced Oxford. In *All's Well That Ends Well*, the less well-born heroine Helena, hopelessly in love with Bertram, that supreme cad, complains:

> My imagination
> Carries no favor in't but Bertram's.
> I am undone: there is no living, none
> If Bertram be away. 'Twere all one
> That I should love a bright particular star,
> And think to wed it, he is so above me.
> In the bright radiance and collateral light
> Must I be comforted, not in his sphere.
> Th' ambition in my love thus plagues itself.
> The hind that would be mated by the lion
> Must die for love [I, i, ll. 81–91].

Bertram carries his objection to being married to her to the king:

> BERTRAM: A poor physician's daughter my wife! Disdain Rather corrupt me for ever.
> KING: 'Tis only title thou disdain'st in her, the which I can build up [II, iii, ll. 116–19].

And this is exactly what the queen did, creating Cecil Lord Burghley.

If Ann is the personification of Anne Page in *The Merry Wives of Windsor*, then she was not without wit herself. There were motions to marry her off to Philip Sidney, who appears as Oxford's milksop character in a number of plays. If he is Slender, who like Sidney had three hundred pounds a year, cousin to Justice Shallow, then Ann is not impressed with the thought of being married to him:

> Alas! I had rather be set quick i' the earth
> And bowled to death with turnips [III, v, ll. 90–91].

Whatever the chances the early years of the marriage might have had, politics intervened. The wedding was originally fixed for September 1571, but in that month the Ridolfi plot broke, and Oxford's cousin, Thomas Howard Duke of Norfolk, was caught in a plot to depose Elizabeth in favor of her Roman Catholic cousin and lineal heiress Mary, Queen of Scots (whom it was planned he should marry), financed by Ridolfi, an Italian banker.

The luckless Ann and Oxford were married on December 15, 1571, and Norfolk's trial began the following month, with every likelihood of conviction followed by execution. To save his cousin, Oxford tried various tricks: literary flattery to the queen and withdrawal of matrimonial relations with Ann so as to drive Burghley wild (and possibly set up an annulment process).[26] This is paralleled by Bertram's attitude to Helen after their wedding in *All's Well That Ends Well*, Act III, scene ii, ll. 19–27. These ploys allied to the pleas of Norfolk's mother and brother nearly worked: after twice signing the death warrant, Elizabeth twice withdrew it. Parliament was recalled and demanded the head of Mary as well. Elizabeth signed a third warrant against Norfolk and again withdrew it in April 1572: to save Mary she had to sacrifice Norfolk. He was finally executed on June 2, 1572. His death was apparently on Oxford's conscience, although it is difficult to see what else he could have done.

Oxford had other problems on his mind. He had reached twenty-one years of age on April 12, 1571, and was entitled to have all his father's estates conveyed to him. However, to secure this happy result he would need to pay the court of wards' fees, in effect a swinging inheritance tax. To pay he would need to sell lands which as yet he had no title to.[27] Temperamentally, as one may logically imagine, Oxford was not disposed to put the discharge of these obligations high on his list, and added to this, Elizabeth had during Oxford's minority put out some of these estates for administration to her principal favorite the egregious Robert Dudley, Earl of Leicester, who was in no hurry to return them.

Added to these pressures may have been the knowledge that the Continent and particularly Italy were in a state of literary ferment: the young Oxford must have been desperate to become part of the scene, knowing that his current writings were deficient because of his lack of contact, and no doubt fired by the writings of Painter and his like (see page 12).

These frustrations would have been enough to unhinge the judgment of any man of his temperament. Oxford began to conduct a somewhat raffish existence[28] both at court and elsewhere. His men assaulted Burghley's servants on the road to Rochester in May 1573 at Gadshill, which I deal with at greater length when I consider *The Famous Victories of Henry V* and related references later in this chapter.

Some of these frustrations he may have been able to take out in tiltyard tournaments. In 1571 Oxford and Sir Christopher Hatton with two others formed a victorious team, which was rewarded by the queen. "The chief honor was given to the Earl of Oxford," records Holinshed. Hatton's prize was a gold bell and chain, and *The Comedy of Errors* Act IV has this seemingly irrelevant reference:

> (Antipholus of Syracuse has been arrested)
> ADRIANA: Was he arrested on a bond?
> DROMIO OF SYRACUSE: Not on a bond but on a stronger thing: A chain, a chain — do you not hear it ring?
> ADRIANA: What, the chain?
> DROMIO: No, no, the bell [iii, ll. 49–52].

Oxford may have amused himself by composing some of the highly stylized tournament poetry that has survived.[29]

Oxford may be the father of the 3rd Earl of Southampton,[30] conceived while the second earl was safely out of the way in the Tower (where he remained until May 1, 1573), and born October 6, 1573, and believed by most the addressee of the first portion of the sonnets. Certainly Oxford was an admirer (at least) of the countess, his mother:

> Thou art thy mother's glass and she in thee
> Calls back the lovely April of her prime [Sonnet 3].

The frustrations of his life are brought out in *All's Well That Ends Well*, where Bertram says:

> I am commanded here, and kept a coil with
> "Too young" and "the next year" and "'Tis too early."
> PAROLLES: An thy mind stand to't. boy, steal away bravely.
> BERTRAM: I shall stay here the forehorse to a smock,
>   Creaking my shoes on the plain masonry
>   Till honour be brought up, and no sword worn
>   But one to dance with. By heaven, I'll steal away [II, i, ll. 27–33].

Which is precisely what Oxford does. He tried for some time to get permission for foreign travel and was refused.[31] In July 1574 he left without permission for Calais. The English Catholic community and indeed the court were under the impression that he had defected to the considerable Catholic exiled group in the Netherlands: Burghley, for some reason, and (Anderson suggests that Burghley might have wanted a Spanish bribe collected for him), supported him to an extent, and the queen appears to have been mollified. Her rage at Oxford's disobedience, as she saw it, did not stop her sending Thomas Bedingfield, who had assisted Oxford with his literary efforts to save cousin Norfolk, hauling him back at the end of the month. However, Burghley noted that Oxford hoped to be forgiven because "He had in his abode so notoriously rejected the attempts of Her Majesty's evil subjects and in his return set apart all his particular desires of foreign travel."

Portrait of Henry, 3rd Earl of Southampton c. 1594.

Oxford's loyalty in the face of immense temptation must have impressed. He was given permission to travel abroad the following year. I think there was a quid pro quo: Oxford had to become a spy. The Catholic nobility trusted him, yet he does not seem to have wavered. Occasionally the cat (or rather the lynx) comes out of the bag. Gabriel Harvey—he of the English hexameters—writes in 1578:

> Not the like discourser for Tongue and head to be found out
> Not the like resolute man for great and serious affairs,
> Not the like Lynx to spy out secrets and privities of states,
> Eyed like to Argus, eared like to Midas, nos'd like to Naso,
> Wing'd like to Mercury, first of a thousand to be employ'd;
> This, nay more than this, doth practise of Italy in one year.

Nashe in *Pierce Pennilesse*[32] (1592) gives us "The Tale of the Beare and the Fox," a political fable and spotted as such by his enemy, the same Gabriel Harvey. The bear is the villain who destroys the other beasts and then conceives a "newfangled lust" for honey. So he can get hold of as much as possible he engages the fox to travel the country, telling everyone that the bees are idle drones and their honey poisonous and corrupt. A passing fly (Nashe himself) overhears their talk, "and buzd in Linceus ear the whole purport of their malice." Linceus — the lynx — is the authority figure. Frustrated, the bear gives up and dies of disappointment. We may identify the extreme Protestant Leicester who died in 1588 with the attitude and crimes of the bear. Oxford is also linked to Linceus by the Puritan Joseph Hall at the time of the so-called War of the Pamphlets (see page 122).

Jonson in *Every Man Out of His Humour*, Act IV, scene iv, has the man-about-town Carlo describe to Puntarvolo (Oxford) the disgusting scene he has witnessed through the keyhole of Sogliardo learning to take tobacco. Puntarvolo is more upset at the spying and betrayal. No one will know, contends Carlo, "What Lynceus can see my heart?"

In 1598 John Marston (who makes occasional references to "Lynceus" in his role as an observer) was engaged in a war of words with Joseph Hall, who had attacked Oxford (see pages 172ff). During a reference to *The Rape of Lucrece*, he (Marston) wrote:

> What icy Saturnist, whose northern pate [Hall was from Leicestershire]
> By such gross lewdness would exasperate?
> I think the blind doth see the flame-god rise [He sees Oxford as
>   Apollo rise as the sun]
> From sisters' couch, each morning to the skies, [the muses']
> Glowing with lust. Walk in the dusky night
> With Linceus eyes, and to thy piercing sight
> Disguised gods will show, in peasants shape, [critical authorities]
> Prest to commit some execrable rape. [Forced to make disgraceful
>   criticisms]

Indeed, Oxford's greatest triumph as a spy came in 1581.[33] He was exceptionally valuable because of his social equality with the Catholic nobility (who entertained hopes — or were fooled into thinking there were hopes — of a conversion). No ordinary middle-class employee of the government could hope to penetrate this section of the community. The same consideration applies later on, with his stage contacts among the middle and lower middle classes.

In 1570 or so there arrived at court Sir Christopher Hatton, who rose rapidly in the queen's favor to become a favorite in the tiltyard, as we have seen, and later captain of her bodyguard in 1573. Before that he had fallen ill and the queen sent him her own physician. In thanks he wrote: "God bless you for ever…. It is a gracious favor most dear and welcome to me; reserve it to the sheep [the queen's nickname for him], he hath no tooth to bite, where the boar's [Oxford's — his crest was the boar] tusk may both raze and tear."

In that same year there was published an anthology, *A Hundred Sundry Flowers*. In it were verses by George Gascoigne, Hatton and Oxford and others, apparently without Hatton's consent. When Oxford was away in Italy, three years later the anthology was reprinted in a revised version, now called *The Posies of George Gascoigne*. The reason for the reprint, as Gascoigne put it, was: "It is very near two years past since (I being in Holland in service with the virtuous Prince of Orange) the most part of these posies were imprinted, and now at my return I find that some of them have not only been offensive for sundry wanton speeches and lascivious phrases, but further I hear some have been doubtfully construed and (therefore) scandalous."[34] Apparently most of the mud had fallen on Hatton. He persuaded Gascoigne to take the blame but persuaded the queen to give the poet laureateship to Gascoigne. Hatton's poems were identified by the signature Fortunatus Infelix — the Fortunate Unhappy. We shall meet him again when *Twelfth Night* is considered.

Gascoigne, who died in 1577, attempted in the introduction to his last work, *The Steel Glas*, to have his revenge. He complained to his patron that because of a "Noble," he lived a "weary life." Gascoigne in this work, recognized as the first satire in English, personifies himself as "Satira" and states that his father was "Plain-dealing." His mother, "Simplicity," and his sister "Poesys," but:

> in the prime of youth
> A lusty lad, a stately man to see
> Brought up in place, where pleasures did abound
> (I dare not say, in court for both mine ears) [risk being cut off]
> Began to woo my sister, not for wealth,
> But for her face was lovely to behold
> And therewithal, her speech was pleasant still
> This Noble's[35] name was called Vain Delight ...

His followers and servants included "False Semblant," "Flearing Flattery," "Destruction Deceit," "Sim Swash" and "False Witness." And:

> I' short tell to make, she gave a free consent
> And forth she goeth to be his wedded mate
> Entic'd percase, with gloss of gorgeous showe
> (or else persuaded by his peers)
> That constant love had harboured in his brest
> Such errors grow where such false prophets' speech.
> How so my sister liked him well
> And forth she goeth, in court with him to dwell ...

But then she wished to see her brother "Satira." "Vain Delight" sent for him and listened to his poetry:

> A spark of lust did kindle in his brest
> And bade him hark to the songs of Satira ...
> Which pleased him so, and so inflamed his heart
> That he forgot my sister Poesys
> And ravished me, to please his wanton mind.

His friends endeavored to persuade him:

> His simple mind from track of trusty truth
> Nor yet deceit could blear his mind through fraud,
> Came slander, accusing me, and said
> That I entic'd Delight to love and lust.
> Thus was I caught, poor wretch that thought none ill.
> And furthermore, to cloak their own offence,
> They clapped me first in cage of misery
> And there I dwelt, full many a doleful day.
> Until this thief, the traitor Vain Delight
> Cut out my song with Razor of Restraint
> Lest I should wray this bloody deed of his.

Before we follow Oxford to Italy, we ought to consider what might be his literary works to date (1575).

We have already mentioned *Ovid's Fable, Romeus and Juliet,* and *Horestes* (page 22). In Cecil's household was Oxford's maternal uncle Arthur Golding, a prominent Latin scholar and translator. Ascribed to him is the translation of Ovid's *Metamorphoses* that was published in 1567. Ovid is the one classical poet on which Shakespeare depends so much. A biographer wrote, "The phraseology of Golding's translation re-appears in Shakespeare's page as almost to compel conviction that Shakespeare knew much of Golding's translation by heart."[36] Recent scholarship indicates that Golding would not have had time during his translation commissions to translate the fifteen books of *Metamorphoses* as well, and in addition, wrote a recent scholar, "It seems strange [i.e., impossible] that this piece of work, excellent for its time, should have proceeded from a puritan and translator of Calvin."[37] The conclusion is inescapable: Oxford was the real translator of *Metamorphoses*. It is not strange that Ezra Pound should judge the work "the most beautiful book in the language," and in expression quite beyond the talent of the otherwise worthy and pedestrian Golding, whose other works were instructional rather than entertaining.[38] The first four books were published in 1565, and the whole in 1567: the verse in the later books, it has been noted, is looser, denoting greater facility in the slightly more mature translator. Pound[39] tells us, "Golding was endeavouring to convey the sense of the original to his readers ... Chaucer and Golding are more likely to find the mot juste than were for some centuries their successors, saving the author of Hamlet."[40] Try this, from book 15:

Two—The Life 1550–1575

> Against the wind and weather cold let wethers yield ye coats
> And udders full of battling milk receive ye of the goats
> Away with springes, snares and g(r)ins, away with risp and net
> Away with guileful feats, for fouls no limetwigs see ye set.

The actual effect of "Golding's" translation on Oxford's verse can be shown over and over again, as this example illustrates:

> that everyman ...
> should direct
> By reason in the way of virtue and correct
> His fierce affection with the bit of temperance least perchance
> They taking bridle in his teeth [XV *Bookes Metamorphoses* b3v].

Compare "The iron bit he crusheth 'tween his teeth" from *Venus and Adonis*, l. 269.

Oxford presumably knew Richard Edwards, director of the Children of the Chapel Royal, who died in 1566. In 1573 there was published posthumously *The Paradise of Dainty Devices*, Edwards' collection of contemporary poetry, containing eight poems signed "E(arl of) O(xford)." These are of limited merit, according to the critics, but were written by Oxford at age seventeen or less. Edwards is also credited the very early *Damon and Pithias* and with the lost play *Palamon and Arcite* (1566),[41] which perhaps reappears as *Two Noble Kinsmen*, and parts of that appear to be a fragment written by Oxford, along with two poems—numbers 33 and 34 on page 40. Miles Windsor (d. 1624),[42] a cousin of Oxford's brother-in-law, was at Oxford University when Oxford acted the part of Pirithous in the 1566 performance before the queen, who lent the royal clothes formerly belonging to Edward VI and Mary I, a mark of signal favor which would not readily be granted to a man of Edwards' standing. Unfortunately, at the performance a staircase collapsed and three people were killed. Perhaps the play was considered unlucky, because it was not revived and ostensibly lost until the Fletcher "collaboration."[43]

Oxford also wrote (with his Latin considered superior to that of the original author Castiglione)[44] a preface in Latin to Clerke's edition of *The Courtier* in January 1571/2 as part of his efforts to secure a permanent reprieve for his cousin the Duke of Norfolk. Later in 1573, as we have seen, to keep himself in the queen's eye he wrote a spoof courtship ridiculing Hatton's relationship with the queen. It was published in *A Hundred Sundry Flowers*, but the authorities stepped in quickly to call in this volume. In that year he wrote an elegant preface to Thomas Bedingfield's *Cardanus Comfort*. Joseph Sobran[45] produces the vocabulary and thought parallels with the plays *Venus and Adonis, The Rape of Lucrece* and the sonnets. "Nearly every word Oxford uses in the Bedingfield letter, including the odd word 'repugn,' is used somewhere by Shakespeare," writes Sobran. For "repugn," compare, from the letter: "this one request of mine ... not to repugn the setting forth of your own proper studies." And: "When stubbornly he did repugn the truth/About a certain question in the law" (I *Henry VI*, IV, iii, ll. 94–95).

It does seem that Oxford's theatrical career starts with those history plays foreseen by Ronsard. In order of history though not necessarily of writing, the following appear to be pre-1575, containing as they do very little of the Italianate influence in the later works. So far as date order is concerned, it might be that with their emphasis on the roles of earlier earls of Oxford, *The Famous Victories of Henry V* comes first, seconded by *The True Tragedy of King Richard III*, and neither has the constant allusions to legal terms of the later plays. This puts these plays prior to Oxford's studies at Gray's Inn in 1567. Much of their general crudity has disappeared by the time we have, say, *Edmund Ironside*, and *Edward III* is placed, as we shall see, after Lepanto (1571). All these plays show no or almost no Italian influence and so are likely to date earlier than Oxford's tour in 1575-76. Below they are listed in order of history (as opposed to composition).

Edmund Ironside: Eric Sams[46] argues for the authorship of this play. Because it shows two archbishops fighting on stage, it may not have been met with much favor. Oxford does not appear to have thought it worthwhile to rewrite. In it there is a completely ahistorical character, an Earl of Southampton: this may have been a mark of appreciation by Oxford to the second Earl of Southampton, a supporter of Canute but otherwise a sympathetic person. In a way this dates the play to before 1572, because, as I mentioned above, after that date Oxford might well have been taking too much interest in Mary Browne, Southampton's wife, from whom he was estranged on his release from the Tower. Oxford did the same thing when he included another ahistorical Lennox in *Macbeth* (see page 113), for the reason suggested when this play is considered. Sams' book contains an exhaustive list of comparisons with later works and language analysis: included above are his remarks on the use of French (see page 49) and Latin. In addition there are nearly three hundred usages first introduced to the language by Shakespeare prior to 1590, of which some 260 appear in plays dated by the "orthodox" to after 1590.

The Troublesome Reign of King John: Arguments for this as an early play of Shakespeare/Oxford have been produced, and for its basis for the canonical *King John*. "The plays match so closely in the selection of characters, the sequence of events, the management of scenes that they cannot have been written independently. Sometimes they parallel not just scene for scene but (substantially) speech for speech," wrote one critic. Even more striking is that in the two plays history is bent in the same way to make a dramatic point. Both plays make the death of Arthur in 1203 the cause of the Barons' Rebellion in 1216, both happening just before John's submission to the pope in 1213.[47]

Edward III: Sams' book *Shakespeare's Edward III*[48] has virtually inserted this play in the canon. It does contain mature rewritten speeches, and its description of the battle of Sluys by "Greek-type" messenger recalls to Sams the Armada of 1588. There was no real set-piece battle in 1588: the obvious and immediate precedent is the battle of Lepanto, October 7, 1571, where the clash of two fleets as at Sluys is described. The defeat of the French ship *Nonpareil* is recounted, and compared incorrectly by Sams to the English victorious ship of the same name in 1588.

Thomas of Woodstock[49]: This play has been recently argued for the canon as Part One of *Richard II*, and also shown to be a rewrite of an earlier version.

Richard II: The play betrays its early origins by its quite static theatrical movement. Heavily rewritten, it is properly enough in textual terms usually dated after *Richard III*. *Richard II*, in contrast to the other "kingly" plays or the first parts of them, begins with nothing by way of introduction, clearly indicating that it was written as a sequel.

The Famous Victories of Henry V: The case for Shakespeare's authorship has been cogently argued,[50] yet no rebuttal has been published. Heavily rewritten parts of the play form the basis of 1 and 2 *Henry IV* and *Henry V*. Perhaps this play is the earliest — certainly it has plenty to appeal to a young playwright. The second most important character is the (eleventh) Earl of Oxford, to whom is given the second most number of lines: amusingly, this situation was amended in the later version. The play also contains the first account of the Gad's Hill incident: in scene 4, the Thief is indicted "for robbing a poor carrier the 20th May last past, in the fourteenth year of the reign of our sovereign lord King Henry the Fourth" (ll. 20–24). This is considerably expanded in Act II of I *Henry IV* and alluded to in *Arden of Feversham*. The important point is that there was no May 20 in the fourteenth year of the reign of Henry IV: the actual fourteenth year began on September 30, 1412, but finished with his death on March 20, 1413. On May 21, 1573, in the fourteenth year of the reign of Queen Elizabeth, two servants of Oxford beat up two of Burghley's servants — at Gad's Hill.

In addition, as one critic puts it: "It might seem implausible to claim that in 1596–98 [when the "orthodox" date the Henry IV plays] (William) Shakespeare could rely on his audience recognizing unexplicit allusions to the Northern rebellion of 1569 and much less likely that he could expect anyone to recall the Pilgrimage of Grace (1536)." As Oxford himself participated in the latter stages of the 1569 event, the "unexplicit allusions" to them would seem natural to him in a play written and revised much closer to the date of the events than the "orthodox" suggested date. Morton is a servant of the rebellious Northumberland in the play and was in fact a Catholic priest, one of the prime movers of the 1569 rebellion. "But," asserts the critic, "the facts suggest otherwise. The continuing relevance and essential identity of the major Tudor rebellions was hammered into the consciousness of the Elizabethan citizen."[51] I would suggest only into the mind of the politically minded Protestant section of society, and anyway the play records the unappealing treachery of Prince John of Lancaster towards the rebels, mirroring that of Henry VIII himself to the leaders of the Pilgrimage of Grace.

1, 2 and 3 *Henry VI*: the very debates about whether these plays are canonical indicate the spread of the demonstration of talent from his apprentice efforts to Oxford's fully mature authorship of the later plays.

True Tragedy of Richard III: Arguments for this play as the basis for *Richard III* have been produced, and the same elements are present for these plays as they are for *The Troublesome Reign* and *King John* above. Dover Wilson agrees that the plays "are strikingly similar in general structure": the second play makes the same historical mistakes and repeats the same basic thoughts of the characters as are contained in the first play in dozens of examples. "Orthodox" critics have been driven to speculate that the plays both derive from a third *Richard III* by a third author, whereas the simpler and rational solution is that the one is the juvenile product of the mature writer of the later. As Ramon Jimenez puts it, "[the two long Jane Shore scenes] are composed in vapid and clanking prose [and are] irrelevant to the story. The play contains many entrance and exit type clues [or cues for amateur actors], such as 'Why, here's Lord'—and 'so, I take my leave.' But ... True Tragedy is full of the artful phrasing, arresting dialogue, and clever turns of speech that are the marks of a superior poet in the making."[52]

Three other plays may be mentioned at this stage. First, the black comedy *Arden of Feversham* in its original guise of *Murderous Michael* shows no Italianate influences, and it was produced at court on Oxford's return in 1578/9. The two murderers, Black *Will* and George *Shake*bag,[53] give an early indication of the use of "Will Shakespeare" as a pseudonym.

Secondly, *A Yorkshire Tragedy* contains some authentic flourishes and may have been adapted to agree with a sensational case in 1605. Perhaps Oxford wrote it for his private delectation; certainly the lines where the Husband character threatens to throw the maidservant downstairs;

> The surest way to charm a woman's tongue
> Is break her neck: a politician did it [V, ll.13, 14].

instantly recall Leicester's involvement with the death of his wife Amy Robsart in the recent past.[54] Incidentally, in *Arden of Feversham* the comic murderer Shakebag while on the run murders his landlady: "I spurned her down the stairs/and broke her neck" [Act V Scene 2, ll.7,8]. Oxford may have enjoyed keeping Leicester's association with this method of murder in the public eye.

The last play is *Titus Andronicus*. There is at Longleat, the palace of the Marquesses of Bath, in Wiltshire a reference to a production in 1574 at Hatfield, the seat of Cecil, being an extract made by that same Henry Peacham (who was at the time curate of a neighboring parish to Hatfield), and to whom I refer on page 63 of a version of this play which bears that date latinized but in an abbreviated form. The interpretation of the symbols I owe to David Roper.[55] The date is set out as "anno m° q° g q^{to}"; in full this becomes "anno millesimo quingentesimo g [equals septuagesimo] quinto": "in the one thousandth five hundredth and seventieth fifth year of Our Lord." Scholars have tried desperately to shoehorn the "g" into another meaning consonant with an acceptable date for William Shakespeare. Their trouble is that "g" is always going to imply "seven." Peacham could not write "s°" as there would be a doubt as to whether sexagesimo (sixtieth) or septuagesimo was meant. Further confirmation of the dating comes from a study of the content of the play: the character who is identified most clearly is the villainous king Saturninus,[56] Saturn being a common name for Philip II of Spain, and the play may well be one of those anti–Spanish compositions which the king complained of, with its reference to the barbarous murderings intended to keep the London populace "informed" about its Spanish enemy. In July 1586, the Venetian ambassador to Spain reported, "But what has enraged him [King Philip II] much more than all else, has caused him to show a resentment such as he has never displayed in his life, is the account of the masquerades and comedies which the Queen of England orders [note that word] to be acted at his expense."[57] The play may well have been rewritten to take on board the massacre known as the Spanish Fury of November 4, 1576, according to at least one student of it.[58] The page on which the scene is reproduced complete with a drawing shows an earlier edition, subsequently rewritten and differing from that which subsequently appears in the 1594 folio and the 1623 folio. Ben Jonson in the Induction to *Bartholomew Fair* (1614) dated the play: "He will swear Jeronimo [i.e., *The Spanish Tragedy*, usually dated to c. 1589] or Andronico, are the best plays yet, shall pass unexcepted here, as a man whose judgment it is constant and hath stood still these five and twenty or thirty years"— that is, since 1589 or 1584. Note it is the auditor's "judgment" which "is constant and hath stood still": a rather earlier date for *Titus Andronicus* is not ruled out.

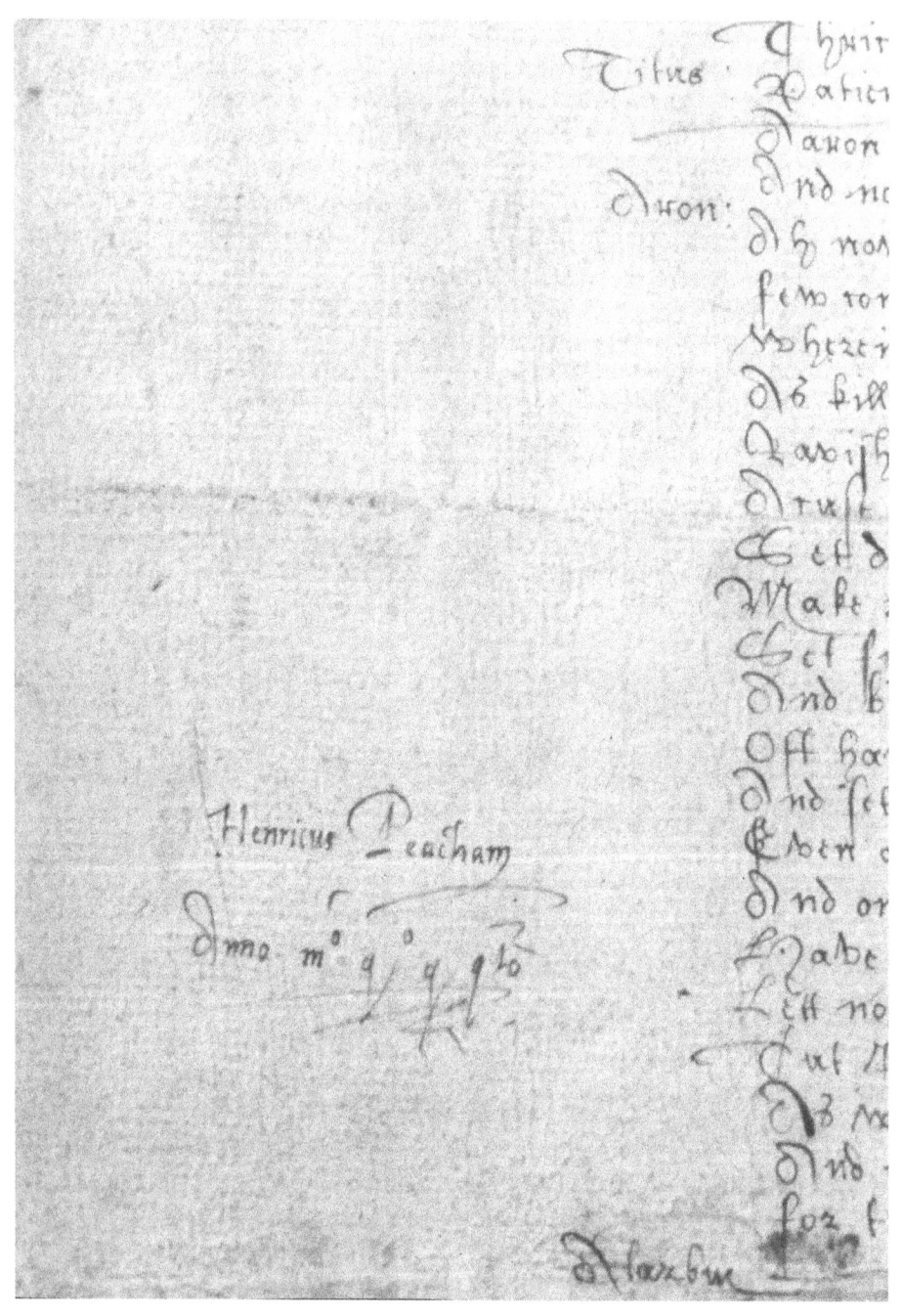

The Peacham manuscript of *Titus Andronicus* (1574).

One of the tests for an early or even juvenile work is the absence of double entendres and obscenity. A playwright needs the confidence of experience and maturity to use these weapons, which are not found at all or in any quantity in these plays.

Because *The True Chronicle of King Leir* may not be one of the strictly historical plays as envisaged by the quotation from Ronsard, I have perhaps arbitrarily postponed consideration of it. Likewise I put back consideration of *The Taming of a Shrew*. Furthermore, in September 1574 Oxford and Lady Lennox, the mother of Darnley, husband (and probably victim by murder) of Mary, Queen of Scots were the guests of Burghley. Mary, Countess of Lennox, probably carried in her possession upon her departure from Scotland the only known manuscript copy of *The Buik of the Croniclis of Scotland*, written some forty years earlier by an illegitimate Stuart relative and containing clear and unique references to the Macbeth story, which I deal with in Chapter Seven. Oxford would have been the only dramatist with any chance of seeing this unique source for the play.[59] Perhaps he made notes for, or wrote, a version of *Macbeth* before his departure for Italy, with a nod to the earl and Countess of Lennox (a nonspeaking part), two ahistorical characters. Compare Southampton in *Edmund Ironside* above.

Here I put in a general cautionary note on the subject of "stylometrics." All composers' or writers' styles alter in their lifetimes: it is unheard of for those styles to regress (indeed, are there any examples?). The evidence is that Oxford was a habitual rewriter. The phenomenon of mixed styles at different times of writing in a play, for not many are consistent in their entirety, can be compared to the span of topical allusions in them. To take an extreme example, from *Hamlet*, c. 1585, may be taken the speech of Polonius on literary drama and acting:

> The best actors in the world, either for tragedy, comedy, history, pastoral, pastorical-comical, historical-pastoral, tragical-historical, tragical-comical-historical-pastoral, scene individable, or poem unlimited ... [I, ii, ll.397–400].[60]

This is a send-up of Sidney's critique of drama in his *Apologie for Poesie*, and of course quite unpublishable in the mouth of a Sidney character by the following year, when Sidney was killed at Zutphen and became a dead national hero, and untouchable but for literary humor (and perhaps conversely a saint above contemporary literary criticism). Oxford no doubt considered the speech too good to lose, so he put it in the mouth of Polonius. (Meanwhile Slender in *The Merry Wives of Windsor* and Aguecheek in *Twelfth Night*, both Sidney's alter egos, having passed into public view from plays written earlier, are saved.)

Then fourteen or so years later he adds, in a sideswipe at William Shakespeare the gentleman,[61] who has recently been roasted by Jonson on the public stage:

> [The little eyases] are now the fashion, and so berattle the common stages — so they call them — that many wearing rapiers are afraid of goose quills, and dare scarce come thither [*ibid.*, ll. 342–45].

I have already contrasted the dramatic force of *Richard III* with that of the less forceful *Richard II*, and the advanced, more mature style of the latter over the former. Rigid dating becomes impossible. Disregarding the numerous similarities between plays dealing with the same scenarios and in the same language and the same ideas, modern critics sometimes consider these early plays genuine sources, sometimes as memorial reconstructions, and sometimes as imitations or adaptations made after the canonical versions. One critic wrote, "The strong probability seems now to be established that in an early quarto entitled *The Taming of a Shrew* we have a mangled version of this early play which Shakespeare refashioned as *The Taming of the Shrew*, although of course we cannot be sure that he may not have been the original author merely expanding and refurbishing his own youthful work."[62]

The last word can be left to another critic, but even he did not perhaps realize that what he said could readily be applied across a wider spectrum: "Several of Shakespeare's (1623) Folio plays, though none of anybody else's, exist in two or more very different versions, including totally different treatments of the same theme. The simple and obvious explanation, now [i.e., 1995] universally overlooked, is that the earlier publications were his first versions."[63]

It is a truism to say that "simple and obvious explanations" stand a much better chance of being right.

February 1574: now Oxford is ready and off to sunny Italy. He reached it in spring 1575.

Note on Early Shakespeare Poetry

One of the most important criticisms of the thesis that Oxford was Shakespeare relates to that slender volume of poetry that is accepted for the most part as by Oxford. The assessment is that this poetry is not up to Shakespearian standards. While Shakespeare's own standards can be variable, this criticism must be met head on. Of course part of the problem is that some of his poems appear in Edwards' anthology *A Paradise of Dainty Devices*— published in 1573, but collected apparently by Edwards prior to his death in 1567, at which time Oxford was at most seventeen years of age. The Oxford poems are very interesting as depicting the path of a poet's evolution. A poet may be "born, not made," but nevertheless he has to exercise his talents and polish his skills, and acquire new ones over time.

So, consider first a poem which looks and sounds like Shakespeare, and is identified as by Oxford:

> If women could be fair and not yet fond,
> Or that their love were firm, not fickle still,
> I would not marvel that they make men bond,
> By service long to purchase their good will;
> But when I see how frail these creatures are
> I muse that men forget themselves so far
>
> To mark the choice they make, and how they change,
> How oft from Phoebus do they flee to Pan
> Unsettled still like haggards wild they range,
> These gentle birds that fly from man to man;
> And who would not scorn and shake them from the fist
> And let them fly, fair fools, which way they list.
>
> Yet for disport we fawn and flatter both,
> To pass the time when nothing else can please,
> And train them to our lure with subtle oath,
> Till, weary of their wiles, ourselves we ease;
> And then we say when we their fancy try,
> To play with fools, O what a fool was I.

The task is to set out a list of those poems which a body of critics think are by Oxford. Here are the first lines:

From the Preface to *Cardanus Comfort* (1572) as enlarged in 1576:
  1. "The labouring man that tills the fertile soil"

From *A Paradise of Dainty Devices* (1573):
  2. "Fram'd in the front of forlorn hope past all recovery"
  3. "The lively lark stretch'd forth her wing"
  4. "The complaint of a Lover wearing black and tawny"
  5. "If care or skill could conquer vain desire"
  6. "The trickling tears that fall along my cheeks"
  7. "I am not as I seem to be"
  8. "Even as the wax doth melt, or dew consume away"
  9. "My meaning is to work what wonders love hath wrought"

From other publications written c. 1575–80, some doubtful and generally published later:
  10. "Who taught thee first to sigh, alas my heart?" "Fain would I sing, but fury makes me fret"
  11. "Were I a king, I might command content"

12. "Come hither shepherd swain"
13. "Whenas my heart at tennis plays"
14. "Winged with desire, I mount on high"
15. "My mind to me a kingdom is, such perfect joy therein I find"
16. "What cunning can express/the favour of her face"
17. "Sitting alone upon my thought in melancholy mood,"
18. "If women could be fair and yet not fond"
19. "In Peascod time when hound to horn gives ear while buck is killed"
20. "What is desire"
21. "Faction that ever dwells/In court, where wit excels"
22. "Doth sorrow fret thy soul"
23. "What plague is greater than the grief of mind?"
24. "What thing is Love: it is a power divine"[64]
25. "When I was fair"
26. "Bewray thy grief, thou woeful heart with speed"
27. "When wert thou born, Desire?"[65]
28. "Fair Cynthia's silver light"
29. "If all the world and love were young"
30. "What cunning can express"
31. "The while we sleep, whereof it may proceed" (entitled *Another Rare Dream*)
32. "Where gripping griefs the heart would wound"
33. "Awake ye woeful wight"

Twelve lines of no. 28 above "When wert thou born, Desire?" are quoted by Puttenham[66] in *The Arte of Poesy* (see pages 123ff), when he discusses the figure "Anthypophora, or the figure or response.... Edward, Earl of Oxford, a most noble and learned gentleman, made in this figure of response and emblem of desire, otherwise called Cupid, which for his excellency and wit, I set down some part of the verses for example: ...." The poem is apparently modeled on an early fifteenth century Italian poem.

Poems numbers 31 and 32 are taken from *Phoenix Nest* (1593). Number 31 was repeated with the first line as "What Shepherd can express" in *England's Helicon* (1600). *Another Rare Dream* is subtitled "learnedly set down by a worthy Gentleman, a brave scholar and M(aster) of Arts at both Universities." While Robert Greene was master of arts at both universities, as was Oxford, he scarcely qualifies as "a worthy Gentleman" to be author of the poem.

Part of number 33 is reproduced in *Romeo and Juliet* (IV, iv, ll. 152–54) and a version is entitled "The song of Emily" (the female lead in *Two Noble Kinsmen*). Number 34 comes from *Damon and Pithias* (1567). Both are ascribed to Edwards, but are claimed by some Oxford supporters.

Many of these poems have direct cross-references, ideas and echoes with works in the canon, including Shakespeare's other poems and the sonnets. The best essay on the subject is that contained in Joseph Sobran's book *Alias Shakespeare* (1997). Appendix 2 sets out some of the endless parallels of wording and thought that appear in the plays and poems attributed to William Shakespeare. An inexperienced poet with defective models influencing him however they might will not write the sonnets, and some of the poems are not much inferior to Berowne on love quoted on page 144: they are merely the predecessors by the same pen.

By way of example, in addition to those given by Sobran a comparison can be made between poem number 24 above, and two quotations with similar build-ups. The poem may be thought superior to the two quotations:

> What plague is greater than the grief of mind?
> The grief of mind that eats in every vein,
> In every vein that leaves such clods behind
> Such clods behind that breed such bitter pain
> So bitter pain that none shall find
> What plague is greater than the grief of mind.

Then from *The Comedy of Errors*:

> The meat is cold because you come not home
> You come not home because you have no stomach;
> You have no stomach, having broke your fast
> But we that know what 'tis to fast and pray
> Are penitent for your default today [I, ii, ll. 47–52].

And from *Two Gentlemen of Verona*, another early play:

> Tut, tut, I mean thou'lt lose the flood,
> And in losing the flood, lose the voyage,
> And in losing thy voyage, lose thy master,
> And in losing thy master, lose thy service
> And in losing thy service ... [II, iii, ll, 45–50].

Scattered about the corpus of late Tudor poetry are many other pieces of work which are anonymous, but some have too many Oxford-Shakespeare touches to be entirely coincidences — for instance the Tournament poetry (see page 26).[67] Many of the poems and songs included in Lyly's plays are claimed for Oxford: their beauty is beyond the powers of Lyly, and they were written at the time of Lyly's association with Oxford. Another one-time employee of Oxford's, Anthony Munday, is touted as the author of *The Pain of Pleasure* (1585), but the argument that it is Oxford's now has a strong champion.[68] The twenty-three pleasures listed come from a wide spectrum, stretching from beauty, riches, humor, love, aristocratic and country sports, music, dancing, fencing, tennis, to studies, law, astronomy, philosophy and divinity — all pleasures open to the aristocrat of the time. Consider also from *Arden of Feversham* a typical Oxfordian early construction piece of versification in which Lady Arden reproaches her lover for not trusting her:

> Wilt thou not look? Is all thy love overwhelmed?
> Wilt thou not hear? What malice stops thine ears?
> Why speakst thou not? What silence ties thy tongue?
> Thou hast been sighted as the eagle is.
> And heard as quickly as the fearful hare,
> And spoke as smoothly as an orator,
> When I have bid thee hear or see or speak,
> And art thou sensible in none of these? [III, v, ll. 123–130].

The academic meter-counting mind also attacks the poetry content of Oxford's poems. In particular, Nelson accuses him of unnatural stress and "galumphing" alliteration. However, Michael Brame and Galina Popova refute these views totally.[69] They point out that where Nelson relying on the iambic ti-tum says the stress is damaging the meaning, Oxford in fact cures this stress defect by inverting the rhythm, and those poems that are accepted as by Shakespeare do exactly the same. For example, four lines from Sonnet 139 begin:

> l. 3 Wound me ...
> l. 5 Tell me ...
> l. 9 Let me ...
> l. 14 Kill me ...

For alliteration, Nelson quotes (where he denounces the use of "f" and "s" and ignores the use of "l"): "He<u>l</u>p <u>f</u>i<u>s</u>h, he<u>l</u>p fou<u>l</u> that <u>f</u>lock<u>s</u> and <u>f</u>eed<u>s</u> upon the <u>s</u>a<u>l</u>t <u>s</u>ea <u>s</u>oi<u>l</u>" from "Fram'd in the front of forlorn hope past all recovery"— poem number 2 above, and from internal evidence written when Oxford was barely into his teens.

Nelson also ignores Sonnet 136 which uses the same letters: "Thu<u>s</u> <u>f</u>ar <u>f</u>or <u>l</u>ove my <u>l</u>ove <u>s</u>uit, <u>s</u>weet <u>f</u>ul<u>fill</u>." No credit for the lack of experience or skill not fully developed is allowed by this type of critic for the fact that the poems accredited to "Shakespeare" are written after Oxford's thirtieth birthday, and most of "Oxford simpliciter" poems are written between five and fifteen years earlier.

I believe that all Oxford and all Shakespeare (where correctly attributed in both cases) were written by Oxford, but the value of this opinion must rest with your judgment. To assist you (some may find this a weasel phrase), you may like to take the test contrived by the late Edward Holmes.[70] It follows the idea of an American, Louis P. Benezet, who devised a similar one, but his was criticized on the ground that there was doubt over the authorship of one or more of the passages selected. The following passages are stanzas taken from a "Shakespeare" or an "Oxford" poem, an equal number from each. Can you identify which is which? Edward Holmes' book gives the answer but I will not: the literary critic should first be able to identify and then explain the reason for his/her distinction — on the basis of his ear rather than foreknowledge or research.

    A. If care or skill could conquer vain desire,
       Or reason's reins my strong affections stay
       There should my sighs to quiet rest retire,
       And shun such sights as secret thoughts betray:
       Uncomely love, which now lurks in my breast
       Should cease, my grief by wisdom's power oppressed.
    B. My reason, physician to my love,
       Angry his prescriptions are not kept,
       Hath left me, and I desperate now approve
       Desire is death, which physic did except.
       Past cure I am, now reason is past cure,
       And frantic mad with evermore unrest.
    C. Fain would I sing, but fury makes me fret,
       And rage has sworn to seek revenge of wrong;
       My mazed mind in malice so is set,
       As patience shall daunt my deadly dolours long;
       Patience perforce is such a pinching pain,
       As die I will, or suffer wrong again.
    D. For if I should despair, I should go mad,
       And in my madness might speak ill of thee;
       Now this ill-wrestling world is grown so bad,
       Mad slanderers by mad ears believed be.
       Love is a discord and a strange divorce
       Betwixt our sense and rest, by whose power,
       As mad with reason, we admit that force
       Which wit or labour never may endower.
    E. My thoughts and discourse are as madmen's are
       As random from the truth vainly expressed;
       For I have sworn thee fair and thought thee bright
       Who are as black as hell and dark as night.
       Why should my heart think that a several plot
       Which my heart knows the wide world's common place?
       Or my eyes seeing this say this is not,
       To put fair truth upon so foul a face?
    F. Who taught thee first to sigh, alas my heart?
       Who taught thy tongue the woeful words of plaint?
       Who filled your eyes with tears of bitter smart?
       Who gave thee grief and made thy joys to faint?

>   Who first did paint with colours pale thy face?
>   Who first did break thy sleeps of quiet rest?
>   Above the rest in court to give thee grace?
>   Who made thee strive in honour to be best?
> G. No drop but as a coach doth carry thee;
>   So ridest thou triumphing in my woe;
>   Do but behold the tears that swell in me.
>   And they thy glory through my grief will show;
>   But do not love thyself; then thou shall keep
>   My tears for glasses, and still make me weep.
> H. And shall I live on earth to be her thrall?
>   And shall and serve thee all in vain?
>   And shall I kiss the steps that she lets fall?
>   And shall I pray the gods to keep the pain
>   From her that is so cruel still?
>   No, no, on her work all your will?
> I. And let her feel the power of all your might,
>   And let her have her most desire with speed,
>   And let her pine away both day and night,
>   And let her moan and none lament her need,
>   And let those that shall her see,
>   Despise her state and pity me.
> J. Let him have time to tear his curled hair,
>   Let him have time against himself to rave,
>   Let him have time of Time's help to despair.
>   Let him have time a beggar's orts to crave,
>   And time to see one that by alms doth live
>   Disdain to him disdained scraps to give.

Deliberately the best of Shakespeare has not been chosen. To those who are defeated, I recommend the purchase of Edward Holmes' book.

There is a volume of further works claimed as by Oxford, some cogently, some less so. In particular the poetry of "Emaricdulfe" deserves full critical attention."[71] A case is made for the anonymous Phaeton sonnet, *To His Friend Florio*,[72] and some claim the work of other poets[73] and that their names are pseudonyms for Oxford. One of the problems may be that plagiarism may support these claims.

Puttenham (d. 1591) in *The Arte of English Poesy* (published 1589) and Sidney (d. 1586) in *The Defence of Poesy* (written c. 1582) preceded by Gascoigne (d. 1577) and Webbe (fl. 1584–91) do not in their works of literary criticism pay much attention to Oxford's poetry. Partly this is because they do not recognize the effect and contribution of his dramatic poetry, and partly because some of Oxford's poetry is juvenile and experimental for its effects. Puttenham and Webbe acknowledge his existence as a poet, but it is difficult sometimes to see if they are merely wishing to flatter or are pleased to pass a favorable judgment (or a mixture of those possibilities). Gascoigne in *The Steel Glas*, as we have seen (page 29) launches a vicious attack on Oxford as a poet, but that does not seem to include a denunciation on technical grounds. Sidney appears to be saying that, as far as poetry is concerned, Oxford and he are of the same mind, as Sidney's *Defence of Poesy* "is a defence of imaginative literature."

I suspect, extrapolating from his attitude to dramatic theory, that Oxford's interest in the nuts and bolts of versification, as opposed to general effect, was limited. "Shakespeare" writes no poetical criticism.

Chapter Three

Oxford in Italy

On February 7, 1574/5, Oxford leaves England, undertaking, as I will show, the most important journeys in literary history. He took with him a great basket of intelligence assets, and the date enables us to consider the paths that his education, general upbringing and experiences have so far brought him, and the use in literary terms to which he put these assets. First we may consider his skills at languages.

Latin[1]

There is a substantial misreading of Jonson's "small Latin and less Greek"[2] phrase. First there are the more than mere competence at Latin and artistry in translation exhibited in the translation of *Metamorphoses*; then there is his grasp and development of the philosophy of the classic authors (e.g., Plautus' *Menaechmi*[3] and other plays applied to, say, *The Comedy of Errors*); and finally there is that element which is in effect in his bones[4]: "Shakespeare, who says nothing to help the audience, evidently has the original before his mind with complete clarity. Never was learning more lightly worn"; "Shakespeare writes like one who can afford not to show off. His academic exercises retain no smell of the classroom. It is pure fun." There is, however, one slight exception to that rule: in the very early play *Edmund Ironside*, the young author plays a show-off trick on his audience:

> I do remember hardy Hannibal
> Did use these words at won Tarentum's loss
> Eadem arte qua prius coepimus[5]
> Tarentum amisimus [IV, iii, 1.1553–1556].

The Latin reads, "By the same trick by which we first begin, we have lost Tarentum." After much cogitation and research, scholars now think this is a spoof quote, nonexistent in original Latin, and a private joke to the author.[6]

Greek

We have seen the probability that Oxford knew biblical Greek (see page 18). The "orthodox" critic comes from a position of total denial that the writer had any knowledge of Greek,[7] or of Greek literature, save through translations. Oxford, as we shall see, was sufficiently competent in Greek to attend the Greek Orthodox services in Venice at the church assigned to the Greek Orthodox community at San Giorgio dei Greci, where he might follow the fiendishly difficult (to an Englishman) pronunciation of the Greek in use. Because the learning is so lightly worn,[8] the clues can be difficult. In *Titus Andronicus*:

> The self-same gods that armed the Queen of Troy
> With opportunity of sharp revenge
> Upon the Thracian tyrant in his tent [I, i, ll. 136–38].

He refers to the revenge of Hecuba in blinding Polymestor for killing her youngest son. The story is apparently from Ovid, but the words "in his tent" are not in the Latin of Ovid — they are in the Greek of Euripides' Hecuba. Again:

> The Greeks upon advice did bury Ajax
> That slew himself; and wise Laertes' son
> Did graciously plead for his funeral [I, i, ll. 376–78].

This is from Sophocles' *Ajax*, where Ulysses is the chivalrous foe, and not *Metamorphoses*, where Ulysses is the villain.

In 3 *Henry VI*, there is a simile for Warwick's scouts:

> That as Ulysses and stout Diomede
> With sleight and manhood stole to Rhesus' tents
> And brought from thence the fatal Thracian steeds ... [IV, ii, ll. 19–21].

The story comes from Homer's *Iliad* and also Euripides' *Rhesus*. To collect elements of the story from Latin, Shakespeare would have had to consult widely — unlikely when there is at least one comprehensive source in Greek.

Erasmus' Latin translation of Lucian's *Misanthrope* is cited as a source for *Timon of Athens*, but the play is devoid of any Latin feel. Likewise the words "academe," "dialogue," "Promethean," "metamorphize," "Olympian," "pander," "ode," and "mimic" are imported directly from the Greek. Greek words are used to identify the characters: Laertes; Dromio (Greek for "run"); Desdemona ("unlucky woman"); Ophelia ("benefit").

The efforts of numerous critics to deny the knowledge of Greek required by the writer, and available to Oxford, are tortuous in the extreme. One non–Greek writer might hit upon a few connections by accident or by borrowing from other writers, but not the volume of sources required for the works of

Shakespeare, but Andrew Werth can point an endless list of connections, from which I take:

> The Greek Anthology: Sonnets 153 and 154
> Homer: *Troilus and Cressida*; *A Midsummer Night's Dream*; *As You Like It*; *The Comedy of Errors*
> Aeschylus: *Macbeth* (and note the typically Greek way in which Duncan's murder is announced).
> Sophocles: *Hamlet*; *Othello*; *Macbeth*

We may add the reporting of the naval battle in *Edward III*, a typical Greek report by messenger.

Jacques Amyot translated Plutarch into French (perhaps the version purchased by Oxford in 1568 referred to above) and Thomas North translated his version into English. Critics however convince themselves that the writer "divined the true spirit of Greek tragedy"[9] through the two idiosyncratic prisms through which Plutarch's *Lives* has to pass to appear in English. They have to ignore this reference:

> Thy promises are like Adonis' garden
> That one day blossom'd and fruitful were the next
> [1 *Henry VI*, I, viii, ll. 6, 7].

This is a direct reference to a question by Socrates; in other words the promises by Joan of Arc were only likely to be fruitful for a short time.[10]

The main argument for Oxford's competence in Greek is his capture of the nuance and irony in Greek tragedy: "[the] conception [of character in Hamlet] is Greek, and Shakespeare got nearer to the spirit of Greek tragedy than did Jonson and the schoolmasters."[11]

Two other critics, who do not entertain for one moment that the author could be other than William Shakespeare of Stratford-upon-Avon, state that his patent intimacy with the classics is "a miracle we cannot explain."[12] Oxford supplies all they and we need to know.

Hebrew[13]

Oxford, as we have seen, obtained his M.A. from both Oxford and Cambridge: there is no evidence as to how much study he did, but one of the arts required in order to have the degree was competence in Hebrew. However, he appears to have gained sufficient knowledge of Hebrew and the customs of Venetian Jewry to make Shylock authentic — far more than strictly necessary for his London audience, then or now. Jessica is a transliteration of the Hebrew Yiscah (just as Rebecca is for Rivcah), but the point is that it is Oxford's own transliteration, as Jessica was unknown as a name before *The Merchant of Venice*.

Shylock may be linked, not with the long *I* in "shyster," but with a shorter sound, as in Shelach in Genesis. The near homonym shalach[14] means a cormorant, that voracious predator of fish: when taxed with the uselessness of the pound of flesh once extracted, the cormorant replies: "To bait fish withal" (III, i, 1.49). Shalach-a means a skinner or meat stripper, and there seems to be a double or treble meaning in the exchange. Shy (with the long I sound)-lock (the name of his non–Jewish Northwest Passage defrauder (see page 99) may have been a later, added bonus for Oxford.

French

Here we meet one of the most interesting aspects of Oxford's life in literature. Critics appear to pass over the poet Ronsard's "astonishing prophesy" (see page 18) in, perhaps embarrassed, silence. Once again, whenever an "orthodox" critic is baffled or amazed by some to him or her inexplicable element or fact to do with Shakespeare, Oxford supplies a more than adequate explanation. Oxford as we learn from Sir Thomas' letter to Burghley of April 25, 1576, was "brought up in my house"; is it too much of a speculation to suggest that the young earl was actually in Paris during some part of Sir Thomas' ambassadorship, also knew Ronsard and was advised by him? If Oxford was at (or even in touch with) the French court at that early age, might he not have been influenced in an Italian direction by the pronounced Italian element there in Catherine de Medici's court? To date I have no evidence to substantiate the suggestion that the barely teenage Oxford was part of Sir Thomas Smith's household in Paris; indeed, it might have been dangerous for him to be there, in case he became a hostage of the Catholic party (of which Ronsard was a supporter). Young aristocrats did, however, as part of their education serve as pages in foreign courts. The English ambassador to Paris in the 1580s was Sir Edward Stafford, who served in one of the (Protestant) Bourbon households.

Consider: we know that Oxford aged 13 was competent in French. There is the letter (with its beautiful penmanship) in the British Library illustrated in Ogbourn, headed "Monsieur très honorable." In full it reads:

> Monsieur i'ay receu voz lettres, plaines d'humanité et courtoysie, et fort resemblantes a vostre grand'amour et singuliere affection envers moy, comme vrais enfans doucement procréez d'une telle mere, pour la quelle ie me trouve de iour en iour plus tenu a v.h. Voz bons admonestements pour l'observation

du bon ordre selon voz appointemens, ie me delibere (dieu aidant) de garder en toute diligence — comme chose que ie cognois et considere prendre especialement a mon propre bien et profit, usant en cela l'admis et autorité de ceux qui font aupres de moy. La discretion dequels i'estime si grande (s'il me convient parler quelque chose a leur advange) qui non seulement ilz se porteront selon qu'un tel temps le requiert, ains (i?) que plus est feront tant que ie me gouverne selon que vous aves ordonné et commandé. Quant a l'ordre de mon estude pour ce que il requiert vn long discours a l'expliquer par le menu, et le temps est court a cette heure, ie vous prie affectueusement m'en excuser pour le present, vous asseurant que par le premier passant ie le vous ferai sçavoir bien au long. Cependant ie prie a dieu vous donner santé.
Edward Oxinford[15]

This letter was written in August 1563, two months after Lawrence Nowell wrote to Burghley, stating, "I clearly see that my work for the Earl of Oxford cannot be much longer required" — that is, he had not much more to teach the boy of 13 (see page 18). The question then arises, Who would be written to in French as an educational adviser?

However, there is an endorsement in Oxford's writing to Burghley. This may be Burghley's file copy or a draft submitted to him for vetting before transmission to France at a politically sensitive time. The heading "monsieur très honorable" may translate as "[to] the Right Honourable Sir [William Cecil]," his correct mode of address at the time. "Admonestements" sounds cecilian, but "l'ordre de mon estude" may indicate something wider. It might appear that the young Oxford is out of the immediate reach of Burghley to be able to write in these terms, so there is just the possibility that the letter was written from France — from the French Court with Ronsard in attendance — to Sir William with its promise of a follow-up "par le premier passant" — by the next person crossing the Channel. Perhaps, though it would certainly seem logical to have him back home in view of the rapid deterioration of English fortunes in the early part of that year, 1563.

What is the effect on Oxford of the French connection? One critic writes: "Shakespeare's French diction is shared with [the play Edmund] Ironside which is itself notable for linguistic invention. The Ironside Gallicisms[16] are at first glance, even at first reading, unobtrusive; but they become conspicuous on closer analysis. They amount to deliberate exploitation of unfamiliar forms." He points out that most apparent is its specialization in reflexive verbs and other Gallic attributes. No such general tendency is noted in any other Tudor writer. He then sets out a long list of examples. Some Oxfordians consider that *Edmund Ironside* was written c. 1571, when Oxford was barely 21 years old, but still virtually at the point of immediate receptivity of the French influence on his education as a literary genius.

As I indicated earlier (page 18), Ronsard's original version of his poem is not an "astonishing prophecy"; it is a reasonable if optimistic estimate in 1564 of future developments in English literature. Great parts of those developments had already by 1585 come to fruition — certainly as far as the literary élite of the two countries were concerned — and are accordingly celebrated by the poet, not just by polishing the original version, but deliberately inserting a substitution for it. Only Oxford and one body of work can qualify as a catalyst for this change and for these praises: and enough of it must have appeared by 1585. Only Oxford meets the tests.

It is fascinating to consider that Ronsard could actually have encouraged the young Oxford in writing the history plays, and approved of his discarding of the continental conventions of drama, so that these plays became more natural and dramatic than the "correct" but impossibly turgid *Gorboduc—* (see page 139).

I suggest Oxford and Ronsard knew (of) each other. The final conclusion may well be that by 1585, Oxford had already become a leading light of English literature, and of European culture generally. So full was Oxford's knowledge of Ronsard that he comes perilously close to plagiarism of Ronsard, who wrote in 1564:

> Le monde est la Theatre, et les hommes acteurs
> La Fortune qui est maistresse de la scene
> Apreste les Habitz, et de la vie humaine.
> Les cieux et les Destins sont les grans spectateurs
> En gestes differens, en differens Langages,
> Roys, Princes et Bergers jouent leurs personages
> Devant les yeux de tous, sur l'escharfant commun ...

All the world's a stage ... [*As You Like It* II, viii, ll. 139 ff].

Italian

From his purchase in 1569 we know that Oxford was interested in Italian[17]: how could he not be as that language was then regarded as the foremost vehicle for drama in Europe? Perhaps he wished to prepare himself in the hope that he might be allowed to travel there at some future date.

One critic is exhaustive on the subject,[18] concluding: "It seems clear, therefore, from the plays which have an Italian source that Shakespeare could read Italian, and that for a surprising number of plays, he read those sources in Italian." He may have taken certain clichés and proverbs, and even borrowed sentences from Florio's *First Fruits* (1578) and *Second Fruits* (1591),[19] but the overwhelming evidence is that Oxford as author was fluent in Italian. Anyway, after the nine months' stay in Italy in 1575-76, how could he not be? The clinching evidence lies in those works in Italian for which no translation into English or French existed, and even where one does exist into French, our critic makes clear that the author bypassed the French version and read straight from the Italian. Thus from *Othello*: "Se non mi fai, dissere, vedere, cogl'occhi quello" (Cinthio), he translates: "Give me the ocular proof" (*Othello* III, iii, l. 360).

Chappuy's contemporary French translation is: "Si tu ne me fais voir ce que tu m'as dit" (If you do not make me see that which you have told me).

Thus a list of sources directly read in Italian would include:

    Cinthio: *Hecatommithi* 1565 — for *Othello, Measure for Measure,*
Epitia 1583 — for *Measure for Measure*
    Bandello: *Novelle* 1554 — for *Othello*
    Ariosto: *Orlando Furioso* 1556 — for *Othello*[20]
    Fiorentino: *Il Pecorone* 1558 — for *The Merchant of Venice*
    Anon: *Gl'Ingannati* 1537 — for *Twelfth Night*

It is noticeable that almost all the dates of these works are prior to Oxford's expedition in 1575-76 to Italy: it is reasonable to assume that he had mastered Italian before his departure, as no one on a cultural expedition would wish to waste time at the destination in learning the language — added to which no Italian resident in Italy is known to have had a command of English at the time.

Spanish

There is no particular evidence for his knowledge of Spanish save that Oxford for a large part of his life had access to Burghley's library, which was reputed to hold a large number of books in Spanish.[21] For a person of his intellectual interests neither Spanish nor Portuguese would present much difficulty.

In summary: "When we approach the romances we catch curious glimpses of extended explorations into source material.... Sometimes we may suppose the peculiar parallels between the plays and works by others may be due to coincidence, to the intermediary of works now lost or to that of conversations with friends, but even when allowance has been made for all such possibilities, enough remains to warrant the assumption that he was easily familiar with Latin, French and Italian, that he read widely in these as in English, and that he frequently took the trouble to examine several renderings of a story before he himself sat down to write."[22]

In addition to those skills at languages, we can add musical and artistic appreciation, law, eloquential skills, his athletic skills at tilting and other aristocratic sports, and not least his aristocratic social skills such as dancing and interludes, which would include his acting ability, all of which he evidenced, and can be demonstrated from the later events of his life.

In music,[23] Oxford has some reputation for competence and patronage. The plays indicate that music was a very important part of the productions, and because the songs in Lyly's early plays are considered superior to anything Lyly wrote, and Lyly was at the time in the employ of Oxford, these songs are thought to be Oxford's as well, and it is more than possible that he wrote the music for them. The productions would contain the actual songs written by the playwright, song fragments and allusions and stage directions for music with the instruments usually specified. *Galliard* is usually attributed to Oxford and the composers Byrd and Farmer were well known to him. Farmer dedicated two sets of songbooks, 1591 and 1599, the second of which reads in part:

> I have presumed to tender these Madrigals only as remembrance of my service and witnesses of your lordship's liberal hand, by which I have so long lived, and from your honourable mind that have so much of all liberal sciences. In this I shall be most encouraged if your lordship vouchsafe protection of my first-fruits, for that both of your greatness you can, and for your judgment in music best may. For without flattery be it spoke, those that know your lordship know this, that using this science as a recreation, your Lordship have overgone most of them that make it a profession.

In law, Oxford's competence is unassailable.[24]

On February 7, 1574/5, Oxford left England for France. His expedition is without exaggeration the most important event in English literature. The revolution was fired by the eloquence in English heard in the public and private theatrical performances of the late 1570s, and the element of Italian sophistication which Oxford brought back from Italy in 1576 is a vital ingredient to that eloquence and the consequent revolution.

He stayed a month in Paris at the court of King Henry III, and was considered to have acquitted himself well, according to the English ambassador there, who wrote to Burghley: "I will assure your Lordship unfeignedly my Lord of Oxford used himself as orderly and moderately as might be desired, and with great commendation."[25]

Next he moved to Strasbourg where he was acquainted, to put it no higher, with the humanist scholar Sturmius. The spring thaw permitted Oxford to cross the Alps into Italy. On April 26 he left Strasbourg, and early in May he reached Venice.[26] Sometime in August or September he visited Genoa, returning effectively to his base in Venice for a short time before visiting Milan at the end of September. Early in October he was back in Venice. At the end of November he wrote to Burghley from Padua. He went back to Venice and on December 12, 1575, set off for Florence. According to an account written fifteen years later, he also visited "the rest of Italy." On January 3, 1575/6, he wrote from Siena, and at the end of February he returned to Venice, which he finally left on March 5. He returned home by way of Milan, Lyons and Paris, and landing, or rather being landed (for which distinction see below, page 60) in April.

There are some suggestions that Oxford might have reached Ragusa (Dubrovnik) and/or Sicily, but the material as opposed to the literary evidence is incomplete. There are, however, substantial gaps in the actual historical record, which is well summarized by the late Philip Johnson[27] thus:

> First tour including Genoa — late July to early September
> Second tour including Milan — September 25–October 6
> Third tour including Padua — October 7–December 10
> Fourth tour including Florence and Siena — December 12–February 25

There would have been time for excursions to Ragusa and the "rest of Italy."

Philip Johnson then adds that Oxford must have gone via Padua on at least one of his journeys, and probably took in Verona, and almost certainly Florence. There is some evidence over which there is a great deal of debate that Oxford went to Palermo, as there is a report in 1590 of him issuing a jousting challenge in that city: "No man durst be so hardy to encounter with him. So that all over Italy he is acknowledged the only Chevalier and Nobleman of England." From the plays, visits are evidenced to Messina as well as to Modena and Mantua. Oxford's geography in the Italian plays has yet to be faulted.[28]

The first point is that millions of visitors since have been struck dumb by the fantastic outpouring of artistic skill on view in the churches and galleries of Italy: Oxford was similarly impressed, and fired to describe in language to match what he saw and its effect on him. While these impressions were blazing hot in his brain he set them down.

His poetry has pride of place beginning with Sonnet 33:

> Full many a glorious morning have I seen
> Flatter the mountain tops with sovereign eye
> Kissing with golden face the meadow grass
> Gilding pure streams with heavenly alchemy.

Clearly this is an Italian not an English dawn.

Then we have *Venus and Adonis*. Noemi Magri has proved that the poem follows the account essentially depicted by Titian, where the adolescent Adonis is importuned by Venus,[29] rather than other accounts including that of Ovid where he takes a more positive role, and it is the Barberini version now in Rome. At the time when Oxford was in Venice the painting was kept by Titian at his studio in Venice: there can be little doubt that Oxford visited Titian, then aged nearly one hundred and virtually a public monument that all travelers of any standing would wish if only for prestige's sake to call upon. This version has Adonis wearing a bonnet just like the poem (ll. 1086–88). Dr. Magri sets out the verbal parallels between the poem and the painting.

Likewise who could doubt that the poet saw the actual painting in the Palazzo del Te at Mantua after reading:

> Look when a painting would surpass the life
> In limning out a well-proportion'd steed
> His art with nature's workmanship at strife,
> As if the dead and living could exceed;
> So did this horse excel a common one
> In shape, in courage, colour, pace and bone.
> Round-hoofed, short-jointed, fetlock shag and long,
> Broad breast, full eye, small head, and nostril wide,
> High crest, short ears, straight legs and passing strong,
> Thin mane, thick tail, broad buttock, tender hide,
> Look, what a horse should have he did not lack
> Save a proud rider on so proud a back [ll. 289–302].[30]

Dr. Magri makes the valuable point that the poem is lighthearted and carefree in tone except those passages relating to the procreation theme (ll.133–74, 727–68, 787–810), which would be added along with and about the same time of the dedication to the third Earl of Southampton (1593). The dedication with its successor *The Rape of Lucrece* looks as if it is a take-off from the genre of such dedications, and quite impossible in its language for a commoner to write to an earl. In their way these dedications are evidence that William Shakespeare had either not come to London or not reached any prominence there: if he had, they would have been worded differently, and more similarly to those of poets of William's age and status. Likewise the actual wording of the dedication includes the phrase referring to the poem as "the first heir of my invention," which can hold only one meaning.[31] The "invention" is not the composition of the poem; nor can it refer to the poet's inspiration or genius as he had written quite a good deal already even by 1576, which is the probable date of the poem. The "invention" is the creation of the pseudonym under which he might write and be anonymous even if published, or under which he might act in public. Having chosen and signed the dedication "William Shakespeare," he also tells us that the poem is "the first heir" of that "invention." In effect he gives the game away by confirming that the name is a pseudonym (probably a necessity for an aristocrat who wished to be published in his lifetime), even if the wording did not give out sufficient signal.

Shortly afterwards Oxford wrote *The Rape of Lucrece*, which contains

Horse by Giulio Romano, 1527–28 — Palazzo del Te.

some two hundred lines of pictorial description of the Trojan mural in the Ducal Palace at Mantua, including where Oxford recalls from the Palazzo del Te the scene where Achilles avenges the death of Patroclus[32]:

> That for Achilles' image stood his spear,
> Gripped in an armed hand, himself behind
> Was left unseen, save to the eye of mind ... [ll. 1424–26].

This seems to touch on the concealment of the face behind the *spear*-shaking arm of the real name (i.e., Achilles-Oxford *behind* Shake-*spear*).

Three — Oxford in Italy

Achilles Avenges the Death of Patroclus by Giulio Romano, c. 1538, Palazzo del Te.

In the Hall of the Giants in the Palazzo del Te at Mantua is a representation by the sculptor and painter Giulio Romano (1499–1546) of a giant dwarf, described in *Love's Labour's Lost* as:

> This wimpled whining, purblind boy
> This senior-junior giant dwarf, Dan Cupid [III, i, ll.182–83].

"Senior-junior" makes no sense at all,[33] but if you replace the phrase with "Signior Giulio's," all is clear.

As we shall see, there are other references to Mantua, including the portrait of the murdered Duke of Urbino by Titian in *Hamlet* (page 111). There are references to Mantuan politics in *Measure for Measure* and *The Merchant of Venice*.

Oxford also carried his artistic experience into his dramatic works, using it in one case to depict an allegory for his own oeuvre which in *The Taming of the Shrew* is entrusted to Sly, the representative at a later stage of William Shakespeare, the rich paintings and other possessions of the lord and attributes of his lordship (Induction 1 and 2). A critic wondered, "Why does the poet lavish such lyrical beauty on so queer a theme?"[34]

Similarly, in *The Winter's Tale*,[35] Giulio Romano has apparently made the representation of Hermione:

> a piece many years in doing and now newly performed by that rare Italian master, Julio Romano, who, had he himself eternity and could put breath into his work, would beguile Nature of her custom, so perfectly is he her ape: he so near to Hermione hath done Hermione, that they say one would speak to her and stand in hope of answer [V, ii, ll. 94–99].

Vasari the artist and art historian reports that his paintings (translation) "do not seem to be painted or imaginary things but they appear to be living and real." One wonders whether Oxford had read Vasari, as that idea is so closely followed in the play. Oxford even hints at the Gonzaga duke's complaint that Romano took an exceedingly long time over his masterpieces for his palace on the island of Te at Mantua, which is where Oxford would have seen them in 1574/5, and picked up the gossip over the delays. Even the phrase "newly performed" would seem to refer to the restoration of the painting on the sculptures at the palace by Bertani in the period 1572–74.[36]

Before departing for Italy, Oxford would have had opportunities to study Italian poetry and drama, and between then and sitting down to write plays on his return, and fortified by the influences and experiences he found in Italy, he took on board the works and ideas of some Italian authors. The effect can be seen in those plays. Italian love poetry is mirrored in the poems and sonnets and *Romeo and Juliet* poetry. The plays' debt to the traditions and even to identifiable texts of Italian *commedia erudita* is well established. They draw on the Italian novelists and playwrights Boccaccio, Ariosto, Bandello, Macchiavelli, Aretino, Cinthio and Florentino. Elements of the plots, by way of example, are taken for *The*

Portrait of Francesco Maria della Rovere, Duke of Urbino, by Titian, 1538, Uffizi.

Merchant of Venice from Florentino's *Il Pecorone*; *The Merchant of Venice* and *Measure for Measure* from Cinthio's *Hecatommithi*; *The Taming of the Shrew* from Ariosto's *I Suppositi*; *Twelfth Night* from Ariosto's *Gli Inganatti*.

There is an interesting test question: to what extent does Giordano Bruno, the secular philosopher murdered by the Inquisition in 1599, influence Oxford, or Oxford Bruno?[37] The latter was resident in London during the period 1581–86. As *The Comedy of Errors, Love's Labour's Lost* and *Two Gentlemen of Verona* can all be dated prior to Bruno's own works, then it would appear that Oxford is the catalyst and Bruno, a known plagiarist, the borrower. Once the dating of Oxford's plays is put right, then this is the substance and logical conclusion. A historian on Bruno's activities in London quotes: "As swift as lead" (*Love's Labour's Lost* III, i. 1.52); "[La barca] parea col sua festina lente tutta di piombo" ("Yet [the boat] seemed to move, hurrying slowly as if it were made of lead") (*La Cena de le Ceneri*, 1584) and also adds a topical political element: the boat (i.e., the Church of Rome) was being crewed by caricatures of Howard and Arundell depicted as senile and incompetent. We shall meet them again.

In addition to the *commedia erudita*, Oxford would have been exposed to the *commedia dell'arte all'improviso*, the vernacular or common form of entertainment, which comes from or is slightly later than the *commedia erudita*. In effect it was street entertainment performed by traveling companies. The plays relied on stock situations laced with topical injections. Occasionally companies ventured outside Italy, including England in the 1570s. The stock situations meant stock characters sometimes in pairs: Old men: Pantalone, the girl's father, rich and pompous; Graziano, the lawyer, old and lecherous; Pairs of lovers; two *zanni*: servants, slapstick and repartee comedians; a "verbal" maid or nurse; a cowardly yet boastful soldier. There are, of course, many examples in Shakespeare in the Italian plays. These characters and the stock situations in which they appear, adapted cunningly as necessarily, form almost the staple of large swathes of the canon.

Oxford, however, seems to have become part of the repertoire in Italy.[38] There is recorded in 1699 a spiel by Dottore Graziano the Bolognese lawyer character, in which he records a farcical tournament at the court of the Emperor Polidor of Trebizond. Among the contestants and other attendant worthies is "Elmond milord of Oxfort." His performance is sent up in fine style: he is unhorsed by Alvida Countess of Edenburg (Edinburgh?). Every contestant, however, receives prizes. Elmond receives Astolf's horn to rout armies.

With the advent of *Venus and Adonis* and those plays with a substantial Italian content we can see how his outlook on life had been widened, and how he viewed his own position not in the social hierarchy but as the cultural icon of his nation. From Siena he wrote on January 1, 1575/6, "I have no help but of mine own, and mine is made to serve me, and myself not mine." This attitude runs directly contrary to the feudal idea of service to the Crown in return for grant of land: Oxford's career as an artist is more important, nay essential, to himself, to culture and to his country generally — breathtaking claims, but in the event justified many times over.

On his way back to England Oxford experienced two important events. He appears to have returned via the Mont Cenis pass or by sea from Palermo to Marseille. He very likely stayed at Tournon-sur-Rhône where the local nobleman, the Count of Rousillon (not to be confused with Rousillon at the base of the Pyrenees), kept a chateau for his guests. The story of Helene de Tournon (a lowborn girl in love with a marquis, whose family persuaded him to renounce her, causing her to die of love) provides the basis for part of the plot of *All's Well That Ends Well*.

Oxford is reported by the English ambassador in Paris to be there on March 31, and on his departure took with him letters from the ambassador to London. Once at sea in the Channel his ship was attacked by pirates. Oxford was taken prisoner, but was saved from any worse fate by being recognized by a Scotsman.[39] As it was he was unceremoniously dumped at Dover wearing only his shirt. The comparison with the similar incident in *Hamlet* (Act IV, scene vi) can readily be made. The scenario comes up again in *Pericles*:

> A gentleman of Tyre, my name Pericles
> My education been in arts and arms,
> When looking for adventures in the world,
> Was by rough unconstant seas bereft
> Unfortunately both of ships and men,
> And after shipwreck driven upon this shore [Scene 7, ll. 76–81].

No doubt, like Pericles in scene 5, he is grateful to the locals who rescue him.

CHAPTER FOUR

The Revolution in English Literature

The introduction suggests that the moment the revolution in English literature takes off is with the return of Oxford from his Italian journey in April 1576, having been unceremoniously dumped by his pirate captors on a Sussex beach wearing only his shirt. Political revolutions have a leader who emerges, and a moment when that leader makes his entry. For example, Lenin appears after a journey from Germany in a sealed train at St. Petersburg station on April 3, 1917, and the rest is recorded history with plenty of eyewitnesses and commentators. The cultural revolution nearly four hundred and fifty years ago is not so fortunate in both the number and quality of its contemporary commentators. It is essential to examine such evidence as we have for that revolution. The conclusion is that in that cultural revolution Oxford is that leader and his return to England is that moment.

Although we may date in effect the revolution in English to 1575/80, there were forerunners, as in Lenin's revolution there were embedded Bolshevik and fellow-traveler cells in czarist Russia prior to 1917. Tyndale asserted in about 1530, in answer to the charge of barbarism in translating the Bible into English, that English did possess grace.

There are a number of examples of early translators who were actually proud of the English tongue. Thomas Phaer (1558) deliberately undertook a translation of the *Aeneid* to defend his native tongue against the charge of barbarism, and to encourage young writers to engage in the composition of poetry by showing them the potentialities of their native language, and his advice was repeated by Barnabe Googe in 1560.

Sir Thomas Smith, the sometime tutor and de facto guardian to the Earl of Oxford and perhaps the leading scholar of his time, wrote in about 1570 that when the use of English "was marked by precision and purity it might even compare with Latin for beauty and force of expression."[1]

George Gascoigne in his anthology *A Hundreth Sundry Flowers* (1573) wants future authors to leave off writing trifling love poems for more serious subjects, "For if quickness of invention, proper vocables, apt epithets, and a store of monosyllables may help a pleasant brain to be crowned with laurel. I doubt not but both our countrymen and country language might be entronized (enthroned) among the old foreleaders unto Mount Helicon."

In Scotland perhaps the revolution was scarcely slower off the ground. For instance, consider Thomas Hudson, who recounts the genesis of his translation of du Bartas'[2] *The History of Judith* (1581) in terms which shed a light on court manners of the time, and the respect given to the barely teenage James VI's view of the language:

> As your Majesty Sir, after your accustomed and virtuous manner was sometime discoursing at table with such of your Domestiques [courtiers of the royal household], as chanced to be attendant. It pleased your Highness [not only to esteem the peerless style of Homer, and the Latin Virgil to be inimitable to us, whose tongue is barbarous and corrupted] but also to allege partly through delight your Majesty took in the haughty style of those most famous writers, and partly to sound the opinion of others, that also the lofty phrase, the grave indictment, the facound [facile, fecund] terms of the French Sallust [du Bartas for the like resemblance] could not be followed, nor sufficiently expressed in our rude and impollished English language. Wherein, I more boldly than advisedly (with your Majesty's licence) declared my simple opinion. Not calling to mind that I was to give my verdict in presence of so sharp and clear-eyed a censure as your Highness is: but rashly I alleged that it was nothing impossible even to follow the footsteps of the same great poet Sallust, and translate his verse (which nevertheless is of itself exquisite) succinctly, and sensibly in our own vulgar speech. Whereupon it pleased your Majesty ... to assign me, the History of Judith, as an agreeable subject to your Highness, to be turned by me into English verse: not for any gift or special science that was in me, who am inferior in knowledge and erudition to the least of your Majesty's Court, but by reason (peradventure) of my bold assertion that your Majesty, who will not have the meanest of your house unoccupied, would have me bare the yoke, and drive forth the penance, that I had rashly procured.... In the which I have so behaved myself, that through your Majesty's concurrence, I have not exceeded the number of lines written by the author: in every one of which, he also hath two syllables more than my English bears. And this notwithstanding, I suppose your Majesty shall find little of my author's meaning pretermitted [missed out]. Wherefore if such be done by me, who am of another profession, and of so simple literature, I leave it to be consired [considered] by your Majesty what such as are consummate in letters and knows the weighty words, the pithy sentences, the polished terms, and full efficacy of the English tongue would have done.

I do hope the depth to which Hudson's tongue went into his cheek did not do him too serious an injury.

And then the revolution happened. Before we consider the elements of it we ought to treat of the effect of the explosion and seek out those commentators who understood, some more than others, the effect and extent of that revolution.

In 1577 Holinshed's *Chronicle* contends that the vernacular had so developed that "there was no one speech under the sun spoken in our time, that hath or can have more variety of words, copie [copiousness] of phrases, or figures or flowers of eloquence, than hath our english tongue." The second edition (1587), produced some years after his death, is widely considered a source for some of "Shakespeare's" history plays and *King Lear*: as we shall see in Chapter Six it may be the borrower from those plays.

In 1580 Jacques Bellot in *The English Scholemaister* writes that though English has as yet no great reputation, the language is so rich that it deserves to be placed among the most famous of the modern languages. The following year, having written a polemic against the detractors of English, George Pettie continues in *The Civile Conversation of Mr. Stephen Guazzo*:

> But how hardly soever you deal with your tongue, how barbarous soever you count it, how little soever you esteem it, I durst myself undertake (If I were furnished with learning otherwise) to write in it as copiously for variety, as compendiously for brevity, as choicely for words, as pithily for sentences, as pleasantly for figures, and every word as eloquently, as any writer should do in any vulgar tongue whatsoever.

This element of eloquence is recognized quite early as the essential ingredient which transforms English into its post–1580 form, or provides the basis for its changed reputation. Henry Peacham, whom we met when the dating of *Titus Andronicus* was considered (page 35), sets out many illustrations from the Bible to indicate clearly that eloquence is possible in the vernacular, in his very early critical essay "The Garden of Eloquence Conteyning the Figures of Grammer and Rhetorick from Whence May Bee Gathered all manner of Flowers, Coulors, Ornaments, Exornations, Formes and Fashions of Speech, very profitable for all those that be studious of Eloquence, and that reade most Eloquent Poets and Orators, and also helpeth much for the better understanding of the Holy Scriptures 1577."

The most eloquent of Peacham's contemporaries would appear to be Richard Mulcaster, headmaster of Westminster School and play producer. In his *First Part of the Elementarie* (1582), he has the confidence to write:

> If the spreading sea, and the spacious land could use any speech, they would both show you, where, and in how many strange places, they have seen our people, and also give you to wit, that they deal in as much, and as great varieties of matters, as any other people do, whether at home or abroad. Which is the reason why our tongue doth serve to so many uses, because it is conversant

to so many people, and so well acquainted with so many matters in sundry kinds of dealing.

He also wrote:

> For is it not indeed a marvellous bondage, to become servants to one tongue for learning sake, the most of our time, whereas we may have the very same treasure in our own tongue, with the gain of most time? our own bearing the joyful title of our liberty and freedom, the Latin tongue remembering [reminding] us of our thraldom and bondage? I love Rome, but London better, I favour Italy, but England more, I honour the Latin, but I worship the English.

And:

> But why not all in English, a tongue of itself both deep in conceit, and frank in delivery? I do not think that any language, be it whatsoever, is better able to utter all arguments, either with more pith, or greater plainness, than our English tongue is, if the English utterer be as skilful in their matter, which he is to utter: as the foreign utterer is. Which methink I durst prove in any most strange argument, even myself, though no great clerk, but a great wellwiller to my natural country. And though we use and must use many foreign terms when we deal with such arguments, we do not any more than the bravest tongues do and even very those, which crake of [grate harshly by] their cunning.... It is our accident which restrains our tongue, and not the tongue itself, which will strain with the strongest, and stretch to the furthest, for either government if we were conquerors, or for cunning, if we were treasurers, not any whit behind the subtle Greek for couching close, or the stately Latin for spreading fair. Our tongue is capable, if our people would be painful [work at it].

From the examples quoted at the beginning of this chapter it might be possible to believe that English and its reputation evolved slowly, but there can be no guarantee of this, especially as stacked against such evolution theory are the opinions of those contemporaries who did not believe that English could attain or surpass the achievements of Latin, Greek, Italian, French and Spanish, or who saw only imitation as the only way to improvement. So there must have been a more accelerated process to provide the catalyst to the revolution. Gavin Alexander wrote:

> When we look back via the prose of Dr. Johnson or the verse of Dryden, it is too easy to view the history of the English language and its literature as a gentle, inevitable evolution towards regularity and refinement, and the idea of English as a world language as a foregone conclusion. But we must not forget what Dryden and Johnson knew well — that Renaissance achievement had been sudden and substantial, and the story of language and literature they wrote ... really began in the sixteenth century.[3]

Elizabethans of the final two decades of the reign recognized that there had been a substantial change,[4] which they put down to the efforts of the poets, and to Sidney's *The Defence of Poesy*. Thus Thomas Nashe wrote in 1592: "The Poets of our time have cleansed our language from barbarism, and made the vulgar sort, here in London ... to aspire to a richer purity of speech than is communicated [among] the Comminalty of any Nation under heaven."[5] Thomas Lodge praises the poets "who brought the chaos of our tongue in frame." George Puttenham, almost certainly the author of *The Arte of English Poesie* (1589), which I comment on in greater depth in Chapter Six, affectionately thanks those poets whom he lists "for their studious endeavors, commendably employed in enriching and polishing their native tongue" which they have "so beautified ... as at this day it will be found our nation is nothing inferior to the French or Italian." Francis Meres' *Palladis Tamia* (1598) gives credit to a long list of poets, by whom "the English tongue is mightily enriched, and gorgeously invested in rare ornaments and resplendent habiliments."

The majority of these poets flourish later than that vital period 1575– 80. This means that there is a void in that vital period, an absence of evidence for literature at that date which is logically unacceptable. Living so close to that period, perhaps those contemporary critics did not perceive fully how the revolution had developed. At an early stage before printing and publication, they or some of them might have had access to manuscript versions of Sidney's poems and Spenser's *Faerie Queen*, and nobody could blame them from being bowled over by the impact of these poems and giving some credit to them for the revolution — incorrectly, I think. I discuss this aspect further below.

However, the effect of the publication of *Venus and Adonis* in 1593 is apparently that "Shakespeare" put himself at the head of a fashion instead of imitating one.[6] For the reasons outlined in Chapter Three, *Venus and Adonis* was certainly written a good deal earlier. Some of the Eclogues in Greene's *Menaphon* (1589)[7] owe something to *Venus and Adonis*.

The revolution without the input of Oxford after 1575 might well have been gradual or delayed or proved stillborn. In addition to a residue of academic critics who would not accept the ascent of English to the first rank of literary languages, there was also another set of conservatives who argued that English was a perfectly good language, but to be put in verse acceptable as literature, it had to be written in classical metres in imitation of the classic Latin poets. Thus William Webbe, author of *A Discourse of English Poetry* (1586), recognizing the part played by prose writers in the refinement of the mother tongue, complains that "only Poetry hath found fewest friends to amend it," so that "our English speech, in some of the wisest men's judgments, hath never attained to any sufficient ripeness, nay not full avoided the reproach of barbarousness in Poetry." He exhorts the poets to abide by the classical rules, whether or not modified to suit the language as necessary.

Chief among the conservatives was Gabriel Harvey who, after the publication of Spenser's *Shepheardes' Calendar* (1579), sought to persuade the author to abide by those rules, and had a (mercifully) short-lived success in that endeavor. Harvey was able to praise Stanyhurst, who like Webbe did permit some modifications in his 1582 translation of the *Aeneid*, with the following result, which trembles between not-too-happy and ludicrous:

> This said, with darksome night shade quite cloudy she vanisht,
> Grisly faces frouncing, eke against Troy leagued in hatred
> Of Saints sour deities did I see.
> Then did I mark plainly the castle of Ilion uplayed
> And Trojan buildings quite topsy turvy removed.[8]

Harvey[9] and his friends labored on, and in 1599 there appeared *The First Booke of the Preservation of King Henry VII*, compiled in English rhythmical hexameters from its preface:

> And to refine our speech, to procure our natural English
> Far to be more elegant; that verse may skilfully flourish.
> Which when it is re'd'ifi'd, eloquent and known to be perfit,
> Unto thee, and to thy realm, (O puissant Prince) what credit!
> Hexameters will amend our speech (thou sacred Eliza)
> Publish an orthography, and teach us true idioma.

Oxford, aided in effect by Edmund Spenser and Philip Sidney,[10] no doubt saw these ideas off. Claims are made that these poets were the authors of the revolution or took some major part in it. Spenser's *Shepheardes' Calendar* was published in 1579 and shortly after that he may have begun *The Faerie Queen*. This appears to have circulated quite widely in manuscript, but was not published until 1589. Sidney's works circulated in manuscript before he died of wounds after Zutphen in 1586, but *Astrophel and Stella* was not published until 1591.

Shepheardes' Calendar comes in for criticism in that, although the many archaisms delighted contemporaries, "they were really alien to their experience"[11] and in effect nostalgic or retrogressive: Spenser attached himself to a fading past of medieval romances, including Arthurian stories. His effects can be studied and over-literary. In summary, he was a one-off, not a leader of a poetic or language revolution, notwithstanding that *The Faerie Queen* is a poetic masterpiece.

John Lyly's *Euphues, The Anatomy of Wit* (1579) and *Euphues His England* (1580) are landmark works in the history of the novel, but his courtly mannerist style of writing, with its reliance on a temporary conversational fad rather than the essential rhetoric element, hardly fills the evidential void in the revolution period. Likewise, Sidney's own prose works of criticism can be ruled out, since they evince a conservative turn of mind and were not published until 1592. Sidney launched an attack on Shakespeare, as will be seen from the next chapter.

Much of this book could have been taken up with examples from minor poets from the last ten or twenty years of Elizabeth's reign. These would merely exemplify the triumph of the revolution, and not necessarily help to identify its causes or take forward the history of its genesis. However this is not to underplay its triumph, which was recognized by the Elizabethans themselves. An eccentric Frenchman calling himself John Soothern, in the service of Oxford himself, in 1584 serenaded his mistress thus:

> My name, quoth I, is Soothern, and
> Madame, let that suffice;
> That Soothern will raise the English language to the skies.
> The wanton of the muses, and
> Whose well composed rime
> Will live in despite of the heavens,
> And Triumph over time.[12]

Then, more seriously, Samuel Daniel wrote in *Poetical Essays* (revised 1599):

> Should we this ornament of glory then
> As th' immaterial fruits of shades, neglect?
> Or should we careless come behind the rest
> In power of words, that go before in worth,
> Whenas our accents equal to the best
> Is able greater wonders to bring forth:
> When all that ever hotter spirits exprest [i.e., Italian, French or Spanish]
>
> Comes bettered by the patience of the North?
> And who in time knows whither we may vent
> The treasure of our tongue, to what strange shores
> This gain of our best glory shall be sent,
> T' enrich unknowing Nations with our stores?
> What worlds in th' yet unformed Occident
> May come refin'd with th' accents that are ours?
>
> Or who can tell for what great work in hand
> The greatness of our style, is now ordain'd?
> What powers it shall bring in, what spirits command,
> What thoughts let out. What humors keep restrain'd
> What mischief it may powerfully withstand,
> And what fair ends may thereby be attain'd.
> And as for Poesie (mother of this force)

> That breeds, brings forth, and nourishes this might,
> Teaching it in a loose, but measured course,
> With comely motions how to go upright:
> And fostring it with bountiful discourse
> Adorns it thus in fashions of delight [*Musophilus*, ll. 939–964].[13]

"Bountiful discourse" is essential, but the real problem is that there is not yet, or not yet enough, eloquential appeal, and with it the declamatory opportunity that the theater gives. The theater's essential contribution is considered in the next chapter.

While poetry is a vital element in consolidating the gains of the revolution and in recording its progress, there is one all-important ingredient needed to complete the picture of the explosion of that revolution. Salinger quotes Heywood:

> "*Elizabethan literature is a literature of the spoken word.* Just as oratory dominated the domestic training of the humanist, so — in the age of the Reformation and popular controversy — the spoken literary forms of preaching and acting dominated the printed forms of journalism and fiction, while in poetry there was the related influence of song." In effect the stage provides the principal setting for that essential eloquential appeal enabling that "discourse" to be or become "bountiful."

Heywood bears this out, writing in his *Apology for Actors* (1607):

> Our English tongue, which hath been the most harsh, uneven and broken language in the world ... is now *by this secondary means of playing*, continually refined, every writer striving in himself to add a new flourish unto it: so that in the process ... it is grown to a most perfect and composed language, that many excellent works and elaborate Poems writ in the same, that many nations grow enamored of our tongue (before despised).[14]

The historian and antiquarian William Camden was perhaps not quite as convinced, but he did write (1605):

> Pardon me and think me not overbalanced with affection, if I think our English tongue (I will not say as sacred as the Hebrew, or as learned as the Greek), but as fluent as Latin, as courteous as the Spanish, as courtlike as the French, and as amorous as the Italian, as some Italianated amorous have confessed.[15]

Perhaps he had Oxford in mind.

Chapter Five

The Revolution in the Theater

The year 1576 is absolutely vital in the history of English language and culture. First, it is the date of Oxford's return from Italy, and secondly, it begins the supply of that vital element of public eloquence lacking as we saw at the end of the last chapter: the opening of the theater in 1576, the most important development in English literature and theater.[1] Now the writers and the players have a permanent forum for experiment as well as rehearsal and performance. This is the "Bastille moment" for the revolution.[2]

Prior to 1576 there were no (or only very short-lived) fixed public theaters. Theatrical companies would travel around England under the protection of some great lord, making one-off performances, mainly of morality plays. These plays must have had some success, but there was no commercial or artistic incentive for a locus where the art of theater could be refined or be the subject of experiment, or even for meeting the need for dramatic works to please a consistently attending and paying public. These traveling theatrical companies might be compared to a one-channel television switched on once a year in the provinces and not much more in London: the sixteenth century could switch on by attending a performance or miss out on the very infrequently available externally produced entertainments. The companies' effective monopoly to a virtually captive audience (to say nothing of the physical effort and management of the traveling, setting up and taking down) would take away the incentive for artistic improvement. The case therefore for low estimation of public performances of plays prior to 1576 seems to be made.[3] The verse in these plays is disfigured by doggerel and fourteen-syllable iambics: doggerel and fourteeners — i.e., seven-foot iambics "died hard, however, thoroughly ill-fitted as they were for dramatic use, and, as readers of *Love's Labour's Lost* know, survived even in the early plays of Shakespeare" (I would say as parodies). "In the lighter parts there are sometimes fair touches of low comedy; in the graver occasionally, though much more rarely, a touching or dignified phrase or two. But the plays as wholes are like Ovid's first fruits of the deluge — nondescripts incapable of life, and good for no useful or ornamental purpose." This view is shared by Samuel Johnson.

In 1576, the first permanent theater opened in London at Shoreditch.[4] Richard Burbage takes the credit, but in order to launch the undertaking and to provide a permanent stage for plays and greater employment for actors, the following were required: (a) finance; (b) political clout; (c) premises; (d) actors; (e) materials (plays, et cetera).

One or more persons with finance and/or political clout would have to be keen enough to join in the project, even though the social status of actors, acting, and even playwriting was very low. If one of those persons were also an actor and/or a playwright, the show could go on. We know it did and all five preconditions were met, as The Theatre lasted at Shoreditch for twenty-two years before being "transferred."

Like the Globe and its successors, it had a broad stage, "well suited both for the rich words and rapid movement,"[5] and for concentration on the richly appareled actors, not on the colorful background as in contemporary Italian theater. (Someone must have realized that.) The actors' companies must have had a substantial repertoire and/or the promise of new plays, otherwise The Theatre would not have come into being.

This theater remained open for some twenty years,[6] and it was followed in 1577 by the Curtain theatre.[7] As the traveling companies' practice of one-off performances was followed, the demand for plays must have been endless.

So it was essential for these theaters to have regular sources for new plays. There are no records for extrinsic sources for these plays, except that plays were regularly produced at court. Other plays which were hawked round the provinces would either be too poor for the sophisticated city and would need rewriting, or, even when made good enough, too few to constitute a repertoire for more than a few weeks.

While there is a case for some evolutionary process from 1560 on, the argument has been thought only to refer to court or private productions. A modern critic is obliged to claim that Elizabethan drama "seems to spring fully formed into existence in the 1580s."[8]

During this time (1576–80) we do have records of plays produced for the court, and these seem to have been one-off performances as well. With both private and public theaters having to meet such enormous demands, it must be sensible to suggest that the court plays put in another appearance in public, perhaps suitably (or unsuitably, depending on the prejudices of the playgoer-critic) adapted. In addition, if the court performance was written or produced by a successful amateur, then the author might welcome a second outing of his masterpiece on the public stage. This would mean that the

Five—The Revolution in the Theater

courtly author would be in contact with the vagabond-status actors.[9] The identities of these authors are on the face of it not revealed to us: it was beneath the dignity of a gentleman to write for the public. No doubt the theater financiers would have been delighted not to have to pay these authors. Less likely, in the beginning the reverse may have happened: a professional play might be translated from the public theater to the court. Again we have no direct or ostensible evidence of any play transferred from the court to the public theater; so the evidence has to be secondary. For example, the play *Murderous Michael* produced at court in March 1578/9 seems to be the precursor of *Arden of Feversham*, a public play printed in 1592 and subsequently reprinted in 1599. The connection is further discussed on page 74.

The public theater clearly attracted a riff-raff element. The Puritan convert Gosson testifies, perhaps involuntarily, to the social success of the playhouses of which the attraction of plays in the new eloquential English of the revolution must have been an element. In his work of 1579 *The School of Abuse* which Gosson dedicated to Sidney, he complains bitterly of the effect of plays on contemporary behavior:

> Our wrestling at arms is turned to wallowing in ladies' laps, our courage to cowardice, our running to riot, our bows to bowls, and our darts to dishes. We have robbed Greece of gluttony, Italy of wantonness, Spain of pride, France of deceit, and Dutchland of quaffing. Compare London to Rome and England to Italy, you shall find the theaters of the one, the abuses of the other, to be rife amongst us.... In our assemblies at plays in London you shall see such heaving and shoving, such itching and shouldering to sit by women: such care for their garments that they be not trodden on; such eyes to their laps that no chips light upon them; such pillows to their backs that they take no hurt; such masking in their ears, I know not what; such giving them pippins to pass the time; such playing at foot saunt without cards; such ticking, such toying, such smiling, such winking and such manning them home when the sports are ended that it is a right comedy to mark their behavior.[10]

Before becoming a Puritan convert, Gosson had also been a playwright, with two plays produced in public, although apparently neither made it to a court performance (perhaps because Gosson was accused by Lodge of plagiarism[11]; from whom is not disclosed). He had become convinced that the theater was evil in its effect on public morality. He therefore attacks the plays and the theater as works of the devil, who "first sent over many wanton Italian books, which being translated into English, have poisoned the manners of our country with foreign delights." So that more could be affected, the devil caused comedies to be devised, "comedies cut by the same pattern [of "Italian bawdries"], which drag such a monstrous tail after them as is able to sweep whole cities into his lap."[12]

In his later work *Plays Confuted in Five Actions* (1582) Gosson becomes more explicit:

> In plays those things are feigned that never were, as Cupid and Psyche played at Paules: and a great many Comedies more at the Blackfriars and in every playhouse in London, which for brevity's sake I over skip.... So was the history of Caesar and Pompey, and the Play of the Fabii at the Theatre, both amplified there, where the drummes might walk, or the pen might ruffle; when the history swelled and the pen ran too high for the number of persons that should play it, the poet with Proteus [error for Procrustes] cut the same fit for his own measure ... I may boldly say because I have seen it, that the Palace of Pleasure, the Golden Asse, the Ethiopean history, Amadis of France, The Round Table, bawdy Comedies in Latin, French, Italian and Spanish, have been thoroughly ransacked to furnish the playhouses in London.... Forsooth saith the Authour of the Play of Plays shown at the Theatre, the three and twentieth of February last: they shall now be purged, the matter shall be good [and Gosson clearly does not trust that "Authour" with the capital A].... As for that glosing play at the Theatre that profers you so fair, there is interfaced in it a bawdy song of a maid of Kent, and a little beastly speech of the new stawled rogue, both of which I am compelled to bury in silence, being more ashamed to utter than they.[13]

"Gosson's importance to us is two-fold: it lies in the facts that he writes about and in the fact that he should have written at all,"[14] wrote Wiggins. From Gosson's point of view, these plays, being the work of the devil, must have been very superior productions: the devil would deploy only the most sophisticated and damaging weapons. These weapons, the metaphor may be continued, would be all the more dangerous in the hand of a playwright (Gosson's unnamed, perhaps noble, "Authour," who is most likely Oxford) who is schooled and confident in the revolutionary use of English being developed at the same time. We do not need to call in the devil; but the effect is the same if we rely on the steady stream of translations of the classics and Italian. The latter were an especially spiky fishbone as we have seen in the throat of Burghley and of Gosson.[15] Nevertheless Gosson makes two named exceptions from his denunciation of all playwriting: one play is called *The Jew*,[16] and can therefore be linked to *The Merchant of Venice*. Nevertheless, as Pearsall-Smith wrote, "The fact is well known that writing for the stage was not regarded as Literature in Shakespeare's time."[17]

Translations must have been made with the encouragement of the nobility, to whom many were dedicated. So the sources for the plays reaching the court literati perhaps by the mid-1580s include the university wits Lyly (c. 1554–1606), Marlowe (1564–93), Greene (1558–92), Peele (1558?–98?), Lodge (1558–1625) and Nashe (1567–1601?), and with them the apparently non–university-educated Kidd (1558–94). These were untranslated works or new

Five—The Revolution in the Theater

translations in post-revolutionary English. These sources are thus employed first by the courtly writers to make plays and those plays would be produced at court. It does seem likely that the producers of public high-quality classic or Italian-based plays would not be involved in the 1575–80 period until those plays were first written and tried out at court and only then adapted/perfected for the public stage; again an unknown university-educated writer could have been the first to produce a play for the public stage. This is evidenced by the patent issued in December 1582 to Edmund Tilney as master of the revels, responsible initially not for censorship but for the entertainments to be set before the queen:

> And furthermore also we have and do by these presents authorise and command our said servant Edmund Tilney Master of his said Revels by himself or his sufficient deputy or deputies to warn command and appoint ... all and every player or players with their playmakers either belonging to any nobleman or otherwise, bearing the name or names of using the faculty of playmakers or players of Comedies Tragedies enterludes or what other shows so ever, from time to time and at all times to appear before him with all such Plays Tragedies Comedies or shows as they shall have in readiness or mean to set forth, and with them to present and recite before our said servant or his sufficient deputy whom we ordain appoint and authorise by these presents of all such shows plays players and playmakers, together with their playing places, to order reform authorise and put down as shall be thought meet or unmeet unto himself or his sufficient deputy in that behalf on pain of imprisonment.[18]

At first these non–court-originated plays had to be recited before Tilney but later, perhaps because it was beneath the dignity of the aristocratic author(s), the delivery of the manuscript (but only from certain authors?) sufficed — like the one for *Sir Thomas More* with the different hands of the secretaries taking dictation. As the *More* manuscript shows, Tilney vetted the manuscript, acting more as a censor than as an artistic examiner. In this way an element of political censorship comes into practice.

So by 1582 there must have been a highly advanced, sophisticated repertoire of plays, including some locally sourced efforts, for the players to draw on for their one-off performances in public — and yet very few of these plays on the face of it survive, according to the critics. They tell us that the great moment was the arrival of Marlowe with Part 1 of *Tamburlaine the Great* in 1587: "The success of this play is perhaps the greatest event in our literary history."[19] Again, "To the Elizabethans, Marlowe's plays must have had all the aural impact of a symphony orchestra taking over from a barrel organ."[20] Gosson, however, is witness that the revolution had already come to the theater: as Wiggins puts it,[21] "His book *Plays Confuted in Five Actions* shows that the emergence of the drama was a phenomenon which was felt to require explanation even before there had been performed a single one of the plays we now consider classics of the Elizabethan stage, and this complicates our notion of the suddenness with which [i.e., "renders invalid our perception of the dates when"] those classics appeared ... Gosson's comments on tragedy and comedy bear witness to the generic diversity the theatre had achieved by the time he left in 1579: these were plays which *evidently bore some similarity* to the kind of drama Marlowe and (William) Shakespeare were writing a decade later." The comparison between such difference and that between an orchestra in 1587 and a barrel organ in 1579 does not have any rational appeal, and moreover the critic writing over four hundred years afterwards has perhaps less chance of being a more perceptive critic than Gosson.

In logic the apparent commercial success of the public performances of these pre–Marlowe plays, allied no doubt to their critical success, makes their alleged non-survival surprising and unlikely, because a commercially successful play would well be followed by a (cheap) revival or succession of revivals, perhaps including successive rewriting. At the same time the absence of the authors' names is also surprising, but if those authors or any one of them were from the nobility, then society would demand that those names be withheld from the public, as it would be thought far beneath the dignity of the nobility for any member to be associated with the public stage.

We may actually have a spiral situation. The revolution may have hit home first at the court plays, making current a more sophisticated and yet respectful and respectable form of English, along with the conversational fad of euphuism. The court plays in public adaptation make revolutionary English flow out into the world, and thus the national confidence in the English language and with it the nation and the people are developed and fortified. This is reflected in the quotations from Mulcaster (himself a producer of plays for the schoolchildren in his care) on page 63. If we add in the element of the actors' rhetoric, persuading the populace of the glories, not to say cultural serviceability, of English, and thus remedying the perceived "eloquential deficiency" referred to in the previous chapter, we arrive at the top of the spiral and find the cause of those choruses of praise for the English language exemplified earlier. Some may say that the public theaters promoted different dramatic tastes — romantic, idealistic, patriotic or religious elements — while the court or private productions leaned towards satiric comedy, but others argue that the repertoires were substantially the same, and therefore cross-pollinating.[22]

The debt to the theater's essential contribution could hardly be fully acknowledged because the social position of the theater, notwithstanding its popularity, continued to be low, certainly as long as Oxford's efforts to improve appreciation of the actors' art were unrecognized[23]: "For Elizabethans with these [political and religious] interests *the drama was the art best fitted to express their deepest convictions, the art most fully designed to appeal to the people.* Poetry could give much, prose pamphlets, some of them approaching the novel in form, abounded, but, in neither was there the opportunity of watching men and women, as though in life, acting out their stories and directly expressing themselves in richly sounding words."[24]

It is all the more important to identify these early plays, and with them their authors: We know the plays' court names, and from these and occasionally from internal evidence we can identify the names by which we now know them or their final rewrite with varying degrees of certainty.[25] Of course if these plays, or some of them under the names we now know them, were produced prior to 1579 when Gosson wrote, then Marlowe is a follower, not a cause, of the revolution in the theater, let alone of the revolution in the English language itself. Like William Shakespeare from Stratford-upon-Avon, Marlowe was only twelve years old when The Theatre opened in 1576 and only in his early twenties when his first plays appeared. Edward Phillips, the nephew of Milton, in his 1675 *Theatrum Poetarum* provides some corroboration as sums up Marlowe's role: "Christopher Marlowe was a kind of second Shakespeare (whose contemporary he was), not only because, like him, he rose from an actor to be a maker of plays, though inferior both in form and merit; but also in his poem *Hero and Leander*, he seems to have a resemblance of that clear and unsophisticated wit which is natural to that incomparable poet."[26] Phillips' Victorian editor Robert Bell, writing two centuries later and, of course, so much better positioned to know, notes, "There is an error of some magnitude in this passage. Marlowe was not the contemporary, but the predecessor of Shakespeare; and it is a still wider departure from the truth to describe him as a second Shakespeare, meaning thereby a follower who nearly equalled his master."[27]

"Orthodox" scholarship tells us that we have the names of plays dating from the immediate post–1576 period and only a handful of texts. Good plays would always survive, if only as fodder for cheap revivals.

CHAPTER SIX

The Life 1576–1590

> *The character of Berowne is sometimes thought ... to be a self-portrait of the young Shakespeare.... Mercifully [David] Tennant does not push the comparisons but he does catch a quicksilver wit, an impatience with solemnity and sudden moments of deeper feeling that suggest the kind of man we all secretly long the elusive and enigmatic Shakespeare to have been.*—Charles Spencer: review of *Love's Labour's Lost, Daily Telegraph* (London), August 2005

In April 1576, Oxford resumed his life at court. We can view his contemporaries' opinions of him at that stage of his career. First we have Gabriel Harvey, as we have seen his cultural opponent. In *Speculum Tuscani*, he clearly characterizes Oxford:

> Since Galateo[1] came in, and Tuscanism 'gan usurp.
> Vanity above all; villainy next her, stateliness Empress.
> No man but a minion, stout, lout, plain, swain, quoth a lording:
> No words but valorous, no works but womanish only.
> For life, Magnificoes, not a beck but glorious in show,
> In deed most frivolous, not a look but Tuscanish always.
> His cringing side neck, eyes glancing, fisname smirking,
> With forefinger kiss, and brave embrace to the footward.
> Large-bellied codpiece doublet, uncodpeas'd half hose,
> Straight to the dock like a shirt, and close to the britch like a diveling.
> A little apish flat couched fast to the pate like an oyster,
> French camarick ruffs, deep with a whiteness starched to the purpose.
> Every one A per se A, his terms and braveries in print,
> Delicate in speech, quaint in array, conceited in all points,
> In courtly guiles a passing singular odd man, ...

Then Harvey gets carried away in admiration:

> For gallants a brave mirror, a primrose of honour,
> A diamond for nonce, a fellow peerless in England.
> Not the like discourser for Tongue and head to be found out,
> Not the like resolute man for great and serious affairs,

Six—The Life 1576–1590

Not like the lynx to spy out secrets and privities of states,
Eyed like to Argus, eared like to Midas,[2] nos'd like to Naso,
Wing'd like to Mercury, fittst of a thousand for to be employed;
This, nay more than this, doth practise of Italy in one year.
None do I name, but some do I know, that a piece of a twelve month
Hath so perfitted outly and inly both body, both soul,
That none for sense and senses half matchable with them.
A vulture's smelling, ape's tasting, sight of an eagle,
A spider's touching, hart's hearing, might of a lion.
Compounds of wisdom, wit, prowess, bounty, behaviour,
All gallant virtues, all qualities of body and soul:
O thrice ten hundred thousand times blessed and happy,
Blessed and happy travail, traveller most blessed and happy ...

It appears that Lyly, who may have been touting for the post of secretary to Oxford (he succeeded), tried to make trouble for his rival Harvey in that endeavor, for in 1592 Harvey wrote in his *Third Letter*:

Another company of good fellows ... would needs forsooth very courtly persuade the Earl of Oxford that something in those letters, and namely, the Mirror of Tuscanismo, was palpably intended against him: whose noble lordship I protest I never meant to dishonour with the least prejudicial word of my tongue, or pen: but ever kept a mindful reckoning of many bounden duties toward the same: since the prime of his gallantest youth, he bestowed angels [coins worth half of a pound] upon me in Christ's College Cambridge, and otherwise vouchsafed me many gracious favours at the affectionate commendation of my cousin, Mr. Thomas Smith, the son of Sir Thomas [and we know him from the references in Chapter Two], shortly after Colonel of the Ardes in Ireland. But the noble earl, not disposed to trouble his jovial mind with such saturnine paltery still continued, like his magnificent self.[3]

At the time in 1592, Harvey was engaged in a furious war of pamphlets with Nash and Lyly, and the earl was distinctly on their side if not actually joining in on their side as Pasquill, as some conjecture, but nevertheless Harvey could write in these terms about a virtually down-and-out enemy whose influence was at a very low ebb.

In July 1578 Harvey had further cause to comment on Oxford. It fell to him to address the queen and the courtiers during her progress that year, at Cambridge University. There is some doubt as to whether this is the actual speech he made, but there seems no reason to doubt he wrote it. Here are some extracts translated from Harvey's Latin:

Thy splendid fame demands even more than in the case of others the services of a poet demanding lofty eloquence. Thy merit doth not creep along the ground ...
O great-hearted one, strong in thy mind and thy fiery will, thou wilt conquer thyself, thou wilt conquer others ... Mars will obey thee ...

For a long time past [i.e., pre–1578 — my italics] Phoebus Apollo has cultivated thy mind in the arts. English poetical measures have been sung by thee long enough. Let that courtly Epistle [i.e., to the reader of the courtier][4] more polished even than the writings of Castiglione himself — witness how greatly thou dost excel in letters. I have seen many Latin verses of thine, yea even more English verses are extant; thou hast drunk deep draughts not only of the muses of France and Italy, thou hast learned the manners of many men, and the arts of foreign countries. It was not for nothing that Sturmius[5] was visited by thee; neither in France, Italy, nor Germany are any such cultivated and polished men.

Now Harvey comes to his point — England is in grave danger:

O thou hero worthy of renown, throw away the insignificant pen, throw away bloodless books, and writings that serve no useful purpose; now the sword must be brought into play....
In thy breast is noble blood, courage animates thy brow, Mars lives in thy tongue, Minerva strengthens thy right hand, Bellona reigns in thy body, within thee burns the fires of Mars. Thine eyes flash fire, thy countenance *shakes spears* [emphasis added]; who would not swear that Achilles[6] is come to life again....

The Latin in the last sentence but one is "*vultus tela vibrat.*" It is accurately translated; the use of the word "vultus" for "countenance" is interesting. The Elizabethan addiction to puns leads me to suspect that there is a pun on the Latin word "vultis": "you will" — "You, Will." Thus we have buried in the Latin "Will, Shakes, Spear(s)," one of the first references to Oxford's use of the pseudonym.

Why did Oxford choose this name? I do not place much weight on academic explanations which attach the name to Pallas Athene, although these might have been useful later on. I think (and I am not quite alone) that the name is a piece of barroom humor on the subject of Oxford's success with the court ladies.[7] About the same time as Harvey's encomium, the two comic murderers in the black farce *Arden of Feversham* are named as Black *Will* and George *Shake*bag.[8]

Then consider this quotation from Barnaby Rich's *Farewell to the Military Profession* (1581):

It was my fortune at my last being at London to walk through the Strand towards Westminster, where I met one came riding towards me on a footcloth nag, apparelled in a French ruff, a French cloak, a French hose, and in his hand a great fan of feathers, bearing them up (very womanly) against the side of his face. And for that I had never seen any man wear them before that day, I began to think it impossible that a man might be found so foolish as to make himself a scorn to the world to wear so womanish a toy; but thought it had been some shameless woman that had disguised herself like a man in our hose and cloaks; but our doublets, gowns, caps, and hats, they had gone long ago.... I began to muse with myself to what end that fan of feathers served, for it could not have been to defend the sun from the burning of his beauty, for it was the beginning of February, when the heat of the sun may be very well endured. No, if it were to defend the wind or the coldness of the air, methinks a French hood had been a great deal better, for that it had been both gentlewomanlike, and being pinned down about his ears would have kept his head a great deal warmer; and then a French hood on his head, a French ruff about his neck, and a pair of French hose on his legs had been right — à la mode de France; and this had been something suitable to his wit.[9]

I note that the rider was going East, in the direction of the Blackfriars theater, perhaps in February 1579/80 or 1580/1; I suspect that the reference to "his wit" means that the writer well knew who the rider was — only the Earl of Oxford ready-dressed for an acting appearance fits.

The third reference as to how Oxford appeared to his contemporaries is contained in the account set down in Chapman's *The Revenge of Bussy d'Ambois* of an encounter with Oxford as he was returning to England. Apart from the account given, there is no evidence that such an encounter between Oxford and Duke Casimir actually took place. Duke Casimir was indeed in command of a Protestant army in alliance with Henry of Navarre (afterwards Henry IV) in 1576, and his army could have been across Oxford's path on his return. The important point is the reflection of Chapman's opinion of Oxford, put in the character's mouth and irrelevant to the plot. Chapman wished to have this opinion preserved in his play published in 1613, nine years after Oxford's death:

> I overtook, coming from Italy
> In Germany, a great and famous earl
> Of England, the most goodly fashion'd man
> I ever saw; from head to foot in form
> Rare and most absolute; he had a face
> Like one of the most honour'd Romans
> From whence his noblest family was derived.
> He was beside of spirit passing great,
> Valiant and learn'd, and liberal as the sun,
> Spoke and writ sweetly, or of learn'd subjects
> Or of the discipline of public weals;
> And 'twas the Earl of Oxford; and being offer'd
> At that time, by Duke Casimir, the view
> Of his right royal army then in field,
> Refus'd it, and no foot was mov'd to stir
> Out of his own free fore-determined course;
> I, wondering at it, ask'd for it his reason,
> It being an offer so much for his honor.
> He all acknowledging, said, "'Twas not fit

> To take those honors one cannot quit..." [match]
> And yet he cast it only in the way
> To stay and serve the world. Nor did it fit
> His own true estimate how much it weigh'd
> For he despised it; and esteemed it freer
> To keep his own way straight; and swore that he
> Had rather make away his whole estate
> In things that crossed the vulgar, then he would
> Be frozen up, stiff like a Sir John Smith
> His countryman, in common noble's fashion
> Affecting, as the end of noblesse were
> Those servile observations [III, iv, ll. 84–115].

In 1584 John Soothern published his *Pandora, The Music of Beautie* of his Mistress Diana. He was at some stage in the household of Oxford and since he is clearly French (he tells us so), some believe he is Denys the Frenchman who took part in the outrage in May 1571 at Gads Hill (see page 33). The little book is dedicated to Oxford and dated June 20, 1584. It contains the following (and note Oxford's interests in poetry and the classics, music, astronomy and athletic pursuits):

> Making speake (her with a sweet brute) [i.e., bruit, rumour]
> The ten divers tongues of my lute
> I will Fredone in thy honor,
> These renowned songs of Pindar [Greek poet c. 500 B.C.]
> And imitate for thee, Dever
> Horace that brave Latin harper.
> As Dever is both wise and virtuous
> As of my harp he is digne. [worthy]
> Muses you have had of your father
> Only, the particular favor
> To keepe fro the reeve infernal:
> And therefore my wantons, come sing
> Upon your best speaking string
> His name that doth cherish you all.
> Come nymphs while I have desire
> To strike on a well sounding lyre
> Of our virtues Dever the name
> Dever that had given him in part
> The love, war, honour and Art
> And with them an eternal fame ...
> Among our well renowned men
> Dever merits a silver pen
> Eternally to write his honor,
> And I in a well polisht verse
> Can set up in our Universe
> A fame to endure for ever [E-ver]

Six—The Life 1576–1590

And filled with a furiae extreme,
Upon a well superbus rhyme
(On a rhyme, and both strong and true)
I will Dever push thy louanges [praises][10]
To the ears of peoples estraunges ...
No, no, I would there were made,
I could take an entire Iliad
Of only his noble antiquity.
But his virtues would blush with shame:
If I should not by his own name
Give him a laud to our posterity
But I will thus like Pindar
In many discourses Egar,
Before I will come to my point:
Or, or touch his infinity
Of virtues in this poesie
Our song will never be conjoint
For who marketh better than he
The seven turning flames of the sky [the planets]
Or hath read more of the antiquity
Hath greater knowledge of the tongues
Or understands sooner the sownes [songs, sounds?]
Of the learner to love Music
Or else has a fairer grace
In the Centaurian art of Thrace [riding]
Half-horse, half-man, and with less pain,
Doth bring the courser indomitable
To yield to the reins of his bridle
Vaulting on the edge of a plain.
And it pleases me to say too
(With a louange I protest true)
That in England we cannot see
Anything like Dever, but he
Only himself must resemble
Vertues so much in him assemble
And nought escapes out of my hand
In this ode but it's veritae
And here I swear Dever 'tis thee
That art ornament of England
Vaunting me of this thing:
Which is, that I shall never sing,
A man so much honored as thee,
And both of the muses and of me.
In means while, take this little thing,
But small as it is, Devere,
Taunt us that never man before
Now in England, knew Pindar's string.

If those were the views of his contemporaries at the period dating from 1575 to 1585, what were his own opinions? These are reflected in a letter he wrote to Burghley from Siena on the first January 1575/6: "I have no help but of mine own, and mine is made to serve me, and myself not mine." Nelson correctly states that this attitude runs counter to the feudal ethos of land grant in return for service to the state and the community. The full interpretation is that Oxford is putting forward his own view of his role, namely that he knew he was to be the cultural flower of the nation and of all time (or at least the foreseeable future), and that was much more important than his position in society. The later Sonnet 62 reflects this attitude: none is so handsome as himself: "And for myself my own worth to define,/As I all other in all worths surmount."

In *All's Well That Ends Well*, Act III, scene ii, Lavatch the countess' servant tells the countess: "I take my young lord [Bertram] to be a very melancholy man.... I know a man who had this trick of melancholy sold a goodly manor for a song" (ll. 3, 8–9).[11]

We note that in 1573 or 1574 Oxford passed over a family estate in Essex to the brother of the composer William Byrd, then organist at the Chapel Royal, subject to the life tenancy of the current tenants, and he somehow lost it to fraud or legal chicanery.

Part of Oxford's time was taken up with jousting at the court tournaments. These required very elaborate verse in the challenges and replies, some of which has been attributed to Sidney, but it is likely that some at least would be Oxford's (see page 26), as he was a frequent participant (and champion).

We come now to one of the more melancholy aspects of Oxford's life. On July 2, 1575, while he was abroad, his wife gave birth to a daughter, Elizabeth, afterwards Countess of Derby. On his return to England he was confronted by open rumors that the child was not his. The reactions of Anne during pregnancy, her father, Burghley, whose letter to the queen in April 1576 betrays his complete panic, Oxford's own policy of non-consummation (see page 25); this, however, might have been honored in the breach), and other surrounding circumstances cause the conclusion that Oxford was indeed not the father. Oxford absented himself from his wife and the Burghley family circle. In the end, as well for form's sake or political or financial support, the parties effected a conciliation — usually described as a reconciliation, which seems inaccurate, and Oxford and Anne began to live together in December 1581. In May 1583 a short-lived son was born. Bridget, afterwards Countess of Berkshire, was born in April 1584. Frances, a short-lived daughter, died in the autumn of 1587. Susan, afterwards Countess of Montgomery, was born in May 1587, and finally poor Anne died, "debilitated by a burning fever," in June 1588.

This scenario is reflected in scenes from the contemporary plays written by Oxford. For their full effect these must have been written soon, even very soon, after that marital rapprochement. Consider those plays where a wronged wife (and daughter whose legitimacy or existence are questioned) is eventually reunited with her errant husband:

All's Well That Ends Well: Helena and Bertram — this contains the bed-trick[12] whereby the wife smuggles herself incognito into the husband's bed. Presumably this was the story put about by the Burghleys and eventually taken on board by Oxford to account for the say-so legitimate conception and birth of Elizabeth. The whole play seems almost an apology for his behavior, and to be effective must have been written in or about 1582.

Comedy of Errors: Egeon and Emilia
Cymbeline: Imogen and Postumus
Measure for Measure: Mariana and Angelo
Pericles: Pericles and Thais, and Marina their daughter
The Winter's Tale: Leontes and Hermione and his rejected daughter Perdita.

There is even a reference to an attempt by the duchess of Suffolk to reconcile Oxford and Anne by showing the baby to Oxford. In Act II, scene ii, Paulina says:

> If she does trust me with the little babe
> I'll show it to the king and undertake to be
> Her advocate to the loud'st. We do not know
> How he may soften at the sight of the child:
> The silence often of pure innocence
> Persuades when speaking fails [ll. 47–52].

The attempt fails and Leontes continues to reject the baby.[13] The duchess of Suffolk's attempt is evidenced by her letter dated December 15, 1577, to Burghley, which Nelson quotes in full and describes as the most deeply human document from the entire Oxford archive.

Much Ado About Nothing: Hero and Claudio; Beatrice and Benedick. In the latter case Beatrice shows command of repartee, which Ann may have acquired as she grew older and more confident. There are those strange exchanges in Act II, Scene i:

> BEATRICE (masked, pretending not to know to whom she speaks): Well this was Signor Benedick that said so.
> BENEDICK (ditto): What's he?

> BEATRICE: I am sure you know him well enough.
> BENEDICK: Not I, believe me.
> BEATRICE: Did he never make you laugh?
> BENEDICK: I pray you, what is he?
> BEATRICE: Why, he is the prince's jester[14] [reflecting the queen's relationship with Oxford]: a very dull fool; only his gift is in devising impossible slanders none but libertines delight in him; and the commendation is not in his wit but in his villainy; for he both pleaseth men and angers them, and then they laugh at him and beat him. I am sure he is in the Fleet [i.e., the Tower] [ll. 120–133].

And later:

> DON PEDRO: Come lady, come: you have lost the heart of Signior Benedick.
> BEATRICE: Indeed, my lord, he lent it me awhile; and I gave him the use for it — a double heart for his single one [a reference to the birth of her daughter Elizabeth]: marry once before he won it of me with false dice, therefore your grace may well say I have lost it [ll. 258–263].

Two Gentlemen of Verona: Silvia and Valentine. I have included this example because it contains this curious reference:

> VALENTINE: I mean that her beauty is exquisite but her favour infinite ... I account her of her beauty.
> SPEED: You never saw her since she was deformed [i.e., visibly pregnant while Oxford was away in Italy].
> VALENTINE: How long hath she been deformed?
> SPEED: Ever since you loved her.
> VALENTINE: I have loved her ever since I saw her, and still see her beautiful [II, i, ll. 50–51, 59–65].

This would be a later interpolation because of course Silvia finishes up with Proteus.

However much the parties might have liked these matters to have remained private, and especially after Oxford and Anne's reconciliation in 1583, the memory seems to subsist underground, however much the playwright might blame himself. As late as 1598 the satirist and puritan divine Joseph Hall (afterwards Bishop Hall) was patently if inaccurately alluding to them as well as praising the father's poetic competence:

> Sith Pontian left his barren wife at home
> And spent two years at Venice and at Rome
> Returned, hearing his blessing asked of three,
> Cries out, O Julian Law, Adultery.

Six—The Life 1576–1590

> Though Labeo reaches right (who can deny)
> The true strains of heroic poetry
> [*Virgedemaria* 6, i, ll. 245–250].

"His blessing asked of three" indicates Oxford's three daughters (Elizabeth, Bridget and Susan) requesting their father's blessing. We shall meet "Labeo" as one of Hall's names for Oxford again (pages 173). "Pontian" is another such name.[15]

The queen herself in this period was under permanent pressure from Parliament and her council to do something about the Roman Catholic element in the upper echelons of the state. Some of those who were anxious were Protestant fanatics, and others were equally concerned but also rightly feared the accession on Elizabeth's death of the legitimate heir Mary, Queen of Scots, which would have plunged the country into civil wars of religion. Elizabeth, thanks to Walsingham and his spy network, knew exactly where each piece stood on the chessboard, and until the pressure became too great could afford a sanguine, laid-back approach. Oxford had returned from Italy evincing no signs of Roman Catholic sympathy—indeed the reverse, as the Venetian Inquisition discovered when it cross-examined Orazio Cuoco. Oxford had brought this boy back to England from Venice as a page, perhaps also to escape the plague which killed his father and mother in Venice. He was possessed of a remarkable singing voice. He stayed in Oxford's household for some eleven months before returning to Venice where the inquisition, knowing he had been in a Protestant country, wished to know what he had been up to. Cuoco told the inquisition that Oxford was not living a Catholic life. Cuoco was not made to eat meat on fast days or listen to the sermons of heretics: he went to mass at the chapels of the ambassadors of Spain or Portugal. Various Italians tried to persuade him towards Protestantism, and so, he says, did the queen before whom he sang. He confirmed that while in Venice Oxford went to Greek Orthodox mass at San Giorgio dei Greci; he was a person who spoke Latin and Italian well. On being asked if Oxford tried to convert him to his faith, Cuoco replied that he let everyone live as they wanted.[16]

Nevertheless, by 1580, Oxford was deeply embedded into the circles of Roman Catholic supporters, including his cousin Henry Howard and other relatives by marriage, Charles Arundell and Francis Southwell. These three plotted to restore Catholicism to England. Then in mid–December 1580 in open court Oxford dropped to his knees in front of the queen and confessed that he and the other three had been reconciled to Rome by a Jesuit priest and afterwards sneaked out of England, courtesy of the French ambassador, who was present and denied everything (as of course he would do). The ambassador's report continues to the effect that Oxford implored the queen to direct the ambassador to tell the truth, that he had asked him to convey the priest out of the country, and that afterwards Oxford had thanked him. The ambassador "had no recollection whatever of the incident."

However, in Elizabeth's court, such an event would only happen if choreographed in advance.[17] Clearly Oxford was the Crown's spy in the group, and he put on the performance of his life. The ambassador was properly skewered: he tried to be more careful in future but was caught out in the Throckmorton plot four years later thanks to his resident priest (and Walsingham's spy), one Giordano Bruno. The three others were put off plotting for good, and a possible nucleus of a plot neutralized. Elizabeth's Protestant critics would be appeased: she would have some breathing space, without having to offend either her Catholic subjects or Spain to any greater degree. Altogether, everyone would agree, a most pleasing "Enterlude."

Well, not quite everyone: Howard and Arundell believed they were fighting for their lives — just what Elizabeth wanted. They tried to hit back, charging Oxford with buggery and bestiality, atheism, slanders on the queen, everything their panicking minds could dream up. None of their accusations were repeated later (nevertheless Professor Nelson eschews the use of salt when dealing with them), but they were of use to their playwright-victim, who followed the wretched Arundell's scheme of accusation with its incoherent enumeration in the mouth of Dogberry in *Much Ado About Nothing*: "Marry, sir, they have committed false report, moreover they have spoken untruths, secondarily they are slanders, sixth and lastly they have belied a lady, thirdly they have verified unjust things, and to conclude, they are lying knaves" (V, i, ll. 208–12). Arundell accuses Oxford of perjury "a hundred times and damned himself into the pit of hell." Dogberry says, "Why, that is flat perjury to call the prince's brother a villain" and "Thou will be condemned into everlasting redemption for this" (IV, ii, ll. 39–40; 54–55).

Although some critics think without any contemporary evidence that there might have been some basis for some of the accusations, the third person named by Oxford, Sir Francis Southwell, wisely kept a low profile and did not support the wilder allegations against Oxford. Sir Francis' cousin was the father of the Jesuit martyr Robert Southwell,[18] who was executed in 1595. Robert composed a letter which was printed and circulated at the time of his arrest in 1592, addressed to "My Loving and Good Cousin" (i.e., Oxford himself) who had encouraged him (Southwell) to publish his own poetry even though the cousin's was much superior. For his part Robert wanted the cousin to write spiritual work, but "still the finest wits are (di)stilling Venus' rose ... playing with pagan toys." The 1616 edition is addressed to "My Worthy

Good Cosen/Maister W.S." There can be little doubt that the author of *Venus and Adonis* is the addressee, who is also exhorted to have some of the Southwell poems set to music to be composed by that addressee. William Shakespeare is not extrinsically recorded as having any such interests. Oxford's interest is summarized on page 53, and in effect referred to on page 82.

I pointed out the five elements required for the success of The Theatre project on its launch in 1576 on page 70. While Oxford is in a position to write or provide writers for it and the Curtain which opened in 1577, and indeed may be acting in public (see the note on page 150ff), he could also have been of assistance to it in terms of finance, perhaps not directly — unless his personal finances were damaged by contributing — and political clout. The latter was very necessary to ward off the assaults of Puritan-minded characters such as successive lord mayors of London.

Equally, at some stage on his return from Italy Oxford had some responsibility for the entertainments put on for the court, presumably under the aegis of the lord chamberlain the Earl of Sussex, whose responsibility it was. Certainly he is recorded as having eight cartloads of goods[19] while on progress with the queen: even his clothing can hardly have needed that amount, and so it is concluded that this impedimenta included the costumes, playbooks, scenery and other props for court productions of plays at the residences of the queen's unfortunate (because of the expense) hosts.

In the same period he was writing, producing and acting in plays at court. We have a record of the production of *Murderous Michael* on Shrove Tuesday (March 3) 1579, when Sussex's Company put on this play "Device by earls Oxford and Surrey, Lord Thomas Howard, and Lord Windsor before the French Ambassador and Simier [Alençon's representative in the French marriage negotiations]. A Morris masque was prepared but not danced." As for the play, Gilbert Talbot reported to his father, the Earl of Shrewsbury, "the device was prettier than it hap to be performed." This play is believed to reappear in 1592 when it was printed as *Arden of Feversham*, one of the key characters being the lord's body-servant, the ruthless yet vacillating Michael, who joins the murderers George *Shake*bag and Black *Will* in the killing of his lord Arden — a matter of great shock, no doubt, to the court audience. The names of the blackly comic murderers, I note again, are a clear pointer to the pseudonym of Oxford: Black Will is in trouble over the Gads' Hill incident, alluded to in *Famous Victories* and I *Henry IV*.[20]

Perhaps it was the incompetence of his fellow aristocratic actors which caused Oxford to take over the Earl of Warwick's players in 1580. The company performed at Blackfriars[21] until the lease of the premises was taken away from him.

At this stage (December 1580) Oxford was riding high in the queen's favor—but he muffed it catastrophically. He became involved with one of the court ladies, Ann Vavasour. She had a miscarriage in the spring of 1580 (apparently unknown to the queen), and was pregnant again in the summer, giving birth finally on March 21, 1580/1. Oxford was arrested and flung into the Tower, being quickly released on June 8, 1581. This provides the answer to one critic's puzzled comment: "But just why (William) Shakespeare alludes more often to the Tower than any other building is another matter."[22]

Again the witty heroine is a stock character who seems to mirror this Ann, or possibly his own sister Mary and sometimes even, as we have seen, Countess Ann. Examples are:

Maria in *Twelfth Night*, married to Sir Toby Belch — possibly a caricature of Oxford's brother-in-law the somewhat bibulous Lord Willoughby, who paid an extended visit to Denmark in 1584; perhaps he brought back local color to the author of Hamlet.

Beatrice in *Much Ado About Nothing*
Rosaline in *Love's Labour's Lost*
Rosalind in *As You Like It*.

In 1581 Oxford appears to have written an apology to the queen entitled *A Compendious or Brief Relationship* "by W.S."[23] Oxford remained out of favor with the queen over the Vavasour affair. Ann Vavasour's uncle Thomas Knyvet succeeded in wounding Oxford quite seriously ("more dangerously"),[24] and there was streetfighting in London of a type mirrored in *Romeo and Juliet* between the Montagues and the Capulets and their servants (with their English names in the plays). Oxford complains of a debilitating lameness in Sonnet 37: "I made lame by fortune's dearest spite...." And Sonnet 89: "Speak of my lameness, and I straight will halt." And Sonnet 66:

> for restful death I cry,—
> As, to behold desert a beggar born ...
> And strength by limping away disabled.

(One reference might be metaphorical but three smack of literal lameness.) In Sonnet 74, he writes of the death of his body: "The coward conquest of a wretch's knife." On March 25, 1595, he wrote to Burghley, "I will attend your Lordship as well as a lame man may at your house."[25]

Romeo and Juliet 1581/2 recalls the Italian fencing master Bonetti, who set up shop in Blackfriars in 1582 to teach the English the art of rapier and dagger fighting, boasting that he "could hit any Englishman with a thrust upon any button." Mercutio compares Tybalt to "the very butcher of a silk button" (II, iv, l. 22).

Raleigh and Burghley made representations to the queen. Burghley reported that the earl had two servants for his wife and her daughter, and a page and "a kind of tumbling boy." Nelson insinuates that this lad was required for sexual purposes; just the sort of detail, were it true, designed to be inferred from a letter to the queen, sent apparently to arouse her forgiveness.

The queen finally received Oxford back into favor on June 1, 1583, by a public display at court. He entertained the hope that he might command the English expeditionary force sent to assist the Dutch in 1585, and was fact made commander of the horse.[26] In September he carried out a tour of inspection. However, the following month overall command was given to Leicester with near disastrous consequences thanks to that worthy's deficiencies. Oxford was recalled to London straightaway.

Oxford's finances had meanwhile gone from bad to worse. He had invested £3,000 in Frobisher's third expedition to find the Northwest Passage around the top of Canada to China. Trinculo in *The Tempest* marvels that "When they [in England] will not give a doit [one-eighth of a penny] to relieve a lame beggar [an autobiographical reference?], they will lay out ten to see a dead Indian" (II, ii, ll. 33–36). Three "dead Indians" were brought home by Frobisher after the second expedition, in 1578. The £3,000 instantly recalls the bond of 3,000 ducats in Act I, scene iii, of *The Merchant of Venice*.

To save expense he had even spent most of the winter 1582/3 at Castle Hedingham. His household was reduced to four, as we have seen. On June 21, 1586, Burghley wrote to Walsingham: "I pray you send me word if you had any commodity to speak with her Majesty to speak of my Lord of Oxford and what hope there is, and if you have any to let Robert Cecil [his son] understand it to relieve his sister, who is more troubled for her husband's lack than he himself."[27]

Suddenly, five days later, the cash-strapped queen made a grant of an annuity to Oxford of £1,000, payable quarterly. There were no overt strings, and no accounting: it has been suggested that the grant was in part to settle some claim Oxford might have had, but the strongest suggestion is that it was to enable Oxford to continue with his productions of patriotic plays on the public stage, and patronage of any new writers. Certainly the productions mightily enraged the king of Spain, whose rage we have already recorded (page 35). Perhaps in view of Walsingham's involvement, the sum was needed to defray Oxford's spying expenses. We have seen how the "lynx"[28] kept tabs on the extreme Protestants with a web of operators.

Elizabeth was a Tudor: she never did anything out of pure generosity, and the size of the grant is amazing — no one else received anything like that sum. Oxford's loyalty was not in question: he sat as a commissioner at Mary,

Queen of Scots' trial in October 1586. The queen was horrified at having to sign the death warrant for her cousin, an anointed queen. She did, and when Mary was executed complained that she was tricked into parting with the warrant. To salve her conscience, Oxford (it is suggested) possibly incorporated into *The Troublesome Reign of King John* a fictitious scene where the king orders the blinding of his child nephew and rightful king Arthur (the son of his elder deceased brother Geoffrey), who is accidentally killed in the process. Mark Anderson suggests that this was the public effort: the private effort is in *Macbeth*, where Macbeth's queen is au fond responsible for the murder of King Duncan, a guest in her palace. Oxford adds the point of "double trust" in Scots law. Macbeth says in revulsion:

> He's here in double trust.
> First, I am his kinsman and his subject,
> Strong both against the deed: then, as his host,
> Who should against the murderers bar the door,
> Not bear the knife myself [I, vii, ll. 12–16].

At some stage in the late 1570s Oxford employed John Lyly (1553–1606) as his secretary, and while in this employ Lyly wrote two of the first novels in the English language, *Euphues: The Anatomy of Wit* (1578) and *Euphues and His England* (1579). Euphues ("good natured"), is a rich and handsome gentleman of impeccable good manners, fluent in the production of long speeches of balanced phrases, which are reproduced in Shakespeare either by way of imitation or in parody. Lyly then turned to playwriting, producing some eight plays, later versions being interlarded with songs, which some think too good for Lyly, and worthy of his master. Indeed, in his dedication of the second Euphues book Lyly wrote that of the "two children" of whom he "was delivered," the first "before my friends thought me conceived" (i.e., able to write such a book), he had sent it "to a Nobleman to nurse, who with great love brought him up for a year, so that wheresoever he wander, he hath his Nurse's name in his forehead." Oxford is almost certainly that nobleman. After writing the plays and quitting Oxford's employ, Lyly saw his career go into rapid decline. As Gabriel Harvey, who may have touted for Lyly's job with Oxford, cruelly but wittily put it, he was "sometime the fiddlestick of Oxford [the man, not the city], and now the very bauble of London" and "once the foil [i.e., the reflection of a jewel in a setting] of Oxford [the man of talent again], now the stale of London," and reminding him, "of thy old acquaintance in the Savoy, when young Euphues hatched the eggs that his elder friend [i.e., Oxford] had laid."

In thanks for the royal £1,000 annuity — there is no evidence but can be no other logical reason — Lyly wrote (or was probably put up to writing) the allegorical play *Endymion* in 1584. Endymion (Oxford) has a secret love affair (Vavasour) that angers his real love Cynthia the moon (the queen). She puts him to sleep (he is in disgrace), but later changes her mind and restores him with a kiss (i.e., the annuity).

Previously the poet Thomas Watson dedicated his *Hecatompathia* (One Hundred Sufferings, 1582) to Oxford. A copy survives with annotations which are the most interesting part of the book.[29] J.P. Collier the scholar and forger recognizes Oxford's authorship. The annotator rolls off quotations from Homer and Xenophon; Horace, Martial, Pliny, Virgil, Ovid, Tibullus and Theocritus[30]; Petrarch and Ronsard, along with the obscure Italian poets Fiorenzuola, Strozza and Parabosco, without apparently breaking into a sweat. Mark Anderson gives a quotation from Susenbrotus in this passage:

> This passion is framed on a somewhat tedious or too much confected continuation of that figure in rhetoric which the Greeks call Palilogia or anadiplosis, of the Latins reduplication: whereof Susenbrotus (if I well remember me) allegeth this example out of Virgil:
> > Sequitur pulcherrimus Austur
> > Austur equo fidens, ...

As Anderson puts it: "If the author of Watson's glosses is not de Vere, an additional Elizabethan literary genius still awaits the light of discovery." In addition, Dover Wilson identified Sonnet 130 as a parody of one of Watson's, and Watson's book might not readily come to the notice of William Shakespeare in Stratford-upon-Avon.

Also in Oxford's theatrical circle was Henry Evans, who with Lyly played a part in the management of the theater at Blackfriars. He appears in *The Merry Wives of Windsor* as the Welsh schoolmaster, instructing young William Page and then the fairies. Act V, scene iv, in its entirety: "Trib, trib, fairies! Come! and remember your parts. Be pold, I pray you. Follow me into the pit, and when I give the watch'ords, do as I pid you. Come, come; trib, trib!"

They appear to have achieved a reputation for producing up-to-date topical shows full of court gossip. One correspondent wrote at the time: "Take heed and beware my Lord Oxenford's man called Lyly, for if he sees this letter he will put it in print or make the boys in Paul's play it upon a stage."

Lyly appears to have doubled as Oxford's financial steward. He was given a terrible run-around by Oxford, even being accused of dishonesty. Oxford's apology for that unfounded slur on his most faithful servant is recorded in *Timon of Athens*, Act IV, scene iii:

> Surely this man
> Was born of woman.
> Forgive my general and exceptless rashness,

> You perpetual sober gods! I do proclaim
> One honest man — mistake me not, but one,
> No more, I pray — and he's a steward [ll. 494–99].

Flavius the steward begs to stay with his master in the forest, but Timon pushes him away: "Fly while thou art blest and free" (l. 536). This would seem to reflect the relationship between Oxford and Lyly.[31]

Unfortunately, Oxford does not appear to have used the annuity for the repair of his finances (or perhaps Burghley diverted some of it for his debts and the children's maintenance). Perhaps he was so constituted that mere household expenses did not figure highly on his personal radar, and he spent the money as he probably believed was the queen's intention on polishing and presenting that great swathe of history plays foreseen and encouraged by Ronsard (see page 18ff), and in propaganda generally. Certainly after 1586 the records are sparse.

Life dealt Oxford bitter personal blows. His son died a baby in 1583, and in September 1587 his infant daughter Frances died aged only two or three. The final blow came when Countess Anne died on June 5, 1588. For some years Oxford was not able to or did not see fit to maintain his three remaining daughters, and the cost and responsibility devolved on the now-aging Burghley (but aided by the annuity?).

Oxford's woes were overshadowed by the prospect of the invasion of England to be effected by the transport of Spanish troops from the Netherlands with the ships of England cleared out of the way by the invincible armada. Oxford, having purchased a ship, *The Bonaventure*, in connection with his Northwest Passage investment, appears to have fitted it out to meet the armada, and to have taken some part in the patrols in the summer of 1588 looking for that fleet without success. Like Hamlet he was not present at his wife's funeral, and his distress (mixed perhaps with guilt, understanding and forgiveness) is recorded:

> I loved Ophelia. Forty thousand brothers
> Could not, with all their quantity of love,
> Make up my sum ... [V, i, ll. 266–68[32]].

After the patrols, Oxford arrived at Tilbury to join Leicester and the queen: it would be fascinating if Elizabeth's great speech was in any way authored by "Shakespeare." It was, however, clearly influenced by the great wave of expression in English which Shakespeare's Revolution would have induced.

With Anne's death Oxford lost his one hold on Burghley, who had done a great deal for his maverick son-in-law in protecting him financially and politically from his enemies, but not unnaturally, as the welfare of the three little daughters would be paramount in Burghley's scheme of things. Since no quotations appear in any of the plays from any book dated after 1588, it appears that Oxford was denied access to a first-rate library which he was formerly using, and Burghley's library is the obvious candidate.[33]

There is no way to explain the developments in Shakespeare's drama in the next period except by postulating that Oxford had a nervous breakdown. His troubles had come, "not as a single spy, but in battalions" (*Hamlet* Act IV, scene v, l. 79). It is indicative of the reliability of this theory that none of the other claimants have any such troubles at the point where their proponents say, "Shakespeare's gloomy period"[34] begins —1601. One piece of evidence is the complete lack of surviving letters written by Oxford between 1588 and August 1590.

For the period 1575–90 I will again consider those plays of which Oxford probably produced first versions. Some of these reflect the first fruit of his Italian experiences, and others his completion of the cycle of history plays. All are works of art, but this does not prevent them from being topical, both as a record and as putting across a policy or policies which ought to be followed. In addition there are the autobiographical references which I have tried to deal with in sequence as they occur and are reflected in the biography, but they are no evidence for an actual date of original composition because they can be readily inserted on a rewriting. Again, this is the period for the first drafts, which are sometimes heavily rewritten at a later stage. They do, however, provide part of the answer to the question of what happened to those immediate post–1576 plays which formed the repertoire of the court revels and the new playhouses, some of the more successful of which are most likely to have survived, rewritten and retitled.

In addition to certain family or general autobiographical references (outside the autobiographical event references above) it is possible to make a link with topical political developments. Eva Turner Clark demonstrates the twists and turns of the stately gavotte of the marriage negotiations between Alençon and the queen can be followed, which accounts for the order in which the plays are treated, which some might otherwise find curious. However, some of these ideas are tortuous to follow. It may be enough to rely on the references selected below.

The comedies were recognized at the time as being the leading works in the genre. Puttenham's *The Arte of English Poesy* makes the point clear enough:

> In these days poets as well as poesie are become subjects to scorn and derision. Whoso is studious in art, and shows himself excellent in it, they call him phantastical and light-headed. Now of such among the Nobility or Gentry as

be very well seen in the making of poesie, it is come to pass that they loath to be known of their skill. So, many that have written commendably have suppressed it, or suffered it to be published without their names: as if it were a discredit for a gentleman to seem learned. And in Her Majesty's Time that now is are sprung another crew of courtly makers, Noblemen and Gentlemen of Her Majesty's own servants, who have written excellently well as it would appear if their doings [i.e., poetry] could be found out and made public with the rest, of which the first is that noble gentleman Edward Earl of Oxford.

And:

That for Tragedy, the Lord Buckhurst [the part author of *Gorboduc*, which puts a question mark over Puttenham's judgment], and master Edward Ferrys (unknown)[35] for such doings as I have seen of theirs to deserve the highest praise. The Earl of Oxford and master Edwards of Her Majesty's Chapel for Comedy and Interlude.

The Comedy of Errors

On January 1, 1576 or 1577, *The History of Error* was shown at Hampton Court enacted by the Children of Powles. I have already noted Hatton's bell and chain and the spoof of Burghley's questions to his wards on geography (page 18). One of those questions was: "Where's France?/In her forehead; armed and reverted, making war against her heir [hair]" (III, ii, ll. 125–27).

This is a clear reference to the wars of religion in France: Henry III was making war against the Protestant princes of Navarre and Condé, who were allied to his heir and brother Alençon.

At a later stage Oxford lost his money in an investment based on the Northwest Passage expeditions at the hands of Michael Lok[36] and his certifying goldsmith John Baptista Agnello. He appears as Angelo who in Act IV is trying to dun Antipholus of Ephesus for a chain he sold to his twin brother, who denies all knowledge.

Timon of Athens

This may well be the *History of the Solitary Knight* shown at Whitehall on February 17, 1576 or 1577. Timon is solitary at first in his grandeur and later on his fall in the wood. One of his debtors says, "I must serve my turn out of my own" (II, i, ll. 20, 21).

This recalls the letter from Siena written just over a year earlier (page 54): "I have no help but of mine own, and mine is made to serve me and myself, and not mine." The play shows evidence of a revising hand and may have been a fragment reconstituted after Oxford's death. There is no case for suggesting direct collaboration between the reviser and Oxford.

Pericles

This play probably existed only as a fragment at Oxford's death in 1604, and was substantially revised and rewritten by a postmortem "collaborator." This reference, however, appears to indicate that Oxford is eager to see his daughter, having decided to accept that Anne is blameless. Perhaps the play is laying the groundwork for the reconciliation:

> PERICLES to his daughter MARINA: Tell thy story;
>   If thine consider'd prove a thousandth part
>   Of my endurances, thou art a man, and I
>   Have suffered like a girl; yet thou dost look
>   Like Patience gazing on kings' graves, and smiling
>   Extremity out of act. What were thy friends?
>   How lost thou them? Thy name, my most kind virgin?
>   Recount, I do beseech thee; come sit by me.
> MARINA: My name is Marina.
> PERICLES: Oh I am mocked
>   And thou by some incensed god sent hither
>   To make the world to laugh at me [Scene 21, ll. 123–133].

A patent fear in the light of the situation; later Pericles is reunited with Thaisa, Marina's mother.

Cymbeline

This play seems readily to relate to *An Historie of the Creweltie of a Stepmother*, shown at court on December 28, 1578. Again there is a reconciliation element: Imogen the king's daughter is married to Postumus, a poor but worthy gentleman, who disbelieves his wife's fidelity and is finally forgiven and reconciled. Oxford/Postumus plays along with the Catholic element, and in effect gives a declaration of his loyalty. In Rome he says:

> I am brought hither
> Among the Italian gentry, and to fight
> Against my lady's kingdom: 'tis enough
> That, Britain, I have killed thy mistress: peace!
> I'll give no wound to thee [V, i, ll. 17–21].

This is Oxford the spy, introduced into that Catholic element, known to the queen as loyal, but warning her Catholic subjects that they were being spied on. (Perhaps this was part of his spymasters' instructions. See my reference to Macbeth on page 196.) No doubt he excused to them the declaration of loyalty which follows easily enough to them as an indication that he needed to keep in the queen's good graces.

The Taming of a Shrew

In 1578 Oxford's sister married Peregrine Bertie, Lord Willoughby, and a year later it is supposed that the first version of this play was performed on January 1, 1578 or 1579, in honor and send-up of their tempestuous relationship. Thomas Cecil wrote in September that he thought the Lady Mary "with that rod which heretofore she prepared for others, serve me, and myself not mine." Lucentio devotes a long speech to the virtues and culture of Padua, Pisa and Florence (I, i, ll. 1–24)— all of which were on Oxford's itinerary three years earlier. The rich gentleman of Padua, Baptista Minola, is clearly a composite of the bankers Baptista Nigrone and Benedict Spinola. Petruchio sounds like the Italian employed by the Lord Chamberlain (if this is a mistaken reference to the Lord Great Chamberlain, then Oxford, the holder of that office, is the actual employer) for the program of court entertainments for the season 1578-79, one Patruchius Ubaldinas.[37] The name of the forerunner play is *A Moral of the Marriage of Mind and Measure*,[38] and much of the play is taken up with the measures taken by Petruchio to subdue the mind of his bride. The similarities between this play and *The Taming of the Shrew* make it most unlikely that a different unknown playwright was the author of this one. The theme, the plot and the subplot, virtually all the characters and most of the action have their counterparts in both plays. "*The Taming of a Shrew* may not be so much the source-play as Shakespeare's first shot at the theme,"[39] wrote a critic. If Shakespeare were not the author, then an unknown playwright would have had to be, and this person in 1593 (I would say much earlier) would have had to be "capable of devising a three-part structure more impressive than the structure of any extant play by Lyly, Peele, Greene, Marlowe or Kyd."[40] I would add that the author would have been "without any known models to learn or copy from."

All's Well That Ends Well

While this play contains a wealth of autobiographical matter which might well have been inserted later, *The Rape of the Second Helen*[41] was shown a few days after *The Moral of Mind and Measure* on January 6, 1578/9. The Roussillon, where the bulk of the action takes place, is twenty miles from Lyons, where there is evidence of Oxford's presence on his way home in the spring of 1576. Resident there was Helene de Tournon, daughter of a lady-in-waiting to Marguerite, queen of Navarre, wife to the heir to the French throne (afterwards Henry IV), who died of love for a young nobleman. Act IV, scene iii, gives a muster of soldiers under the names of those providing them with so many men each. The first is Spurio, who appears in Act II, scene i: "You shall find in the regiment of the Spinii one Captain Spurio, with his cicatrice, an emblem of war on his sinister cheek" (ll. 42–44).

This Henri, Duke of Guise with his regiment Spinii or *épineux*, the French for thistle, the emblem of the Lorraine Guise family, had been wounded in the left cheek in 1575. In the later scene two Captain Dumains appear, the French title being duke de Mayenne, who is identified as "a botcher's prentice in Paris" (l. 190), an assistant to his brother the extreme Catholic duc de Guise, an instigator of the St. Bartholomew's Day massacres in Paris in 1572. Helena is abandoned by her husband and in Act III resolves to go on pilgrimage to Saint Jacques to be near her husband. This is assumed to be one of "Shakespeare's" blunders, that he thought the shrine of St. James[42] at Compostela in Spain was somewhere near Florence where Helena arrives in Scene v:

> WIDOW: God save you, pilgrim. Whither are you bound?
> HELENA: To Saint Jacques Le Grand. Where do the palmers lodge, I beseech you? [ll. 33–35].

In fact "Shakespeare's" geography is always right — thirty miles west of Florence is the shrine of San Giacomo Maggiore at Altapascio.

In the play, Krapp writes, "Parolles the gentleman-soldier whose tongue is mightier than his sword cultivates a virtue of manner exemplified by vivacity and novelty of phrase. Pompous words are not his stock-in-trade: he speaks a courtly idiom which by [1590] had ceased to be learned and pedantic. A 'snip taffetted fellow' (IV, v, l.1) in speech as well as dress he knows how to use the language of the smart set of his day."[43] By 1590 this language was hopelessly dated; effectively this language dates the play to an earlier period.

Two Gentlemen of Verona

This play may have some link with *A History of the Duke of Millayn [Milan] and the Marquess of Mantua*[44] produced at court on December 26, 1579, or the Boccacio novella *Tito and Gysippo*, a version of which under the title *Titus and Gysippus* was performed two days later. Kenneth Branagh has sought to explain the unevenness of the writing of the play by suggesting that two hands are at work, but the simple solution to this type of problem (which always looks more persuasive than any other) is that the mature Oxford was rewriting part of his apprentice efforts for public performance by (and as) Shakespeare.

Love's Labour's Lost

Parts of this play mirror the negotiations at Nerac in August 1579[45] between the Protestant Henry of Navarre, Marguerite, his Catholic queen, and her mother Catherine de' Medici, by which Henry and Catherine were allowed to resume marital relations. At the time Henry's friends included Biron, anglicized to Berowne, and de Longueville (Longaville), and an enemy de Mayenne (Dumain). Henry could not enter a Catholic town nor could his wife enter a Protestant one, so they had to meet in open country:

> KING: Fair Princess, welcome to the Court of Navarre.
> PRINCESS: "Fair" I give you back again, and "welcome" I have not yet. The roof of this court is too high to be yours, and welcome to the wide fields too base to be mine [II, i, ll. 90–94].

The negotiations begin with the princess handing over a letter from her father (i.e., her brother the king of France) or mother, Queen Catherine de' Medici:

> KING: Madam, your father here doth intimate
> The payment of a hundred thousand crowns,
> Being but one half of that entire sum
> Disbursed by my father in his wars.
> But say he or we — as neither have —
> Received that sum, yet there remains unpaid
> A hundred thousand more, in surety of the which
> One part of Aquitaine is bound to us,
> Although not valued to the money's worth.
> If the king your father will restore
> But that one half which is unsatisfied,
> We will give up our right in Aquitaine
> And hold fair friendship with his majesty [*ibid.*, ll. 128–140].

Part of the play also deals with the current state of the Alençon/Elizabeth marriage negotiations and with Don John's (Armado's) career in the Netherlands. At the time he was contemplating an invasion of England, a plan scotched by his brother Philip II, but nevertheless a continuing danger to Protestants everywhere.

> This Armado is a Spaniard that keeps here in court.
> A phantasim, a Monarcho, and one that makes sport
> To the Prince and his bookmates [*ibid.*, IV, i, ll. 97–99].

Monarcho was a crackbrained Italian hanging around the court in England at the time — a contemporaneous reference as Monarcho died shortly afterwards.

The play concludes with the Pageant of the Nine Worthies which, with elements in the main body of the play, sends up the Russian delegation sent to Elizabeth by Ivan the Terrible to ask for the hand of Lady Flora Hastings for Ivan the Terrible in September 1582.[46] There would be no point in writing and producing this prolonged skit unless it was immediately topical.

The Merchant of Venice

On February 2, 1579/80, *The History of Portio and Demorantes*[47] was produced at Whitehall, and this may readily linked with Gosson's reference to *The Jew* of roughly the same date, both now known to us as *The Merchant of Venice*. There is an early clear reference to Oxford when Graziano says to Antonio: "Why should a man whose blood is warm within/Sit like his grandsire cut in alabaster" (I, i, ll. 83–84).

Not too many people have their grandfather's effigy cut in alabaster like that of John, 15th Earl of Oxford in St. Nicholas Church, Castle Hedingham.

Portia's marriage chances were circumscribed like those of the queen by the will of her deceased father: "So is the will of a living daughter curbed by the will of a dead father" (I, ii, ll. 23–24).

Some have connected the (non–Jewish) fraudster Michael Lok,[48] with whom and on whose misrepresentations Oxford invested £3,000 in the third Northwest Passage expedition in May 1578, with Shylock the Venetian moneylender. While the play displays the Christians' visceral anti–Semitism (and some of the characters were probably déraciné Jews themselves, like Bassanio), there is no evidence that Oxford shared these sentiments; he seems to have had no such problem himself. He dealt with the Italian bankers and no doubt realized that there were concealed Jews among them, such as Baptista Nigrone and Benedict Spinola, the composite of the sympathetic Baptista Minola in *The Taming of the Shrew* (practically a Pantalone character from the *commedia dell'arte*), to say nothing of the lead character Bassanio himself. The wooing of Jessica and Lorenzo excites no racial attention from him at all, save for the jocular comment that the conversion of Jews to Christians will raise the price of pork (Act III, scene v, l. 20). No other non–Jewish playwright would have dealt with that aspect in that way, then or now. Shylock is merely doing business until his desire for revenge (nothing particularly Jewish in that, and in the circumstances, understandable, if not excusable) becomes irrational and corrupts his reasonable desire to take commercial advantage of his fallen persecutor. Oxford had to borrow from the Spinola representative while he was in Venice himself. The play itself did not provoke any anti–Jewish feeling in the city, notwithstanding the quite large Jewish community in London. Gosson describes *The Jew* as "representing the greediness of wordly choosers and bloody-minded usurers," which does not seem that severe, or particular to the Jewish community. We may contrast Oxford's view with that of Marlowe in *The Jew of Malta*.

While Oxford was cozened to the extent of £3,000, Antonio was in bond for 3,000 ducats. No serious commentator has doubted the accuracy of the author's knowledge of Venetian law on the enforcement of bonds and mortgages,[49] even by noncitizens such as Shylock (in which at the time Venetian law was apparently unique).

The evidence for the playwright's actual knowl-

Alabaster tomb of John, 15th Earl of Oxford, St. Nicholas Church, Castle Hedingham.

edge[50] of Venice is shown by his selection of the name Gobbo for the father and son characters, the Gobbo being a gargoyle at the end of the Rialto bridge, and by the use of the name "traject" (*traghetto*) for the Grand Canal ferries, miscopied as "tranect" by the later compositors, and distinguished from the "common ferry" below.

The indefatigable researches and scholarship of Dr. Noemi Magri have been able to place Belmont, Portia's country residence,[51] a clear indication that Oxford knew exactly the geography of the area. The "common ferry" began from the mouth of the river Brenta, along which all the aristocratic palaces were built at the time, five miles across the lagoon to Venice itself. In Act III Portia has to travel to Belmont: "we must measure twenty miles today," meaning there and back. The journey is five miles across the lagoon and five miles up the river, and back. Exactly in place is Villa Foscari and two miles from it is the Ca' delle Monache or Nuns' House, where Portia and Nerissa are:

> to live in prayer and contemplation:
> there is a monast'ry two miles off
> And there we will abide ... [III, iv, ll. 24, 31–32].

Because of the line "the light we see is burning in my hall," Dr. Magri can identify the hall on the north side of the building through which that light shines to a traveler on the road. In Act I Nerissa recalls that one of Portia's suitors was Bassanio, "a Venetian (a scholar and a soldier) that came hither in the Company of the Marquis of Montferrat" and Dr. Magri identifies the marquis as the Duke of Mantua using one of his subsidiary titles, who was entertained at the Villa Foscari with the new King Henry III of France in 1573. By coach or by ferry in the 1570s from, say, Padua to Venice you would have to pass the villa which is on a bend in the road, and in the river, so Oxford would have seen the villa on his travels and the light on in the hall.

In a derivation of the plot from the play, in Part III of Munday's *Zelauto* (1579)[52] the usurer Truculento is thwarted in his desire for the Lady Cornelia, and insists on obtaining the eyes of the two young men who owe him money. Truculento respects "cruelty more than Christian civility" (l. 174).

Antony and Cleopatra

Eva Turner Clark thinks this play could be the "Ptolome"[53] (i.e., Cleopatra, a queen from the Ptolemy dynasty) referred to by Gosson and/or the play with the title mistranscribed as *The History of Serpedon* produced at court on February 16, 1579/80, and ties it in with the political situation after Alençon's visit courting the queen in August 1579. Critics have linked the stirring descriptions of Cleopatra and Queen Elizabeth at the height of her powers. Then there is the curious passage of dialogue between Cleopatra and the Clown,[54] when the Clown brings in the asp with which Cleopatra is to kill herself. The asp is referred to as a "worm," and the word is repeated nine times in thirty-six lines. The French for worm is *ver*, pronounced "vair," likely the contemporary pronunciation of Vere. The Clown in an apparent slip says "truly I would not be the party that should desire you to touch him, for his biting is immortal" (V, ii, l. 250). The Clown is Oxford in his "allowed fool" role, and the "worm" is the personification of his works which will make Cleopatra/Elizabeth "immortal," and, says the Clown: "I wish you all joy of the worm" (*ibid.*, l. 265).

Twelfth Night

A publisher named Peck announces that he proposes to publish a manuscript called "A pleasant conceit of Vere, Earl of Oxford, discontented at the rising of a mean gentleman in the English Court c.1580." Sir Christopher Hatton, the captain of the queen's bodyguard, is the best fit for time and social level, and indeed their rivalry had begun before Oxford's departure for Italy. The letter forged by Maria (possibly Oxford's sister married to the boozy Willoughby, Sir Toby Belch) is signed "The Fortunate-Unhappy," precisely the translation of "Fortunatus Infelix" noted by Gabriel Harvey in his copy of Gascoigne's *Posies* as "lately the posy of Sir Christopher Hatton." Poor Hatton must have been mightily displeased to be shown as being taken in by the manifestly obscene content of the letter ("these be her very C's, her U's, and ['n'] her T's; and thus she makes her great P's" [II, v, ll. 85–86]). The play is littered with contemporary allusions. Sir Andrew Aguecheek "had as lief be a Brownist as a politician" (III, ii, l. 34), which refers to Burghley's sheltering of his cousin Thomas Browne,[55] an anti-Episcopalian campaigner, from the wrath of his superior the bishop of Ely in 1581. The point would be lost if the play were written after 1583, by which time the Brownists had virtually collapsed. There is another reference in *Sir Thomas More* below (page 121).

Sir Toby says, "My lady is a Cataian,[56] we are politicians" (II, iii, l. 72) and this draws attention to the fact that the queen was also an investor in the Northwest Passage expeditions to find a route to Cathay or China.

The Clown's "Primo, secundo, tertio, is a good play; and as the saying is the third pays for all: the triplex, sir, is a good triping measure; or the bells of St. Bennet, sir, may put you in mind; one, two, three" (V, i, ll. 33–36).

The bells of the three Churches of St. Bennet[57] in London would ring for Sunday afternoon prayers and sermon, precisely as The Theatre trumpet would sound to advertise the plays on a Sunday and the triplex dancing with them. Performances on a Sunday were not finally banned until 1581.

Orthodox critics usually date *Twelfth Night* to 1601, but attention has been drawn to Mitis' speech in Jonson's *Every Man Out of His Humour* (1599) at the end of Act III, scene i:

> MITIS: I travail with another objection, signior, which I fear will be enforced against the author, ere I can be delivered of it.
> CORDATUS: What's that, sir?
> MITIS: That the argument of his comedy might have been of some other nature, as of a duke in love with a countess, and that countess to be in love with the duke's son, and the son to love the lady's waiting-maid; some such cross wooing, with a clown to their servingman, better than to be thus near, and familiarly allied to the time.

One critic has described the speech as an "alarmingly prescient account"[58] of the plot of *Twelfth Night*, which wrecks the "usual" dating of the play.

Coriolanus

The suggestion is that this play reflects the political position on the return of Drake from his round-the-world expedition in 1581. His mother says: "Methinks I hear hither your husband's drum" (I, iii, l. 31); there is no mention in Plutarch, the principal source, of a drum, and, similarly unsourced, there are the several references to drums in the play, and to sea and fish.

The great Catholic fear had descended on England and very strict anti–Catholic laws were proposed by the Commons, meeting with much opposition in the Lords. Sir Walter Mildmay, Chancellor of the Exchequer, made a speech in 1581 which gave rise to this reference:

> SICINUS: It is a mind
>   That shall remain a poison where it is,
>   Not poison any further.
> CORIOLANUS: "Shall remain"!
>   Hear you this Triton of the minnows? Mark you
>   His absolute "shall"?
> COMINIUS: 'Twas from the canon.
> CORIOLANUS: "Shall"?
>   O good, but most unwise patricians! Why,
>   You grave, but reckless, senators, have you thus
>   Given Hydra leave to choose an officer,
>   That with his peremptory "shall," being but

> The horn and noise of the monster, wants not spirit
> To say he'll turn your current in a ditch,
> And make your channel his? [become the religious dictator]
> [III, i, ll. 89–100].⁵⁹

Measure for Measure

The play probably reflects Oxford's protest against the rigorous laws being enacted, and the enforcement in 1581 of old laws which had fallen into desuetude.

> This new governor
> Awakes me all the enrolled penalties
> Which have, like unscoured armor, hung by the wall
> So long that nineteen zodiacs have gone round
> And none of them have been worn; ... [I, iv, ll. 153–57].

The nineteen years referred to take us nearly back to the Elizabethan Act of Supremacy in 1559 and the penalties in it for nonconformity, which had not been rigidly enforced in the interim.

The play is riddled with associations with the Paris of the 1580s. All these characters can be identified. The duke is Henri III given to flights of religious mania, which make him take on the role of friar Lodowick (Louis), since St. Louis IX is his ancestor. Angelo is Argenoust, a rapporteur of the Paris court. Juliet is the pregnant accused Julietta. Claudio is the accused Claude Tonart. The duke's lords mentioned in Act IV, scene v:

Varrius is Guillaume de Vair Flavio is La Roche-Flavin;

Valencius is de la Marcke, the grandson of Dianne de Poitiers, the mistress of Henry II and duchesse de Valentinois;

Rowland is Rowlandson, a Catholic propagandist at the French court;

Barnardine is Bernardo de Mendoza, formerly a Spanish ambassador to England but in 1584 an ambassador to France;

Ragozine is the Papal legate Ragasoni;

Lucio is d'Espinay de Saint-Luc, who slandered the king and was married off to a morally corrupt hunchback.⁶⁰

"Orthodox" critics suggest it was written in 1604, but the clear topicalities of the trial of Tonart and Julietta and the transposal of all the other French names suggest a much earlier date. Unlike the post–1591 plays (or revisions of plays) it has a happy ending—of a sort, depending on the reader's view of life.

Romeo and Juliet[61]

The play reflects under the guise of the affrays between the Capulets and the Montagues the continuing problems that Oxford was having with the Knyvet family even after his release from the Tower. Romeo tries not to be involved:

> For I am proverbed with a grand-sire phrase,
> I'll be a candle-holder and look on [I, iv, ll. 37–38].

A candle holder or trussel, archaism for "trestle," is a stand or frame for candles that was at one time used in church. Oxford's grandmother's maiden name was Trussel.

There was a small and rather unmemorable earthquake in England in 1580. A much larger and destructive one took place in Northern Italy in 1570, destroying Ferrara, and more particularly described in *The Tempest*. The reference in *Romeo and Juliet* helps date this play to 1581: "Tis since the earthquake now eleven years" (I, iii, l. 25).

As You Like It

This play appears to reflect the political situation[62] on the temporary acceptance of the duke Francis Hercules of Alençon as husband for the queen, who in his guise as Orlando is wished well by Rosalind in his bout with the usurping duke's champion: "Now, Hercules be thy speed, young man" (I, ii, l. 198).

When he wins, Rosalind congratulates and rewards him with a chain: "Gentleman, Wear this for me; one out of the suits of fortune, That could give more, but that her hand lacks means" (*ibid.*, ll. 224–26).

Both the chain and the suitor (Alençon) with "but a little beard" (III, ii, l. 213) are referred to later in the play, but there was an incident whereby the queen presented Alençon's envoy with a "belle jartiere" which may be reflected by the chain.

As we have seen, Oxford was in Siena in January 1575–76, where he cannot fail to have seen the mosaic *Seven Ages of Man*,[63] then a hundred years old but then inserted in the newly consecrated cathedral. From it he derived with his usual accuracy the famous "All the world's a stage" speech (Act II, scene vii). Incidentally, there is a translation in similar terms, virtually a parallel, taken from the Plato-type Greek dialogue *Axiochus*,[64] and there is a suggestion that Oxford may have had a hand in the translation by "Edw. Spenser"; his (Spenser's) authorship has long been disputed.

In the play, the two run-down courtiers Jaques and Touchstone seem to be a composite of Oxford, wanting to carry on with his acting career:

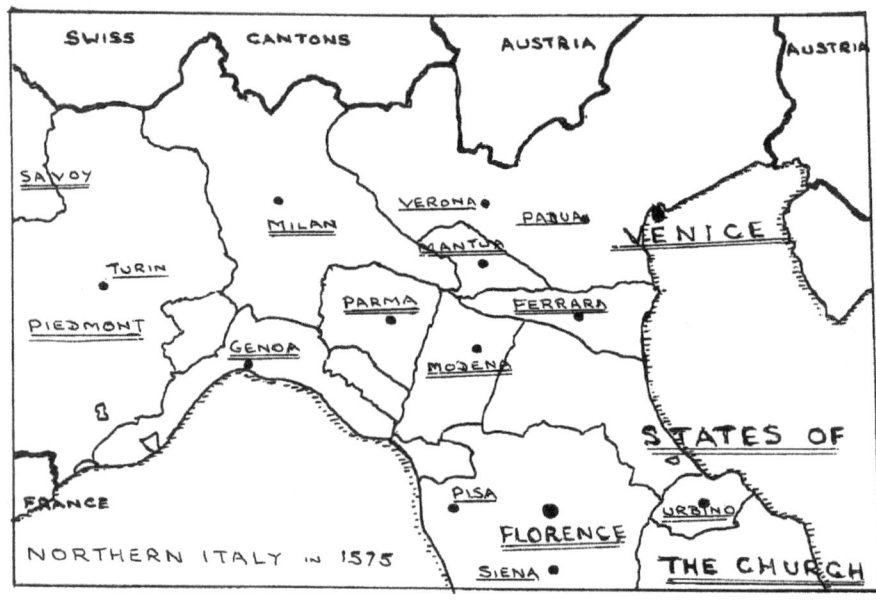

Map of northern Italy, 1575.

JAQUES: O worthy fool! One that hath been a courtier,
   And says, "if ladies be but young and fair,
   They have the gift to know it." And in his brain,
   Which is as dry as the remainder biscuit
   After a voyage, he hath strange places crammed [the theaters]
   With observation, the which he vents
   In mangled forms. Oh that I were a fool,
   I am ambitious for a motley coat.
DUKE SENIOR: Thou shalt have one.
JAQUES: It is my only suit [the only thing I want]
   Provided you weed your better judgments
   Of all opinion that grows rank in them
   That I am wise. I must have liberty
   Withal, as large a charter as the wind,
   To blow on whom I please, for so fools have;
   And they that are most gall-ed with my folly
   They most must laugh. And, why, sir, must they so?
   The why is plain as way to parish church:
   He that a fool doth very wisely hit
   Doth very foolishly, although he smart,
   Seem aught but senseless of the bob. If not,
   The wise man's folly is anatomised
   Even by the squandering glances of the fool.
   Invest me in my motley. Give me leave

> To speak my mind, and I will through and through
> Cleanse the foul body of th' infected world
> If they will patiently receive my medicine.
> DUKE SENIOR (portraying the authority figure not wanting Oxford to play that role): Fie on thee, I can tell what thou wouldst do.
> JAQUES: What, for a counter, would I do but good?

And the duke tells him that his record is so bad that publicity for him would infect "the general world" (II, vi, ll. 36–63, 70).

Touchstone is most remarkable for the later inserted dialogue with William, alias William Shakespeare, "You are not ipse, for I am he" (see page 189). It would have been too revealing if Jaques in the light of the extract above had played this part as well, and so Touchstone has to be introduced as a separate character.

An intermediate rewriting probably caused the insertion of Sir Oliver Martext, probably a Puritan minister named Oliver Pigge,[65] who was ridiculed for seeking to alter, or mar, the text of the fourth chapter of the Epistle of St. Peter, c. 1586. His claims to religious legitimacy are mocked in Act II, scene iii, by both Jaques and Touchstone.

Julius Caesar

This is thought to be *The historie of fferrar*[66] played at court on January 6, 1582/3, the mistranscription caused in much the same way as Cleopatra for Serpedon earlier. The play presents important evidence for Oxford's acting and views on actors generally, and further consideration is given to these aspects in the section *Note on the Author as Actor* at the end of Chapter Six (page 150).

Much Ado About Nothing

A large part of the plot of this play is covered by Ariosto's *Orlando Furioso*, the principal characters in which are Ariodante and Genevora.[67] A play of that name was produced at court on February 12, 1582/3. As we have seen, there is much by way of direct autobiographical reference (page 87).

Othello

While this play may reflect the complex political situation in the Netherlands in 1583, there are two references to the Sagittary in Venice (I, i, l. 159 and iii, l. 115).⁶⁸ This was apparently a part of the Doge's Palace which was burned down in 1577. In effect it was the assayer's office or possibly a courtroom, and would only be known to a pre–1577 visitor. With that thought in mind in that latter scene, a senator says: "This cannot be,/By no reason of assay" (ll. 18, 19).

And Iago says:

> If the balance of our lives had not one scale of reason to poise another of sensuality, the blood and baseness of our natures would conduct us to the most preposterous of conclusions. But we have reason to cool our raging motions, our carnal stings, our unbuttered lusts; whereof I take this, that you call love, to be a sect, or scion [ll. 326–332].

Burghley and the Privy Council had been much exercised by the activities of an Anabaptist sect, the Family of Love,⁶⁹ founded in 1539 and operating in Suffolk, next to Oxford's home county of Essex. One of its disciples in about 1580 produced a work of which only the title survives: *Testimony of Sion*. Iago's "scion" is a pun on Sion in the title of the book and the sect is thus attacked—a true topical reference as the sect was then at its strongest. Iago's hypocrisy, and his references to virtue, will and lust, tar him with the excesses of the sect, which declined into a figure of fun later on.

The orthodox date for *Othello* is 1604, but refers to *Every Man in His Humour* (1598). Kitely's speeches are "often disquietingly prescient of Othello,"⁷⁰ says one critic. Kitely appears in the anglicized edition of Jonson's play, replacing the near homonym of Othello/Thorello in the original Italian version, which should have disquieted our critic further along with the dialogue:

> BIANCHA (replacing Desdemona—the white wife): I pray thee (good muss) we stay for you.
> THORELLO: By Christ I would not for a thousand crowns.
> BIANCHA: What ail you sweetheart? Are you not well? Speak good muss.
> THORELLO: Troth, my head agues extremely on a sudden [I, iv, ll. 184–191].

Compare:

> DESDEMONA: How now, my dear Othello!
>   Your dinner and the generous islanders
>   By you invited, do attend your presence.
> OTHELLO: I am to blame.
> DESDEMONA: Why do you speak so faintly? Are you not well?
> OTHELLO: I have a pain upon my forehead here [III, iii, ll. 283–88].

A Midsummer Night's Dream

*A Pastorall of Phillyda and Corin*⁷¹ was presented to the court on December 26, 1584. This can be identified with *A Midsummer Night's Dream* because of Titania's lines in Act II:

> Then I must be your lady: but I know
> When thou hast stol'n away from fairy-land,
> And in the shape of Corin sat all day
> Playing on pipes of corn, and versing love
> To amorous Phillyda [i, ll. 64–65].

In addition, the musk-rose[72] had only recently (1582) been introduced into England: the only three references to it in the whole of the canon are in *A Midsummer Night's Dream*.

A great part of the play sends up the courtship of Elizabeth by Alençon; Bottom repeatedly gives fairies Alençon's French title as heir to the French throne — Monsieur.[73] Then there is this splendid exchange:

> BOTTOM: I will discharge it [the part of Pyramus] either in your straw-coloured beard, your orange-tawny beard, your purple-in-grain beard, or your French-crown-coloured beard, your perfect yellow.
> QUINCE: Some of your French crowns have no hair at all [I, ii, ll. 85–89].

The reference to "French crown" having "no hair at all" is a standard English joke on the effect of syphilis, the "French disease," as well as a mention of the French *ecu* coin.

Some authorities think that the play was slightly rewritten for the marriage of Sir Thomas Heneage and Southampton's mother on May 2, 1594, perhaps as part of the campaign to suggest matrimony to Southampton along with the first tranche of the sonnets (see page 177).

Troilus and Cressida

On December 27, 1584, *The History of Agamemnon and Ulysses*[74] was presented at court. In the court records £6 13s. 4d. was paid on a warrant for this performance "by the Children of the Earl of Oxford (Harry Evans)." The play is heavy with topical political resonances, but it also contains the earliest mention of the potato (introduced to England in 1584): "How the devil Luxury, with his fat rump and potato-finger,/tickles these together" (V, ii, ll. 56–57).[75]

Hamlet

There are a number of plays which might or might not be earlier versions of *Hamlet*, but there is a speech that can be dated to 1585 or 1586:

> The best actors in the world, either for tragedy, comedy, history, pastoral, pastoral-comical, historical-pastoral, tragical-historical, tragical-comical-his-

torical-pastoral, scene individable or poem unlimited. Seneca cannot be too heavy or Plautus too light. For the law of writ and the liberty, they are the only men [II, ii, ll. 397–404].[76]

The literati of the court circle would readily recognize this as a send-up of Sidney's prolix literary criticism, with its attempts at classification of "Poesy," which:

> may be subdivided into sundry more special denominations, the most suitable be the Heroic, Lyric, Tragic, Comic, Satiric, Iambic, Elegiac, Pastoral, and certain others, ... Now in his parts, kinds, or species (as you list to term them), it is to be noted that some poesies have coupled together two or three kinds, as the tragical and comical, whereupon is risen the tragicomical. Some in the like manner have mingled prose and verse, as Sannazzaro and Boethius. Some have mingled matters heroical and pastoral.

Sidney, because of his heroic death after the battle of Zutphen (1586), comes beyond criticism for whatever his views — even of matters of literature, let alone caricature, parody or mockery. Oxford clearly did not want to lose his speech mocking Sidney's genre of literary criticism, so he puts it in the mouth of his father-in-law in the guise of Burghley-Polonius. In this way the original caricature is lost but the parody saved. Sidney's other caricatures, Slender in *The Merry Wives of Windsor* and Aguecheek in *Twelfth Night*, being earlier and out in the public domain, are saved in their full glory of ineptitude.

It is notable that Oxford's brother-in-law Lord Willoughby (alias Sir Toby Belch) in July 1583[77] led a mission from the queen to the king of Denmark in July 1583, which gives Oxford and *Hamlet* an immediate nexus. Horatio is clearly the soldier Horace de Vere, Oxford's cousin,[78] who is bid in a later version:

> Report me and my cause aright
> To the unsatisfied.
>
> And in this harsh world draw thy breath in pain,
> To tell my story [V, ii, ll. 291–92, 300–01].

We will see how well Horace de Vere was able to fulfill his commission.

Many critics have identified Polonius with a caricature of Burghley, not altogether a wise thing on the part of an author unless one's own position is secure. Oxford sets out the then unpublished advice given by Burghley to his eldest son on his departure for study in Paris (I, iii), which much resembles that in the subsequent printed edition (see page 10).

In Act I, scene i, in order to ascertain the time of the ghost's appearance, Bernardo refers to:

> yond same star that's westward from the pole had made its course t' illume that part of heaven where it now burns [ll. 34–36].

Shakespeare astronomists identify this star as Tycho Brahe's supernova of 1572, the memory of it revived for the play.[79] The references to stars and astronomical events have been tallied with the works of Shakespeare, and it is significant that none date after 1604, the year of Oxford's death.

Rosenkrantz and Guildenstern[80] were real-life courtiers in Denmark in the last two decades of the sixteenth century. Unlike most Danish nobles who went to study at Rostock or Leyden, these men went on to Wittenberg, as did their fictional namesakes and Hamlet. This must be a further example of the local knowledge supplied by Lord Willoughby.

The players' play *The Murder of Gonzago*,[81] although written in "very choice Italian" (III, ii, l. 250), has not survived either in Italian or English, although "the story of the play is certainly taken from the murder of the Duke of Urbino[82] by [a relative of his wife] Luigi Gonzago in 1538, who was poisoned by means of a lotion poured into his ears." A biography of the murdered duke was in circulation in Italy in the 1570s but it had little detail of his death save that he was poisoned. The first two quartos refer to the victim as duke, and duke becomes king in the 1623 folio. In *Hamlet* the player Murderer is Lucianus, and the murder is by poison into the king's ear. The connection is clear, and not immediately available to any other playwright of the period. Titian's portrait of the Duke (which was available for Oxford to see in Florence in 1575) is followed in the description of his father's ghost. The Duke was buried in full armour, and:

> Enter the Ghost in complete armour, holding a truncheon, with his beaver up [Stage direction before I, i, l. 37]
> HORATIO: A figure like your father Armed at all points exactly, cap-à-pie.... A countenance more in sorrow than in anger.
> HAMLET: ... And his eyes fixed upon you?
> HORATIO: Most constantly.
> HAMLET: His beard was grizzly, no?
> HORATIO: It was as I have seen it in his life, A sable silvered [I, ii, ll. 199–200, 228–29, 238–40].

The Merry Wives of Windsor

The character of Slender[83] looks like a caricature of Sidney. If so, the play must be before 1586 because it would otherwise be impossible to caricature a deceased hero. Otherwise, apart from the comments included when *Henry V* is studied below so far as they touch on this play, there are no particular elements of evidence which would help to fix a first date for this play, but it relies on the existence of the two plays on the reign of Henry IV, which feature the same mock hero, Falstaff. It does, however, show a familiarity with Windsor and its environs where Oxford spent some part of his childhood and convalescence in the period 1569-70. The reference to a "saw-pit" into which the children are to hide themselves (IV, iv, l. 53) before their assault on Falstaff is echoed by the location of a timberyard in Windsor Great Park on Norden's map (1607).

The Winter's Tale

This play reflects, among other matters, upon the rise of Sir Walter Raleigh[84] at court in the period 1585-86, beginning with this recorded exchange between Raleigh (the boy Mamillius) and the queen (Leontes):

> LEONTES: Mamillius, Art thou my boy?
> MAMILLIUS: Ay, my good lord.
> LEONTES: I'fecks! Why that's my bawcock. What, hast smutch'd thy nose.
>   They say it's a copy of mine. Come captain, We must be neat;—not neat, but cleanly, captain [I, ii, ll. 121–25].

The queen offered to wipe the captain's nose (aquiline, just like hers), but Raleigh removed the smut himself.

In March 1584, Raleigh was given a license to export a certain number of woolen cloths, which was regranted and extended in later years. We know that in 1581 the price of a tod of wool (a quarter of a hundredweight) varied from a pound to twenty-two shillings, and it probably remained stable until the hostilities with Spain began in 1586. The Clown says: "Let me see: every 'leven wether tods; every tod yields pound and odd shilling: fifteen hundred shorn, what comes the wool to?" (IV, iii, ll. 31–33). In other words, what is the license worth to Raleigh?

On the death of the Earl of Bedford in 1585, Raleigh received the Lord Wardenship of the Stannaries, and the Clown says: "I must have saffron to colour the warden pies" (*ibid.*, l. 44).

Slightly later in 1586 Raleigh received the very substantial lands and goods forfeited by the convicted plotter Babington, with the exception of a curious clock[85] which the queen kept for herself:

> HERMIONE: I love thee not a jar of the clock behind. What lady, she her lord [I, ii, ll. 42–43].

Walter Raleigh's home village in Devon was Fardel: the archaic word "fardel," meaning bundle, is found six times in this play and only once elsewhere. A further oblique reference:

OLD SHEPHERD: Would any but these boiled-brains of nineteen and twenty-two hunt this weather? They have scared away two of my best sheep, which I fear the wolf will find sooner than the master. If anywhere I have them, 'tis by the seaside, browsing of ivy [III, iii, ll. 62–65].

It should not be impossible to ascertain the two young hunters: the sheep may be identified with Sidney and Fulke Greville who dodged out of court to join Drake's 1583 expedition. Oxford may have been commenting on their immaturity. However the reference to "ivy" is to Ivybridge in Devon whence the expedition was to set out. Fardel is two miles northwest of Ivybridge.

Macbeth

In 1567 an agent of Burghley in Scotland sent to him a drawing of the death of Darnley's assassination on February 9, 1566-67,[86] which is now in the State Papers. In the Northeast quarter are laid the bodies of Darnley and his servant with a bloody dagger floating in the air near them, recalling:

> Is this a dagger I see before me
> The handle toward my hand? Let me clutch thee:
> I have thee not, and yet I see thee still [II, i, ll. 33–35].

In the Northwest quarter the infant James (afterwards James VI and I) is shown sitting up in his cradle, praying with a flagged message ("Judge and avenge my cause, O Lord"), and Macbeth says:

> What is this
> That rises like the issue of a king
> And wears upon his baby brow the round
> And top of sovereignty? [IV, i, ll. 102–05].

At the time of the assassination Oxford was in Burghley's household aged sixteen, and it seems unlikely that the events and even the drawing were not discussed and shown then. Sometime in September 1574, Oxford visited Burghley at Theobalds, his country seat. Also staying was the Countess of Lennox, Darnley's mother. She was the aunt of Mary, Queen of Scots, and after James VI the next in succession to the Scottish throne. There is in the Royal Library at Windsor *The Buik of the Cronicles of Scotland* in manuscript,[87] written by an illegitimate Stuart cousin some thirty years earlier, and the most probable way the book came to England was with the countess in 1567. It is a clear source for great tracts of *Macbeth* with its own dramatic account of the witches and with passages of dialogue adapted to the play. Details of the Darnley murder taken from the depositions at the time also reappear in *Macbeth*. Much is repeated in *Holinshed*, second edition, 1587. The play is full of contemporary references to Scotland. In the middle of the eleventh century there was no Lord Lennox and no Setons — the family did not become royal armor-bearers until much later — but both appear in *Macbeth*.

Another contemporary event which appears in the play and would be in an early version for topicality's sake is the St. Bartholomew's Day[88] massacre of the Protestants in Paris and provincial France. Although the weakling king Charles IX gave the actual order, the common consensus was that without the determination of his ghastly mother, Catherine de' Medici, he would have continued to waver. This is reflected in the determination of Lady Macbeth (mirroring the same pertinacity as Lady Arden in the earlier play *Arden of Feversham*). This hesitation is reflected at length in *Macbeth* and terminates with the ringing of a bell:

> MACBETH: Go bid thy mistress, when my drink is ready
> She strike upon the bell.
> While I threat, he lives;
> Words to the heat of deeds too cold breath gives.
> I go, and it is done; the bell invites me.
> Hear it not, Duncan, for it is a knell
> That summons thee to heaven or to hell [II, i, ll. 32–33, 60–63].
> LADY MACBETH: Hark! Peace!
> It was the owl that shrieked, the fatal bellman [II. ii, ll. 2, 3].

Catherine, the Queen Mother, still feared her son might relent, and after suggesting that he was a coward angered him into giving the order. Catherine herself gave the order for the bell of St. Auxerrois to be rung as the signal for the start of the St. Bartholomew's Day massacre.

King Lear

This play appears to contain a number of references to the state of France in 1589. Henry III's massacre of his Guise opponents[89] led to his own excommunication and left him friendless, so that he had to take refuge in effect with his Protestant heir Henry of Navarre. As illustrated in Act IV, scene iii:

> KENT: Why the king of France is so suddenly gone back — know you the reason?
> GENTLEMAN: Something he left imperfect in the state which since his coming forth is thought of; which imports to his kingdom so much fear and danger that his personal return was most required and necessary.
> KENT: Who hath he left behind him general?
> GENTLEMAN: The Marshall of France, Monsieur La Far [IV, iii, ll. 1–8].[90]

"Monsieur," the king's heir, and "La Far" tell us that this commander is Henry of N(L)av(F)arre, Henry III's then actual heir.

King Leir with its "happier ending" may represent an early version. This play contains twoscore parallels of language, thought and expression that go "far beyond what we should necessarily expect in any two dramatic versions of a common theme." In *King Lear* there is a reference to "That lord that counselled thee/to give away thy land." In the 1608 quarto of that play (*The History of King Lear*, scene iv, ll. 135–36), no one does (the lines and the whole of the Fool's song are not in the folio), but in *King Leir* Skalliger[91] gives just that advice — Oxford forgot to repeat it in his rewrite, or resurrect Skalliger.

Two Noble Kinsmen

This is one of two plays deemed to be a collaboration between Fletcher and Shakespeare — evidenced by the 1634 title page. It could be based on a lost play entitled *Palamon and Arcite*, said to be by Richard Edwards (d. 1566), at a performance of which the press of spectators and the collapse of a wall and a staircase caused the death of three people (see page 31). Equally, it might be the play described by Henslowe's diary as "Palamon and Arsett" described as "ne" on its first recorded performance on September 17, 1594. Further consideration is discussed in Chapter Eight.

Of course there are missing plays from the list like *The Three Sisters of Mantua* (see page 122). *Arden of Feversham* and *A Yorkshire Tragedy* are considered in Chapter Two.[92]

The History Plays[93]

The early plays *Edmund Ironside*, *Edward III* and *Famous Victories* are considered in Chapter Two as well. The history plays do not lend themselves so much to autobiographical reference or political topicality as do the comedies and tragedies, but there is nevertheless one matter which is significant: the treatment of de Vere's ancestors. There is no doubt that in the reign of Richard II an unaffected dramatist would conceive Robert, the ninth Earl of Oxford, as the villain of the piece, certainly if he were writing *Thomas of Woodstock*, and his influence would continue in the later play *Richard II*. He is not mentioned, as no doubt being a disgrace to the author's family. Conversely, in *Famous Victories*, his successor Richard, the eleventh earl, plays such an overbearing part that, when the play was revised and divided between 1 and 2 *Henry IV* and *Henry V*, no doubt under pressure the role was cut altogether. In actuality Lord Richard appears to have played a minor part. He died aged thirty-two in 1417. In the Wars of the Roses, the twelfth earl was at all times a loyal Lancastrian. He and his son were executed by Edward IV, and they are shown as the heroic victims by John, the thirteenth earl (3 *Henry VI* III, iii ll. 101–107). John is shown as playing himself, a heroic role on the Lancastrian side repeatedly acclaimed by his descendant in 3 *Henry VI* and *Richard III*. In 1471 the efforts of the earls of Warwick and Oxford, and of the egregious Clarence, resulted in the short-lived restoration of Henry VI. At the battle of Barnet, John made a fatal mistake. In a fog he attacked Warwick's force, causing the final rout of the Lancastrians and John to desert his own troops. The suggestion in the play that John made a valiant attempt to aid Henry's queen is a total fabrication by the playwright. His role at Bosworth in 1485 at the final triumph of Henry VII is not clear in the historical evidence but very important in the play *Richard III*. This consistent glorification[94] of his predecessors and suppression of negative matter can only lead to the conclusion that the writer was the seventeenth Earl of Oxford.

King John

The process of the rewriting of this play is considered below (page 137). The second euphuistic section of the First Citizen's speech went in during the early 1580s when the fashion for such speaking and writing was at its height, and the later, more mature section quoted before belongs in date to the next chapter.

Richard II, 1 *Henry IV* and 2 *Henry IV* are considered in Chapter Two, along with *Edmund Ironside*, *Edward III* and *Thomas of Woodstock*.

Henry V

This play was put on in 1599 to speed the departure of Essex and his expedition to Ireland to put down the very serious O'Neill Tyrone rebellion. Oxford, who had his reasons for not wanting to be associated with Essex (see page 181), would not have had anything to do with this production which in effect was a revival of his earlier play written in 1584 and itself a rewrite of part of *Famous Victories*. The Chorus at the start of Act V switches from the triumphant welcome to the king from the city of London:

> As by a lower but by loving likelihood,
> Were now the general of our gracious empress —
> As in good time he may — from Ireland coming,
> Bringing rebellion broach-ed upon his sword [ll. 29–31].

The word "broach-ed"[95] is significant: to "broach" is to skewer, to stick something on a point. In 1583 the second Desmond rebellion in Ireland was reaching its climax: after some years of desultory fighting, Elizabeth appointed Thomas Butler 10th Earl of Ormonde to command a force to bring the rebellion to an end. After a vigorous campaign he succeeded in his task, and finally the Desmond earl was captured and beheaded in November. His head was put on a sword point — "broached" — and sent to Ormonde. He sent it to the queen, who had it exhibited on a pole on London Bridge. She wrote to him at the end of December, inviting him to London to receive her thanks, and he duly arrived "as in good time he may" in May 1584. So a play about the triumph of a glorious predecessor coupled with that of a "lower ... general" written by the restored-to-favor playwright would be particularly apposite and acceptable. The contrast with the miserable effort by Essex in 1599 is inescapable. If the whole play was performed in early 1599, no wonder the Chorus speeches and much else were missed off when the quartos were printed anonymously (Oxford may not have wanted even his pseudonym associated with it) in 1600 and 1602.

I now refer to Sidney's *Apologie for Poetry*, probably written about 1583, and presumably circulating in manuscript, with its diatribe against the practices of existing playwrights (see page 41). He objected to the mingling of kings and clowns (*Famous Victories* must have done his digestion no good at all), and the mocking of "strangers because they speak not English so well as we do." It is apparent that Oxford did not agree with one word of this nonsense, and went out of his way to pile on the clowns led by Falstaff and to mock Welsh, French and other accents in the history plays and *The Merry Wives of Windsor*, and indeed throughout the canon. Sidney hated the representation of battles on the stage: "While in the meantime two armies fly in, represented by four swords and bucklers."[96] Oxford has Chorus say:

> Can this cockpit hold
> The vasty fields of France?
> Or may we cram within this wooden O
> The very casques
> That did affright the air at Agincourt [pre I, ll. 10–14].

And:

> and so our scene must to the battle fly
> Where — O for pity! — we shall much disgrace

> With four or five most vile and ragged foils
> Right ill-disposed in brawls ridiculous,
> The name of Agincourt. Yet sit and see,
> Minding true things by what their mockeries be [pre IV, ll. 48–53].

Thus the opinions of tiny minds are routed (and the date of their debacle established as well).

I Henry VI

In Holinshed's first edition (1577)[97] there is no account of the career of Joan of Arc, but there are numerous references in the 1587 posthumous edition (Holinshed died in 1580). There is a good case for placing the play before, and as a source for, the second edition, in the same way that *Arden of Feversham* alias *Murderous Michael* (1578) precedes the version of events in Holinshed (1587). Act I, scene iii, lines 40–47, recounts the scene where the dauphin tests Joan by putting up a courtier to act his part to her which she immediately realizes, and this is followed by Holinshed:

> Lo, while I waited on my tender lambs,
> And to the sun's parching heat display'd my cheeks,
> God's mother deigned to appear to me,
> And in a vision full of majesty
> Will'd me to leave my base vocation
> And free my country from base calamity;
> Her aid she promis'd and assur'd success;
> In complete glory she revealed herself ... [ll. 55–62].

Holinshed:

> Now recounting altogether, her pastoral bringing up, rude, without any virtuous instruction, her campestrall conversation with wicked spirits, whom in her first salutation to Charles the Dolphin [i.e., the scene in the play above], she uttered to be our Lady, St. Katharin and St. Anne, that in this behalf came and gave her commandments from God her maker as she kept her father's lambs in the fields [iii, 604/2/23].

Same scene:

> I am prepared: here is my keen-edg'd sword,
> Deck'd with five flower-de-luces on each side:
> The which at Touraine, in Saint Katharine's churchyard,
> Out of a great deal of old iron I chose forth [ll. 77–80].

Holinshed:

> then at the Dolphin's sending me by her assignment, from St. Katharin's church of Fierbois in Touraine (where she never had been and knew not) in a

secret place among old iron, appointed she her sword to be sought out brought her (that with five floure de lices was graven on both sides) wherewith she fought ... [iii, 600 2/2].

The dauphin takes her aside for a long talk, and a courtier speaks:

My lord, methinks, is very long in talk ...
Shall we disturb him since he keeps no mean? [ll. 118, 122].

Holinshed:

she picked him out alone who thereupon had her to the end of the gallery, where she held him an hour in secret and private talks, that of his privy chamber thought very long, and therefore would have broken it off but he made them a sign to let her say on [*ibid.*].

2 Henry VI

In Holinshed's first edition (1577) there is no account of the Yorkist claim, but the second edition follows the play, just as the play *Arden of Feversham* in the same way may precede the account of the murder in Holinshed's second edition. The Yorkist claim is dealt with exhaustively in Act II, scene ii, and this version is faithfully followed in Holinshed (1587).

In Act II, scene iv, at line 16 there is a stage direction whereby the duchess of Gloucester traverses a street in London in penance "with a taper burning in her hand." Holinshed: "Polychronicon saith she was enjoined to go through Cheapside with a taper in her hand" (iii, 657/2/51).

An episode at court in 1579 where the queen boxed the ears of the Countess of Leicester is paralleled by the scene where Queen Margaret boxes the ears of the duchess of Gloucester (I, iii).

3 Henry VI

The very young thirteenth Earl of Oxford plays a small but heroic part in Act III, scene iii.

Richard III

Again there are references in Holinshed's second edition which are not in the first. In Act I, scene iii, the newly ennobled Marquess of Dorset says to the court about and in the presence of the deposed Queen Margaret:

DORSET: Dispute not with her, she is lunatic
QUEEN MARGARET: Peace, master Marquess, you are malapert.
  Your new fire-stamp of honour is scarce current
  Oh, that your young nobility could judge
  What 'twere to lose it and be miserable ... [ll. 252–56].

Holinshed:

... created the Lord Thomas, Marquess Dorset before dinner, and so in the habit of marquess above the habit of knighthood, he began the table of knights in St. Edward's Chamber [iii, 702/2/8].

In Act V, scene ii:

BLUNT: He hath no friends but what are friends for fear,
  Which in his dearest need will fly from him [ll. 20, 21].

Holinshed:

... wishing and working his destruction: who otherwise would have been the instrument of their casting away.

(marginal note) "some who hated Richard came to him through fear" (745/2/42).

Holinshed's chief copying of *Richard III* comes in scene v where Richmond and the king give their respective orations to their forces: these in *Holinshed* contain many direct transpositions from the play. He had no other authority for these speeches.

Henry VIII

The only evidence for an early date is a list of costumes in the possession of Edward Alleyne, apparently datable prior to 1592. These include a "Harry VIII gown" and a "Cardinall's gown." Again because of the strong connection and alleged collaboration with Fletcher, further consideration is postponed to Chapter Eight.

Sir Thomas More[98]

Recent research suggests that the play shows clear signs of dictation, with passages written in the hands of several scribes. As in *Hamlet*, the author resisted the temptation open to a member of the middle class to "send up" the noble actor/producer (see the quotation on page 156). There is a good argument for giving the whole of the play to Shakespeare. The language consistently used is an excellent argument for this view. In Addition IV the rogue Faulkner has his long hair forcibly cut in prison, to his disgust: "Here's a lousy jest! But if I notch not that rogue Tom barber, that makes me thus look like a Brownist, hang me!" (III, ii, ll. 278–79).

This reference to the Brownist sect[99] makes the play contemporaneous with *Twelfth Night*, written not later than 1583. However, the play could be two or so years earlier, as it contains very marked Catholic sympathies: this could have been calculated to give Oxford cover for his spying activities. There is no doubt where Oxford himself stood: the anachronistic figure of the Earl of Surrey,[100] who was only seventeen when More was executed in 1535, was his uncle by marriage and the brightest poetic star in the reign of Henry VIII, until he too was judicially murdered just before the king's own death in 1547. In the play, Surrey signs the king's articles under which the pope's jurisdiction to interfere in England was abrogated, but More and the bishop of Rochester refuse. Surrey says:

> 'Tis strange that my Lord Chancellor should refuse More
> The duty that the law of God bequeathes
> Unto the King [IV, ii, ll. 114–16].

And when More goes off to his execution, in the last speech of the play:

> A very learned worthy gentleman
> Seals error with his blood [V, iv, ll. 134–35].

In a nod to his own affairs Oxford has Surrey say to More:

> Oh my noble Lord, you tax me in that word poet of much idleness.
> It is a study that makes poor our fate.
> Poets were ever thought unfit for state [Scene 8, ll. 216–17].

More himself, although in high office, has not lined his pocket:

> That part of poet that was given me
> Made me a very unthrift
> For this is a disease that attends us all,
> Poets were never thrifty, never shall [V, iii, ll. 63–66].

Interestingly, Oxford portrays More as being sensitive about his "humble" birth. In point of fact More came from substantial gentry, his father being knighted and obtaining for his son as his first leg up in his political career a post in the household of Cardinal Morton. But Oxford has him say:

> Good God, Good God, that I from such a humble bench of birth
> Should step up as 'twere to my country's head ... [III, ii, ll. 6, 7].

This seems a gratuitous comment lying only in the mouth of an aristocratic (and young, snobbish) author.

This summary unfortunately can only give a taste of the mind of the author and cannot be comprehensive. For example, there exists *An Exposition upon the Epistle of St. Paul to the Ephesians* by St. John Chrysostom translated anonymously from the Greek with an introduction clearly by Oxford littered with the same usages and thought as are seen in Oxford's letters and some of the plays. Published in 1581 and dedicated to Countess Anne, it looks like some form of repentance gift on the part of the author. The usages serve as a link to common authorship of 2 *Henry VI*, *King John*, *Measure for Measure*, and probably other works. Other critics applaud *Doctor Doddypoll* for its Shakespearean poetry.[101] In addition there are the possibilities in the lost plays such *Harthacanute*. One authority has suggested that the play *The Three Sisters of Mantua*,[102] a tragedy clearly based on the politics of that duchy in the 1530s, would be within the ambit of Oxford's experience. It was produced at court at Richmond on December 28, 1578.

After 1590 Oxford seems to have devoted himself in part to the sonnets, and also to his playwriting. Many of the plays were revised in the final period, 1590–1604, and we cannot tell to what extent these revisions encompass the whole spectrum, from minor touching up to substantial rewriting. Certainty of dating is impossible and the study of chronology in stylometrics[103] as a base for dating the plays is as a result a waste of time.

He was also of use to the authorities in the role of supervisor of the drafting of anti–Puritan pamphlets (if not the writer himself). The evidence for his role is really only his connection from 1588 on with the anti–Martinist writers Lily, Greene and Nashe and later in the War of the Pamphlets with the same writers. The Martinists were extreme Puritans and the campaign against them was apparently turned over to Oxford and his associates by the church authorities. Nashe's reference to "Lynceus" quoted above (page 27) appears to confirm the point directly, but much research and analysis remains to be done. Certainly Oxford's role annoyed Joseph Hall (again), who wrote in 1598: "That Lynceus may be matched with Coward's fight,/That sees not Paris for the houses' height" (*Virgedemarium* IV, I, ll. 25–26).

At the end of the last chapter, I left the question as to what happened to those plays which were successful in the immediate post–1576 period (where apparently we have only the names and very few texts). No early "Shakespeare" texts survive, except that part of *Titus Andronicus* covered by the Peacham cryptogram (see page 35).

The obvious answer to the conundrum of the apparent (but unlikely) failure of those quality plays to survive is that some of them did, either as near originals or modernized with (successive) rewriting, as my review above shows. It is no great leap to link them to the numerous productions of the period whose exact date of writing as opposed to being acted or printed is obscure. To make life more difficult, frequently the titles of the plays were altered, perhaps when being adapted or rewritten. Some have more than one title. The original title for *The Tempest*, we now can see, was *The Spanish Maze*,[104] a play produced under that name at court during the 1604/5 court revels.

There is, I think, one play which calls for consideration in priority to the others, even though it is not identified in the records of the court revels. This is *Love's Labour's Lost*. Critics wrote:

> Nothing is more remarkable in [William Shakespeare's] earliest productions than their perfect polish and urbanity. The principal characters in *Love's Labour's Lost* are princes and nobles, true to the models he might have found in contemporary society.... The creator of such personages must have been in better company and enjoyed a wider outlook on society than can easily be believed attainable by an actor or a resident in a single city ... that knowledge of good society (and) easy and confident attitude towards mankind which appears in Shakespeare's plays from the first and which (we must concede this much to the Baconians) are so unlike what might have been expected from a Stratford rustic or London actor.[105]

Another critic gave his readers a choice, either to reject William Shakespeare as the author or to believe in miracles[106] — yet most people do not believe in secular miracles (as opposed to divine ones). The case is made stronger because the critic did not take into account the faithful reproduction of events in the French court in 1578, as they appear in the play (see page 98). The current (1575–85) fad of euphuism, that elegant conversational mechanism, is either set out or indeed may be being sent up. Elements of the *commedia dell'arte*,[107] the Italian street play art, are synthesized along with an apparent relationship with Giordano Bruno's cast of mind,[108] and the whole is quite beyond the education and life experiences of William Shakespeare as we know them. By the time of the "orthodox" date 1592, the euphuism fad was long gone and the French king Henry III had been assassinated three years earlier.

If we take William Shakespeare and the 1592 date out of the equation, then it is clear that the play was written during the period 1578–80. We have certainly come closer in the review above as to how and why Oxford came to write it (page 99).[109]

Then we have a prime piece of evidence. In 1589, *The Arte of English Poetry*,[110] almost certainly by George Puttenham, appeared. This is a work of considerable scholarship, not to say pedantry, and part of it is devoted to illustrating by examples grammatical figures of speech and idioms. It is suggested that the book took some twenty years to produce. In its method, it is heavily influenced by the work of the first Tudor critic, Sir Thomas Wilson, who also used these figures.

We are indebted to William Lowes Rushton and his book, *Shakespeare and "The Arte of English Poesie."* Mr. Rushton was a barrister who diligently trawled *Arte* (as I shall now refer to it) for examples of the various figures, or idioms, employed in the plays, and set these out in his book.

Arte was published in 1589. It contains the famous lines: "Noblemen and Gentlemen of Her Majesty's own servants, who have written excellently well, as it would appear if their doings could be found out and made public with the rest, of which is first that noble gentleman, Edward, Earl of Oxford."

There is no mention of Shakespeare in *Arte*, but "knowledge of [*Arte*], with which Shakespeare was very familiar," Rushton writes on page one of his book, "has enabled me to illustrate many obscure passages and words and expressions of doubtful meaning. Shakespeare not only introduces in his Plays many of the Figures which Puttenham describes, but he also uses the same words which appear in the examples Puttenham gives of the Figures."

Mr. Rushton wants us to imagine that William Shakespeare consulted *Arte* extensively whenever he required a grammatical figure or an example to illustrate it. This runs counter to all our conceptions as to how the author worked. It is probably an oversimplification to say that in "Shakespeare" grammar takes a far second place to the words employed, and both are well behind the requirement for dramatic effect and/or lyrical intensity. About Puttenham's predecessor, Sir Thomas Wilson, one critic says:

> When a man writes ... a good piece of prose, he does not say to himself, "Now I shall throw in some hyperbaton; now we shall exhibit a little anadiplosis; this is the occasion, surely, for a passage of zeugma." He writes as the spirit moves him, and as the way of art leads.[iii]

But *Arte* is very important, because it appeared in 1589, by which time I say some considerable part of the canon had been written but not published, for the reason given by its author above. Equally I believe that for the most part the plays written up to that date were primarily for the court, yet they may well have had public performances as well. The author, I believe, is using his memory of those court performances to illustrate his figures. Study of Puttenham and Rushton affords valuable evidence of the dating of the plays prior to 1589 and, because of the sheer volume of such evidence, strengthens the view that at least some of them date back to ten or more years earlier. Puttenham was writing a book of analysis and criticism, not a manual for budding authors.

By way of extreme example of his approach, he constructs the figure Pillar from which, Rushton suggests (p. 151), William Shakespeare obtained the ideas for these lines:

The Janssen engraving purportedly of William Shakespeare, c. 1610s.

> Yet let us all together to our troops,
> And give them leave to fly that will not stay;
> And call them *pillars* that will stand to us [3 *Henry VI* II, iii, ll. 48–51].
>
> Brave peers of England, *pillars* of the state [2 *Henry VI* I, i, 1.75].
>
> I wonder how yonder city stands,
> When we have here her base and *pillar* by us [*Troilus and Cressida* IV, vii, ll. 94–95].

Rushton quotes *Arte* without giving a reference — he seldom does.

> The *Pillar* is a figure among all the rest of the Geometrical most beautiful, in respect that he is tall and upright and of one bigness from the bottom to the top. In architecture he is considered with two accessory parts, a pedestal or base, and a chapter or head, the body is the shaft. By this figure is signified stay, support, rest, state, and magnificence; your ditty being reduced to the form of a *Pillar*, his base will require the breadth of a metre of six or seven syllables: the shaft of four: the chapter egal with the base, of this proportion I will give you one or two examples which may suffice —
>
> Her Majesty resembled to the crowned *pillar*. Ye must read upward.
>
>> Is bliss with immortality.
>> Her trimest top of all ye see,
>> Garnish the crown
>> Her just renown
>> Chapter and head,
>> Parts that maintain
>> And womanhead
>> Her maiden reign
>> Integrity:
>> In honor and
>> With verity:
>> Her roundness *stand*
>> Strengthen the state.
>> By their increase
>> Without debate
>> Concord and peace
>> Of her support,
>> They be the base
>> With steadfastness
>> Vertue and grace
>> Stay and comfort
>> Of Albion's rest,
>> The sound Pillar
>> And seen afar
>> Is plainly exprest
>> Tall stately and straight
>> By this noble portrait [2, 12].

It is fatuous to imagine Oxford would gain anything from this fatuous exercise, but the writer shows at least a passing knowledge of some existing work(s), which as Mr. Rushton gives out unawares, must be the already written plays from which the original quotations come (or early versions). This clearly fortifies the argument in the paragraph above. Of course, as evidence these examples standing by themselves constitute only a very small connection, which would be probatively almost negligible; some of the others selected and quoted below are no better, and some rather more impressive. The point is that it is the volume of examples which forms the reliability of the evidence. Let us see what can be found (the page references are from Rushton, and the names of the figures are from *Arte*). Note also that the *Arte* author puts in examples using Shakespearean words and phrases — but disguised in verse[112] which may well be that author's own — to conceal the borrowing of the original idea found in that low-class (to Puttenham) form of literature — drama.

1. Surplusage (page 2):

I saw the wound, *I saw it with mine eyes* [*Romeo and Juliet* III, ii, l. 52].

He hears with ears [*Merry Wives of Windsor* I, i, l. 137].

ARTE: The first surplusage the Greeks call Pleonasmus, I call him "too full speech," and no great fault, as if one should say, *I heard it with mine ears, and saw it with mine eyes* [3.22].

2. Cacozetia or Fond Affection (page 4):

> Oh, never will I trust to speeches penn'd,
> Nor to the motion of *a school boy's* tongue;
> No, never come in vizard to my friend;
> Nor woo in rhyme, like a blind harper's song:
> Taffeta *phrases*, silken terms precise,
> Three-piled hyperboles, spruce *affection*,
> Figures pedantical: these summer-flies
> Have blown me full of maggot ostentation
> [*Love's Labour's Lost* V, ii, ll. 402–09].

... nor no matter in the *phrase* that might indict the author of *affectation* [*Hamlet* II, ii, ll. 447].

ARTE: Ye have another intollerable ill manner of speech, by which the Greeks original we may call fond *affectation*, phrases other than the good speakers allowed, and is the common fault of *young scholars* before not half well studied they come from the University or schools, and when they come to their friends, or happen to get some benefice or other promotion in their countrys, will seem to coign fine words *out of the Latin, and to use new fangled speeches, thereby to show themselves among the ignorant the better learned* [3.22].

3. Metaphora or Transport (page 10):

> This rudeness is sauce to his good wit,
> Which gives men stomach to *digest* his words
> With better appetite [*Julius Caesar* I, ii, ll. 300–02].

ARTE: There is a kind of wresting of a single word from his own right signification, to another not so natural, but yet of some affinity or convenience with it, as to say, I cannot *digest* your unkind words for I cannot take them in good part [3.17].

4. Catachresis or Figure of Abuse (page 12):

Lean, raw-boned *rascals* [1 *Henry VI* I, iii, l. 14].

ARTE: ... or as one should in reproach say to a poor man, thou *raskal* knave, where raskal is properly the hunter's term given to a young deer, *lean* and out of season, and not to people [3.17].

5. Atanaclasis or Rebound (page 16):

A young man *married* is a man that's *marred* [*All's Well That Ends Well* II, iii, l. 295].

> would I might never
> O'ertake pursued success, but I do feel,
> By the *rebound* of yours, a grief that *smites*
> My very heart at root [*Antony and Cleopatra*, V, ii, ll. 101–104].

ARTE: Ye have another figure which by his nature we may call the *Rebound*, alluding to the tennis ball which being *smitten* by the racket rebounds back again, ... this [figure] playeth with one word written all alike but carrying divers senses, as thus — The maid that soon *married* is, soon *marred* is [3. 19].

This looks like an example of the author's "disguised borrowing" referred to above.

6. Prosonomasia or the Nicknamer (page 21):

SPEED: But Launce, how sayest thou, that my master is become a notable *lover*?
LAUNCE: I never knew him otherwise.
SPEED: Than how?
LAUNCE: A notable *lubber*, as thou reportest him to be [*Two Gentlemen of Verona* II, v, ll. 36–40].

ARTE: And we in our Interlude called the Wooer, played with these two words, *lubber* and *lover* thus.... They be *lubbers* not *lovers* that so used to say [3. 19].

This is another "disguised borrowing."

7. Disabler (page 34):

CLOWN to AUTOLYCUS: I will swear to the prince, thou art a *tall fellow with thy hands,* and that thou wilt not be drunk; but I know thou art no *tall fellow with thy hands*, and that thou will be drunk [*The Winter's Tale* V, ii, ll. 161–63].

Six—The Life 1576–1590　　　　　　　　　　　　　129

ARTE: As he that said to a bragging ruffian, that threatened he would kill and slay, no doubt you are a *tall fellow with your hands* [3. 19].

8. Pragmatographia (misspelled by Rushton "Pragmatoria") or Counterfeit Action (page 43):

> and I was I like to be apprehended for the witch of Brentford; but that my admirable dexterity of wit, *my counterfeiting the action* of an old woman, delivered me, the knave constable would set me i' the stocks, i' the common stocks, for a witch [*The Merry Wives of Windsor* IV, v, ll. 109–112].

ARTE: But if such description be made to represent the handling of any business within the circumstances belonging thereunto as the manner of a battle, a feast, a marriage, a burial, or any other matter that lieth in feat and activity: we call it then the *Counterfeit action* [3. 19].

9. Barbarismus or Foreign Speech (page 48):

COSTARD: Go to; thou hast it ad dunghill, at the fingers' end, as they say.
HOLOFERNES: O, I smell false Latin: dunghill for unguem.
COSTARD: Arts-man, perambulate we will singuled from the *barbarous*. Do you not educate youths from the charge-house on the top of the *mountain*? [*Love's Labour's Lost* V, i, ll. 73–78].

ARTE: The Italian at this day by like arrogance calleth the Frenchman, Spaniard, Dutch, English and all other breed behither their *mountains* Appenines, Tramontani, as who would say *Barbarous* [3. 22].

I am trying to resist the temptation to identify the author of *Arte* with Holofernes—not very successfully!

10. Fantasy (page 50):

> Thou hast no figures, nor no *fantasies*,
> Which *busy* care draws in the *brains* of men;
> Therefore sleep'st so *sound* [*Julius Caesar* II, i, ll. 230–32].

ARTE: For as evil and vicious disposition of the *brain* hinders the *sound* judgement and discourse of man with *busy* and discordant *fantasies*....

11. Exargasia or the Gorgeous (page 55):

> There is a divinity that shapes our ends,
> *Rough-hew* them how we *will* [*Hamlet* V, ii, ll. 11].

ARTE: Exargasia ... a term transferred from these polishers of marble or porphyrite, who after it is *rough hewn* and reduced to that fashion they *will* [3. 20].

Some think this couplet refers to hedge-coppicing, rather than stone.

12. Climax or the Marching Figure (page 68):

> O, when degree is shaked,
> Which is the *ladder* to all high designs,
> Then enterprise is sick ...
> Then everything includes itself in power,
> Power into will, will into appetite;

> And appetite, an universal wolf,
> So *doubly* seconded with will and power,
> Must make perforce an universal prey,
> And last eat up himself. Great Agamemnon,
> This chaos, when degree is suffocate,
> Follows the choking.
> And this neglection of degree it is
> That by a *pace* goes backward, with a purpose
> It hath to *climb*. The general's disdain'd
> By him one *step* below, he by the next,
> That next by him beneath; so every step,
> Exampled by the first *pace* that is sick
> Of his superior, grows to an envious fever
> Of pale and bloodless emulation
> [*Troilus and Cressida* I, iii, ll. 101–134].

ARTE: Ye have a figure which as well by his Greek and Latin originals, and also to the manner of a man's gate or going may be called the marching figure, for after the first *step* all the rest proceed, by *double* the space, and so in our speech one word proceeds *double* to the first that was spoken, and goeth as it were by strides or *paces*: it may as well be called the *Climbing* figure, for Climax is as much as to say as a *ladder* [3.19].

13. Epitheton or the Qualifier (page 71):

ARMADO: I spoke it, tender juvenal, as a congruent *epitheton* appertaining to thy young days, which we nominate tender.
MOTH: And I, tough senior, as appertinent title to your old time, which we may name tough.
ARMADO: Pretty, and *apt*.
MOTH: How mean you, sir? I pretty and my saying *apt*? Or I *apt*, and my saying pretty? [*Love's Labour's Lost* I, ii, ll.13–20].
ARTE: Your *Epitheton* or qualifier, whereof we spake before, placing him among the figures auricular, now because he serves also to alter and enforce the sense, we will say somewhat more of him in this place, and conclude he must be *apt* and proper for the thing he is added to, ... [3.16].

14. Tautologia (page 78):

HOLOFERNES: I will sometimes affect the *letter*, for it argues *facility*. "The preyful princess pierced and pricked a pretty pleasing pricket" [*Love's Labour's Lost* IV, ii, ll. 55–56].
ARTE: Many of our English makers use it too much, yet we confess it doth not ill but prettily becomes the metre, ... For such composition makes the metre run away smoother, and passes from the lips with more *facility* by iteration of a *letter* than by alteration ... [3. 22].

15. Epigram (page 81):

Good then save me a piece of *marchpane* [*Romeo and Juliet* I, v, l. 8].
Is this a prologue, or the *poesie* of a ring? [*Hamlet* III, ii, l. 14].

> Of folded schedules she had many a one,
> Which she perus'd, sigh'd, tore, and gave the flood;
> Crack'd many a *ring* of *posied* gold and bone
> [*A Lover's Complaint*, l. 45].

ARTE: There be also other like Epigrams that were sent usually for new year gifts, or to be printed or put upon their banqueting dishes of sugar plate, or of *march paines*, ... We call them *Poesies*, ... or use them as devices in *rings* and arms about such courtly purposes [I. 30].

16. Counterchange (page 99):
> Bring me into your city,
> And I will use the olive with my sword,
> Make war breed peace; make peace stint war; make each
> Prescribe to *other* as each *other's* leech
> [*Timon of Athens* V, v, ll. 86–89].

ARTE: Rushton writes that peace and war are the words which are used in the second example Puttenham gives in illustration of this Figure; besides, according to Puttenham, this Figure plays with a couple of words, peace and war, making them "change and shift one into *other's* place" [3. 19].

17. Indent or Condition (page 110):
> Shall we buy Treason and *indent* with Fears,
> When they have lost and forfeited themselves?
> [1 *Henry IV* I, iii, ll. 86–87].

ARTE: Right so in negotiating with Princes we ought to seek their favour by humility and not by way of sternness, nor to traffick with them by way of *indent* or condition, but frankly and by manner of submission to their wills, for princes may be led but not driven, ...

18. Use of demons, etc. (page 113):

O thou *eternal mover of the heavens* [2 *Henry VI* III, iii, l. 18].
If that same *demon*, that hath gulled thee thus, ... [*ibid.*].
> Thy *demon* (that's thy spirit which keeps thee) is
> Noble, courageous, high, unmatchable,
> Where Caesar's is not: but near him, thy *angel*
> Becomes a fear, as being o'erpowered; ...
> [*Antony and Cleopatra* III, ii, ll. 17–20].
> By a divine instinct men's minds mistrust
> Ensuing danger; ... [*Richard III* II, iii, ll. 42–43].

ARTE: Poets are of great antiquity. Then forasmuch as they were the first that entended to the observation of nature and her works and specially of the Celestial courses, by reason of the *continual motion of the heavens*, searching after the first *mover*, and from thence by degrees coming to know and consider of the substances separate and abstract, which we call *devine intelligences* or good *Angels (Demones)* they were the first that instituted sacrifices of placation, with invocations and worship to them, as to Gods; ... they came by *instinct devine*, and deep meditation ... to be made apt to receive visions ... [1. 3].

19. Ornament (page 116):

> So may the *outward shows* be least themselves;
> The world is still deceiv'd with *ornament* ...
> In religion,
> What damn'd error, but some sober brow
> Will bless it, and approve it with a text,
> Hiding the grossness with fair *ornament*?
> There is no vice so simple, but assumes
> Some mark of virtue on his *outward parts*.
> ...
> Thus *ornament* is but a guiled shore
> To a most dangerous sea [*The Merchant of Venice* III, ii, ll. 73–98].

ARTE: This *ornament* is of two sorts, one to satisfy and delight the ear only by a goodly *outward show* set upon the matter with words, ... [3. 3].

20. Lion and lamb (page 122):

> In peace, there's nothing so becomes a man
> As modest stillness, and humility;
> But when the blast of war blows in our ears,
> Then imitate the action of the *tiger* [*Henry V* III, i, ll. 3–6].

He hath borne himself beyond the promise of his age; doing in the figure of a *lamb*, the feats of a *lion* [*Much Ado About Nothing* I, i, ll. 13–15].

IAGO to DESDEMONA: You are pictures sent out of doors,
  Bells in your parlours, wild-cats in your kitchens,
  Saints in your injuries, devils being offended,
  Players in your housewifery, and hussies in your beds
  [*Othello* II, i, ll. 111–15].

ARTE: And touching a person, we may say it is comely for a man to be a *lamb* in the house, and a *Lion* in the field, ... we limit the comely parts of a woman to consist in four points, that is, to be a shrew in the kitchen, a saint in the Church, an angel at the board, and an ape in bed, ...

Although there is no direct quotation from Iago's speech, the source of the thought is clear.

21. Mincing Measures (page 138):

> And that would set my teeth nothing on edge,
> Nothing so much as *mincing* poetry —
> 'Tis like the forced gait of a shuffling nag
> [*1 Henry IV* III, i, ll. 129–131].

ARTE: I rather wish the continuance of our old manner of Poesy, scanning our verses by syllables rather than by feet, and using most commonly the Iambic and sometimes the Trochaic, which ye shall discern by their accents, and now and then a dactyl keeping precisely our symphony or rime without any other *mincing* measures, which an idle inventive head could easily devise [2. 15].

Six—The Life 1576–1590

22. Insultatio (page 140):

LUCIANA: If thou art changed to aught, 'tis to an ass.

DROMIO OF SYRACUSE: 'Tis true; she *rides* me and I long for grass [*The Comedy of Errors* II, ii, ll. 202–23].

ARTE: Ye have another figure much like to the Sarcasmus, or bitter taunt we spoke of before; and is when with proud and insolent words, we do upbraid a man, or *ride* him, as we term it: for which cause the Latines also call it Insultatio [3. 19].

23. Staff (page 143):

HOLOFERNES: Let me hear a *staff*, a *stanza*, a verse [*Love's Labour's Lost* IV, ii, l. 104].

ARTE: *Staff* in our vulgar Poesy I know not why it should be so called, unless it be for that we understand it for a bearer or supporter of a song or ballad, not unlike the old weak body that is stayed up by his *staff*, and were not otherwise able to walk or stand upright. The Italians called it *Stanza*, as if we should say a resting place: and if we consider well the form of this Poetical staff, we shall find it to be a certain number of verses allowed to go together and join without any intermission ... [2. 2].

This is a good example of *Arte*'s style.

24. Purchase (page 148):

GADSHILL (one of the thieves): Give me thy hand: thou shalt have a share in our *purchase*, as I am a true man [1 *Henry IV* II, i, l. 91–92].

They will steal anything and call it *purchase* [*Henry V* III, ii, l. 40].

ARTE: All this I do agree unto, for no doubt the shepherd's life was the first example of honest fellowship, their trade the first art of lawful acquisition or purchase, for at those days robbery was a manner of *purchase* [1. 18].

25. Singularity (page 159):

> Some villain,
> Ay, and *singular in his art*,
> Hath done you both this cursed injury
> [*Cymbeline* III, iv, ll. 120–22].

ARTE: Thus far therefore we will adventure and not beyond, to the intent to show some *singularity in our art* that everyman hath not heretofore observed.

26. "*Jets*"[113] (page 160):

Contemplation makes a rare turkey-cock of him: how he *jets* under his advanced plumes! [*Twelfth Night* II, v, ll. 29–30].

To which I would add:

And bravely *jets* it in his silken gown [*Arden of Feversham*, I, l.30].

And:

YORK: Tell me, kind Cheyney
How does thy master, our good brother Woodstock

> Plain Thomas, for by the rood so all men call him
> For his plain dealing, and his simple clothing.
> Let others *jet* in silk and gold, says he,
> A coat of English frieze, best pleaseth me
> [*Thomas of Woodstock* I, i, ll. 99–105].
>
> ARTE: All singularities or affected parts of a man's behaviour seem undecent, as for a man to march or *jet* in the street more stately, ... [3.14].

The word may have passed into common speech. Gosson's *School of Abuse* (1579) records the use: "Players, which stand at reversion at vi s(hillings) by the week, *jet* under Gentlemen's noses in suits of silk"; and in *An Apology of the School of Abuse*: "Patroclus may *jet* in Achilles' armor"—possibly a reference to *Troilus and Cressida*.[114]

In *Arte*, Chapter 3, p. 303, Puttenham discourses on Art's relationship to Nature:

> In some cases we say *art* is an aid and coadjutor to *nature* ... and the gardener by his *art* will not only make a herb or flower or fruit come forth in his own season without impediment but will also embellish the same in virtue, shape, odor and taste, that nature of itself would never have done; as to make a single gillifloure, or marigold, or daisy, double; and the white rose, red, yellow or *carnation*.

Perhaps he remembers Perdita the gardener[115]:

> the fairest flowers of the season
> Are our *carnations* and streaked *gillivors*,
> Which some call nature's bastards ...
> POLIXENES: You see sweet maid, we marry
> A gentler scion to the wildest stock,
> And make conceive a bark of baser stock
> By bud of nobler race. This is an *art*
> Which does mend nature — change it rather; but
> The *Art* itself is *nature*.
> PERDITA: So it is.
> POLIXENES: Then make your garden rich in *gillivores*
> And do not call them bastards [*The Winter's Tale* IV, iv, ll. 81–83, 92–98].

I have chosen the examples from no fewer than 24 plays which some believe were written before 1589 that seem most obvious to me; in many other examples from those plays the idea in the canon is reproduced but in the same or similar words, perhaps to disguise the borrowing. In some of the post-1589 plays, Rushton quotes sometimes a match in ideas but not in wording employed. After all, the author of *Arte* knew the writer and his literary reputation — see my contention above. Rushton seldom gives examples from named authors, and it is curious that his quotation from Insultatio (23 above) continues,

I choose to name him Reproachful or Scorner, and when Queen Dido saw, that for all her great love and entertainments bestowed upon Aeneas he would needs depart, and follow the Oracle of his destinies, she broke out in a great rage and said very disdainfully—

> Hie thee, and by the wild waves and the wind,
> Seek Italy and Realms for thee to reign;
> If piteous Gods have power amidst the main,
> On ragged rocks thy penance thou mayst find.

These lines are not in Marlowe's *Dido, Queen of Carthage*, and once again it appears that the author of *Arte* may be creating his own examples, perhaps prompted by Marlowe's play—apparently Marlowe's earliest, written about 1583/4.[116]

There is another possibility so far as the "Shakespearean" canon is concerned, that the author was citing, not the version of the particular phrase or speech which we now have, but an earlier version current in 1589. Thus we consider that *Famous Victories* or *Troublesome Reign* are early attempts at their much greater successors and, as has been pointed out, in *As You Like It* there are the fossils of a verse version[117]: rewriting was a continuous process. This can be shown from Nashe's *Introduction to Menaphon* (1589): "Yet English Seneca [i.e., 'Shakespeare'] read by candlelight yields many good sentences, as 'Blood is a beggar,' and so forth; and if you entreat him fair in a frosty morning, he will afford you whole Hamlets, I should say handfuls, of tragical speeches." Now "Blood is a beggar" does not appear in Hamlet or anywhere else in the corpus of "Shakespeare," nor anywhere else apparently in contemporary literature. The idea is perhaps buried in the rewriting, perhaps in *Hamlet* II, ii, l. 265: "Then are our bodies beggars, and our monarchs and outstretched heroes the beggars' shadows." There are of course other examples of the rewriting process which from the stylistic point of view complicate or render impossible dating a play by mere style considerations, especially where a play bears signs of only partial rewriting. Consider in this respect the Peacham document version of the passage from *Titus Andronicus*, which I mentioned on page 35.

Anyone who might seek to oppose the rewriting hypothesis will have to deal with the perceived developments of "Shakespeare's" style. As Granville Barker wrote:

> Then, with Hamlet—and with Hamlet's own speech particularly—we come within reach of a seeming spontaneity. Shakespeare allows him all possible scope of expression, both in prose and verse; and in the choice between them, and in the form and colour of the verse as well as its content, his every mood, of contemplation, irony or despair, will be sensitively reflected. It is of course only a "seeming spontaneity." People do not naturally speak blank verse; and

even in prose, and for the simple speech of citizen or peasant, Shakespeare never lapses into an imitated spontaneity, so as to forfeit all the aids of form and accepted convention. It is a consonant part — this reaching towards a seeming spontaneity — of Shakespeare's general development as a dramatist, and it necessarily tends to loosen and break down the verse.... It is when the character and emotion gain complexity and extraordinary force that — as a stream in flood eats its banks away — the verse breaks bounds; and Shakespeare himself has developed from the poet writing plays into the true dramatic poet.

As if amazed at what he had written, the author adds a note: "Really, it sometimes seems as if Shakespeare must have had all the secrets of his art stored in him from the beginning, as if he only had to enlarge upon what he already knew."[118] This suggestion cannot be logical, as it totally ignores the development from juvenilia to masterpiece writing, and only serves to highlight the inherent improbability and unsustainability of the "orthodox" position.

The analysis above produces a result that means that the following plays (or early versions of them) had already been written by 1589 in addition to the ones I listed from the court revels (pages 93ff): 1 *Henry IV*, *Henry V*, 1, 2 and 3 *Henry VI*, *The Merry Wives of Windsor*, *Richard III*, *The Comedy of Errors*, *Julius Caesar*, *Much Ado About Nothing*, *Hamlet*, *Othello*, *Romeo and Juliet*, *Timon of Athens*, *Twelfth Night*, *Troilus and Cressida*, *The Winter's Tale*. Nor should we forget *A Lover's Complaint*.

Rushton finds examples of these grammatical figures in these plays and the rest of the accepted canon, but they are not exemplified by such direct quotation as the examples picked out above. Plays from which Rushton apparently takes no examples are *King Lear*, *Pericles*, *Titus Andronicus* and (of course, since they were not generally thought "canonical") *Edward III* and *Two Noble Kinsmen*. There should be an interesting field for research to find *Arte*-type examples from these last two plays and from *Famous Victories*, *Edmund Ironside* and *A Yorkshire Tragedy* and more from *Thomas of Woodstock* and *Arden of Feversham*.

I suspect that this list is by no means complete, and would expect to find, when the texts of the plays are considered for autobiographical and topical connections along with linguistic and construction elements, that other "Shakespeare" plays were to be added. While autobiographical elements can be slipped in on a rewrite as well as figure in the first draft, topical connections are most likely to appear in the first draft, for obvious reasons like commercial appeal. These further plays might well include: *King John*, *Richard II*, *2 Henry IV*, *Henry VIII*, *As You Like It*, *A Midsummer Night's Dream*, and *Pericles*.

As studied in *Arte*, many of these plays may be early (or at least pre–

1589) efforts at the more polished versions[119] we have today under the name of Shakespeare. To show the extent of my contentions which I expand in regard to the history plays, I set out a list with the versions as we know them today:

Famous Victories expanded into 1 and 2 *Henry IV* and *Henry V*
Edmund Ironside apparently not rewritten; no rewriting survives
Harthacanute lost but probably "Shakespeare's" sequel to *Edmund Ironside*
The Troublesome Raigne King John
Edward III the only surviving version
Thomas of Woodstock incomplete — apparently not further rewritten[120]
Richard II, 1, 2 and 3 *Henry VI* the only surviving versions
The True Tragedy Richard III
Sir Thomas More the only surviving version.

Early versions also exist of *King Lear* (as *King Leir*) and *The Taming of a Shrew*, as *The Taming of the Shrew*.

At this stage I note those plays which are generally thought to be so-called collaborations.[121] There is much agreement that the versions we have of *Timon of Athens, Pericles, Two Noble Kinsmen* and *Henry VIII* are the product of "Shakespeare" and lesser hands, and other plays are suggested as similar. In what circumstances we do not know, but my suggestion is that they are not the production of true collaboration between two or more living and cooperating authors but the fruit of partial rewriting or completion by these lesser hands after the death of Oxford in 1604, without of course the consent or approval of the man himself. Why would the world's greatest literary genius have need of a collaborator in his lifetime?

I make no further effort now to date the plays listed above; it is enough here to say that they are pre–1589. Some, like *Hamlet* and *King Lear*, underwent probably several rewrites in the next decade, and indeed in the light of the playwright's health and circumstance afflictions, even recasting. Some, perhaps, like *Macbeth*, give almost no ground for suggesting that they too might be pre–1589. Until a play is printed, there is no final text, and efforts to establish a terminus a quo for the first draft are likely to be unsuccessful and a waste of time and effort. How can anyone aspire to date to a single year *King John*, let alone this speech of the First Citizen:

> The daughter there of Spain, the Lady Blanche,
> Is niece to England:—look upon the years
> Of Louis the Dauphin, and that lovely maid;
> If lusty love should go in quest of beauty
> Where should he find it fairer than in Blanche?
> If zealous love should go in search of virtue,
> Where should he find it purer than in Blanche?
> If love ambitious sought a match of birth,

> Whose veins bound richer blood than Lady Blanche?
> Such as she is, in beauty, virtue, birth,
> Is the young Dauphin every way complete [II, I, ll. 424–434].

There then follow a couple of dozen lines of frankly substandard "Shakespeare," which were clearly written at an earlier, less accomplished time in the writer's career. The speech is undatable to a single year, and so as a result is the whole play. Here is an extract:

> If not complete of, say he is not she;
> And she again wants nothing, to name want,
> If want it be not, that she is not he;
> He is the half part of a blessed man
> Left to be finished by such a she;
> And she a fair divided excellence,
> Whose fullness in perfection lies in him ... [*ibid.*, ll. 435–442].

It does not improve.[122]

Certain recent critics have suggested that "Shakespeare" actually wrote plays in a five-act form for in-house productions at court or in private houses.[123] This is an "assumption — commonly stated as though it were a fact — that [*The Winter's Tale, The Tempest, Cymbeline* and *Pericles*] were written for the indoor Blackfriars Theatre at which Shakespeare's Company began to act in 1610. Since the assumption has a good deal of scholarly support, perhaps it may prove salutary, at the very start, to stress that all available evidence is either completely negative or runs directly counter to such a supposition."[124] The first quarto of *Pericles* (1609) "specifically states that the play had been "divers and sundry times acted ... at the Globe on the Banck-side." Furthermore, it was at "the Glob" that Simon Forman saw *The Winter's Tale* on May 15, 1611, and where he probably saw *Cymbeline* the month before. "For *The Tempest* no evidence is forthcoming [it was performed at court in 1604/5], but we know that when the first Globe went up in flames on June 26th 1613, *Henry VIII* was the play being presented." My critic writes that, except for *Two Noble Kinsmen*, issued in 1634 as by Shakespeare and Fletcher and as "presented at the Blackfriars," "we have no justification whatsoever for associating Shakespeare with the Blackfriars at all — even the *Two Noble Kinsmen* presents an element of doubt since the title page ascription of 1634 need not necessarily apply to the original production of the play."

Additionally, another critic contends that as the rebuilt Globe did not alter "Shakespeare" as a playwright, neither would the new Blackfriars[125]: he means he detects no attributable difference in the writings, but "like everything else, the drama evolved, and fashions changed but that there was a much greater uniformity of theatrical taste and production methods within periods of a few years than [critics] would have us believe is becoming apparent."

In addition to the extrinsic evidence and the conclusions which by the application of logic can be drawn from it, there is the intrinsic evidence, by which I mean the conclusions we can draw from the actual pre-revolutionary plays. Contemporary literary criticism is limited to Ronsard, Gosson and Sidney, and the conventionalized listings of Webbe and Puttenham, and so modern scholarship[126] has a vital role in throwing light on this area.

We have already seen the "Marlowe clap of thunder" school exemplified. A contrasting school saw a more evolutionary process. Eloquence acquired a deeper meaning: "Instead of merely fulfilling its outward function as a polished, highly adorned and effective technique of oratory, eloquence comes to mean the ability to communicate by the medium of words a variety of man's deepest emotions. This ability we find in 'Shakespeare,' but we should not find it had not the playwrights who preceded him [i.e., the author(s) of the plays listed below] already contributed to dramatic verse that wealth of expression and of effect the potentialities of which were to be completely realised only after their time."[127]

To begin with, *Gorboduc* (1562) demonstrates that the stage entirely relies on rhetoric, consisting of monologues, soliloquies and set speeches, reporting action elsewhere and reaction to it, with an ultimate didactic purpose, rather than being a drama of entertainment illustrating conflict and action between the characters. *Gismond of Salerne* (1567) is a romantic comedy in the footsteps of *Gorboduc*. The beginnings of a freer or more realistic style may be seen in Gascoigne's *Jocasta* (1565). Thomas Preston's *Cambises* (c. 1562) represents a hybrid between the "pure" style of *Gorboduc* and the rough dramas of the touring morality plays with their appeal to popular taste; in *Cambises*, "Everything is cruder and clumsier," and there is a "relish for coarse jests and violence of expression and graceless stage effects."[128]

Wolfgang Clemen in a chapter titled "Popular Drama and History Plays" (before "Shakespeare," as he sees it) comments on this *Cambises*, and also on an anonymous play called *Jack Straw*, dated to 1592 but actually probably much earlier and "much less impressive than *Famous Victories*." The remainder of Clemen's chapter treats this play and four other "anonymous" plays, namely, *The Troublesome Raigne of King John, The True Tragedie of Richard the Third, Thomas of Woodstock* and *King Leir and His Three Daughters*. Clemen demonstrates that these plays (and he could have added *Edmund Ironside* and *Edward III*, and possibly *The First Part of Sir John Oldcastle*—see Chapter Two, note 24) are the steps by which drama in England evolved into the glory of "Shakespeare": "*The transition from the rhetorical tragedy of the early period to the Shakespearian type of drama is bound up with the most striking and impressive developments in form that English drama has undergone in the whole of its history"* (my italics). He does not consider whether these plays were "Shakespeare's" apprentice efforts, by which he taught himself (there could be no English mentors for him)— the groundblocks of his art. Clemens is nevertheless profoundly impressed by the strides away from the earlier crudities, both in writing and presentation, which these plays represent in that evolution, so that it is logical for his readers to see them as such apprentice efforts of a writer teaching himself without exemplars and feeling towards the mature works we find in the "Shakespeare" canon.

The "orthodox" critic is confronted with, to him (but not to me) a paradox. At every stage in "Shakespeare's" early and middle plays there are conventional usages, forms of style, literary artifices, and so on, which have origins and parallels in "pre–Shakespearian drama," which make them appear to be merely an evolutionary phenomenon. Clemen notes that this would be an entirely wrong conclusion: "We constantly feel that we are in the presence of something entirely new and unexpected, something that belongs to him alone.... One of the distinctive features of Shakespeare's development is his constant modification of the existing dramatic kinds and of the styles of expression that lay ready to hand." The paradox is an illusion if you discard all those authors and works which Clemen thinks are pre–"Shakespeare," but which are post-revolution (i.e., Marlowe), and consider only those works, perhaps juvenile or experimental, that are referred to in the previous paragraph.

Of course individually, especially if dated to be contemporaneous with the "orthodox" Shakespeare of the 1590s, these works are correctly not highly rated artistically: put in as a group as forerunners to the "orthodox" canon, they are immensely significant for the development of drama, since they have no predecessors worthy of the name. They are important foundation elements of Shakespeare's revolution. If the seven plays mentioned earlier are Shakespeare's early efforts, they are not particularly like the more finished article (but there is nothing more similar, even remotely so), however much they may resemble it in terms of plot, use of vernacular and naturalism, and rejection of the Seneca-Gorboduc school. It is tempting to suggest that the young author Oxford realized their deficiencies and sought additional inspiration from foreign sources, whence he profited to such an extent he was able to rewrite his earlier plays and begin his career as the "best for comedies"; this is precisely how his life developed, as we have seen.

In effect Clemen, by placing the beginning of Shakespeare's career in 1590, brings in as his predecessors instead of his followers the author of *Locrine*,[129] Thomas Hughes, Lodge, Marlowe, Peele and Greene, and demonstrates that these authors, although sometimes superior in poetical terms, are sometimes less advanced in the technique of drama than that Shakespeare, the author of the seven pre–1575 plays.

We should note that these early efforts could not by themselves cause the revolution. There were no permanent public theaters before 1576. It is a nice point as to whether there were sufficient plays for the public theaters then, or did the theaters come first as a speculative leap in the dark by their entrepreneurs, or did those entrepreneurs know that a supply of adequate plays would be forthcoming?

This chapter shows the course of the revolution, and some of the contemporary evidence with some criticism of it. In setting out the history of the revolution we have in effect reached 1585/90. The revolution has happened: the wave has hit the shore. In the next decades the revolution, along with Shakespeare's contribution as a catalyst, is taken for granted, as we shall see in the next chapter.

A peripheral question then arises: Excepting the works of "Shakespeare," do we have any pieces of literature available for judgment by those early critics of the 1580s? Lyly's *Euphues* and its sequel, and his early plays, cannot, I think, make him that catalyst: Spenser's *Shepheardes Calendar* (1579) and *The Faerie Queen* would not, as we have seen, be influential. At this early stage (say, 1580) Spenser was also being influenced by Gabriel Harvey and those scholars who wished English to imitate Latin hexameters. Sidney's *Apology for Poetry*[130] may be thought to make him a candidate, but nothing of his was printed before 1592. His manuscript may well have had wide circulation, but it does contain substantial if concealed criticism of existing plays and therefore of Shakespeare.

One critic puts it bluntly: "Follow Sidney, and goodbye to Faustus [Marlowe], to Hamlet, to Philaster [Beaumont and Fletcher], to The Duchess of Malfi [Webster], to the Changeling [Middleton], to The Virgin Martyr [Dekker], to The Broken Heart [Ford]. We must content ourselves with Gorboduc [Buckhurst] and Cornelia [Kidd], with Cleopatra [Daniel] and Philotas [Daniel], at the very best with Sejanus and The Silent Woman [both Jonson]."[131] It can be safely said that *Apology for Poetry* is a reaction verging on the pedantic as well as a by-product of the revolution. Indeed, Sidney justifies the critic's opinion when he writes a swipe at Oxford (again unnamed):

> How all their [modern writers'] plays be neither right tragedies nor right comedies, mingling kings and clowns, not because the matter so carrieth it, but thrust in the clown by head and shoulders to play a part in majestical matters, with neither decency nor discretion, so as neither the admiration and commiseration nor the right sportfulness is by their mongrel tragic-comedy

obtained.... So it falleth out that, having indeed no right comedy, in that comical part of our tragedy, we have nothing but scurrility, unworthy of any chaste ears, or some extreme show of doltishness, indeed fit to lift up a loud laughter, and nothing else; where the whole trace of a comedy should be full of delight, as the tragedy should be still maintained in a well-raised admiration.[132]

While using plenty of elocution in his own poetry, he criticizes "that honey-flowing Matron Eloquence apparelled or rather disguised in a courtesan-like painted affectation."[133]

Sidney, after he died fighting the Spanish at Zutphen in 1586, had become the peerless national hero: his views on any subject including literature and the stage and his reputation as a cultural icon seemed therefore to acquire an aura of unchallengeability to his contemporaries, and they cloud the appreciation of "Shakespeare's" contemporaries, and are rightly exposed by the critic.

"Of course," writes Clemen, "a *highly gifted* playwright will *on his own initiative* begin discarding the accepted forms with all their rigid limitations, and will handle the existing conventions in such a way as to gain the most vivid dramatic effects" (emphasis added).[134] Most importantly, Clemen does not attempt to identify a candidate. We have to follow his logic as we still need to find such a candidate, bearing in mind that Sidney and his circle would try to lean very heavily on any unsupported university wit who might step out of line to discard any of the "accepted forms" at least while Sidney lived (until 1586), unless (as was in fact the case) there were already a substantial writer by way of precedent who was likely to defend the errant young writer's method and choice: clearly an argument for, and an element of, the Shakespeare revolution. The plays which are the product of the revolution with the impact of the new eloquence (as we have seen in Chapter Two) must have revolutionized the science and art of acting at the same time. Clemen, if he applied his own logic, could only have had in mind the author(s) of the seven plays mentioned on page 139. Oxford is certainly the only extant candidate.[135]

Sidney also wrote: "But for the uttering sweetly and properly the conceit of the mind which is the end of speech ... [English] hath it equally with any other tongue in the world."[136]

The question is, where did he get his examples, evidence for that opinion, except from existing literature including the early plays of Shakespeare?

For the modern critic, Sidney's denunciation of tragic-comedy is a "major heresy," but, it is suggested, he may in part be excused. Saintsbury wrote: "His classical authorities were quite clear on the point, and as yet there was nothing to be quoted on the other side — at least in English."¹³⁷ The critic has missed the point: if there was nothing to be quoted in opposition, then Sidney's denunciation (which seems only directed at plays in English) was unnecessary — there should be no one to have gone astray. The true position is that by 1580 there was a volume of drama that included tragic-comedy, and it did attract Sidney's "heretical" denunciation.

Sidney actually lets the cat out of the bag. He wrote:

> For where should the stage should always represent but one place, and the uttermost time presupposed in it should be, both in Aristotle's precept and common reason, but one day, there is both many days and places, inartificially [i.e. unskillfully] imagined....
>
> But if it be so in Gorboduc, how much more in all the rest? where you have Asia of the one side, and Africa of the other, and so many underkingdoms, that the player, when he comes in, must ever begin by telling you where he is, or else the tale will not be conceived. Now you have three ladies walk to gather flowers and then we must believe the stage to be a garden. By and by we hear news of a shipwreck in the same place and then we are to blame if we accept it not for a rock. On the back of that comes our a hideous monster with fire and smoke and then the miserable beholders are to take it for a cave. *While in the meantime two armies fly in, represented with four swords and bucklers,* and what hard heart will not receive it for a pitched field? [my italics].¹³⁸

What plays prior to 1585 with battles portrayed on the stage other than existing ones by Shakespeare could Sidney be referring to? Only *Cambises* (Preston, c. 1562) and *Horestes*¹³⁹ (1568?) come to mind; but Sidney is certainly sneering at the recently produced early versions of the history plays of Shakespeare.

Then there is Marlowe with his magna opera, the two Tamburlaine plays (1587/8).¹⁴⁰ He does not appear to have written anything before those plays which would detonate or be part of a series of detonations to begin the revolution. Marlowe brings many assets to the literary table but, according to Saintsbury, "it is usual to say that had he lived, and had his lot been happily cast, we should have had two Shakespeares. This is not wise. In the first place Marlowe was totally destitute of humour — the characteristic which, united with his tragic and imaginative powers, makes Shakespeare.... In other words [Marlowe] was absolutely destitute of the first requisite of self-criticism." Sir John Gielgud agrees: "Marlowe's stagecraft is crude or non-existent when compared to Shakespeare's know-how. Is there a character in Marlowe which makes one smile, let alone laugh outright?"¹⁴¹

The cause of the revolution, however, must be contained in the stage plays, both private and public. Other genres, poetry or general prose, be it criticism or creative writing, circulated in manuscript, or where printed appeared in those few and expensive books of the period. What those other genres lack is the element of rhetoric. No doubt Spenser read his poetry aloud to his admirers and they could well have been inspired, but his poetry could not have competed in effect with the aural effect of a production of, say, *The Comedy of Errors* or *Tamburlaine*, any more than it does now.

Therefore we must take into consideration those plays, some produced at court and subsequently in public, others in public alone, for which there is some evidence of their production before 1590. These I have reviewed above, and take them as examples of the poet-dramatist gradually feeling his way towards that sublimity that marks out "Shakespeare." We have a problem: because of "Shakespeare's" apparent propensity for rewriting, the pre-1590 version may not be the one we have now, for the passages I wish to rely on. That original version may contain the bones of any one of the poetic and dramatic triumphs (and disasters) in the early plays.

Earlier in this chapter, I discussed *Love's Labour's Lost*: it is only right that I should take from that play an extract to exemplify my case for the revolution. You will no doubt have your own favorite and possibly even more effective passages for it, taken from the same or another play.

Now I want to conduct an experiment. As *Love's Labour's Lost* is a court play, I want each of you to imagine that you are the queen or a grizzled, cynical statesman like Burghley or Walsingham, or a member of the court glitterati or literati, or a musician or a servant, and for the first time, you are about to hear the passage I have selected declaimed by an actor of some competence. Remember the passage comes to you in your imagined state as a virgin revelation, an example (perhaps your alter ego's first experience) of the power and the glory, the nuance and the endless possibilities of English. Please now read it aloud in full voice:

Berowne on the Power of Love

But love, first learned in a lady's eyes
Lives not alone immurèd in the brain;
But with the motion of all elements,
Courses as swift as thought in every power;
And gives to every power a double power,
Above their functions and their offices.
It adds a precious seeing to the eye;
A lover's eyes will gaze an eagle blind;
A lover's ear will hear the lowest sound,
When the suspicious head of theft is stopp'd;
Love's feelings are more soft, and sensible,
Than are the tender horns of cockled snails;
Love's tongue proves dainty Bacchus gross in taste;
For valour, is not love a Hercules
Still climbing trees in the Hesperides?

> Subtle as sphinx, as sweet and musical,
> As bright Apollo's lute, strung with his hair;
> And, when love speaks, the voice of all the gods
> Makes heaven drowsy with the harmony.
> Never durst poet touch a pen to write,
> Until his ink were temper'd with love's sighs;
> O, then his lines would ravish savage ears,
> And plant in tyrants mild humility [IV, iii, ll. 303–325].

No one can attempt to describe in imagination the effect of such English on those first auditors: we have reached one of the moments of detonation of the revolution, and we can recognize that "Shakespeare" himself is the leader, the detonator of that revolution.

I ought to touch on a wider question: to what extent did the revolution influence the nation's politics as well as its cultural development? Members of an aspirational middle class would find themselves listening to the most seductive and yet grand language describing, not only the faults of the king's servants, which they and their ancestors had no doubt chewed over and in their ignorance excused the king for centuries, but also the character, and, indeed, title, defects of the king himself, anointed and appointed by God himself. Had God saddled the English with the morally reprehensible and/or incompetent kings John, Edward II, Richard II, Henry VI and Richard III and the Lancastrians with their defective title in payment for their sins? As Shaw put it:

> Surely a more mercilessly exposed string of scoundrels never crossed the stage. The very monarch [Claudius in *Hamlet*] who paralyses a rebel by appealing "to the divinity that hedges a king" [IV, v, l. 122], is a drunken and sensual assassin, and is presently killed contemptuously before our eyes in spite of the hedge of divinity.

Once a member of the audience says to himself that that is unfair and likely to be foreign to the nature of God, and looks to the character and conduct of rulers of his/her own time who claim divine right, a political revolution will follow as night follows day.

How far can the revolution in the theater claim to be an element of that political revolution? It should share a place with the Protestant religious revolution, parts of whose message would be less palatable to that aspiring middle class than the ideas broadcast by the Shakespearean theater.

Note on Marlowe

One of the most interesting studies that arise from the perception that Oxford was the catalyst for the revolution is the realization that all scholarship purporting to show Oxford as the student or borrower from Marlowe is rendered useless. This idea did not arise until after Malone's studies on the dating of "Shakespeare's" plays: before that Marlowe only achieves a modest mention. Thus a recent critic can write: "We have been able to account for a Marlovian influence in promoting Shakespeare's intoxication with words and the discovery of new ways of ordering them. Interestingly [there are] passages in Titus Andronicus, King John, and The Merchant of Venice where Shakespeare tries to write in the manner of Marlowe. Yet even in these passages his own stylistic characteristics surface, giving us a solid means for defining the traits that make him and his fellow writers distinctive.... Marlowe acted as a catalyst in Shakespeare's disregard of standard expectations in a given genre."[142] Because he does not question "Shakespeare's" dating and accepts Marlowe's precedence in time, he does not consider that Marlowe is the imitator and perhaps not competent to imitate those stylistic characteristics which surface unimitated by Marlowe in "Shakespeare." Significantly, the critic gives the game away. In his acknowledgments, he writes:

> In a study of influence, the danger and advantage are one and the same: tunnel vision. Because I have restricted myself primarily to Marlowe's influence on Shakespeare, I have spoken only infrequently of the multiplicity of other cultural and literary influences on Shakespeare.... But the chief reason is that Shakespeare himself had a kind of tunnel vision when he saw or read Marlowe's works.

Because Marlowe has to be so much younger than "Shakespeare" the writer, the critic is looking through the tunnel from the wrong end. Marlowe was the man saddled with tunnel vision. When he started to write there was only one predecessor of any consequence: Oxford.

Oxford was, however, a shameless and witty parodist of Marlowe. These examples would have been tucked in at later rewrites of his original play.

From 1 *Tamburlaine*:

> By this my sword that conquer'd Persia,
> Thy fall shall make me famous through the world
> [III, iii, ll. 82–83].

This is picked up in *The Merchant of Venice*, spoken by the comic braggart Morocco:

> By this scimitar,
> That slew the Sophy, and a Persian Prince
> That won three fields of Sultan Solyman,—
> I would outstare the sternest eyes that look,
> Out-brave the heart most daring on the earth,
> Pluck the young sucking cubs from the she-bear,

Yea, mock the lion when he roars for prey,
To win thee, lady [II, iii, ll. 24–31].

From 1 *Tamburlaine*; Bajazeth has dashed his brains out on the bars of his cage.

> ZABINA (his queen): What do mine eyes behold? My husband dead!
> His skull all riven in twain! His brains dashed out
> The brains of Bajazeth, my lord and sovereign!
> O Bajazeth! my husband and my lord!
> O Bajazeth! O Turk! O Emperor!
> Make ready my coach, my chair, my jewels.— I come, I come!
> (She brains herself against the cage.)
> [V, ii, ll. 242–258].

Naughty "Shakespeare" writes in *A Midsummer Night's Dream* in the rustics' playlet:

> THISBE: Asleep, my love?
> What dead, my dove?
> O Pyramus arise.
> Speak, speak. Quite dumb?
> Dead, dead? A tomb
> Must cover thy sweet eyes.
> These lily lips
> This cherry nose
> Those yellow cowslip cheeks
> Are gone, are gone ...
> Tongue, not a word,
> Come trusty sword,
> Come blade, my breast imbrue [she stabs herself]
> And farewell friends
> Thus Thisbe ends
> Adieu, adieu, adieu [she dies] [V, i, ll. 319–28, 337–42].

From 2 *Tamburlaine*:

> Now walk the angels on the walls of heaven,
> As sentinels to warn th' immortal souls
> To entertain divine Zenocrate:
> Apollo, Cynthia, and the ceaseless lamps
> That gently looked upon this loathsome earth,
> Shine downwards no more, but deck the heavens
> To entertain divine Zenocrate:
> The crystal springs, whose taste illuminates
> Refined eyes with an eternal sight,
> Like tried silver run through Paradise
> To entertain divine Zenocrate [II, iv, ll. 16–26].
> (and so on, for three more verses)

Morocco again in *The Merchant of Venice*:

> The Hyrcanian deserts and the vasty wilds
> Of wide Arabia are as thoroughfares now
> For princes to come view fair Portia:
> The wat'ry kingdom, whose ambitious head
> Spits in the face of heaven, is no bar
> To stop the foreign spirits; but they come,
> As o'er a brook, to see fair Portia [II, vii, ll. 39–47].

2 *Tamburlaine* again:

> Holla, ye pamper'd jades of Asia!
> What, can ye but draw but twenty miles a day,
> And have so proud a chariot at your heels,
> And such a coachman as brave Tamburlaine,
> But from Asphaltis, where I conquer'd you,
> To Byron here, where I thus honour you [IV, iii, ll. 1–6].

This is mercilessly sent up in 2 *Henry IV* by Pistol:

> Shall packhorses,
> And hollow pamper'd jades of Asia,
> Which cannot go but thirty miles a-day,
> Compare with Caesars, and with Cannibals,
> And Trojan Greeks? nay, rather damn them with
> King Cerberus: and let the welkin roar [II, iv, ll.148–153].

Doctor Faustus:

> Was this the face that launched a thousand ships,
> And burnt the topless towers of Ilium? [V, i, ll. 89–90].

This becomes, in the mouth of (or is derived from) Richard II:

> Was this face the face
> That every day under his household roof
> Did keep ten thousand men? Was this the face
> That, like the sun, did make beholders wink?
> Was this the face that fac'd so many follies,
> And was at last outfac'd by Bolingbroke? [IV, i, ll. 281–86].

The original may have been taken by Marlowe from *Troilus and Cressida*:

> Why, she is a pearl,
> Whose price hath launch'd above a thousand ships
> [II, ii, ll. 82–83].

This too might be intended as a parody in the light of the following line "And turn'd crown'd kings to merchants." It was reused in *King Lear*:

> Was this a face
> To be oppos'd against the warring winds? [IV, vii, ll. 32–36].

From *Hero and Leander*: "Who ever lov'd, that lov'd not at first sight?" (I, l. 176).

It appears in *As You Like It*, spoken by Phebe the shepherdess:

> Dead shepherd! now I find thy saw of might:
> Who ever lov'd that lov'd not at first sight [III, v, ll. 81–82].

Lines from *The Passionate Shepherd to His Love*:

> By shallow rivers, to whose falls
> Melodious birds sing madrigals.
> And I will make thee beds of roses,
> And a thousand fragrant posies; ...

are wickedly sent up by the comic Welshman Evans in *The Merry Wives of Windsor*:

> To shallow rivers, to whose falls,
> Melodious birds sing madrigals;
> There we will make our peds of roses,
> And a thousand fragrant posies [III, i, ll. 16–19].

Where these parodies or borrowings must by their nature be later than the Marlowe originals, the dates will have been added on the occasion of rewriting by "Shakespeare." The original play may well have an earlier date than the Marlowe play on which the parody is based.

The band of Marlovians[143] points to more than two hundred examples of plagiarism by "Shakespeare" from Marlowe. The revolution which establishes the primacy in date as well as talent of "Shakespeare" makes this impossible, and to be polite some references are more appreciable than others. Where there is a putative date for a prior "Shakespeare" play, the actual reference may have been incorporated at the time of rewriting, but "Shakespeare" is clear when he puts in an element which is not his own or extraneous to the plot: we have seen this with Phebe's remark on love in *As You Like It* quoted above. It seems unlikely that in his rewritings "Shakespeare" would incorporate anything else of Marlowe's without some acknowledgment, and the vast majority of the references put forward by Marlovians are to or from early "Shakespeare" plays.

It is right that references should be considered to those plays for which no clear pre–1587 reference can be established.

Thus in *Macbeth*, we need to look at this:

> Shake off this downy sleep, death's counterfeit,
> And look on death itself [II, iii, ll. 76–77].

And Zenocrates in 2 *Tamburlaine*:

> And might, if my extremes had full events,
> Make me the ghastly counterfeit of death [III, ii, ll. 16–17].

But a reference in *Edward II* to *Macbeth* can be discounted if *Edward II* is written after *Macbeth*, subject to the caveat on *Macbeth* being rewritten incorporating the reference. In *Othello*:

> Not poppy, nor mandragora
> Nor all the drowsy syrups of the world [III, iii, ll. 334–35].

is apparently the descendant of, from *The Jew of Malta*: "Poppy and cold mandrake juice" (V, i, l. 80).

Finally, in *As You Like It*, "A great reckoning in a little room" (III, iii, l. 11) is often thought to be a reference to Marlowe's murder, but surely not when matched with its near contemporary from *The Jew of Malta*: "Infinite riches in a little room" (I, i, l. 37).

These are scarcely mind-blowing comparisons. They and that earlier volume of references from "Shakespeare's" plays seem more to bear out the truth of Nashe's sarcasm in his introduction to Greene's *Menaphon* (1589):

> Yet English Seneca [Shakespeare] read by candlelight yields many good sentences...; and if you entreat him fair on a frosty morning, he will afford you whole Hamlets, I would say handfuls of tragical speeches.

So, if the direct verbal references to Marlowe inside "Shakespeare's" works are in the main discounted, what is left? There is a substantial critical apparatus which seeks to show, for example, that "without Marlowe's examples to inspire him, Shakespeare might not have developed to such a potent level of effectiveness the device of ambiguity in his portrayals of character and event."[144] However, the revolution in English, and the clear priority in dating of a large part of "Shakespeare's" plays, indicate that Marlowe is the follower. If one discards the "orthodox" dating scheme, then it is impossible to say whose was the greater influence on whom. On the other hand, the studies in this book enable a clear picture of "Shakespeare's" priority in time and influence to appear. The absence of verbal references to borrowings by "Shakespeare" from Marlowe would seem logically to negate the suggested literary influences as well. The borrowing of words in the quantities that the Marlovians suggest "Shakespeare" did suggests that he would have also borrowed the ideas: the boot is on the other foot, both for word- and idea-borrowing, and the terrible critical confusion illustrated by note 77 of Chapter Eight arises.

Note on the Author as Actor

Some critics such as Professor Bate have sought to dismiss the authorship claims of Oxford by suggesting that he had no "hands-on" connection with the stage.[145] Indeed, Professor Bate seems to suggest that this element provides incontrovertible evidence of the authorship of William Shakespeare of Stratford-upon-Avon. The evidence of the plays entirely supports their underlying premise that the connection between the writer and the actor is essential, so we can all agree that the author was an experienced actor and producer as well, as the players scenes in *Hamlet* would indicate beyond much doubt. Peter Brook put the point even more succinctly in private conversation: "Would actors never discuss their lines? Would authors never reply to their questions, argue, laugh, cut, rewrite and adapt scenes on the spot? Hour after hour, day after day, year after year, were Shakespeare's fellow actors so dumb they never smelt a rat?"[146] Of course not: the actors would know their position exactly.

From a slightly different angle, Coleridge's reported opinion is persuasive: "It is my persuasion — indeed my firm conviction — so firm nothing can shake it — the rising of Shakespeare's spirit from the grave, modestly confessing his own deficiencies, could not alter my opinion — that Shakespeare in the best sense of the word, was a very great actor; nothing could exceed the judgment he displays on that subject.... Great dramatists make great actors."[147] The only example he can quote is the "tradition" that Shakespeare played the minor part[148] of Adam in *As You Like It*, which would devalue his opinion if it were applied to William of Stratford. Apply the opinion to Oxford and it is totally justified.

The evidence for William Shakespeare himself in the roles of actor and/or producer is slight indeed. Practically all the references can be shown to be to an unqualified investor rather than to an actor/producer/impresario — or are at least, and perhaps deliberately, capable of more than one interpretation. Indeed, in any of the roles other than a silent partner/investor, he would have been a formidable and possibly dangerous figure to the up-and-coming Ben Jonson; yet Jonson in his *Every Man Out of His Humour* satirizes him as a newly—and undeservedly—rich, rustic cultureless buffoon and a criminal grainhoarder and speculator, and ridicules his pretensions to a grant of arms; his acting is given the most awful hammering (see page 255). This and the absence of any worthwhile evidence rules out the Stratford man as actor and therefore, by extension of the logic of the argument, as writer too.

In contrast, Oxford's experiences with the stage and acting must surely begin at his ancestral home, Hedingham Castle. His father kept a troupe of actors and it is reasonable to deduce that the Great Hall at Hedingham Castle was put to dramatic use. It follows that this set of influences upon a child would affect the career of the adult. We have seen the influences and experiences that befell Oxford, which would amply provide him for his careers both as dramatist and actor. I do need to reiterate that Oxford's cast of mind was that of a post-medieval nobleman, to whom laws, customs and conventions did not apply. Thus (to put it mildly) he was cavalier towards his legal, financial and social obligations as a citizen, estate owner and aristocrat. As a husband, as we have seen, he was under additional strains. In spite of being an earl, he may well have had no objection in himself to being a playwright or an actor, indeed quite the reverse.

In 1576[149] on his return from Italy he again took up his court life. I am satisfied that he wrote a number of the plays listed in the court revels and that when he revised these for public performance later the titles, too, were altered.

In 1579 the court revels list the play *Murderous Michael*[150] which has been identified as *Arden of Feversham*, which in turn is considered Shakespearean by several critics, including Swinburne. Although the construction of the play is not on the face of it Shakespearean, the language most definitely is, and it may represent a blind alley in the dramatist's development. The play must have been particularly shocking to the court as it portrayed Michael, the lord's body-servant, who is a secondary character, as being in league with his master's adulterous wife, her lover, and the hired murderers Black *Will* and George *Shake*bag. Black Will (did Oxford play that part?) on the run delivers as his last lines of the play:

> For the constable had twenty warrants to apprehend me:
> Beside that I had robbed him and his man at Gads Hill.
> Farewell, England. I'll go to Flushing[151] [V, iv, ll. 12–14].

We are reminded of *Henry IV Part 1* (to say nothing of *Famous Victories*) in which are repeated Oxford's own exploits in 1572. The point is that this production is reported by one Gilbert Talbot, who writes in March 1579 to his father, the Earl of Shrewsbury, the custodian at the time of Mary, Queen of Scots:

> At Shrove-tide were shews presented at court before her Majesty that night. The chiefest was a device presented by the persons of the Earl of Oxford, the Earl of Surrey, the Lords Thomas Hayworth and Windsor. But the device was prettier than it had hap to be performed.

In other words, good play, poor production.

In 1580 the Earl of Oxford took over the Earl of Warwick's professional troupe. He can now do anything theatrical he pleases, although perhaps he makes a nod to the court in the "invest me in my motley" speech, with the duke's reply, in *As You Like It* (see page 106). For the purpose of public performances he would have had to use a pseudonym, and no doubt the appearance in 1593 or so of William Shakespeare in London would have had its uses

Six—The Life 1576–1590

as a body on which to stick the existing pseudonym. From this possibility arises the whole erroneous deduction that William Shakespeare was in fact an actor. The evidence, or rather the counterevidence, is described in the appendix on pages 255ff.

The company acted at Blackfriars, and Oxford took on the lease in 1584, only for the owner to close the theater down later that same year. Among his associates was Thomas Edwards, who wrote:

> Adon defly masking thro' [Adonis/Oxford acting — incognito?]
> Stateley tropes rich conceited [in high-class plays]
> Show'd he well deserved to
> Loves delight on him to gaze
> And had had not love herselfe intreated [the queen?]
> Other nymphs had sent him baies.
>
> Eke in purple roabes destain'd, [in his actor's royal robes]¹⁵²
> Amidst the Centre of this Clime
> I have heard saie doth remain
> One whose power floweth far, [Oxford]
> That should have bene of our rime
> The only object and the Star. [Star — part of Oxford's arms]
>
> Well could his bewitching pen
> Done the muses objects to us,
> Although he differs much from men [ordinary actors]
> Tilting under Friaries, [acting at Blackfriars]
> Yet his golden art might woo us [his superior acting]
> To have honoured him with baies.

Oxford is clearly shown as writing and acting in high-class plays: he is very different from ordinary actors. The phrase "Tilting under Friaries" shows that the poem refers to a period predating the closure of the Blackfriars theater in 1584.

The whole poem was not published until 1595. However, it does contain references to Colleyn (i.e., Spenser), and Leander (i.e., Marlowe) as the author of *Hero and Leander*, as well as to Shakespeare/Oxford as the author of *Venus and Adonis*, which would indicate a substantially earlier date of composition.

Here I note again Oxford's "greatest acting Triumph" in the exposure of the court Catholic element in 1581 dealt with in Chapter Six, page 85. We return to the artistic acting.

Hamlet (written 1585/6) contains the famous scenes (II, ii; III, ii) of instructions to the players which clearly show the author's knowledge of dramatic production. The scenes are played absolutely straight: surely in the hands of an author of less social standing, the aristocratic know-all producer would have been sent up. Even Polonius praises him: "'Fore God, my lord, well spoken, with good accent and good discretion" (II, ii, ll. 469-470).

This may impute a not particularly congenial opinion to Burghley by way of an Oxford joke. One of the best pieces of evidence for Oxford acting is that contained in the Epilogue to 2 *Henry IV*.[153] There is a passage, ll. 24-32, that is for public production to be spoken by the comic Will Kemp, conflated by the printing compositor with an earlier passage which critics contend can only have been spoken at a court production by William Shakespeare, the author/actor himself. However, they omit the intermediate reference in ll. 20-23: "All the gentlewomen here have forgiven me; if the gentlemen will not, then the gentlemen do not agree with the gentlewomen, which was never before seen in such an assembly." What journeyman actor would dare to comment in this way to the queen and court?

Critics also contend that William Shakespeare was so close to the acting company that he wrote parts with specific actors in mind[154] to display their strengths and/or cover their weaknesses. However, it appears that Oxford as actor or director was at times on hand to rewrite and adapt his already written plays in this way.

Before reviewing the further evidence, it may be instructive to consider the effect of the actor/producer's experience on the plays and on the formation of the character of some of the role in the plays. First I consider *Shakespeare and the Idea of the Play* by Professor Anne Barton (aka Anne Righter),[155] from which I take the passage below. I believe that it fortifies my view that Oxford was a, if not the, leading actor from 1580 onwards. She shows in effect how acting and the stage permeate the writer's bones, in the same way as did his profound classical and legal education, his attachment to Italy and to aristocratic pursuits, and his class attitudes. She discusses the practice of other dramatists in the first decade of the seventeenth century of effortlessly referring to the theater in their plays, but in contrast "Shakespeare" is almost unique among his contemporaries in his refusal to employ references of this type, with one very significant exception, namely the passage in *Hamlet* which deals with the little eyases and their depredations. The passage may therefore be a deliberate (and late, say, 1600) insertion. It finishes with the "little eyases ... berattling the common stages that many wearing rapiers [i.e., would-be gentlemen] are afraid of goose quills and dare scarce come thither" (II, ii, ll. 342-45). This is a cut at William of Stratford after he appears to have absented himself from London from 1599 on a regular basis and after the publication of Ben Jonson's vicious caricature in *Every Man Out of His Humour*. The unique and deliberate nature of the reference is also commented on by Professor Bradbrook in her *Elizabethan Stage Conditions*, and my argument is further supported:

As it is only when they interfere with the straightforward movement of the play and clash with its dominant mood that it is profitable to consider his concessions to the audience, so it is only when they stand out from the body of the writing, when the particular intention has altered the quality of the style, that there is any point in recognising personal allusions. Shakespeare's one allusion to theatrical matters (the "little eyases" speech in *Hamlet*) proclaims itself for what it is: it seems probable that he would have made any other allusions equally unambiguous.

Professor Barton maintains that the London stage did build itself deeply into Shakespeare's imagination and, in ways more subtle than those used by contemporary dramatists, into the structure of his plays. To her, *The Taming of the Shrew*, with its deliberate enhancement of the actor's dignity, the new skill and competence of men who had been mocked in the original play,[156] offers perhaps the first suggestion of Shakespeare's own attitude towards the theater with which his life was to be involved, with ever-increasing force culminating in *Hamlet*. Then shortly after the turn of the century [her date, not mine], she detects a strange and precipitous reversal, when the theater and even the idea of imitation inexplicably went dark for Shakespeare, and the actor, all his splendor gone, became a symbol of disorder and futility. She illustrates this progress first from *King John* where the Bastard decides that the citizens of Angiers are mocking the kings of France and England. They

> stand securely on their battlements
> As in a theater, whence they gape and point
> At your industrious scenes and acts of death [II, i, ll. 374–76].

The quotation gives a vivid image of the interior of a London theater, a view from the stage of the galleries and pit, of an audience open-mouthed with excitement.

Likewise a sense of familiarity with small details of the acting profession is conveyed by that passage in the last act of *Richard II* which describes the erstwhile king, riding through the streets of London in the train of Bolingbroke, a minor actor who suffers by comparison with a more impressive performer (*Richard II*, V. ii. 23–30). Professor Barton links those lines with those that begin Sonnet 23:

> As an unperfect actor on the stage
> Who in his fear is put beside his part
> So I, for fear of trust, forget to say
> The perfect ceremony of love's rite [ll. 1–2, 5–6].

Correctly she identifies in both cases that a quite precise and special observation about the theater has become a natural means of expressing something "which, to a man less deeply involved with the stage, might seem unrelated or far removed."

No one can show that William of Stratford was so involved. The comment on the "strange and precipitous reversal" fits Oxford perfectly, apart from the "dating" references, such as "shortly after the turn of the century," which I deal with below.

At this point I put in the quotation from *Richard III*, Act III, scene v, which Professor Barton might have had in mind, where Buckingham says:

> True, I can counterfeit the deep tragedian,
> Speak and look back and pry on every side,
> Tremble and start at waging of a straw,
> Intending deep suspicion; ghastly looks
> Are at my service, like enforced smiles [ll. 5–9].

And also from *Hamlet*, Act II, scene ii, where Hamlet says of the players to Polonius, the chief minister of the Kingdom of Denmark: "Do you hear, let them be well used, for they are the abstract and brief chronicles of the time. After your death you were better have a bad epitaph than their ill report while you live" (ll. 526–29).

The social aspect of this command should be noted. Indeed, he sees himself as directly engaged with them. His greeting to them is both several and individual, and incredible from a prince to a player without some rationale:

> You're welcome, masters all.—I am glad to see thee well.—Welcome, good friends,—O, my old friend! Thy face is valanced [a boy actor has grown a beard] since I saw thee last. Comest thou to beard me in Denmark?—What my young lady and mistress. By'r Lady, your ladyship is nearer heaven than when I saw you last by the altitude of a chopine. Pray God your voice, like a piece of uncurrent gold, be not cracked within the ring. Masters, you are all welcome [II, ii, ll. 422–435].

Then there is Hamlet's comment on the success of *The Mousetrap*:

> Would not this, sir, and a forest of feathers, if the rest of my fortunes turn Turk with me, and two Provincial roses on my raised shoes on my raised shoes, get me a fellowship with a cry of players, sir?
> HORATIO (sardonically?): Half a share.
> HAMLET: A whole one, I [an autobiographical reference; III, ii, ll. 263–68].

Although scene 9 of *Sir Thomas More*[157] is not generally considered as by Shakespeare, its inclusion is irresistible in the argument. The players are rehearsing a play for an entertainment they are to give. One Luggins is sent out on an errand. While he is away, More takes his part and exits; and on Luggins' return:

> LUGGINS: ... and by my troth, I ran so fast that I sweat againe.
> A PLAYER: Doo you hear, fellows? Would not my lord make a rare player?

Six—The Life 1576–1590

> Oh, he would uphold a company beyond all hoe, better than Mason [chief actor in Henry VIII's court] among the king's players! Did ye mark how extemprically he fell to the matter and spake Luggins's part almost as it is in the very book set down?
> ANOTHER PLAYER: Peace: do ye know what ye say? My lord a player! Let us not meddle with such matters: yet I may be a little proud that my lord hath answered me in my part [IV, i, ll. 293–305].

One would expect a non-noble author in *Hamlet* and *Sir Thomas More* to have "sent up" the noble amateur actor/producer, but it is the noble who shows himself a true professional. There is probably no contemporary report of the incident: it must be Oxford's own invention. As an early reference to actors it is notably condescending like the references in *The Taming of a Shrew*.

Professor Barton directs our attention to *Julius Caesar*. This idea of the actor's greatness works itself out in conjunction with the familiar theme of the Player King, where the scene in which Mark Antony offers Caesar a crown before the dubiously enthusiastic populace, the common people "clap and hiss him, according as he pleas'd and displeas'd them, as they use to do the players in the theatre" (*Julius Caesar* I, ii, ll. 256–260). This illustrates Shakespeare's usual attitude—the theatrical imagery in this speech expresses the insecurity of the ruler's position. There again, "the actors appear in Julius Caesar in another and more honorific guise, however, one which reflects Shakespeare's attitude towards the Elizabethan theater itself. Brutus actually bids the conspirators model themselves upon the players:

> Let not our looks put on our purposes,
> But bear with it as our Roman actors do,
> With untir'd spirits and formal constancy [II, i, ll. 225–27].

Professor Barton points out that the actors are no longer the frail, shadowy figures of *Love's Labour's Lost* or *A Midsummer Night's Dream*; they are the creators and guardians of history. Then the conspirators, bending down to bathe their hands in his blood, glory even in the moment of violence the fame which is now theirs:

> BRUTUS: Stoop, Romans, stoop,
> And let us bathe our hands in Caesar's blood
> Up to the elbows.[158]
> CASSIUS: Stoop then and wash. How many ages hence
> Shall this our lofty scene be acted over.
> BRUTUS: How many times shall Caesar bleed in sport,
> That now on Pompey's basis lies along
> No worthier than the dust [III, i, ll. 103–105; 112–17].

As Professor Barton puts it:

> It [this passage] serves, pre-eminently, to glorify the stage. The actors, Shakespeare's own companions and friends, have become the chroniclers of man's great deeds. It is in the theater that the noble actions of the world are preserved for the instruction of future generations.

This attitude cannot be found in the other plays of the era.

It is clear that Oxford is seeking to glorify the stage to raise the status of the profession and to justify the apparent disgrace of his own appearances. There would be no need for any other dramatist to do this, as we know of no other whose social standing would be so greatly prejudiced by acting in public. It is legitimate to inquire whether a player of the social standing of William of Stratford would see himself as a creator and also a guardian of history, or create characters who see themselves thus. In effect and in contrast, Oxford is constructing his own apologia.

For the period 1588–91 (as we have seen in Chapter Six, by which date the probability is that the plays quoted above had been written in at least a first version) we have seen a dramatic decline in Oxford's fortunes. His wife, the daughter of Burghley, dies: presumably Burghley was less interested, to put it mildly, in Oxford's cultural career (even his library was apparently no longer open to Oxford), let alone defending Oxford's lifestyle. His finances appear to have reached their nadir: the facts might well indicate something like a nervous breakdown. Certainly both Spenser in *Tears of the Muses* ("Our pleasant Willy/Ah, is dead of late") and Nashe in *Alarum Call to Sleeping Euphues* (both 1589) are together eager to recall him as a writer, and perhaps also as an actor. Nashe continues:

> Sundry other sweet gentlemen I know, that have vaunted their pens in private devices and tricked up a company of taffeta fools with their feathers, whose beauty had not our poets picked up with the supply of their periwigs. They might have antickt it until this time up and down the country with the king of the Fairies, and dined every day at the pease-porridge ordinary with Delphrigus [the poorhouse].
>
> But Tolossa hath forgot it was sometime sacked, and beggars that they ever carried their fardles on footback; and in truth no marvel, when as the deserved reputation of one Roscius of force to enrich a whole rabble of counterfeits. Yet let subjects [i.e., lesser actors], for all their insolence, dedicate a De Profundis every morning to the preservation of their Caesar, lest their increasing indignities return them ere long to their juggling to mediocrity, and they bewail in weeping blanks the wane of their monarchy.

In Greene's *Groatsworth of Wit* (see below) the author suggests that Greene was introduced to playwriting by a player magnificently dressed who was an author as well as an actor, one of whose parts was "The King of the Fairies." I suggest that Oxford played the part in London and others played it in repertory in the country. Is this part Oberon in *A Midsummer Night's Dream*? Roscius was the chief classical actor of Rome, not known for any literary productions.

Incidentally, Nashe supplies the answer to Peter Brook's questions in the first paragraph of this section: of course the actors knew he was the 17th Earl of Oxford, and that by 1592 he was virtually down and out. Only Oxfordians can make sense of *The Epistle Dedicatorie to Strange Newes* (1593) as it shows Oxford's relationship to the cultural set to which the actors and authors such as Nashe[159] belonged. Everyone knew his place and knew better than to reveal publicly what their noble colleague was doing — no conspiracy theory is required or need be entertained today.

Professor Barton believes that the change in Shakespeare from regarding actors as noble to actors as parasites takes place about 1600. Oxfordians, however, would date the change to, say, the period 1588–91. There is nothing in William Shakespeare's material biography in 1600 that would suggest a change — quite the reverse. From down-and-out at the start of *The Taming of a Shrew* of 1594 he had enjoyed continuous financial success and was about to make even greater strides in the coming decade, which might in part mitigate for the loss of his son in 1596. At this stage I suggest that Greene's *Groatsworth of Wit* is also evidence of Oxford's acting.[160] The reference by Chettle, who was in fact the author and also at the beginning of his career ignorant of the relationship of the three playwrights and the actor, can be shown to demonstrate that Oxford has to be the "upstart crow with his tiger's heart in a player's hide," who "supposes" he can write. Chettle was misled into thinking Oxford an "upstart crow" because Chettle misinterpreted his recent return to the stage as the beginning of the career of a new actor not fully known to him. His apology (*Kind-Heart's Dream*) indicates that the art (of acting) by Oxford was justified by his playwriting.

The mid- to late 1590s was the era of furious pamphleteering, culminating in the bishop's book-burning of 1599. Although the works of Marlowe, Nashe and Marston went up in the blaze, *Venus and Adonis*, *The Rape of Lucrece* and the blasphemies and obscenities of the plays were for some reason (i.e., because they were by Oxford) preserved. The puritan anti-playhouse, anti-blasphemy, anti-obscenity Joseph Hall[161] was banned from publishing further his *Virgedemarium*, from which I take this quotation:

> One higher pitch'd doth set his soaring thought
> On crowned kings that Fortune hath low brought:
> Or some upreared high-aspiring swain
> As it might be the Turkish Tamberlaine.
> Then weeneth he his base drink-drowned spright,
> Rapt to the threefold loft of heaven hight,

> When he conceives upon his fained stage
> The stalking steps of his greate personage,
> Graced with huf-cap[162] termes, and thundering threats,
> That his poore hearers hayre quite upright sets.
> Such some as some brave minded hungrie youth
> Sees fitly frame to his wide-strained mouth,
> He vaunts his voice upon an hyred stage,
> With high-set steps and princely carriage;
> Now sooping in side-robes of Royalty,[163]
> That earst did scrub in lowsie brokerie.
> There if he can with terms Italianate,
> Big-sounding sentences, and words of state,
> Faire patch me up his pure Iambicke verse.
> He ravishes the gazing scaffolders,
> Then certes was the famous Corduban [Seneca]
> Never but half so high tragedian
> Now, least such frightful showes of fortune fall,
> And bloody tyrants rage, should chaunce appal
> The dead stroke audience, midst the silent rout,
> Comes leaping in recommendation self-misformed lout,
> And laughs, and grins, and frames his mimik face,
> And jostles straight into the princes place
> Then doth the theater echo all aloud
> With gladsome noyse of that applauding croud.
> A goodly hotch-poch when vile russettings
> Are match with monarchs and with mightie kings;
> A goodly grace to sober tragic muse,
> When each base clowne his clumbsie fist doth bruise,
> And show his teeth in double rotten-row,
> For laughter at his self-resembled show [I, 3, ll. 9ff].

The suggestion in the poem is quite clear: the author referred to is a high Tudor aristocrat who is also acting in public — both roles outside the usual conventions of Oxford's social class and a particular distress to Hall.

Professor Barton notices the change in the plays' attitude towards actors themselves which I believe had by the time of Hall's publication (1598) taken place. Oxford perhaps continued to produce new or revised plays while still acting, as the quotation from Hall shows. Perhaps the references in the sonnets are pertinent. While he personally had no care for his reputation — "For what care I who calls me well or ill" (112) — he was worried that the addressee of the sonnets would be shamed by association with him. But the admission of acting is there in Sonnet 110:

> Alas, 'tis true, I have gone here and there
> And made myself a motley to the view,
> Gor'd mine own thoughts, sold cheap what is most dear.

"Gor'd mine own thoughts" means, I think, "disgraced respect for me"; "gored" being a heraldic term for disgrace, and not one which would readily occur to a small-town tradesman.

Another autobiographical reference appears in *The Winter's Tale*:

> LEONTES: Go, play, boy, play,— thy mother plays, and I
> Play too; but so disgraced a part, whose issue
> Will hiss me to my grave [I, iii, ll. 187–89].

Professor Barton traces the decline in regard for the dignity of the theater through *All's Well That Ends Well, Measure for Measure, Troilus and Cressida, King Lear, Othello, Coriolanus* and finally *Macbeth*:

> Out, out brief candle;
> Life's but a walking shadow, a poor player
> That struts and frets his hour upon the stage
> And then is heard no more. It is a tale
> Told by an idiot, full of sound and fury
> Signifying nothing [V, v, ll. 22–27].

The last plays, culminating in *The Tempest*, may provide evidence of the author's attitude to the stage but, significantly, do not seem to show the author acting.

There are other pieces of evidence to show Oxford acting. First, John Davies' poem. It was published in 1610 and is in the present tense, but there is a case for saying it was written in (late) 1604:

> To Our English Terence [1], Mr. [2] Will. Shake-speare. [3]
> Some say (good Will), which I, in sport, do sing,
> Hadst thou not played some Kingly parts in sport,
> Thou hadst been a companion [4] for a King;
> And been a King among the meaner sort
> Some others rail, but, rail as they think fit,
> Thou hast no railing, but a reigning Wit:
> And honesty thou sowst, which they [5] do reap;
> So to increase their stock which they do keep.

1. P. Terentius Afer,[164] an African slave believed in classic Roman times to be the cover author for the dramatic productions of a Roman noble (compare the role of William Shakespeare).

2. "Mr.," that is, at least a gentleman (unlike William Shakespeare of Stratford-upon-Avon, whose armigerous and class aspirations were the subject of Ben Jonson's humor in *Every Man Out of His Humour* and of "Shakespeare" himself— see *The Winter's Tale* Act V, scene 2, where the aspirations of the Clown and his father the Old Shepherd are wickedly mocked — not a rendition which would appeal to William).

3. Hyphen — showing (with the other indications) a pseudonym being used.

4. "hadst" — past tense — Oxford is dead. "Companion," "comes" in Latin, later companion to the king, count, or earl in England; as if an actor could ever have been a companion for a king, unless he already was "comes."

5. Plagiarists who take the profit.

A different John Davies wrote in 1603, "Although the stage doth stain pure gentle blood," and both can only refer to Oxford. However, I ought to deal also with the 1623 folio in which the author dying in harness is described as "not having the fate ... to be the executor to his writings." Contrast this with the final period of William Shakespeare of Stratford-upon-Avon. Jonson in his ode compares Shakespeare to Terence (see above) and says he outranks Kidd, Lyly and Marlowe. Jonson also ignores the dramatists of 1595 on, and then we have this reference: Jonson summons all the great dramatists of classical literature back to hear him act.

> To life again, to hear thy buskin tread
> And shake a stage, or when thy socks were on
> that is, when you were doing the actual acting
> Leave thee alone for the comparison
> Of all that insolent Greece or haughty Rome
> Sent forth or from their ashes come.

Of the supporting poems, one is by Holland. In it is the remark "Dried is the Thespian spring," meaning the acting career is over. Then there is I.M.'s poem:

> To the memory of Master William Shakespeare
> We considered, Shakespeare, that thou went'st so soon
> From the world's stage to the grave's tiring-room [1].
> We thought thee dead, but this thy printed worth
> Tells thy spectators that thou went'st but forth
> To enter with applause. An actor's art
> Can die [2], and live to act a second part.
> That's but an exit of mortality,
> This, a re-entrance to a plaudite.

1. Actor's dressing room; note (apparently) directly from "the world's stage to the grave's tiring-room," not via retirement at Stratford-upon-Avon.

2. Why refer to "it," unless "Shakespeare" was an actor, too?

The folio introduction concludes with the names of the principal actors in all these plays. The first name is "William Shakespeare," not because, as Ogburn says, of his social rank,[165] which was ostensibly still being concealed, but because he was in fact the best actor.

I note again Barnaby Rich's description which can only be of Oxford on his way to the playhouse in 1581 which is quoted in Chapter Six, page 78.

In conclusion, there is more than enough to show that the author of "Shakespeare" had a substantial acting career. No such argument can be made on behalf of William of Stratford-upon-Avon. In contrast, the pieces of evidence and the application of logic to "orthodox" criticism establish Oxford the actor as having sufficient hands-on experience for authorship as well. Indeed, the argument may be taken further. Oxford, by his revolution in playwriting (see pages 138ff), may have forced an accompanying revolution in acting to accommodate his new-style plays. We can only suspect what part he might have taken in promoting those changes.

The only outstanding point is the question as to whether the premier Earl of England would appear on the public stage even anonymously. Oxford had many virtues but he was consistent in that he always endeavored to please himself, and if that and his self-regard and exhibitionism coincided with desired literary and artistic advancement, so much the better. There was not the constant media attention that there is now when someone is perceived to be performing out of his or her class. In Tudor times people knew their place and well knew the dangers of talking out of turn.[166] In addition, those who needed to know the real name of the actor knew already, and those who did not (like Chettle at the start of his career, see page 241), did not.

There was no conspiracy of silence or need for it.[167] By way of corroboration, Oxford's failure to make headway politically in the last twenty years of his life, let alone be appointed a knight of the garter (which elevation should have come to him readily enough as the premier Earl of England), may well reflect the new nobility's abhorrence of him and his theatrical activities.

Nowadays, if there is a secret, everyone, including those who comment four hundred years later, outside that secret is apt to cry "Conspiracy!" when it is revealed. To take two modern examples of secrecy, those who needed to know knew that it was the queen's cousin's wife who was performing on the concert stage, and that a prominent conductor was looking after his new family abroad, while his wife, a prominent performer herself, was dying slowly and painfully in England. Everybody else was outside those circles.

"Orthodox" critics writing four centuries after Oxford's death do not seem to want to grasp the point, and are apt to suggest that Oxford's supporters have to engage in conspiracy theories. This is clearly unnecessary and counterproductive to a clear analysis.

CHAPTER SEVEN

The Life 1590–1604

Charles Spencer: Do you feel that Shakespeare had personal experience of clinical depression? Depression makes it terribly hard to do anything — one of the great themes of the play [Hamlet]. Michael Grandage: I suffered depression early in my life, and see it very strongly in the play.... What's extraordinary is that Shakespeare didn't have labels like depression and paranoia. [Yet] he clearly had a great depth of understanding about the way the mind can sink.—Daily Telegraph (London), May 27, 2009

There is an absence of evidence for the period 1588–90 for Oxford's political or cultural biography, which is reflected in the absence of contemporary references to him. Nelson, typically, suggests he merely purveys an excuse not to come and see Burghley on business, yet Oxford's letter of September 8, 1590, confirms, "I have not had my health," and other literary references confirm my suggestion that he had had a nervous breakdown and was effectively out of circulation. Nelson lists no letters from Oxford between those dated June 25, 1586, and August 5, 1590 — the longest gap since Oxford attained eighteen years of age.

There are, however, substantial literary references. First, after Spenser went back to Ireland after the publication of *The Faerie Queen*, his publisher brought out in 1591 his *Complaints*, containing "sundrie small poems of the world's vanities" and written generally in the period beginning two years or so earlier. The second poem is entitled *Tears of the Muses*, a general lament on the state of culture in England. It is worth noting that Spenser had been absent from Ireland for some nine years and perhaps the full effect of the revolution had passed him by. He had been good friends with Harvey and was happy to be a follower of Leicester and his nephew Sidney.

The first muse in the poem is Clio, the muse of history. She says in her lament:

> It must behoves the honorable race
> Of mighty Peers true wisdom to sustain,
> And with their noble countenance to grace

Seven—The Life 1590–1604

> The learned foreheads, without gifts or gain;
> Or rather learned themselves behoves to be,
> That is the girlonde of nobility.
> ...
> But they do only strive themselves to rise
> Through pompous pride, and foolish vanity;
> In th' eyes of people they put all their praise
> And only boast of Arms and Ancestry,
> But virtuous deeds, which did these Arms first give
> To their grandsires, they care not to achieve.
>
> So I, that do all noble feats profess
> To register, and sound in trump of gold,
> Through their bad doings and base slothfulness
> Find nothing worthy to be writ, or told;
> For better far it were to hide their names
> Than telling them to blazon out their blames.

Spenser is highly critical of Oxford's approach to the history plays as they were in 1589: like *The Famous Victories* with its emphasis on Oxford's forebear, they were toned down and heavily rewritten after 1590 to make them actable and publishable.

Oxford might well be criticized for including "bad doings," but "base slothfulness" was never one of his defects, unless the depression which he seems to have suffered from made him appear in this light. Clio finishes:

> So shall succeeding ages have no light
> Of things forepast, nor moniments of time ...

Note the use of the word "moniment," meaning archive or record, as used by both Jonson and Digges, as we shall see in Chapter Eight.

Spenser's next muse is Melpomene, the muse of tragedy. There seems to be a element personal to Oxford in her lament:

> Most miserable creature under the sky
> Man without understanding doth appear
> For all the world's affliction he thereby,
> And Fortune's freaks, is wisely taught to bear;
> Of wretched life the only joy she is
> And th' only comfort to calamities.
> ...
> She solaceth with rules of Sapience
> The gentle minds, in midst of wordly smarts [noble]
> When he is sad, she seeks to make him merie

("he" [introduced at this point without previous reference, and therefore a specific person] may well be Oxford)

To the memory of my beloued,
The AVTHOR
Mr. WILLIAM SHAKESPEARE:
AND
what he hath left vs.

TO draw no enuy (Shakespeare) on thy name,
  Am I thus ample to thy Booke, and Fame:
  While I confesse thy writings to be such,
As neither Man, nor Muse, can praise too much.
'Tis true, and all mens suffrage. But these wayes
Were not the paths I meant vnto thy praise:
For seeliest Ignorance on these may light,
  Which, when it sounds at best, but eccho's right;
Or blinde Affection, which doth ne're aduance
  The truth, but gropes, and vrgeth all by chance;
Or crafty Malice, might pretend this praise,
  And thinke to ruine, where it seem'd to raise.
These are, as some infamous Baud, or Whore,
  Should praise a Matron. What could hurt her more?
But thou art proofe against them, and indeed
  Aboue th' ill fortune of them, or the need.
I, therefore will begin. Soule of the Age!
  The applause! delight! the wonder of our Stage!
My Shakespeare, rise; I will not lodge thee by
Chaucer, or Spenser, or bid Beaumont lye
A little further, to make thee a roome:
  Thou art a Moniment, without a tombe,
And art aliue still, while thy Booke doth liue,
  And we haue wits to read, and praise to giue.
That I not mixe thee so, my braine excuses;
  I meane with great, but disproportion'd Muses:
For, if I thought my iudgement were of yeeres,
  I should commit thee surely with thy peeres,
And tell, how farre thou didst our Lily out-shine,
Or sporting Kid, or Marlowes mighty line.
And though thou hadst small Latine, and lesse Greeke,
  From thence to honour thee, I would not seeke
For names; but call forth thund'ring Æschilus,
Euripides, and Sophocles to vs,
Paccuuius, Accius, him of Cordoua dead,
  To life againe, to heare thy Buskin tread,
And shake a Stage: Or, when thy Sockes were on,
Leaue thee alone, for the comparison

Above and following page: The two *Moniments* from the preface to the 1623 folio.

TO THE MEMORIE
of the deceased Authour Maister
W. Shakespeare.

Shake-speare, at length thy pious fellowes giue
The world thy Workes: thy Workes, by which, out-liue
Thy Tombe, thy name must: when that stone is rent,
And Time dissolues thy Stratford Moniment,
Here we aliue shall view thee still. This Booke,
When Brasse and Marble fade, shall make thee looke
Fresh to all Ages: when Posteritie
Shall loath what's new, thinke all is prodegie
That is not Shake-speares; eu'ry Line, each Verse
Here shall reuiue, redeeme thee from thy Herse.
Nor Fire, nor cankring Age, as Naso said,
Of his, thy wit-fraught Booke shall once inuade.
Nor shall I e're beleeue, or thinke thee dead
(Though mist) vntill our bankrout Stage be sped
(Impossible) with some new straine t'out-do
Passions of Iuliet, and her Romeo;
Or till I heare a Scene more nobly take,
Then when thy half-Sword parlying Romans spake.
Till these, till any of thy Volumes rest
Shall with more fire, more feeling be exprest,
Be sure, our Shake-speare, thou canst neuer dye,
But crown'd with Lawrell, liue eternally.

                                                    L. Digges.

To the memorie of M. W. Shake-speare.

WEE wondred (Shake-speare) that thou went'st so soone
    From the Worlds-Stage, to the Graues-Tyring-roome.
Wee thought thee dead, but this thy printed worth,
Tels thy Spectators, that thou went'st but forth
To enter with applause. An Actors Art,
Can dye, and liue, to acte a second part.
That's but an Exit of Mortalitie;
This, a Re-entrance to a Plaudite.
                                                    I. M.

> And doth refresh his sprights when they be werie
> But he that is of reason still bereft
> And wants the staff of wisdom him to stay
> Is like a ship in midst of tempest left
> Withouten helm or Pilot her to sway ...
> My part is and my professed skill
> The stage with Tragic buskin to adorn
> And fill the scene with plaint and outcries shrill
> Of wretched persons to misfortune borne;
> *But none more tragic* matter can I find [my italics]
> Than this, *of men deprived of sense and mind.*
> ...
> But I that am in true Tragedies am skilled,
> The flower of wit, find naught to busy me ...

Next up is Thalia, the muse of comedy. She is even more direct:

> O! All is gone; and all that goodly glee,
> Which wont to be the glory of gay wits
> Is laid abed, and nowhere now to see [? ill, and/or slothful again]
> And in her room unseemly sorrow sits, [unbecoming]
> With hollow brows and grisly countenance,
> Marring my joyous gentle dalliance
> And him beside sits ugly Barbarisms
>   ["him" is likely to be Oxford in the guise of "unseemly sorrow"]
> And brutish Ignorance.

The muse laments the current state of the stage and continues:

> And he, the man whom Nature self hath made
> To mock her self, and Truth to imitate,
> With kindly counter under mimic shade,
> Our pleasant Willy,[1] ah! is dead of late
> With whom all joy and jolly merriment
> Is also deaded, and in dolor drent.
> ...
> But that same gentle Spirit, from whose pen
> Large streams of honey and sweet Nectar flow
> Scorning the boldness of such baseborn men
> Which dare their follies forth so rashly throw,
> Doth rather choose to sit in idle Cell
>   [idle again — see "slothfulness" above]
> Than so himself to mockery to sell.

These two verses admit no other interpretation: Oxford is out of circulation — "gentle Willy" (noble "Shakespeare") is silent, "scorning ... baseborn men."

The next piece was intended to be in some ways similar. It is Thomas Nashe's preface to Robert Greene's *Menaphon*,[2] written in 1589, entitled

Seven—The Life 1590–1604

"Camilla's alarum to slumbering Euphues, in his melancholic cell at Silexdra." The addressee appears to be Oxford as Lyly's Euphues in melancholic cell (or "idle cell," as Spenser calls it) at Silexdra, which is the name of the place in Lyly's novel where Euphues can be contacted. The preface itself is curious and seems to have been the victim of severe censorship or correction. In the first place there is no alarum call in it, nor any suggestion that the addressee is idle or melancholic or needs awakening from his cell. First, it contains this denunciation in an appeal to "The Gentlemen Students of Both Universities" against the overrich eloquence of:

> every mechanical mate [who] abhors the English he was born to, ... which I impute not so much to the perfection of arts as to the servile imitation of vainglorious tragedians, ... But herein I cannot so fully bequeath them to their folly as their idiot art-masters, that intrude themselves to their ears as the alchemists of eloquence, who (mounted on the stage of arrogance) think to outbrave better pens with the swelling bombast of a bragging blank verse.... Mongst this kind of men that repose eternity in the mouth of a player, I can but engross some deep-read grammarians who, having no more learning in their skull than will serve to take up a commodity [i.e., follow the latest fashion], nor art in their brain than was nourished in a serving man's idleness, will take them to be the most ironical censors of all, when God and Poetry doth know they are the simplest [i.e., stupidest] of all.

This appears to be a denunciation of a type of dramatic bombastic verse, favored by Marlowe and Kidd the (supposed) author of *The Spanish Tragedy*, but it would be over the top for Oxford as it contains an implied attack on the cultural status of actors. Certainly Chettle who, I show in the appendix, almost certainly wrote Greene's *Groatsworth of Wit*, borrowed the tone of his directed attack. If Nashe consulted Oxford, it may be that Oxford repented of his earlier enthusiasm for actors as becomes clear, save that Oxford did not amend the acting-reference portions of *Hamlet* in the later versions. Nashe carries on a page or two later:

> It is a common practice nowadays amongst a sort of shifting companions, who run through every art and thrive by none, to leave the trade of Noverint [the trade of scrivener or engrosser of legal documents — a crack at Kidd[3]] whereto they were born, and busy themselves with the endeavors of art.... Yet English Seneca read by candlelight yields many good sentences, as "blood is a beggar" and so forth; and if you entreat him fair[4] in a frosty morning, he will afford you whole Hamlets, I should say handfuls, of tragical speeches. But O grief! Tempus edax rerum [Time, eater of things], what's that will last always? The sea exhaled by drops will in continuance be dry, and Seneca let blood line by line and page by page, at length needs must die to our stage; which makes his famished followers to imitate the Kid in Aesop, who enamoured of the Fox's new fangles, forsook all hope of life to leap into a new occupation; and these

men renouncing all possibilities of credit or estimation to intermeddle with Italian translations.

"English Seneca" can only be the leading playwright of the day — Oxford. I cannot find the sentence "blood is a beggar,"[5] which need not necessarily come from *Hamlet*; it could have been rewritten to read "Then are our beggars bodies and our Monarchy and outstretched heroes the beggars' shadows" (*Hamlet* II, ii, l. 265). The most important item is the reference to *Hamlet* in 1589, by then a play well enough established with the theatrical public to be worthy of an offhand pun without explanation, and presumably by a writer of some repute. Only Oxford fits.

"Seneca ... must needs die to our stage" gives rise to the suggestion that "leaching blood," or plagiarism, will cause Oxford finally to cease writing for the stage, and cause the plagiarists to turn to Italian translations.

Later Nashe denounces these translators as "bungling practitioners," with a few minor exceptions, the chief of which is "aged Arthur Golding for his industrious toil in Englishing Ovid's *Metamorphoses*, besides many other exquisite editions of Divinity turned by him out of the French tongue into our own." As we have seen, the translation of *Metamorphoses* is claimed as Oxford's own juvenile work.

From there Nashe turns to the state of contemporary English poetry: "What should I come to our court, where the otherwhile vacations of our graver nobility are prodigal of more pompous wit and choice of words than ever tragic Tasso could attain to?" He mentions Spenser, and with him Roydon and Atchelow (from whom nothing survives) and Peele, which might indicate he did not know in 1589 of *Venus and Adonis* or *The Rape of Lucrece*. He adds:

> Sundry other sweet gentlemen I know, that have vaunted their pens in private devices and tricked up a company of taffeta fools with their feathers, whose beauty if our poets had not picked with their periwigs, they might have antickt it until this time up and down the country with the king of the Fairies [possibly Oberon in *A Midsummer Night's Dream*], and dined every day at the pease-porridge ordinary with Delphrigus [i.e., in the poorhouse].
>
> But Tolossa hath forgot that it was sometime sacked and beggars that ever they carried their fardles on footback; and in truth no marvel, when as the deserved reputation of one Roscius is of force to enrich a rabble of counterfeits. Yet subjects, for all their insolence, dedicate a De Profundis every morning to the preservation of their Caesar lest their increasing indignities return them ere long to their juggling to mediocrity and they bewail in weeping blanks the wane of their monarch.

Note their Caesar needs preserving, in the first place from, I suggest, his illness: if he be not preserved by prayers, "de profundis," from those in the lower ranks of society, then they, the actors and dramatists, have only mediocre examples to follow both in acting and in dramatic writing and "bewail in weeping blanks" the collapse of their careers, just like the "base born men" in the quotation from Spenser. Caesar is introduced in place of Roscius, and is portrayed as the literary and cultural leader. Like his alter ego Seneca, he must also be in danger from plagiarism.[6]

Just when Nashe seems to be working himself up to a finale with a clarion call to Oxford to come to the rescue and resurrect the cultural scene, as foreseen by the title *Alarum Call to Sleeping Euphues*, Nashe contents himself with a promise to continue to persecute the third rate, and a modest little plug for his recent pamphlet *Anatomie of Absurdities*. Perhaps the first version was too revelatory of the identity of Seneca, Roscius and Caesar as Oxford and was amended.

Sometime earlier the poet Thomas Churchyard[7] had entered into a lease of property near St. Paul's Cathedral with Oxford as guarantor. Churchyard could not pay, and neither could Oxford. The queen's annuity apparently was not available, and it may be that payment was understandably being diverted by Burghley for the maintenance of the three daughters. This episode is alluded to by Nashe in the Epistle Dedicatorie to his *Strange News*,[8] published in 1593 and written slightly earlier. It begins:

> To the most copious carminist of our time, and famous persecutor of Priscian [a Latin grammarian], his verie [Vere-y] friend, Master Apis Lapis [Apis, the Egyptian bull god, Lapis, a stone, but also an idle fellow: Oxford in idleness]: Tho: Nashe wishes new strings to his tawnie purse [i.e., better financial state, "tawnie" being one of Oxford's heraldic colors], and all honourable increase of acquaintance in the Cellar [of Silexdra?].
>
> Gentle [Noble] M. William, that learned writer Rhenish wine and sugar [this writer is identified later as William Elderton, a ballad writer who celebrated the taverns of London and a lover of Latin phrases] in the first book of his Comment upon Red-noses hath this saying: veterem ferendo injuriam invitas novam [by bringing in an old injury you invite a new one]; which is as much in English as one cup of nipitaty [strong beer] pulls on another. In moist consideration whereof, as also in zealous regard of that high countenance you show unto Scholars, I am bold, instead of wine, to carouse to you a cup of news; Which if your worship (according to your wonted Chaucerism)[9] shall accept in good part. I'll be your daily Orator[10] to pray that that sanguine complexion of yours may never be famished with pot luck, that you may taste to your last gasp, and live to see the confusion of your special enemies,[11] Small Beer and Grammar rules.

Nashe carries on in this splendid fashion, which must have been a tonic to a sick Oxford, with a long encomium on his generosity and literary patronage ("an infinite Maecenas"). In this is included a coded reference to Churchyard's troubles: "An honest man of Saffron Walden [Harvey's father] kept three sons at the University together a long time; and you kept three maids together in your house." In the second edition (no doubt after Oxford's remarriage), this becomes:

> all poor scholars acknowledge you as their patron, providitore, and supporter, for there cannot be a threadbare cloak sooner peep forth, but you straight press it to be an outbrother of your bounty; three decayed students you kept attending upon you a long time.
>
> Shall I presume to dilate of the gravity of your round cap [only top-ranking wore this] and your dudgeon dagger [this relates to the sword of state carried in procession by the hereditary Lord Great Chamberlain, the Earl of Oxford]?
> ...

There was a secondary purpose in all this praise, of which I have only taken select quotations, which is covered only in the penultimate paragraph:

> Thou art a good fellow, I know, and hadst rather spend jests than money. Let it be the task of thy best terms, to safeconduct this book through the enemy's country.

Then Nashe finishes with this:

> However I write merrily, I love and admire thy pleasant wity humour, which no care or cross can make unconversable. Still be constant to thy content, love poetry, hate pedantism. Vale, vale, cave ne titubes, mandataque frangas [Cheerio, take care not to stumble, or break these commandments],
> Thine entirely,
> Tho: Nashe.

The next edition has the Epistle Dedicatorie in very small type and later ones drop it altogether.

This introduction paints a picture of the decayed aristocrat almost slumming it with the clever university wits, and being their example and icon—a complete contrast to the libels poured out on Oxford by modern critics. The contrast and attraction of him as Berowne in his prime and this picture and the received version of him is totally compelling. Curiously (to some), Nashe never mentions (William) Shakespeare at all.

The reviewer[12] in some confusion in *Shakespeare Survey 35* (1982) reports:

> In 1980 John Tobin noting some eleven unusual words in Romeo and Juliet are also found in Nashe's Have with You to Saffron Walden advanced the thesis that (William) Shakespeare borrowed these terms from Nashe. Tobin returned to this thesis this year [1982], finding seven names of persons or things and some thirty words common to Two Gentlemen of Verona and Have With You. This is a more impressive catalogue than that for Romeo and Juliet, yet it is one that causes more trouble, for acceptance of Tobin's thesis necessitates a date of 1595 or 1596 for Shakespeare's play. Since it seems unlikely that the indebtedness is reversed — that Shakespeare's play influences

Nashe's prose — one is *almost* [my italics] forced to conclude that Shakespeare read Nashe's attack in Manuscript in 1593 or 1594 (although Nashe says it circulated for only three months prior to publication in 1596) or that the concatenation is not unusual.

The Pamphlets War[13] also lets out other hidden allusions. Here is Gabriel Harvey ostensibly attacking Nashe and through him Oxford (as his hidden principal author):

> Where Nashe, there his Nisus, his Laelius, his Damides, his Archiadas, his Musidorus, his companion, with whose puissant help he conquereth wheresoever he indivisible rangeth. Na, Homer was not such an author for Alexander; nor Xenophon for Scipio; nor Virgil for Augustus; nor Justin for Marcus Aurelius; nor Livy for Theodosius Magnus; nor Caesar for Selimus; nor Phillipe de Commines for Charles Vth; nor Macchiavelli for some late princes; nor Aretine for some late courtesans; as his Author for him; the sole author of renowned victorie.

"Laelius" is one of the supposedly aristocratic author of Terence; "renowned victorie" is a reference to Oxford's play *The Famous Victories*, which had just been printed, and tells us that the author is Nashe's mentor.

Nashe in the body of *Strange News* refers to "one of my fellows Will Monox. Hast thou never heard of his great dagger?" This is the "dudgeon dagger" referred to in the introduction above.

Harvey persists and refers to Oxford as the "old ass" in his pamphlet *Pierce's Supererogation* (1593), subtitled *A New Praise for an Old Ass*, the old ass being the dominating figure of the literary scene. Consider (from page 79 of the pamphlet):

> Marvel not, that Erasmus has penned the encomium of folly, or that so many singular learned men have laboured the commendation of the Ass[14]: he it is the godfather of writers, the superintendant of the press, the muster-maister of the innumerable band, the general of the great field; he and Nashe will confute the world.... He has christened so many notable authors; censured so many eloquent pens; enrolled so many worthy garrisons and encamped so many noble and reverend Lords, may be bold with me. If I be an ass, I have company enough: if I be no ass, I have favour to be enrolled in such company.

The Puritan divine Joseph Hall (afterwards Bishop Hall) joined in at a later stage. His denunciation of Oxford's acting and playwriting is at page 159, but he had some more good goes at Oxford as a writer in his book *Satires Virgidemarium* from 1597 on:

> For shame, write better Labeo, or write none, [Oxford]
> Or better write, or Labeo, write alone [i.e., otherwise just
>   write privately for yourself]

> Nay call the Cynick but a witty foole [Oxford again, like
>   Diogenes in his tub giving away his last possession]
> Thence to abjure his handsome drinking bowl [his "handsome"
>   fortune is spent]
> Because the thirsty swain with hollow hand
> Convey'd the stream to wet his dry weasand [throat].

In the same satire come the lines:

> Then Labeo write little or write none, ...
> For shame or better write or Labeo, write none ...
> For shame write cleanly, or write none [II, I, ll. 1–6, 24, 54, 64].

And later:

> Labeo is whip't, and laughs me in the face,
> Why? for I smite and hide the galled place,
> Gird but the Cynick's helmet on his head, [Diogenes again]
> Cares he for Talus and his flail of lead:
> Long as the crafty cuttle lieth sure
> In the black cloud of his thick vomiture;
> Who list complain of wronged faith or fame
> When he may shift it to another's name [IV, 1, ll. 17–24].

This is a clear reference to the concealed use of just William Shakespeare's name and nothing else by or on behalf of Oxford. It is the only reference attributable to William Shakespeare on the contemporary scene, save for the one to the speculating farmer (see pages 252ff).

We can tell where Hall came from, when he wrote:

> Though Labeo reaches right (who can deny)
> The true strains of Heroic Poesy [praise indeed]
> For he can tell how fury reft his sense
> And Phoebus filled him with intelligence [Apollo, god of poetry]
> He can implore the heathen deities
> To guide his bold and busy enterprise
> Or filch whole pages at a clap for need
> From honest Petrarch clad in English weed
> While huge "But Ohs" each stanza can begin [as in *Venus and Adonis*]
> Whole trunk and tail slutish and heartless been;
> He knows the grace of that new elegance,
> Which sweet Philisides fetch't of late from France [Sidney]
> That well beseemed his high-styled Arcady [his book Arcadia]
> Though others mar it with much liberty
> In epithets to join two words in one [VI, I, ll. 249–263].

To Oxford's defense came Marston. I have already quoted his attack on Hall in the reference to Lynceus on page 27. Here he is again in parody of Hall:

> My soul adores judicial scholarship
> But when to servile imitatorship
> Some spruce Athenian pen is prenticed
> Tis worse than apish. Fie, not be flattered,
> With seeming worth. Fond affection
> Befits an ape and mumpkin babion
> O what a tricksy learned nicking strain
> Is this applauded, senseless modern vein
> When late I heard it from sage Mutius' lips[15]
> How ill one thought such wanton juggling skips [by others]
> Beseemed his graver speech. [i.e., imitation damaging Oxford's original composition]
> Then in quotation marks, he broke out in his own voice:
> Far fly thy fame
> Most, most of me beloved, whose silent name
> One letter bounds. Thy true judicial style
> I EVER honour, and if my love beguile [my capital letters]
> Not much my hopes. Then thy unvalued worth
> Shall mount fair place, when apes are turned forth
>   [*Scourge of Villainy* IX, ll. 38-52].[16]

Mutius, the silent name, with the medial "I," denoting nobility, is Oxford (Edward de VERe) and "E" or "O" is the "letter" that "bounds."

Things began to turn very much better for him. One of the queen's maids of honor, Elizabeth Trentham, became his second wife in late 1591, and she apparently did not attempt to alter his lifestyle. Probably as a result of her brother Francis' efforts, a settlement for the children's maintenance was negotiated involving the transfer of Hedingham Castle to trustees for the daughters in return for their maintenance being no longer Oxford's responsibility. Francis sorted out his other properties. This acrostic[17] dates from this period:

> T ime made a stay when highest powers wrought
> R egard of love where virtue had her grace
> E xcellence rare of every beauty sought
> N otes of the heart where honor had her place;
> T ried by the touch of most approved truth,
> A worthy saint to serve a heavenly queen
> M ore fair than she that was the fame of youth,
> E xcept the one, the like was never seen.

Trentame is an alternative spelling of Trentham, and the poem contains a nod to the queen as well.

We have these rueful references in *King Lear*:

> FOOL: I can tell why a snail has a house.
> LEAR: Why?

> FOOL: Why, to puts' head in [Hed-ing-ham] and not to give to his daughters and leave his horns without a case [I, v, ll. 28–31].

And in the storm:

> FOOL: He that has a house to put's head in has a good head-piece [III, ii, l. 25].

In due course the Trentham family was able to buy back Castle Hedingham and settle it on Oxford's son and heir by his new wife, with a transfer in the event of that son having no heir to the Trentham family. With the childless heir Henry, the eighteenth Earl of Oxford, killed at Maastricht in 1625, this is what happened, and archive-minded supporters of Oxford's claim continue to hope that a box of documents may appear with a silver bullet in it in the muniments of some Trentham descendant. I find this attractive but likely to contain as little by way of evidential substance as the portrait of Francis Trentham's great-granddaughter (nude, by Sir Peter Lely).[18]

Curiously, this heir was named Henry. There were no Henrys in the de Vere family tree, and the name Henry would not seem appealing since in return for the support Oxford's predecessor the fourteenth earl had given Henry VII as shown in his play *Richard III*, that monarch heavily taxed him to the extent that the family finances were always precarious.

Portrait of Elizabeth Trentham, Lady Cockayne, by Sir Peter Lely, c. 1670.

Seven — The Life 1590–1604

In this day and age we are familiar with the parent whose child can do no wrong; when the infant is caught with stolen goods, says it is someone else's fault; when ticked off at school, rushes off to abuse (and worse) the teacher. This behavior is reduced to an obsessional absurdity when we consider Oxford's attitude to his son, not his newborn heir nor the Vavasour bastard he packed off to his cousin Horace to become a soldier, but Southampton.

Henry Wriothesley, third Earl of Southampton, was seventeen in 1590 and already Burghley as his official guardian must have been thinking of his marital prospects, and he would not have been human if he did not consider the eldest daughter of his beloved Anne as a suitable choice. The trouble was that Southampton at seventeen was showing little interest in the girls at court, as Sonnet 1 makes clear, and one scenario might be that the matter was clearly of some concern to his mother, the beautiful countess, who called on Oxford, the boy's likely natural father (see page 26). Oxford resurrected the two old poems *Venus and Adonis* and *The Rape of Lucrece* and gave them to Southampton, the one showing a young boy's reluctance in the face of inordinate desire on the part of Venus, and the other the victimization of Lucrece by that of Tarquin.

C.S. Lewis wishes to know, "What man in the whole world, except a father or a potential father-in-law, cares whether any other man gets married?"[19] So why otherwise is Oxford if he is not the father so passionately concerned? In this way the homosexual interpretation appears irrelevant. Sonnet 3 praises the young boy's mother, beginning:

> Look in thy glass, and tell the face thou viewest
> Now is the time that face should form another ...
> Thou art thy mother's glass, and she in thee
> Calls back the lovely April of her prime.

Two absolutely non-homoerotic sentiments are set out, the second a remembrance of the fun the mother and the author had some twenty years earlier. I am not alone in thinking that the resemblance between Oxford and Southampton is marked — see the pictures on pages 22 and 27.

These early sonnets[20] are all for the furtherance of the first idea, and culminating in Sonnet 10: "Make thee another self for love *of me*" — what else can this mean? By way of further corroboration of the non-homosexual element, consider this from the rather obscure Sonnet 20:

> And for a woman wert thou first created [not the
>   first thought of a homosexual lover]
> Till nature as she wrought thee fell a-doting
> And by addition me of thee defeated [i.e., by adding
>   the male organ nature kept me as a man away from you]

> By adding one thing to my purpose nothing [i.e., from my
>   point of view it did not matter for the purposes of this
>   poem whether you were son or daughter]
> But since she pricked thee out for women's pleasure
> Mine be thy love and thy love's use their treasure.

Whatever would be the point of Sonnet 10, quoted above, unless the poet wanted his same nature reproduced for the next and future generations? A legitimate baby, and Oxford had already lost one infant male heir, was a dangerously weak base to rely on to build a dynasty of talent — whereas Southampton had reached early manhood, and the poet's hopes are raised. He also hopes that Southampton may reciprocate his love, but there is a problem. Burghley wants to marry his granddaughter Elizabeth to Southampton. On the face of it the poet should be delighted, but there are two obstructions: too many people know or imagine that Southampton might be the half-brother of Elizabeth — not a problem if you reveal that Elizabeth is not the child of Oxford.[21] Southampton turns down Burghley's plan and is fined by Burghley as his crown guardian five thousand pounds. Did he ever have to pay, I wonder, because it was in no one's interest to have the full story in the open?

Astonishingly for such a private matter, there is some other evidence for this scenario. In 1597 William Burton, the elder brother of Thomas Burton, the author of *Anatomy of Melancholy*, dedicated to Southampton his translation of Achilles Statius' *History of Clitophon and Leucippe*. In part this tells the story of Clitophon's father's plans for his marriage to his half-sister, and his passion duly reciprocated for Leucippe. No doubt the innocently ignorant author hoped that the work might receive approbation from Southampton, who was involved with and had to marry against most approval Elizabeth Vernon, another of the queen's maids of honor.[22] The book appears to have been all but suppressed; it must have been a very hot potato indeed.

Oxford reveals his attitude in Sonnet 36:

> I may not evermore acknowledge thee
> Lest my bewailed guilt should do thee shame
> Unless thou take that honor from thy name [give up your earldom]
> But do not so. I love thee in such sort
> As, thou being mine, mine is the good report.

That is, my bewailed guilt is a secret, you keep your earldom and so the "good report" of us both is kept.

This is evidence that both were from the same social background. A poet from a lower class discovered in an apparently homosexual relationship would have had no "honor" nor "good report" to keep. Consider also from Sonnet 37:

Seven — The Life 1590-1604

> As a decrepit father takes delight
> To see his active child do deeds of youth.
> So I made lame by fortune by fortune's dearest spite
>   [perhaps the wound inflicted by Knyvet — see page 88]
> Take all my comfort of this worth and truth
> ...
> So that I am not lame, poor nor despised
> While that this shadow doth such substance give.

"Shadow" indicates the reflected glory of the younger earl.

The next section of the sonnets are written to the "lovely boy" (Sonnet 126) at arms' length, and Oxford sways from suggesting that his verse is immortal as in Sonnet 55: "But you shall shine more bright in its contents" to that it is a "shame" in Sonnet 72.

The secret is hardly in safe hands if Sonnet 55 becomes public. Sonnet 76 will tell you the author's name:

> Why write I still alone, eVER[23] the same, [my capitals]
> And keep invention in a noted weed [i.e., use my imagination
>   for more poems in the same well-known dress]
> That eVERy word doth almost tell my name
> Showing their birth and whence they did proceed.

I would add that these quotations as reasons for identifying Oxford as the author of the canon often attract derision in default of rational argument, but as no compelling alternative is suggested, and until one is, they stand as respectable pieces of evidence.

In the later sonnets Oxford departs from the reason given in these earlier sonnets — perhaps the birth secrets were reasonably safe — and contents himself with running down his unacceptable role as an actor on the public stage, and pointing up his unworthiness in more general terms. Sonnet 110:

> Alas, tis true, I have gone here and there,
> And made myself a motley to the view,
> Gor'd my own thoughts, sold cheap what is most dear,
> Made old offences of affections new.
> Most true it is, that I have looked on truth
> Askance and most strangely:
> But there is an upside:
> But, by all above
> These blenches gave my heart another youth.

In other words his interest in Southampton took him out of his depression. (This is the only use of "blench" [aberration] as a noun. There are a few uses as a verb in Shakespeare.)

Consider also from Sonnet 111, from public appearances: "Thence comes it my name receives a brand/And almost thence my nature is subdued."

A critic wrote: "Actors as well as those who wrote for the public theatres might be applauded in the theatre, but they were, particularly by the rising Puritan groups, widely considered as amoral pariahs, if not rogues and vagabonds and 'vile esteemed' (Sonnet 121) by the middle and upper levels of Society,"[24] and much more so if the actor/writer were an aristocrat.

I think this thought was in Oxford's mind when he wrote the "disgrace" references in Sonnet 25: "Whilst I, whom fortune of such triumph bars...."

And Sonnet 29:

> When in disgrace with Fortune and men's eyes,
> I all alone beweep my outcast state,
> And trouble deaf heaven with my bootless cries,
> And look upon myself and curse my fate,
> Wishing me like to one more rich in hope,
> Featured like him, like him with friends possessed
> Desiring this man's art, and that man's scope,
> With what I most enjoy contented least; [acting?]
> Yet in these thoughts myself almost despising,
> Haply I think on thee, and then my state
> (Like to the lark at break of day arising
> From sullen earth) sings hymns at heaven's gate;
> For thy sweet love rememb'red such wealth brings
> That then I scorn to change my state with kings.

Nevertheless Oxford's aging is a continuing theme in the sonnets, for example: "My glass shall not persuade me I am old" (22, l. 1).

But: "But when my glass shows me myself indeed/Beaten and chopped with tanned antiquity" (62, ll. 9, 10).

And Sonnet 73:

> That time of year thou mayst in me behold
> When yellow leaves, or none, or few, do hang
> Upon those boughs that shake against the cold,
> Bare ruined choirs, where late the sweet birds sang.
> In me thou seest the twilight of such day
> As after sunset fadeth in the west,
> Which by and by black night doth take away,
> Death's second self, that seals up all the rest.
> In me thou seest the glowing of such fire
> That on the ashes of his youth doth lie,
> As the death-bed whereon it must expire,
> Consumed with that which it was nourished by.
> This thou perceiv'st, which makes thy love more strong,
> To love that well which thou must leave ere long.

The concept of oblivion for the author Oxford and everlasting glory for the dedicatee Southampton is summarized in, for example, Sonnet 81:

> Your name from hence immortal life shall have,
> Though I (once gone) to all the world must die;
> The earth can yield me but a common grave[25]
> When you intomb-ed in men's eyes shall lie....

The whole idea of aging and death comes to its head in Sonnet 107, quoted below.

From the mid–1590s on Oxford made various efforts to repair his finances by seeking offices under the Crown.[26] These were mostly nonstarters, as Oxford had no intention of leaving London to become governor of Jersey or Wales: these were not the sinecures as Oxford would have liked to treat them (appoint a deputy to reside and do the work, while Oxford draws the fee). He attempted to obtain a tin-mining concession and also an interest in the forfeited estates of one of Essex's supporters after the attempted putsch of 1601.

Southampton eventually impregnated and married another maid of honor, Elizabeth Vernon, but Oxford was able to do one further service for Southampton's mother, the dowager countess. Her second husband, Sir Thomas Heneage, died on October 17, 1595. He had been treasurer to the chamber, responsible for paying out to the acting companies the fees awarded to them for the entertainments given, but on his death the accounts were in a sad mess. The queen wrote to the widow that there was a deficit of £518 18s.7d due. The accounts then produced show a payment of £20 to "Will Kempe Will Shakespeare and Richard Burbage servants to the Lord Chamberlain ... for two several comedies or interludes shewed by them before Her Majesty ... upon St. Stephen's day and Innocents' day [December 27 and 28, 1594]."[27] On this is built the evidence for the dizzyingly steep rise of William to a position of management in the lord chamberlain's company, but there is a flaw: On December 28, 1594, other records show, the admiral's company performed before the queen, and the lord chamberlain's company was putting on *A Comedy of Errors* at Gray's Inn. Strangely, Lady Heneage, formerly the dowager countess, was in no further trouble: Oxford's support as earl and as the real "Will Shakespeare" (and known as such to anyone who needed to know) appears to be sufficient cover.

Elizabeth Oxford's putative daughter had married William, Earl of Derby, but was unfaithful to him allegedly with the Earl of Essex.[28] That was one reason for Essex to incur Oxford's dislike; but there was another. Essex began to exercise a maleficent influence on Southampton to the anguish of Oxford as expressed in sonnets 78 to 86; Essex is disguised as a rival poet. While he was not in Shakespeare's league as a poet, he did have sufficient talent and learning to qualify as a rival for Southampton's affections, at any rate in Oxford's no doubt sensitive eyes.

The next tranche of sonnets, 87 to 100, appears to reflect the next stage in

Oxford's relations with Southampton. Sonnet 87 begins: "Farewell...": Southampton is off to Paris for a career of dissipation. He is summoned back for a short interval to marry his countess. Oxford has a few choice words for his behavior (which would hardly lie in the mouth of the man from Stratford), even pointing out that he is disgracing his name while about to be a father. Sonnet 95:

> How sweet and lovely dost thou make the shame [ironic]
> Which, like a canker in the fragrant rose [*Rose*-ley/Wriothes-ley]
> Doth spot the beauty of thy budding name [i.e., your expected heir
>   may well be tainted — scarcely a homoerotic thought]
> ...
> Take heed, dear heart, of this large privilege;
> The hardest knife ill-used doth lose his edge.

Oxford made the point in another reference in Sonnet 69:

> But why thy odor matcheth not thy show
> The soil is thin and thou dost common grow

Imagine a person of any lower class writing that in 1600 to an earl, and living on in one piece.[29] Then likewise consider from Sonnet 84:

> You to your beauteous blessings add a curse
> Being fond on praise, which makes your praises worse.

And 94:

> For sweetest things turn sourest by their deeds
> Lilies that fester smell far worse than weeds.[30]

Essex in 1599 was completely overblown with conceit, but it suited Burghley's son Sir Robert Cecil to have him away from court while Cecil consolidated his position as successor to his father who had died the previous year. Essex was given the command of the campaign in Ireland with the largest army Elizabeth ever sent abroad and he took Southampton with him. The Chorus speech at the beginning of *Henry V* is supposed to evidence the contemporary patriotic view of the occasion which Oxford cannot have enjoyed: indeed, some commentators see the whole play as a fairly ancient effort celebrating the departure of a more successful expedition in 1583/4[31] resurrected by Essex's friends for performance in 1599.

Against the express command of the queen Essex appointed Southampton commander of the horse. When she heard of it she caused Essex to revoke the appointment, so Essex to her rage did away with the post altogether. The whole expedition dissolved into a very expensive farce. Without orders, Essex made a truce with the Irish leader and came home to London, with his army still in Ireland.

Oxford's comments on Essex were scarcely subtle. His admirers had repeatedly portrayed him as Achilles, so he appears in *Troilus and Cressida* as sulking in his tent with his "male whore"[32] Patroclus. Perhaps he then rebased his Coriolanus on Essex and his career: how arrogance and ambition finally defeats a man however privileged.

Finally, Essex completely overplayed his nonexistent hand by attempting a putsch against the ruling Cecil faction in February 1601. He hired the Lord Chamberlain's men to do a performance of *Richard II* by way of propaganda: Oxford was never implicated, and would have been totally unsympathetic. He did have two roles in the aftermath. First, when the actors were called upon to explain themselves over their subversive performance of *Richard II* with every prospect of some very nasty punishments being handed out to those involved, they were represented by Augustine Phillips, one of its senior actors (one wonders if the Burbage family had absented themselves from the enterprise). He explained that they did not wish to do the performance, but it was made worth the actors' while by Essex. Neither William Shakespeare, the putative author, safely ensconced in Stratford, nor Oxford himself were required to give evidence, and there can be little doubt that, thanks to their connection with Oxford and probably Oxford's own representations behind the scenes, the actors escaped without a scratch.

Even luckier was Southampton. At Essex's trial Essex and he had been condemned to death for their leading parts — a more open-and-shut case could hardly be imagined. Somehow, and again Oxford's hand, or desperate pleading, may be suspected, the sentence on Southampton was reduced to life imprisonment in the Tower and attainder — loss of his earldom.

It may be that at this stage, with his health apparently failing, that Oxford may have decided to put together his sonnets to be given to Southampton after his death with the following dedication:

> To. The. Only. Begetter. Of.
> These. Insuing. Sonnets.
> Mr. W.H. All. Happinesse.
> And. That. Eternity.
> Promised.
> By.
> Our. Everliving. Poet.
> Wisheth.
> The. Well-Wishing.
> Adventurer.
> In. Setting.
> Forth.

The mighty tribe of cryptographers have been much exercised by this dedication, and I have a rooted objection to accepting any solution achieved by their aid as evidence. We shall see on page 222, with the Bacon cryptogram on William Shakespeare's memorial in Westminster Abbey, that the intention of the cryptographer is the real test of the evidence and what he writes is not necessarily the truth. However, buried in this wording and extractable from a couple of rectangles created from transliterating the words, is the name HENRY WR-IOTH-ESLEY, rendered in separate syllables,[33] and the odds of these occurring by accident are astronomical. Note that the name given is that borne by the Earl of Southampton before he succeeded to the title, and *after he was attainted*— that is, during most of the short period that remained of de Vere's life. The best bet for the much-disputed name of Mr. W.H. is Mr. H.W., or Henry Wriothesley, the then-current name of the attainted Earl of Southampton.[34] In due course the book came into the possession of Thomas Thorpe, who probably added the remaining sonnets and published it in 1609. Oxford, who could well be the cryptographer in expectation of his own approaching death (Sonnet 107 below), called himself "our EVERliving poet." He believed his work to be immortal and that the book would appear in print only after his death. It illustrates his wish for happiness and immortality for "Mr. W. H."—and for whom apart from Southampton would he want these blessings?

On March 25, 1603, the queen died, and shortly after that Southampton was released from the Tower. Oxford carried on writing his sonnets to him. Sonnet 107 reflects Oxford's present state:

> Not mine own fears, nor the prophetic soul
> Of the wide world, dreaming on things to come,
> Can yet the lease of my true love control
> Supposed as forfeit to a confined doom. [Southampton is out
>   of the Tower]
> The mortal moon hath her eclipse endured [The queen is dead]
> And the sad augurs mock their own presage,
> Incertainties now crown themselves assured [All the fears on her
>   death prove groundless]
> And peace proclaims olives of endless age
> Now with the drops of this most balmy time
> My love looks fresh, and Death to me subscribes [Death is
>   contemplated but I will triumph over it]
> Since spite of him I'll live in this poor rhyme,
> While he insults o'er dull and speechless tribes
> And thou in this shall find thy monument,
> When tyrants' crests and tombs of brass are spent.

The other sonnet which bears signs of topicality is 125, written after the queen's funeral, with its reference to obsequies: "Let me be obsequious in thy heart."

It begins:

> Were't aught to me I bore the canopy
> With my extern the outward honouring, ...

Because he was now the premier Earl of England, there would be no question of him taking a pole of the canopy to carry it over the bier in the queen's funeral procession.[35] This comparatively menial task would be reserved for some lesser dignitary, and anyway what the phrase means is that although it was his right to be the commander of the coffin party, he did not exercise it, and it did not matter to him that he did not. Significantly there are in the College of Arms no less than three drafts of the funeral procession. The first two show Oxford in the commanding position, leading the canopy detail, and the third shows that he was no longer carded for this task: politics or his own reluctance, even illness, may have intervened. In point of fact, the ten syllables of that first line are a wonderful compression of ideas, with the all-important, to the poet, repetition of the vowel sound. Equally it mattered not to him that he had not "laid great bases for eternity [i.e., of mansions, or of fame]/Which proves more short than waste or ruining."

Sonnet 126 is interesting in that it is only twelve lines instead of the regulation fourteen. Some think the poem complete; others think that Thorpe the producer left off the last two lines as being revelatory of the identity of the "lovely boy" of the first line. It may be that they were too revelatory of the poet himself.

That concludes the "Southampton" sonnets, the richly obsessional outpourings of a besotted but concealed father frustrated by his inability to claim his relationship with his splendid son. So far we have seen Southampton in his worst light: it is worth pointing out that Southampton learned a lot from his experiences and became a clever and wise politician for the remaining twenty years of his life.

The twenty-eight remaining sonnets in the 1609 production include the "Dark Lady" section. From the aspect of mere literary criticism it does not really matter who she was. Oddly enough there seems to be a literary exercise element in some of the sonnets: Sonnet 130 is apparently a parody of Watson's Hecotompathia VII[36]; a version of Sonnet 138 appeared in 1599, when *The Passionate Pilgrim* was published; sonnets 153 and 154 are clearly literary exercises. The 1996 Cambridge edition has this interesting headnote (or very uninteresting, if you think William Shakespeare wrote a word of the sonnets):

> Sonnets 153 and 154, anacreontic in character,[37] are ultimately alternative variations on the central conceit of an epigram of the Greek Anthology

(Planudean Anthology IX 627) attributed to Marcianus Scholasticus (fifth century A.D.).

In addition to this literary exercise element, there is some autobiographical element, but it is not so easily defined, some part being overlaid with naughty (or obscene) rather than narrative references.

I have deliberately dealt with the sonnets in a block, to the detriment of the biographical order in literature, but at about the same time as the appeal in Sonnet 1, Oxford was resurrecting his long poem *Venus and Adonis* in the hope that the young Adonis in the shape of Southampton would be interested. In the front of it he inserted a spoof dedication in the manner of the university-wit poets seeking patronage from a rich noble. Only a writer twenty-five years older and of the same social standing could produce such an effort, with its obvious tongue-in-cheek element: "I leave it to your honorable survey, and your honor to your heart's content, which I wish may always answer your own wish and the world's hopeful expectation."

He also resurrected *The Rape of Lucrece* with similar dedication, but with the growing paternal love obsession more evident:

> The love I dedicate to your lordship is without end, whereof this pamphlet without beginning is but a superfluous moiety. The warrant of your honorable disposition, not the worth of my untutored lines, makes it assured of acceptance.

Both dedications are signed: "Your honor's in all duty, William Shakespeare." In the first dedication is the well-quoted phrase: "But if the first heir of my invention prove deformed...."[38]

Now that means either that *Venus and Adonis* is the first thing that the author ever wrote, or it does not. *Venus and Adonis* is 1,194 lines based on Ovid's version of the story, but with elements of two other stories, those of Salmacis and Hermaphroditus and of Narcissus (*Metamorphoses* X, IV and III); in the description we must not forget the bonnetted version of Adonis in Titian's painting (see page 55). The digressions are an imitated feature of the Alexandrian idylls; the poet's imagination is fired by a vision of perfect youth and beauty, the clash of wills, pain and danger, lust and the rejection of it. It is a sophisticated feast of ideas and the poetic rendering of them by a genius — from scratch? That is what critics would wish us to accept when William Shakespeare of Stratford-upon-Avon is touted as the author.

"The first heir of my invention" refers not the work but to the use of the pseudonym "William Shakespeare" as the author for publication in 1592, otherwise the phrase makes no sense at all. I have already indicated those small scraps of evidence showing that Oxford was known as Will, or Willy, and "shake" and "spear" are associated with his name (see pages 34, 78, 87, and 168).

Venus and Adonis by Titian (Barberini version), c. 1560.

Lucrece published in 1593 is half as long again as *Venus and Adonis*, more elaborate in style and in the depiction of emotion, and in moralization. One of the perceived defects of the poem is the long interruption (ll. 1366–1456), the raped Lucrece's disquisition on a remembered painting of the siege of Troy, readily identified with the paintings by Giulio Romano in the private rooms of the ducal palace at Mantua. One particular extract stands out: Achilles is avenging the death of Patroclus with his spear raised up so his arm hides his face—an allegory that might appeal to Oxford hidden behind a "-spear" of his own:

> For much imaginary work was there,
> Conceit deceitful, so compact, so kind,
> That for Achilles' image stood his spear

> Gripped in an arm-ed hand, himself behind
> Was left unseen, save to the eye of mind [ll. 1422–26].

Such a detail, and there are others in the ninety-line description, would only be available in the memory of Oxford, who was of sufficient standing to be given a private viewing of Romano's masterpiece.

The social imperatives of Elizabethan society made it impossible for a person of gentle birth to be overtly, in his own name, associated with the stage, or indeed write poetry or academic prose, except as an amateur or even in a dilettante way, at least until he were dead, like Sidney. To an exhibitionist like Oxford this would have been a most frustrating convention, and by using his pseudonym he tried to evade it, with some success. However, as nothing else was published under the pseudonym until after Burghley's death in 1598, we may suspect that even that avenue for the publication of the plays was for the time being closed.

For the next five years there are only anonymous Shakespeare publications, but in 1598, with his formidable former father-in-law out of the way, Oxford was able to publish at least under the name of his pseudonym. However, sometime in 1593 or so, there appeared in London "William Shakespeare" (variously and inconsistently spelled). He seems to have been introduced or to have attached himself to the lord chamberlain's company with nothing, as far as can be ascertained, to commend him but the similarity or near similarity of his name to that of Oxford's pseudonym. One imagines there was a kind of crisis — too many people knew who William Shakespeare the author was, and yet it was unthinkable that he should be allowed to publish or suffer to be published works dedicated to another earl, and of such character.[39] We shall never know the terms of the arrangement that were reached with William from Stratford-upon-Avon, but it is logical to suppose that it might have contained conditions whereby he is to be referred to as the author and/or the actor but was to adopt a low profile in return for a capital sum. While Burghley was alive, even the name "William Shakespeare" was to be kept out of the limelight, but the publication in print anonymously of some of the plays (then an even lower form of literary life for an aristocrat to be involved in) was either allowed or crept under Burghley's net. William appears to have kept his part of the bargain: he resided in London only intermittently, escaping the attentions of the London rate-collectors, and beginning his successful business career back in Stratford with the purchase of New Place in 1597.[40]

For Oxford's view of the arrangement and how it was working out, we need only to look at scene i in Act V of *As You Like It*, and William's famous conversation with Touchstone[41] (who, with Jaques, is Oxford's composite self-caricature):

TOUCHSTONE: Good ev'n, gentle friend ["gentle" is a piece of mockery investigated in the Appendix]. Cover thy head, cover thy head. Nay prithee, be covered. How old are you, friend?
WILLIAM: Five-and-twenty, sir.
TOUCHSTONE: A ripe age. Is thy name William?
WILLIAM: William, sir.
TOUCHSTONE: A fair name. Was't thou born i' the forest?
WILLIAM: Ay, I thank God.
TOUCHSTONE: Thank God — a good answer. Art rich?
WILLIAM: Faith, sir, so-so. [One might wonder how a peasant became even "so-so" rich]
TOUCHSTONE: So-so is good, very good, very excellent good. And yet it is not, it is but so-so. Art thou wise?
WILLIAM: Ay, sir, I have a pretty wit.
TOUCHSTONE: Art thou learned?
WILLIAM: No, sir.
TOUCHSTONE: Then learn this of me: to have is to have. For it is a figure in rhetoric that drink, being poured out of a cup into a glass, by filling the one doth empty the other.
(turns to the audience): For all your writers do consent that ipse is he.
(turns back to WILLIAM): Now you are not ipse, for I am he [from ll. 16–43].

For ease I have omitted Audrey and put in some staging directions. The only explanation for this otherwise baffling and irrelevant (as always, "irrelevant" means when the playwright is telling us something he wants us to know) passage is that of Oxfordians. Oxford is talking to William of Stratford-Upon-Avon.[42] When unable to provide any rational "orthodox" explanation, Schoenbaum and other critics claim that interpretation of this crux (to them) will always escape us. If a logical explanation is the only one in the field of interpretation, it deserves respect from every critic unless and until it is trumped by a more logical effort. One critic suggests that it is an imagined conversation between William as his rural self and William as the playwright, but this reeks of academic desperation.[43] William hardly seems the kind of man who would want his rustic self on parade before the court and on the public stage in any guise.

The plays appearing anonymously in print before Burghley's death on August 4, 1598 (with their subsequent non-1623 folio editions added — note that the 1598 editions are given an author: they are probably immediately post-Burghley), are:

1591— *The Troublesome Reign of King John*: the 1611 edition is written by "W. Sha." and the 1622 edition "written by W. Shakespeare"
1592— *Arden of Feversham*: 1599 and 1633 anonymous
1594— *Titus Andronicus*: 1600 and 1611 anonymous
1594— *The Taming of a Shrew*: anonymous

1594 — 2 *Henry VI*: 1600 anonymous; 1619 "written by W. Shakespeare Gent."
1595 — 3 *Henry VI*: 1600 and 1619 anonymous
1596 — *Edward III*: 1599 anonymous
1597 — *Richard III*: 1598 "by William Shake-speare"; 1602, 1605 and 1612 "newly augmented"; 1622
1597 — *Romeo and Juliet*: 1599 and 1609 anonymous; after 1609 "Written by W. Shakespeare"
1597 — *Richard II*: 1598 Q2 and 3 "By William Shake-speare"; 1608 and 1615 "With new additions."

By 1597 the lord chamberlain's company was in deep financial trouble, and in late 1598 the shareholders decamped to the south side of the Thames, taking the whole of their theater building with them and re-erecting it as the Globe. William's money was required, and with no Burghley on the scene, the anonymous publication of plays could no longer be prevented. Indeed, the William Shakespeare cover, if indeed there was one, was effectively blown by Meres, who in his *Palladis Tamia* (1598)[44] revealed the authorship in the name of Shakespeare of five comedies. These can readily be identified as *Two Gentlemen of Verona*, *The Comedy of Errors*, *Love's Labour's Lost*, *A Midsummer's Night Dream* and *The Merchant of Venice*, and a sixth, *Love's Labour's Won* (which has so far defied identification). He also named six tragedies: *Richard II*, *Richard III*, *Henry IV*, *King John*, *Titus Andronicus* and *Romeo and Juliet*. Meres was composing less a work of criticism or scholarship than a work of art, with for instance six comedies balanced by six tragedies. To use him as evidence for dating the unmentioned plays as later than 1598 is proving not to be scientific. So there must have been a change of policy, or Meres lifted a lid which was meant to be closed. The plays' author could be identified as William Shakespeare.

Between then and 1604, the printings of *Richard III* and *Richard II* and the following appeared in print:

1598 — *Famous Victories of Henry V*: anonymous; also in 1617
1598 — *Love's Labour's Lost*: "newly corrected and augmented by W. Shakespere"[45]
1598 — 1 *Henry IV* anonymous; 1599 "Newly corrected by W. Shake-speare"; 1604, 1608, 1613 and 1622
1599 — *The Passionate Pilgrim*: by "W. Shakespeare"
1600 — *Henry V*: anonymous; 1602 and 1619 anonymous. It is interesting that "W. Shakespeare" is not associated with this most successful play, no doubt because of its association with Essex's career in the public mind.
1600 — *Much Ado About Nothing*: "Written by William Shakespeare"
1600 — 2 *Henry IV*: "Written by William Shakespeare"
1600 — *The Merchant of Venice*: "Written by William Shakespeare" 1619

1600—*A Midsummer Night's Dream*: "Written by William Shakespeare" 1619
1601—*The Phoenix and the Turtle*: anonymous poem attributed to "Shakespeare" 1601 *The Merry Wives of Windsor*: by "William Shakespeare"
1603—*Hamlet*: by "William Shake-speare," the "bad quarto"; 1604 the "good quarto" (see page 199) by "William Shakespeare."

Oxford's brush with what seems to have been a nervous breakdown left him with a different outlook on life. In general, depression accompanied by alcoholism (suspected in Oxford's case) can play havoc with the sufferer's creative and artistic drive. In part this can be seen in his view of the acting profession discussed in my note at the end of the previous chapter, and the symptoms of this change are indicated by and in his writings. As this "change" is so generally accepted, the need to set out the evidence for this attitude at great length is obviated. Perhaps the view of the teenage Harold Pinter will suffice: "Shakespeare writes of the open wound ... the fabric breaks. The wound is open. The wound is contained. The wound is peopled."[47]

One can see that whereas *The Winter's Tale* and *Pericles* are tales of calamities in which all comes right in the end, *King Lear*, *Macbeth*, *Hamlet*, *Coriolanus*, *Timon of Athens* and *Othello*, in the versions that we now have, end for the title characters in final disasters: certainly in the first three we have Oxford's last version, being his final revisions along with those for *Henry V* and *Measure for Measure* and those incorporating put-downs or revelations for William Shakespeare: *The Winter's Tale*; *The Merry Wives of Windsor*; *As You Like It* and *The Taming of the Shrew*. Only *The Tempest* seems to be an entirely fresh conception from this final period 1590–1604.

Incidentally, the problem for commentators and supporters of William Shakespeare and other contenders for his honors (who generally agree that there was this "change") is that they have great difficulty in relating it biographically to their candidate. First, the date they all choose is 1601, to fit in with the play-dating schedule inflicted on them by Malone and Chambers. William at that date was safe in Stratford, with his finances improving from year to year, and his material circumstances would have beyond his wildest imagination ten years earlier.[48] True, he had lost his only son five years earlier, in 1596, and his father more recently, but these were natural hazards of life, and there is no evidence that either of or both these losses had any particular effect on him. Of course they could well have, and he kept himself busy making money in various ways. This appears to have been his principal, perhaps sole, interest. He and the other authorship candidates cannot produce that succession of family, and financial and social disasters which afflicted Oxford ten to twelve years earlier. He continued to pursue the wish for a grant of arms to his father, soon after the death of his own son; he had of course, three younger brothers available to carry on the great armigerous name.[49]

Barton wrote, "Shakespeare's disillusionment with the stage ... is [with] the whole conception of the play, of something imitated, reproduced at second hand, which seems to disgust him. The actor is a man who cheapens life by the act of dramatizing it; the shadows represented on the stage are either totally corrupt or totally without value 'signifying nothing.'"[50] Those sentiments are reflected in the plays which Oxford rewrote in the last decade of his life.

In *Henry V* the opening Chorus speech illustrates the chasm between reality and the stage's imitation of it in the unrealistic illusion that the stage retails — how different to the speeches on the "wonder role" of actors as the guardians of history, exemplified in *Julius Caesar*.

In *Measure for Measure*, the duke distrusts his subjects, and the futility of rigid judgments is exposed. In *Troilus and Cressida* this basic cheapening and futility element is apparent again and again. Often in the plays the villains Iago, Richard III, Edmund and Macbeth are examples which illustrate this argument.

There are topical references in these plays: *Macbeth* contains a reference to Oxford's spying work, with its concomitant instruction to warn off those who might be tempted. Critics date *Macbeth* after the Gunpowder Plot of 1605; that is, after Oxford's death, because of its reference to the Jesuit practice of "equivocation,"[51] disregarding the fact that "equivocation" was laid down as a permissible ruse as early as 1584. The word "equivocation" occurs in *Hamlet* as well, in the grave-digger scene, where the practice is lampooned by the grave-digging clown, causing Hamlet to say: "We must speak by the card or equivocation will undo us" (V, i, l. 132).

There would be no point in the exchange if the practice were not well known to the audience. The trial of Father Garnett in 1606 may have brought the idea more to the public attention, but Oxford would have known all about it even earlier — there were trials in 1596 when it was also revealed.[52]

Equally Jonson reminds himself of the Porter's lines: "Here is a farmer that hang'd himself in the expectation of plenty" (II, iii, ll. 4–5) when he put in the farcical (and again, irrelevant) scene of Sordido (one of the composite parts of Jonson's caricature of William Shakespeare) hanging himself and being cut down by the despised locals. Jonson's play *Every Man Out of His Humour* dates from 1599, and the scene records the decent improvement in the harvest in 1598, and the date of *Macbeth* is similarly evidenced (see Appendix, note 56). The incident of the speculative farmer seems to have had considerable currency. Joseph Hall wrote:

> Each muckworm will be rich with landless gain,
> Although he smother up mows of seven years gain
> And hanged himself when corn grows cheap again
> [*Virgedemarium* IV, 6, ll. 23–25].

This sentence firmly places *Macbeth* at an earlier date, and there is nothing that can be specifically dated to a post-plot reference:

> Light thickens, and the crow
> Makes wing to the rooky wood [III, ii, ll. 51–52].

"Crow" is a reference to the Jesuits, and indeed it may be to a specific one. In 1600 Ambrose Rookwood, one of the two noble conspirators in the Gunpowder Plot, inherited Coldham Hall in Worcestershire, and made the house "a common refuge of priests." Their visitations were obviously known, and the line is a clear warning to Rookwood to back off. Had it been written after the Gunpowder Plot, it would have been entirely useless, and in the poorest possible taste in view of Rookwood's subsequent grisly execution.

Anyway, the play is markedly anti–Scottish, and full of witches, which James I, who came to the throne in 1603, would have found completely repugnant, so any later date is most unlikely.[53]

The other play which "orthodox" critics use for dating is *The Tempest*. There seems to be a move away from the old reliance on alleged verbal parallels with the so-called Strachey letter, allegedly written in 1610 but not published until 1625, two years after the first printing in the 1623 folio. These verbal parallels have largely been exploded by analysis.[54] For contemporary evidence predating 1610, "orthodox" commentators rely on a report given to the board of directors of the Virginia Company of the wreck of the *Sea Venture* the previous year. How this document reached William Shakespeare in Stratford-upon-Avon is not explained, except through some tenuous connection between one of the director's families and the overseer of William Shakespeare's will.

Recent critical analysis has established that the play is the same one known as *The Spanish Maze*[55] performed at court as part of the Christmas revels in 1604-05. The play is ostensibly about the dynastic quarrels of the Spanish ducal families ruling Milan and Naples at the time, both being Spanish fiefdoms since 1535 and 1503 respectively, and the names of the noble characters all being Spanish. So Prospero must be thought of as a high Spanish noble whose Castilian accent is mocked by Ariel, a joke well appreciated no doubt by the court. Ariel remembers that Prospero had called him up from the nook where the ship is hidden "to fetch dew from the still vexed Bermoothes" (I, ii, l. 229) — an apparently unnecessary task involving a long journey, even for a fairy.

The phrase gives the lie to the location of Bermuda and the 1609 shipwreck there as the basis for *The Tempest*. The location of the island, as is clear from the play, is somewhere in the Mediterranean Sea between, say, Tunis and Southern Italy in the area of Pantellaria or Lampedusa.

Once the characters are on dry land a maze is a very good description of what they find on the island. From the ship, which is not wrecked after all, there come, first the juvenile lead Ferdinand, then the other nobles, then their households, typified by Trinculo and Stefano, and finally the crew, who are all saved without any knowledge of one another. All land on the island or enter the maze by four separate entrances. In the middle are Prospero and Miranda, Caliban and Ariel. The maze is both geographic and psychological.

The noble characters overtly compare their sojourn of the island as being in a maze:

> GONZALO (an elderly courtier with a Spanish name):
> By'r lakin, I can no further go, sir;
> My old bones ache: here's a maze trod indeed,
> Through forth-rights and meanders [III, iii, ll.1–3].

> ALONSO: This is as strange a maze as e'er men trod
> And there is in this business more than nature
> Was ever conduct of: some oracle
> Must rectify our knowledge [V, i, ll. 242–45].

> GONZALO (blessing FERDINAND and MIRANDA):
> Look down. You gods,
> And on this couple drop a blessed crown;
> For it is you that have chalked the way [V, i, ll. 201–03].

For the 1610 production before the court, the play could not be called *The Spanish Maze* in view of its anti–Hispanic name and content; both could well be disguised behind its new name *The Tempest*.

In 1596 Florio (born in England of an Italian Protestant father, and who never himself set foot in Italy) translated Montaigne's essay *Des Sauvages*.[56] Gonzalo's speech (II, i, ll. 153ff) is a direct lift therefrom:

> In a nation, would I answer Plato, that no kind of traffic, no knowledge of letters, no intelligence of numbers, no name of magistrate, nor of politic superiority; no use of service, of riches or of poverty; no contracts, no successions, no partition, no occupation but idle; no respect of kindred, but common, no apparel but natural, no manuring of lands, no use of wine, corn or nectar. The very words that import lying, falsehood, treason, dissimulation, covetousness, envy, detraction and pardon were never heard among them.

The critic J.-M. Maguin goes on to point out, "Curiously, Miranda's exclamation about that 'Brave New World' (V, i, l. 186) is close in statement to a

Latin quotation added in the 1595 posthumous edition of Montaigne's Essays — the one Florio translated — and omitted in his English version"; this is clear evidence that Oxford was using a French version as well as the translation. Montaigne applies the phrase to savages: Miranda's salutation is aimed at the sophisticated and perverse Old World race as it appears to her.

There is a topical reference to Raleigh's 1595 Guyana expedition, when his description of the inhabitants was much mocked at the time, and Gonzalo says:

> Who would believe ...
> Or that there were such men
> Whose heads stood in their breasts? [III, iii, ll. 44, 46–47].[57]

Burghley had the habit of taking off his lord treasurer's cloak at the end of his day, putting it down and saying: "Lie there, Lord Treasurer." In the conception of his son-in-law, Prospero removes his coat of magic, and says: "Lie there, my art" (I, i, l. 25).[58] It is a clear reference and of limited import once Burghley died in 1598.

The play is ostensibly the last that Oxford wrote with its intimations of finality: it is the culmination of his plot invention career with much less in the way of extraneous sources.

Critics are apt to date certain other plays as being written after Oxford's death in June 1604, in addition to *Macbeth* and *The Tempest*. Some suggest that *Cymbeline*, *Pericles* and *The Winter's Tale* were written specifically for an indoor theater such as the new Blackfriars Theatre. As we have seen on page 138, this assumption, commonly stated as if it were a fact, by, for instance, Professor Bate, "that these romances [i.e. the last three mentioned plays and *The Tempest*] were written for the indoor Blackfriars at which Shakespeare's Company [and we will see in the Appendix what precisely was William's connection with the profession in 1610] began to act in 1610. Since the assumption has a good deal of scholarly support, perhaps it may prove salutary at the very start, to stress that all available evidence is either completely negative or else runs directly counter to such a supposition." The critic then reviews the evidence which justifies his contention, per my earlier quotation.[59]

Apart from *The Tempest*, Oxford in the final ten or twelve years of his life appears to have written very little from scratch, preferring to rewrite or touch up earlier efforts and incorporate in those improved versions some topicalities, including revelations on his relationship with William Shakespeare.

On June 18, 1604, he died at Hackney.[60]

It would be cowardly (yet understandable) if I did not try to sum up Oxford's religious attitudes. I see him as reacting against the Protestant upbringing provided by Burghley and being attracted to Roman Catholicism.[61] His primary loyalty to England, its peace and security, saw him reject the blandishments of the Catholics to defect in 1573 (see page 27). He was able to reconcile his conjectured employment as a spy so he could be allowed to go to Italy, because he saw that the English Catholic politicians of the day were even worse crooks than the queen, Burghley and Walsingham, and a dreadful danger to the peace of England. Demonstrated by the plays and in his life, he had the greatest sympathy with the Catholic martyrs, and none towards the Puritan activists; from one group he received Father Southwell's pleas and gave a warning to Ambrose Rookwood (see page 192): from the other he denounced and used his spy ring against Leicester and his sympathizers and Essex. They and the Catholic extremists were all his enemies as divisive threats to the peace of England: their general incompetence no doubt did not appeal to him either. Perhaps he was an early pre–Laudian Anglo-Catholic.

CHAPTER EIGHT

Aftermath

[I have] profited from the reminder that the past bears a shape we have afterwards imposed upon it. It did not have that shape at the time. — Matthew Parris, former member of Parliament and political journalist, the *Times* (London), June 20, 2008

Matthew Parris' aperçu is true of the revolution: plays continued to pour out from dramatists, obscuring almost immediately its effect on its contemporaries.

But not entirely while Oxford was still alive: in *The Arte of English Poesie* (1589) its reputed author George Puttenham wrote: "In her Majesty's time that now is, are sprung up another crew of courtly makers [i.e., poets], noblemen and gentlemen of Her Majesty's own servants, who have written excellently well, ... with the rest, of which number is first that noble gentleman, Edward Earl of Oxford" and he mentioned "doings as I have seen of theirs ... to deserve the highest praise, the Earl of Oxford for Comedy and Interlude."[1] This means that by 1589 "Shakespeare" had a recognized track record for excellence, which I think can only be based on his works set out in Chapter Six.

As we have seen (pages 164ff), Spenser's reaction is comparable.

In *England's Mourning Garment* (1603) "Shakespeare" is criticized by Henry Chettle for failing to honor Elizabeth the dead queen:

> Nor doth the silver tongued Melicert[2]
> Drop from his honeyed muse one sable tear
> To mourn her death that graced his desert
> And to his lays opened her Royal ear.
> Shepherd remember our Elizabeth,
> And sing her rape, done by that Tarquin, Death.

But later in the main body of the work (a "conversation" between two shepherds), dealing at one point with the causes of the Anglo-Spanish wars, he writes: "For thou hast heard the songs of that warlike poet Philisides [Sidney] ... and smooth tongued Melicert, tell us what thou hast observed in their sawes, seen in thine own experience, and heard of undoubted truths touching those accidents [i.e., the causes of the wars]: for that they add, I doubt not, to the glory of our Eliza." Thus he places "Shakespeare" as a contemporary of Sidney (wrong — he has to be Sidney's predecessor — a typical example of Matthew Parris' point quoted above), who was killed at Zutphen in 1586. However, William Shakespeare has to be too young and with no track record for this reference to be relevant. Yet, with its reference to *The Rape of Lucrece*, the first reference has to relate to the author of the canon, who perforce cannot appear to be the same person: but of course with the same pseudonym, Melicert, he must be.

Melicertus is also the joint hero of Greene's *Menaphon* (1589), which recounts the poetic competition between Menaphon (Greene himself) and Melicertus, who is later renamed Maximius ("the greatest"), as if in imitation of a noble Roman family name.

In 1599 John Weever proclaimed: "Honey-tongued Shakespeare when I saw thine issue [i.e., the plays] I swore Apollo got them, and none other."[3]

Francis Meres reviews writers in a section of his book "A comparative discourse of our English poets, with the Greek, Latin and Italian Poets" (1598).[4] He is perhaps more laudatory of Sidney and Spenser, but he writes "The sweet, witty soul of Ovid lives in mellifluous and honey-tongued Shakespeare — witness his Venus and Adonis, his Lucrece, his sugared sonnets among his private friends...," and then the famous passage:

> As Plautus and Seneca are accounted the best for comedy and tragedy among the Latins, so Shakespeare among the English is the most excellent in both kinds for the stage: for comedy, witness his Gentlemen of Verona, his Errors, his Love's Labours Lost, his Love's Labour's Won, his Midsummer Night's Dream, and his Merchant of Venice; for tragedy, his Richard the Second, Richard the Third, Henry the Fourth, King John, Titus Andronicus, and his Romeo and Juliet.

Meres was anxious more to produce a work of art than a scholarly record: thus "Shakespeare's" six comedies are balanced by six tragedies. He also simply without comment repeated Puttenham's earlier statement. Enoch Powell makes the valuable comment that either Meres was among "Shakespeare's" friends and had access to the sugared sonnets and was able to justify the comparison with Ovid or he was merely reporting something secondhand; the remark is odd because Meres is generally discussing "Shakespeare's" reputation as a playwright entertaining public audiences.

Oxford's burial is recorded as being at Hackney Parish Church on July 6, 1604. While there is no extant account of his funeral, two important events

Eight—Aftermath

Hamlet 1604 quarto page with Royal Arms at top.

are linked to his death. The first is the publication in late 1604 of the so-called Good Quarto of *Hamlet*, distinguished by the Royal Arms on the second page by superscripture in which the Royal Arms are prominent. This clear and unique signal of royal approval is not found on any other contemporary work of literature, and indicates the importance of the work and its author. It would be pleasant to think, but there is no evidence, that Horace de Vere, Oxford's military cousin, obeyed Hamlet's charge to Horatio in Act V, scene ii: "Report my cause aright/To the unsatisfied" [ll. 291–92].

Secondly, the Christmas revels of 1604-05 at court bear all the signs of a Shakespeare-fest, a good-bye and thank-you celebration to the recently deceased author (sometimes listed as "Shaxberd"). The list of plays performed at court[5] is below. Note that eight out of ten are Shakespeare's, including *The Merchant of Venice* twice:

November 1: *Othello*
November 4: *The Merry Wives of Windsor*
December 26: *Measure for Measure*
December 28: *The Comedy of Errors*
January 7: *Henry V*
January 8: *Every Man Out of His Humour* (Jonson)

January 9: *Love's Labour's Lost*
February 2: *Every Man in His Humour* (Jonson)
February 10: *The Merchant of Venice*
February 11: *The Spanish Maze*, known to us as *The Tempest* (see page 193)
February 12: *The Merchant of Venice*

On this punishing schedule one critic writes, "I find it hard to believe that so unrelenting a piece of Jonsonian improvisation as *Every Man Out of His Humour* had retained its popular appeal for the five years since its first performance, but there are few plays so hard to memorize in the whole history of English drama. If this piece was revived in a hurry it was an astonishing feat." As usual, when "orthodox" critics are puzzled there is an obvious explanation. The play contains the most direct and complete refutation of the pretensions of William Shakespeare as author, and Jonson, probably the artistic director of the court revels, may well have wanted this aspect set out in the clearest terms to the court, along with the gentle caricature of Oxford as Puntarvolo[6]; its numerous spoofs of Shakespearean situations and parodies of quotations would make it instantly recognizable to the audience, and a very good choice for the Shakespeare-fest.

Also in 1604, James I wrote to Sir Robert Cecil reporting that Lord Sheffield did not think his pension of £1,000 adequate: "As I told him, never greater gift of that nature was given in England. Great Oxford[7] ... got no more of the late queen."

At the same time the acting company was in trouble for the first time without the protection of Oxford, because of the production of *Gowry*, a play about scandal in the king's administration in Scotland.[8]

In 1607, William Barksted wrote of Shakespeare in the past tense, as of a dead poet, but addressing his own muse:

> His song was worthy merit (Shakespeare he)
> Sung in fair blossom, thou the withered tree.
> Laurel is due to him, his art and wit
> Hath purchased it; cypress thy brow will fit.[9]

In the same year, Marston, who throughout his career seems to have displayed a greater regard for the author of Shakespeare's plays, published his own play *What You Will*. In Act II, scene i, the Marston character says:

> No, sir. Should discreet Mastigraphos [i.e., himself]
> Or that dear spirit acute Canaidos [Oxford]
> (That Aretine, that most of me beloved
> Who in rich esteem I prize his soul
> I term myself) ...

Eight—Aftermath

Clearly "that most of me beloved" has died between the first reference in 1599 (see page 175) and this one in 1607, where Oxford is compared to Pietro Aretino, the best Italian for ribald verse.

After Oxford's death in 1604, however, Jacobean taste and demand meant that Webster could only find praise for "Shakespeare's" "right happy and copious industry."[10]

In the next nineteen years, up to the publication of the 1623 folio, only four canonical (or, with *A Yorkshire Tragedy*, possibly five) further plays were printed for the first time, namely:

1608 — *King Lear*: Q1 "William Shakespeare"; Q2 "M. William Shak-spear"; 1619
1608 — *A Yorkshire Tragedy*: Q1 "Written by W. Shakspeare"; Q2 1619[11]
1609 — *Pericles*: Q1 and 2 "By William Shakespeare"; 1611; 1619
1609 — *Troilus and Cressida*: Q1 and 2 "By William Shakespeare"
1622 — *Othello*: "Written by William Shakespeare."

From the publication point of view, eighteen of the plays (half the canon) were apparently not printed until 1623. At the end of the sonnets as published in 1609, there appeared *A Lover's Complaint*.

Note that *King Lear* was twice printed in 1608, the first edition by "William Shakespeare" but the second by "William Shak-spear," an interesting amendment. *Troilus and Cressida*'s first printing states that the play had been performed at the Globe, but the second printing had this curious appeal:

> A never writer [i.e. William Shakespeare, but yet an eVER writer], to an ever reader [no doubt an eVER reader]. Newes. You have hear a new play (untrue as we have seen), never staled with the stage, never clapper clawed with the palms of the vulgar ... and were the vain names of comedies changed for the titles of commodities, ... you should see all those grand censors that now style them such vanities, flock to them for the main grace of their gravities: especially this author's (not actually named in this preface), that are so framed to the life, that they serve for the most common commentaries of all our lives, showing a dexterity, and power of wit, that th(os)e most displeased with plays are pleased with his comedies.

The writer finishes:

> And believe this, that when he is gone [a nod to the fiction that William is the author], and his comedies out of sale,[12] you will scramble for them, and set a new English Inquisition [i.e., buy them now, before they are no longer obtainable even with the help of the tortures of an English inquisition]. Take this for a warning, and at the peril of your pleasure's loss, not being sullied with the smoky breath of the multitude, but thank fortune for the scape it hath made amongst you. Since for the grand possessors' wills, I believe you should have prayed for them rather than been prayed.

Some have tried to suggest that the "grand possessors" must have been the acting companies, socially an unlikely imaginative effort. The implication must be that the play must have been removed from wherever it was in high-placed custody.

The sonnets appeared in 1609 in a similar, slightly clandestine production with the same printer as *Troilus and Cressida*, George Eld, who might have proved difficult over the copyright for the 1623 folio. *Pericles* came into the possession of another printer, Henry Gosson, in 1609, and this time the play was overlooked altogether, either for copyright reasons or because it had been too mucked about to be included. Anyway, for twelve years or so no new play from the canon appeared.

A shorter version of *Othello* appeared in print in 1622, and then the great 1623 folio records all the usually accepted plays except *Pericles* and *Two Noble Kinsmen*, with *Troilus and Cressida* put in as such an afterthought that it does not appear in the index at the front.

Of the other plays that had already appeared in print, *Edward III, The Famous Victories, Arden of Feversham* and *A Yorkshire Tragedy* were not included; *Edmund Ironside, Thomas of Woodstock* and *Sir Thomas More* existed in manuscript, not to be revealed for many years. *Harthacanute* and *The Three Sisters of Mantua* are lost, and the sole manuscript of *Cardenio*[13] was accidentally burned a hundred years later. The sonnets and other poems do not appear. With no one to protect the name or even the pseudonym of the dead writer — certainly William Shakespeare does not appear to have taken any interest at all — other plays appeared whose authorship is now always rejected. These appeared in print as "by W S" or "by William Shakespeare": *The London Prodigal* (1605); *The Puritan Widow* (1607); *Sir John Oldcastle* (1619); and a number of post-1623 efforts, of which only parts of *Two Noble Kinsmen* ("by Mr. John Fletcher and Mr. William Shakespeare Gent") first printed in 1634 have received any approval. To these spurious Shakespeare plays we should add the earlier ones: *Locrine*, 1595 ("Newly set forth, overseen and corrected by W S") and *Thomas Lord Cromwell* 1602 ("Written by W S") with a second quarto in 1613.

Were it not for the sterling work of Jonson as editor (if indeed he were),[14] the final versions of these plays might well have been lost if the 1623 folio had not seen the light of day: *The Comedy of Errors; The Taming of the Shrew; Two Gentlemen of Verona; As You Like It; Twelfth Night; All's Well That Ends Well; Measure for Measure; Henry VI*, part I; *King John; Henry VIII; Julius Caesar; Macbeth; Antony and Cleopatra; Coriolanus; Timon of Athens; Cymbeline; The Winter's Tale* and *The Tempest* would have to take their chances as a survival in manuscript or be reduced to the evidential level of *The Three Sisters of Mantua, Harthacanute* and *Cardenio*.

Some plays provide clear examples of completion and/or rewriting by authors subsequent to Oxford's death.[15] These plays with their suggested lesser hands include:

Pericles with portions by Wilkins
Two Noble Kinsmen with portions by Fletcher
Timon of Athens with portions by Middleton
Henry VIII recast by Fletcher.

Wilkins and Middleton need not detain us.

In regard to Fletcher's contribution I go some way with Clare Asquith.[16] She suggests that the play manuscripts fell into the hands of the militant Protestant government of Robert Cecil, who turned over to John Fletcher the fragment of *Henry VIII* to produce an acceptable "heroic" version, which, because of its success, had to be included in the 1623 folio as a genuine all–William work.[17] It finishes with the arrival of the baby Princess Elizabeth, presumably from a much earlier pure Oxfordian version: King James would not want too much emphasis on the glory of his predecessor in case it compared with his own shortfall from that standard, let alone on that predecessor as executioner of his own mother. Fletcher was at least ostensibly extremely successful in his adaptation.

Some would add *Cardenio* or *Double Falsehood*,[18] a play "adapted" by Lewis Theobald in 1728 from a manuscript subsequently lost in a fire, said to be a "collaboration" between "Shakespeare" and Fletcher. Some detect "Shakespearean" portions, but others may reflect Professor Wells' magisterial opinion: "There's more reason to believe the play preserves bits of Fletcher than Shakespeare. However there might be a bit of Shakespeare DNA in it."

Fletcher had a go at *Two Noble Kinsmen*,[19] which like the "collaborative" *Pericles* and *Cardenio* was excluded from the 1623 folio, even going so far as to try to make his efforts clearly Shakespearean and applicable to William Shakespeare back in Stratford. Here is a specimen of his try, which has no bearing on the plot of the play (i.e., we are being told something the writer wants us to know):

> I was acquainted
> Once with a time when I enjoyed a playfellow.
> You were at wars when she the grave enriched
> Who made too proud the bed; took leave o' th' moon —
> Which then looked pale at parting — when our count
> Was each eleven.
> But I
> And she sigh and spoke of were things innocent,
> Loved for what we did ... [I, iii, ll. 49–54, 55–57].

A more clunking effort to relate to the loss of one of William's twins, his only son, in 1596, aged eleven, and to attach the play to him, can scarcely be imagined.

The prologue of this play provides further evidence that it is not a collaborative effort by making out that it starts life as a work of a single original "breeder," contrasted later on with the writer of "witless chaff."

> We pray our play may be so. [like an innocent bride on honeymoon]
> For I am sure ["I," the author of the prologue]
> It has a noble breeder and a pure ["noble," i.e. Oxford]
> A learnèd, and a poet never went [a single academically
>   distinguished author]
> More famous yet 'twixt Po and silver Trent [ll. 9–12].

The author of the prologue, a third person, identifies the play with one "noble breeder," "pure," "learned" and "a poet never went/more famous yet 'twixt Po and silver Trent"—precisely Oxford's principal stomping grounds. The author (Jonson, I suggest) put in these concealed Oxford references, while damning Fletcher and the play. Fletcher (d. 1625) was not around to object to the prologue in the 1634 printed edition.

Chaucer cries out from his tomb:

> O fan
> From me the witless chaff of such a writer [i.e., Fletcher]
> That blasts my bay and my famed works makes lighter
> Than Robin Hood [ll. 18–21].

When speakers are plural, it is the actors in the cast who "pray" for the audience's sympathy and cry out to be "saved."

Consider also these lines on war:

> O great corrector of enormous times;
> Shaker of o'er rank states; thou grand decider
> Of dusty and old titles, that heal'st with blood
> The earth when it is sick and curs't the world
> O' th' pleurisy [superabundance] of peoples [V, i, ll. 61–65].

And compare them with Barnabe Barnes in his *Four Books of Offices* (1606—too early for Fletcher): "[War] is the noble corrector of all prodigal states, a skilful bloodletter against all dangerous obstructions and pleurisies of peace."

And in the scene where Claudius and Laertes plot Hamlet's death, Claudius says: "For goodness, growing to a pleurisy/Dies in his own too much" (V, vii, ll. 118–19).

Fletcher made a bad continuity error in Act II, scene i.[20] "Orthodox" critics say this shows that the parts allotted to the writers were being written simultaneously but separately. However, with no Oxford around to correct the error, it would seem to show that Fletcher was writing carelessly or incompetently. William Shakespeare was far way in Stratford.

In 1610 Fletcher tried his hand at pastoral verse drama in *The Faithful Shepherdess*, with its "Arcadian daintiness," and later on produced a sequel to *The Taming of the Shrew*, *The Tamer Tamed* (1611). Neither receive much critical acclaim. Jonson waxed eloquent:

> Poor poet Ape, that would be thought our chief,
> Whose works are e'en the frippery of wit,
> From brokage is become so bold a thief,
> As we, the robb'd, leave rage, and pity it.
> At first he made low shifts, would pick and glean,
> Buy the reversion of old plays; now grown [a cut at government instigation?]
> To a little wealth, and credit in the scene,
> He takes up all. Makes each man's wit his own;
> And, told of this, he slights it. Tut, such crimes
> The sluggish gaping auditor devours;
> He marks not whose 'twas first: and after-times
> May judge it to be his, as well as ours.
> Fool! As if half eyes will not know a fleece [a double entendre on fleece?]
> From locks of wool, or shreds of the whole piece [*Epigrammes* LVI].

Strangely, this poem is sometimes quoted as a jealous outburst by Jonson on the success of William Shakespeare. It looks like a vicious mirror of Fletcher's career to date.

In 1612 Jonson wrote a pastoral verse counterblast to *The Faithful Shepherdess*[21] with Shakespearean allusions (Asquith calls it *A Pastoral Tribute*) called *The Sad Shepherd*, or *A Tale of Robin Hood* (note the reference in *The Two Noble Kinsmen* prologue above) which is incomplete, suspiciously so — perhaps the lost ending contained too much of a revelatory nature. Anyway, the prologue for *The Sad Shepherd* contains this similarly vicious passage:

> Or that the man who made who made such one poor flight
>   [i.e., *The Faithful Shepherdess*]
> In his whole life, had with his winged skill
> Advanced him upmost on the muses' hill
>   [i.e., as far as his little talent let him]
> When he like poet yet remains, as those
> Are painters who can only make a rose.

Jonson continued to be loyal to Oxford's memory.[22] Here is an extract from *The Devil Is an Ass* (1616) showing the court fixer Meercraft suggesting ducal titles to his dupe Fitzdotterell:

MEERCRAFT: I think we have place to fit you now, sir — Gloucester.
FITZDOTTERELL: Oh, no, I'll none.
MEERCRAFT: Why, sir?
FITZDOTTERELL: Tis fatal.
MEERCRAFT: That you say right in, Spenser, I think, the younger [one of Edward II's favorites] had his honor thence. But he was but an earl.
FITZDOTTERELL: I know not that, sir. But Thomas of Woodstock
I'm sure was Duke, and he was made away
At Calice, as Duke Humphrey was at Bury
And Richard the third, you know what end he came to.
MEERCRAFT: By my faith, you are cunning in the chronicle, sir.
FITZDOTTERELL: No, I confess I have it from the playbooks
And think they are more authentic [II, i].

"Playbooks" is a clear reference to Oxford's history plays: note that Fitzdotterell is unfamiliar with Marlowe's *Edward II*, but does know of *Thomas of Woodstock*.

Beaumont wrote a verse letter to Jonson in about 1615 (my italics):

> Here I would let slip
> (If I had any in me) scholarship
> And from all learning keep these lines as clear
> As Shakespeare's *best* are which our heirs shall *hear*
> *Preachers apt to their auditors* to show
> How far sometimes a mortal man may go
> By the dim light of Nature.

These lines are quoted sometimes to show that William as the author was lit "by the dim light of Nature" alone, and then with the words in italics ignored: Beaumont makes the contrast between these "best" lines which low critics suited "to their auditors" will pass on, and the remainder, the most intellectually sophisticated of the age.

Jonson also made an effort when he published his own works in 1616 to keep the name of Shakespeare before the public as a superlative actor — the first actor in his plays, when he and everyone else would know that William Shakespeare had no credit in that art or any other. He was reminding his readers of the excellence of Oxford, and he repeated his ploy with a similar list in the 1623 folio.

In 1612 Henry Peacham,[23] the son of the Henry Peacham whom we met both as a reflector of the revolution (page 63) and also the transcriber of the 1575 fragment of *Titus Andronicus* (page 35), wrote an emblem book. Emblem books were a continental fashion full of cryptic cartoons and drawings to puzzle the reader. Peacham's was the first published in English, entitled *Minerva Britanna* [sic] *or A Garden of Heroical Devices*. The central design of the title page consists of an oval intertwined with two phrases in Latin. The first reads

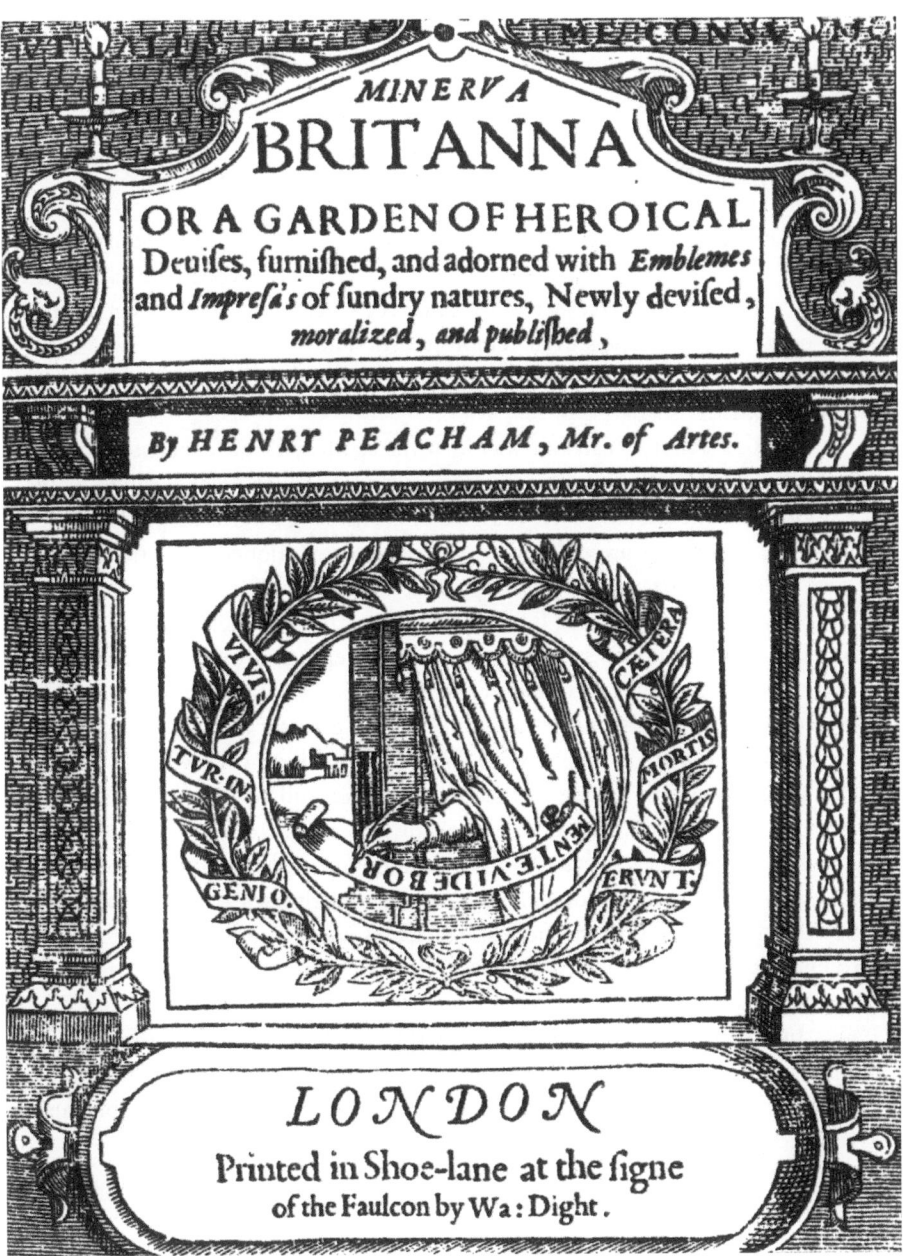

Mente Videbor: Title page with engraving from *Minerva Britanna* by Henry Peacham (1612).

"vivitur ingenio," which can be translated as "he lives in his art," and the second, "cetera mortis erunt," "everything else will be of death"; in other words, this man's art is immortal; everything else will perish. The central design is of a stage curtain around which a right arm protrudes, the hand writing with a pen on a scroll "mente videbor" (I will be perceived/appreciated in the mind). At the end of the second word the pen is in effect adding a further "i," to make the word "videbori" a nonexistent word in Latin. Some think "mente videbori" is an anagram of "tibi nom de Vere"—"your (the concealed writer's) name is de Vere." I remain to be convinced, but that explanation is the only one that makes even remote sense. The vital point is that this all appeared while William Shakespeare was very much alive, residing far away in Stratford.

In 1622 Henry Peacham was in print again with an exhaustive list of English poets in *The Compleat English Gentleman*, which went through many editions without alteration. At the head of his list is "Edward, Earl of Oxford." Nowhere is Shakespeare or William Shakespeare mentioned, even though the great folio appears the following year in his name. Peacham does not use Meres' list, preferring that of Puttenham and writing in almost the same terms, but Peacham modernizes Puttenham's list by repeating Oxford, Buckhurst, Paget, Sidney and Dyer, dropping Fulke Greville, Gascoigne, Britton (possibly Nicholas Breton) and Turberville, and adding Spenser and Daniel; there is no mention of William Shakespeare. Peacham, who lived till 1643, had opportunities to revise his listing in the two unaltered subsequent editions in his lifetime, those of 1627 and 1634.[24] The only logical conclusion is that Peacham knew that Shakespeare was Oxford's pseudonym, and there was no need to mention that secondary name. Incidentally, Buckhurst's name is no doubt preserved because his grandson was Peacham's patron, and might be flattered to find his name as the part author of *Gorboduc* mentioned in the same breath as that of the author of *Hamlet*.

In about 1619 Sir George Buck[25] wrote *The History of King Richard III*. The words in square brackets come from a reconstituted transcript after a fire in Buck's papers. The words in round brackets are the editor's reasonable (and very clever) insertions:

> And in much (shorter time than his) life's time [i.e., less than the lifetime of the thirteenth Earl of Oxford who died in 1513 aged seventy-one], that great and stately (earldom of Oxenford, with the) very opulent and princely patri(mony was dissipated) and wasted, and it was suddenly (and swiftly u)sed and consumed, and como sal en agua, (as the Spaniar)ds say in the refrain. But not by the fault (of the earl t)hen lord thereof, but rather by the fate of the (divine) ordinance. For certainly the earl was (a dev)out and a magnificent and very learned and religious (nobleman) and so worthy in every way, as I

have heard some grave and (di)screet and honorable persons, who knew this earl from his (youth) and could very well judge of the hopefulness and the(springt)imes of young men, say and affirm that he was much more likely to raise and to acquire and to establish a new earldom than to decay (and) waste and lose an old earldom. And in a word he was a (Vere) in deed as in name, vere nobilis. For he was (verily) and truly noble, and a most noble Vere.... And I speak (that) which I know, for he vouchsafed me with his familiar (acquaintance). And whereas I call this earldom a stately (earldom) and a princely patrimony, who being pleased to do me the honour to come to my lodging at Hampton C(ourt).

The remainder is an unreliable reference to Oxford's financial affairs in his youth, compounding the errors in the above account.

The exclusion from the 1623 folio[26] of the poems, usually at the time thought more worthy products of a writer than mere plays, is indicative of the opposition that their inclusion might have encountered. Thus the two dedications to Southampton of *Venus and Adonis* and *The Rape of Lucrece*, the reference to Mr. W H in the sonnets' dedication and the suspicion of overt homosexual desire or concealed paternity would draw too much attention to Southampton himself: the last thing that the godfathers of the whole undertaking to publish the works in a single volume would want would be to lose any support in their endeavors. It is clear that there was a strong political motivation in the production. At the time King James was seeking to marry off his heir to one of the Spanish infantas,[27] in the teeth of considerable Protestant opposition spearheaded by the Earl of Pembroke and his brother Montgomery, the husband of Oxford's daughter Susan, supported by Southampton and Oxford's son Henry, the eighteenth Earl of Oxford, by his second wife. Southampton spent a time under house arrest and Henry had two short periods in the Tower during 1621 and 1622, with the Spanish ambassador requiring the king to cut off his head. Perhaps the conspirators thought they could make the position clear to the public when they managed to have *Othello* published in 1622 with the villainous Iago (him with a Spanish name), playing on the fears of the foreign-born leader Othello. So as to make the position even clearer, it appears that Pembroke and Montgomery wanted the play *The Tempest*, or *The Spanish Maze*, republished with its generally appalling picture of Spanish political mores, but to conceal their objective they apparently agreed to publish the whole canon, with *The Tempest*, the last play to be written, appearing first in the book, so as to be the first read, and its political (to them) message broadcast. No "orthodox" commentator can produce a reason for the first play in the folio being *The Tempest*. Indeed, for some equally curious reason the last play in the folio is *Cymbeline* which in one stratum recounts a war of independence from Rome. The last lines of the play, and those of the folio are the peace treaty spoken by the king:

The two Henrys, the 18th Earl of Oxford and his (putative) half-brother the 3rd Earl of Southampton, c. 1624.

Eight—Aftermath

> Publish we this peace
> To all our subjects. Set we forward, let
> A Roman and a British ensign wave
> Friendly together ...
> Set on there. Never was a war did cease,
> Ere bloody hands were washed, with such a peace
>   [V, vi, ll. 479–82, 485–86].

Modern biographies of King James I pass over the roles of Southampton and the eighteenth Earl of Oxford as leaders of the Patriot Coalition against the Spanish marriage arrangement. The 1623 folio is altogether in part a fairly overt effort to transmit their case.

There is little doubt that Jonson was the editor of the volume and that he saw to it that as little connection with William Shakespeare as possible was included, and that the case was put not too blatantly, both to please "The most Noble and Incomparable Pair" and prevent the project from being aborted for overexposure of things they would wish concealed. However, to provide clues to the identity to the real author he was able to insert the following:

> But since your lordships have been pleased to think these trifles something heretofore, and have prosecuted them and their author living, with so much favour [not much evidence of that, but even less i.e. nil, towards William Shakespeare], we hope that, they outliving him, and he not having the fate, common to some, to be executor to his own writings, you will use the like indulgence [careful choice of word] toward them as you have done unto their parent.

The phrase "he not having the fate ... to be executor of his own writings" reflects exactly the circumstances, so far as we know them, of the end of Oxford's acting and writing career.

Now there can be no question that had William Shakespeare been the author he would have had ample time to edit and perfect himself, but he seems not to have cared.[28] The volume of spurious works dated between 1604 and 1616 demonstrates that they were published as they were without his objection, along with the all too revelatory sonnets. Jonson incorporated I.M.'s poem, which some think is perhaps a rejected prologue to the *Hamlet* "Good Quarto" (see page 199) written soon after Oxford's death in 1604 by John Marston (or with the words "this thy printed worth" a later adaptation):

> We wondered, (Shake-speare), that thou went'st so soon [hyphenated]
> From the world's stage to the grave's tiring room [actors' dressing room]
> We thought thee dead, but this thy printed worth[29]
> Tells thy spectators that thou went'st but forth
> To enter with applause. An actor's art

> Can die, and live to act a second part.
> That's but an exit of mortality;
> This, a re-entrance to a plaudite.

And Hugh Holland:

> His days are done that made the dainty plays
> Which made the globe of heav'n and earth to ring.
> Dried is that vein, dried is the thespian spring,
>   [the acting ends at the same time]
> Where fame, now that he gone is to the grave —
> Death's public tiring house — the nuntius is ... messenger.

Without the 1623 folio we would know only of the titles of some of the plays, or they might even have been lost forever. Furthermore, the chances are that, had there been no political impetus, most of these plays listed on page 202 would have been lost as well.[30] In contrast to the Middleton part of *Timon of Athens*, Jonson as putative editor may have considered *Pericles*, *Cardenio* and *Two Noble Kinsmen* too contaminated for inclusion. Fletcher's association with these plays may not have commended them to Jonson. *Henry VIII* as a patriotic play, even though partly by Fletcher, would have to be included as it had been such a success.

Then in the 1623 folio, there appeared the "portrait" with the right front of his jacket made up from the left back of it — which must be telling readers not to rely on it, an opinion reinforced by the poem on the opposite page:

> This Figure, that thou here seest put,
> It was for gentle[31] Shakespeare cut
>   ["for" meaning in the place of, i.e., not a real portrait;
>   "gentle" meaning noble, and hardly applicable to William]
> Wherein the graver had a strife
> With Nature, to outdo the life ...
> Oh, could he but have drawn his wit
> As well in brass, as he hath hit
> His face; the print would then surpass
> All that was ever writ in brass
>   [a bit of a backhanded compliment, I think]
> But since he cannot, Reader, look
> Not on his picture, but his book.

(i.e., do not bother with the picture, read the book if you want to know what sort of person the author was).

Before turning to Jonson's *Ode* in the preface to the 1623 folio, we need to note that other hands also put in their two cents' worth of praise in that preface. Leonard Digges writes:

> Nor shall I e'er believe or think thee dead —
> Though missed — until our bankrupt stage be sped —
> Impossible — with some new strain t'outdo
> Passions of Juliet and her Romeo,
> Or till I hear a scene more nobly take
> Than when thy half-sword parleying Romans spake.

Digges also provides on the face of it the best evidence for William Shakespeare's alleged literary career, but Shake-speare is hyphenated as a pseudonym three times:

> Shake-speare, at length thy pious fellows give
> The world thy works, the works by which outlive
> Thy tombe thy name must: when that stone is rent
> And time dissolves thy Stratford moniment[32]
> Here we alive shall view thee still.

The first is presumably Hemmings and Condell, but Jonson in his ode seems to link them with "silliest ignorance," "blind affection," or even "crafty malice." In the second the true author is resurrected. In the third we are meant to think of Stratford-upon-Avon, but note the use of "i" in "moniment": this archaic word means "oeuvre," or body of work. The phrase means that time dissolves the false Stratford ascription: the true works by which thy name shall outlive the actual tomb: the "moniment" survives to be appreciated by those who live on. Altogether these lines are a brilliantly clever piece of hidden evidence.

Some critics think that there is a link between Digges and William Shakespeare. In 1600 the manor at Alderminster, four miles from Stratford, came into the family via Thomas Russell who may or may not have married Leonard Digges' mother.[33] Digges was twelve years old; at fifteen he went up to Oxford University. Thus for a short period time in his early teens he might have known William Shakespeare, who was twenty-four years older. The lease of the manor ran out in 1612, and while Russell became an overseer of William's will on his death in 1616 there is no reason to think there was any particular link between him and Russell's putative stepson Digges. Digges was much better known to the "Incomparable Pair" of dedicatees of the 1623 folio, to whom he addressed his translation of a Spanish novel in the previous year. He was a convinced Protestant and his dealings (if any) with the apparently Catholic Shakespeare family would be affected accordingly.

Jonson must continue to be the best witness of "Shakespeare's" worth to those who knew him[34]:

> I confess thy writings to be such
> As Neither man, nor Muse, can praise too much.
> Tis true, and all men's suffrage.

The question is to whom is Jonson referring in this panegyric? He gives no biographical details except the name of the author, and the reference to "the Swan [a mute bird] of Avon," and the adjective "gentle" meaning "noble," and not applicable to William. Then some of his readers might spot the comparison between those lines and these:

> Thus, then, to show my judgment to be such
> As can discern the colours black and white,
> As alls to free my mind from envy's touch,
> That never gives to any man his right,
>   [perhaps a bit of rueful biography there]
> I here pronounce this workmanship is such
> As that no pen can set it forth too much.

This is the third verse of an introductory commendatory poem in the front of Spenser's *The Faerie Queen*, published in 1590 but certainly written earlier. The poem is signed "Ignotus," meaning by an unknown poet. As there would be no reason for William to conceal his authorship, the only candidate for "Ignotus" must be "Shakespeare" himself. "Ignotus" must have been a poet of recognized and track-record talent to be invited to contribute to the preface of *The Faerie Queen*— this would not be William in 1589 or any other time. Ergo Jonson is not praising William but the real "Shakespeare."

Jonson continues:

> Soul of the Age!
> The applause! The delight! The wonder of our Stage!
> *My* Shakespeare, rise: I will not lodge thee by [*My*: the real one]
> Chaucer,
> [an ancient predecessor]
> or Spenser,
> [a contemporary]
> or bid Beaumont lye
> [a modern follower]
> A little further, to make thee a roome:
> Thou art a Moniment, without a tombe,
> And art alive still, while thy Booke doth live,
> And we have wits to read and praise to give.

Again "moniment" and tomb are contrasted.

The same idea was picked up by Basse[35] probably in imitation both of Jonson's thought and Digges' fancy:

> To lodge all four in one bed make a shift
> Until doomsday, for hardly will a fifth
> Between this day and that by fate be slain
> For whom your curtains need be drawn again.

Back to Jonson:

> For if I thought my judgment were of years
> [i.e., would be sufficient to cover the whole history of literature]
> I should commit thee surely with thy peers,
> [your equals, the classical masters below]
> And tell, how far thou didst our Lyly outshine
> Or sporting Kidd, or Marlowe's mighty line.[36]
> And not of course with your three followers.

And then, more ink is washed over the next phrase, which after construing could hardly be clearer: "And though thou hadst small Latin, and less Greek."

It is an obvious untruth to say that "Shakespeare" the playwright was unlearned by Elizabethan standards.[37] The line in effect begins: "And even if (but that is not the case)...." Compare "Though I speak with the tongues of men and of angels [but I do not], ..." as St. Paul tells the Corinthians (I, 8 v.1)].

> From thence to honour thee, I would not seek
> For names: But call forth ...

That is, "I would not seek for examples from that literature, but immediately summon the great writers themselves":

> thund'ring Aeschylus,
> Euripides and Sophocles to us,
> Paccuvius, Accius, him of Cordoba dead [Seneca]
> To life again, to hear thy buskin tread,
> And shake a Stage:
>   [These are his peers with whom Jonson commits him]
> Or, when thy socks were on, [acting]
> Leave thee alone, for the comparison
> Of all, that insolent Greece, or haughty Rome
> Sent forth, or since from their ashes come,
> Triumph, my Britain, thou hast one to show
> To whom all scenes of Europe homage owe.
> He was not of an age, but for all time!
> But stay, I see thee in the Hemisphere
> Advanced, and made a Constellation there!
> Shine forth, thou Star of Poets, and with rage,
> Or influence, chide, or cheer the drooping Stage,
> Which, since thy flight from hence, hath mourned like night,
> And despairs day, but for thy volumes light.

In 1624 Thomas Vicars[38] published a second edition to his *Manual of Rhetoric*, in which he listed the most outstanding English poets. Once again

Shakespeare's name does not appear (and neither does Oxford's). The third edition (1625) contains an amendment in Latin: "istis annumerandos censeo celebrem illum poetam qui a quassatione et hasta nomen habet…," — "To these I believe should be added that famous poet who has his name from 'shaking' and 'spear,' John Davies, and my namesake, the pious and learned poet John Vicars." Here we have a member of the literati clearly establishing that the name the poet used is a pseudonym, a name made up from its parts. The feeble reply to the suggestion that there is a clear reference to a pseudonym is to the effect that "Shakespeare" undivided into its two syllables was too difficult for the writer to render into Latin. Jonson had no problem in his memorial *De Shakespeare Nostrati*, but we can understand that *Shakespurius* might create a difficulty.

In 1627 Michael Drayton wrote to his friend Reynolds a verse letter listing the poets in this order: Surrey, Wyatt, Gascoigne, Churchyard, Spenser, Sidney (taking over from Lyly), Warner, Marlowe, Nash, Daniel, Shakespeare, Jonson, Chapman. Of Shakespeare, he writes:

> and be it said of him,
> Shakespeare, thou had as smooth a comic vein
> Fitting the sock, and in thy natural brain [acting]
> As strong conception and as clear a rage
> As any that trafficked with the stage.[39]

The young John Milton[40] shows no doubts in his epitaph in the 1632 folio:

> Thou in our wonder and astonishment
> Hast built thyself a lasting monument, …
> And so sepulchred in such pomp dost lie
> That kings for such a tomb would wish to die.

An anonymous poem in that folio:

> Spectator: this life's shadow is; to see
> The truer image and a livelier he.
> Turn, Reader. But observe his comic vein
> Laugh, and proceed next to a tragic strain,
> Then weep: So when thou findst two contraries,
> Two different passions from thy rapt soul rise,
> Say (who alone such wonders could)
> Rare Shake-speare to the life thou dost behold.

I.M.S.[41] indicates "Shakespeare's" singularity in the same volume:

> These [the nine muses] jointly woo'd him, envying one another
> (Obeyed by all as spouse, but lov'd as brother)
> And wrought a curious robe of sable grave …

> there run
> Italian works whose thread the sisters spun ...
> [The designs] ... were living drawn
> Not out of common Tiffany or Lawne.
> But fine materials, which the muses know,
> And only know the countries where they grow.

Then we can draw only one deduction from Richard Brome's[42] *The Antipodes* (1638):

> I tell thee that
> These lads can act the Emperors' lives all over
> And Shakespeare's chronicled histories, to boot.
> And were that Caesar, or that English earl, [even if or otherwise]
> That lov'd a Play and Players so well, now living,
> I would not be outvysed in my delight [excelled] [Recto C2 ll. 32–37].

He appears to be distinguishing between Shakespeare and Oxford, but the inclusion of the reference to the virtually buried "English earl" (with no apparent track record for the history plays) is a deliberate pointer to the correct position: they are one and the same. Read: "were that Caesar," that is, "Shakespeare," otherwise "that English earl...."

In 1640 John Benson produced a collection of "Shakespeare's" poems, and again various odes and poems were inserted by way of preface. This extract from an anonymous effort seems to hark back to the proposition that "Shakespeare" was the first ("the age has lost in thee her chiefest tutor") in the revolution era as well as achievement as poet and dramatist:

> Nature herself did her own self admire
> As oft as thou wert pleas-ed to attire
> Her in her native lustre, and confess
> Thy dressing was her chiefest comeliness.
> How can we forget thee, when the age
> Her chiefest tutor, and the widowed stage
> Her only favorite, in thee has lost,
> And nature's self what she did brag of most?

Under a "portrait," a "shadow" of Shakespeare, a poem appears dotted with curious question marks[43]:

> This Shadow is renowned Shakespeare's? Soul of th'age
> The applause? delight? the wonder of the Stage
> Nature herself was proud of his designs
> And joyed to wear the dressing of his lines.
> The learned will Confess, his works are such
>   [there could be another question mark in this line]
> As neither man, nor Muse can praise too much,

> For ever live thy fame, the world to tell:
> Thy like, no age shall ever parallel.

What buries Oxford as the concealed poet-dramatist was not just the death of the generations who knew him or knew of him, but the shutting of the theaters between 1642 and 1660 and the suppression of dramatic art in the period. A new generation sprang up with different demands from and tastes in its theater, and ignorant of its predecessors' concerns. This is reflected in Anthony Wood's references[44] in 1691 to Oxford, the most full being to "an excellent poet and Comedian as several matters of his composition, which were made public, did shew, which I presume are now lost or worn out."

In the eighteenth century, Horace Walpole the critic[45] (1717–97) wrote, "The Earl of Oxford and Dorset (Buckhurst) struck out new lights for drama without making the multitude laugh or weep at the ridiculous representations of Scripture ... we owe ... to the latter two Taste — what do we not owe to [Buckhurst]; our historic plays are allowed to have been found on the heroic narratives in the Mirrour for Magistrates; to that plan and the boldness of Lord Buckhurst's new scenes perhaps we owe Shakespeare." Apart from some references to Oxford the poet and some repeatings of his name taken from Meres and Puttenham, the silence is complete.

So then Oxford is dead, and for three hundred years his reputation is underground. Above ground are the innumerable artifacts of his revolution, waiting for literary archaeologists to rediscover and reanalyze.

In 1642, with the closure of the theaters, the cultural life of England as well as the memory of Oxford was seriously compromised. There was apparently no record of "Shakespeare's" life preserved, and when the Restoration came, William Shakespeare's dates were apparently unknown to Fuller in 1662.[46] Fuller records only his birth town as Stratford-upon-Avon, and that he was "never any scholar." Notwithstanding the latter preserved opinion, his reputation seems hardly to suffer. The marchioness (subsequently duchess) of Newcastle wrote a long letter of praise in 1664:

> Shakespeare's wit and eloquence was general, for, upon all his subjects, he rather wanted subjects for his wit and eloquence to work on, for which he was forced to take some of his plots out of history, where he only took bare designs, the wit and language being all his own; and so much he had above others, that those, who writ after him, were forced to borrow of him, or rather to steal from him.[47]

In the same year Richard Flecknoe in his *Discourse on the English Stage* tells us: "For plays, Shakespeare was one of the first [he does not name any others] who inverted the dramatic style from dull history to quick comedy."[48]

For the most part, apart from technicalities of taste and complaint of unevenness, Dryden is the guardian of the critical reputation and of historical priority. He wrote, "The homogeneous character of Restoration and early eighteenth century criticism has long been recognised. The earlier critics (Dryden, for example) must have been conversant with the conditions of the Elizabethan stage, verbal traditions of which still survived."[49] Dryden records the opinion of Suckling given at court in about 1638 and with him "the greater part of the Courtiers" that Shakespeare should be set "far above Jonson." His own opinions include (my italics):

> So from old Shakespeare's honored dust, this day
> Springs up and buds a new reviving play.
> Shakespeare, who *(taught by none)* did first impart
> To Fletcher wit, to laboring Jonson Art ...
> But Shakespeare's Magic could not copied be;
> Within that circle none durst walk but he ...
>   [Prologue to *The Tempest*, 1667].[50]

To begin then with Shakespeare: he was the man who of all Modern, and perhaps Ancient poets, had the largest and most comprehensive soul ... Shakespeare was the Homer, or father of our dramatic poets; Jonson was the Virgil, the pattern of elaborate writing: I admire him, but I love Shakespeare [*Essay on Dramatick Poesie*, 1668].[51]

And that he who began dramatic poetry amongst us, *untaught by any*, and, as Ben Jonson tells us [did Dryden seriously believe him?], without learning, should by the force of his own genius perform so much, that in a manner that left no praise for any who come after him [Preface to *All for Love*, 1678].[52]

> But spite of all his [the author's, i.e., Dryden himself]
>   pride, a secret shame
> Invades his breast at Shakespeare's sacred name:
> Aw'd when he hears his godlike Romans rage,
> He, in a just despair, would quit the stage
> And to an age less polish'd, more unskill'd,
> Does with disdain the foremost Honors yield
>   [Prologue to *Aurung-Zebe*, 1675].[53]

The actor Betterton acting as the ghost of "Shakespeare" evidences "Shakespeare's" priority:

> *Untaught, unpractis'd,* in a barbarous age,
> I found not, but *created first* the stage ...
>   [Prologue to *Troilus and Cressida*, 1679].

Betterton was employed by Nicholas Rowe, who produced an edition of "Shakespeare's" works in 1709, to go on pilgrimage to Stratford-upon-Avon in search of relics of the author, but without much scholastic profit. Rowe, from a somewhat academic perspective, has criticisms of "Shakespeare," but in no sense attacks his primacy or his priority. Rowe sees the Elizabethan world as little removed from barbarism: "We are to consider him [Shakespeare] as a Man that liv'd in a state of almost universal Licence and Ignorance.... *There is not one play before him of a Reputation* good enough to entitle it to an Appearance in the present Stage." (Emphasis added.) Thus Rowe "did nothing to initiate the enormous task, essential to Shakespearean biography, of reconstructing the historical, cultural, and theatrical context in which the poet lived and worked." At least he did not tear up the established critical opinion of the century since "Shakespeare" ceased to write, that "Shakespeare" was the all-surpassing poet who created the modern theater out of virtually nothing.[54]

However, Rowe's biography of William Shakespeare finally appeared to fix him and "Shakespeare" as the same man, born in Stratford-upon-Avon in 1564 and dying there in 1616. No doubt this was the received opinion in 1709, just as it is in 2009. Even so, there is a woodcut of the comic actor Tarleton who died in 1588, describing him as "one of the first actors in Shakespeare's plays."[55]

One debate concerning "Shakespeare's" academic skills raged. Alexander Pope produced an edition of "Shakespeare" with a biographical and critical preface, following Jonson in his apparent allegation of "want of learning." The biography with minor amendments was mainly lifted from Rowe, which was treated as the basic text right up to 1790 without much in the way of biographical inquiry. As for criticism, Pope in his preface praised his originality and penetrating insights, but said, "His sentiments are not only in general the most pertinent and judicious upon every subject; but by a talent very peculiar, something between penetration and felicity, he hits upon that particular point upon which the bent of each argument turns, and the force of each motive depends. This is perfectly amazing from a man of no education or experience in those great and public scenes of life which are usually the subject of his thoughts." As for primacy in terms of time this is Pope's view:

> If any author deserved the name of an Original, it was Shakespeare. Homer drew not so immediately from the fountains of nature: it proceeded through Egyptian strainers and channels, and came to him not without some tincture of learning or some cast of models of those before him.[56]

It does not matter that Pope was wrong about the "the tincture of learning." He perceives the absence of "the cast of models." He however considered the popularity of Jonson's opinion as it was received ("small Latin, less Greek") as owing much to the popularity among the learned of Jonson's own works.[57]

In 1742 a monument to William Shakespeare was erected in Westminster Abbey, and Pope was one of the four main promoters of this exercise, no

The six signatures of William Shakespeare.

doubt because of his position as chief cultural icon of his generation. The inscription, it is claimed, purports to show that Bacon was the true author, and Pope therefore a supporter of his claims. Since the middle of James I's reign there appears to have been a body of Rosicrucians in England that probably included Bacon: they wished to establish Bacon as "Shakespeare." The Bacon cryptogram appears to be the work of this group: as biography it is quite valueless as are all codes of this type, once the hidden motive or motives of the encryptographers are perceived.[58]

However, the view that "Shakespeare" was academically undistinguished received considerable support from Richard Farmer, whose *Essay on the Learning of Shakespeare* (1767)[59] convinced many (but not Samuel Johnson entirely) that "Shakespeare" lacked skills in classical and modern languages which Farmer demonstrated from his own knowledge of contemporary literature.

But the view of his priority in time was unaffected: even so, consider Samuel Johnson's prologue (spoken by Garrick) for the opening of the Drury Lane Theatre 1747: "When *Learning's* Triumph o'er her barb'rous foes/First reared the stage, immortal Shakespear rose...."

In 1756 Johnson produced an essay, *Proposals for the Printing of the Dramatic Works of William Shakespeare*,[60] from which these extracts (with my italics) are taken:

> Every age has its modes of speech and its cast of thought; which, though easily explained when there are many books to be compared with each other, becomes sometimes unintelligible and always difficult when there are no parallel passages that may conduce to their illustration. Shakespeare is the first considerable author of sublime or familiar dialogue in our language.
>
> The English nation, in the time of Shakespeare, was yet struggling to emerge from barbarity. The philology of Italy had been transplanted hither in the reign of Henry the Eighth; and the learned languages had been successfully cultivated by Lilly [i.e. Lyly the grammarian, thought to be the grandfather of the dramatist/novelist], Linacer and More; by Pole, Cheke and Gardiner; and afterwards by Smith, Clerk, Haddon and Ascham. Greek was now taught to boys in the principal schools; and those who united elegance with learning, read, with great diligence, the Italian and Spanish poets. But literature was confined to professed scholars, or to men and women of high rank.
>
> But the greater part of (Shakespeare's) excellence was the product of his own genius. He found the English stage in a state of utmost rudeness; *no essays in either tragedy or comedy had appeared*, from which it could be discovered to what degree of delight either one or other might be carried. *Neither character nor dialogue was yet understood. Shakespeare may truly be said to have introduced both amongst us*, and in some of his happier scenes to have carried both to the utmost height.
>
> Other writers borrow their characters from preceding writers, and diversify

them only by the accidental appendages of present manners; the dress is a little varied, but the body is the same. *Our author had both matter and form to provide*; for except the characters of Chaucer, to whom I think he is not much indebted, there were *no writers in English,* and perhaps not many in other modern languages, which shewed life in its native colors.

Perhaps it would not be easy to find any author, except Homer, who invented so much as Shakespeare, *who so much advanced the studies which he cultivated,* or effused so much novelty upon his age and country. *The form,* the characters, the language, and the shows *of the English drama are his.* He seems ... to have been the very original ear of our English tragical harmony, that is, the harmony of blank verse.

This however is certain, that he is the first who taught either tragedy or comedy to please, *there being no theatrical piece by any older writer,* of which the name is known, except to antiquaries and collectors of books, which are sought because they are scarce, and would not have been scarce, had they been much esteemed.

To him must we ascribe the praise, unless Spenser may divide it with him, of having first discovered to how much smoothness and harmony the English language could be softened.

Johnson mentions only Gorboduc as a pre–"Shakespeare" play.

"Shakespeare's" cultural triumph was omnipresent. The Garrick celebrations of 1769 of the bicentenary of his birth[61]—five years late and in September—at Stratford are clear evidence of contemporary adulation. Even Garrick, however, injected a note of academic criticism in his oration[62] at the event itself, which some say was probably written for him by his friend Edmund Burke. Following is an extract, emphasis added:

> Shakespeare is, above all others, allowed to be the poet of nature; and is therefore, as an author, he stands highest in the highest class. The beings exhibited by the poet of nature are men: they are not creatures of the imagination, acting from principles by which human actions are never produced, and suffering distress which human beings suffered; but partakers of the same nature as ourselves, to whose hearts our own sensations are a clue.
>
> It was happy for Shakespeare, and for us, that in his time there was no example by the imitation of which he might hope to be approved. He painted nature as it appeared to his own eye, and not from a transcript of what was seen in nature by another. The genius looks not upon nature, but through it; not at the outline only, but the differences, nice and innumerable within it: at all that the variation of tints and the endless combinations of light and shade can express. As the perception is more, more is perceived in the inexhaustible varieties of life.
>
> As there was *no poet to seduce Shakespeare into imitation,* there was no critic to restrain his extravagance; yet we find the force of his own judgment sufficient to rein his imagination, and to reduce to system the new world which he made.

If criticism such as Burke's (if it be his) as to priority in time as well as art is treated as part of a larger biographical survey, it must carry far more value than the defective dating efforts that are found in "Shakespeare's" biographies since the publication of Edmond Malone's *An Attempt to Ascertain the Order in Which the Plays of Shakespeare Were Written* (1778). Malone had one great virtue; as Schoenbaum wrote: "Whether right or wrong, Malone sets forth in every instance the data on which he bases his conclusions. In the case of Henry VIII, for example, the reader is furnished with all the evidence for a later date than Malone's; he is also given Malone's reasons, which he may or may not accept, for rejecting that evidence — but, and this is most important, he is in a position to form his own conclusion. Malone never claims infallibility."[63]

While more recent critics have tinkered with Malone's dating schedule, the question remains. How can we reconcile this dating schedule with its commencing date of (say) 1590, and its acceptance of William Shakespeare as the author, though he was still only twenty-six in 1590, with the clear evidence of the primacy of "Shakespeare" in terms of both date priority, accepted as such, as we have seen, by Ben Jonson (by inference), Dryden, Rowe, and Dr. Johnson, and in effect by Malone himself?

It is instructive to see how Malone copes with the question, and, although he seems to make it appear that it did not trouble him directly, the very fact that his solution is so absolute and direct leads one to suspect that he was well aware of it. As part of his further studies on "Shakespeare," he produced in 1790 his *Historical Account of the English Stage*. He appears to accept "Shakespeare's" cultural primacy, and therefore William Shakespeare's (whom, of course, he does not differentiate from Shakespeare) but also maintains his priority in date. By an astonishing sleight of understanding, he in effect postpones the revolution until 1590. So what does he say of those playwrights, the immediate followers of "Shakespeare" in the revolutionary period 1585 on?

Critics today tell us that Malone was no critic himself[64] and perhaps he took his curious opinion from Rowe (above). On the first page of *The Historical Account of the English Stage*, Malone dismisses as contemptible all plays produced before 1592: "The titles are scarcely known, except to antiquaries; nor is there one of them that will bear a second perusal."[65] It seems curious that a man of his culture and intelligence should dismiss the works which he takes the trouble to list (as evidence for his opinion, according to Schoenbaum) including Peele's *The Arraignment of Paris*, Kidd's *The Spanish Tragedy*, Greene's *Friar Bacon* and *Friar Bungay* and every word that Marlowe wrote. One critic says, "The general contempt for Shakespeare's contemporaries remained: a little earlier Johnson had been quite ignorant of Marlowe and thought [correctly, as it happens] Gorboduc typical of the pre–Shakespearian stage."[66] She cannot be entirely right about this "general contempt": we have seen Edward Phillips on Marlowe on page 75, and Malone's own correspondence presents a different picture. Malone's own listing (which on the face of it contradicts his own thesis), is evidence for knowledge of Marlowe and others.

The suspicion is that Malone was attempting to muddy the waters, and wanted his readers to include Marlowe, Peele, Greene and Kidd among the authors of the "titles ... scarcely known." He apparently believed (or at any rate argued, in order to protect his own chronology) that those authors wrote before "Shakespeare" had begun to write, yet were so inconsequential as not to influence at all their purported successor. This view commanded no support then and none now. Of course their influence would be limited or nonexistent, if they began to write after "Shakespeare" had already begun—which is the case.

Whatever he may have thought, Malone's play-dating has to suggest a dim period for the stage between 1570 and 1590, and "Shakespeare" springs up unheralded (correctly), at a date after that (incorrectly). The new problem is to what works of literature does Malone think were Peacham and Mulcaster and their followers (see Chapter Four) alluding; needing the element of rhetoric supplied by the stage to provide and start the engine of the revolution, the language needed the plays supplied by someone. The others are too late (1585 on); the author can only be "Shakespeare." Malone must have been aware of the development of the language and the import of the opinions of these early critics. Perhaps he (or perhaps his later collaborator, James Boswell the younger) tried to deal with the problem in this way:

> From some words spoken by Polonius in *Hamlet*, I think it probable that there was an English play on *Julius Caesar* before Shakespeare commenced as a writer for the stage. Stephen Gosson in his *Plays Confuted in Five Actions* published about 1582 mentions a play entitled the *History of Caesar and Pompey*.... It should also be remembered that our author has several plays founded on subjects which had been previously treated by others. Of this kind are *King John, Richard II*, 1 *Henry IV*, 2 *Henry IV, Henry V, Richard III, King Lear, Antony and Cleopatra, Measure for Measure, Taming of the Shrew, Merchant of Venice*, and I believe *Timon* and 2 and 3 *Henry VI*, whereas no proof has hitherto been produced that any contemporary writer ever presumed to new-model a story that already employed the pen of Shakespeare.[67]

So "Shakespeare" is branded as a plagiarist on a big scale: a "fact," let alone an unevidenced opinion, that attracted no notice in 1590 or the two following decades, or before Malone's book, with its squid-like fudge above, revealed it. We might as well ignore it, especially as Malone tells us of these earlier plays: "Their titles are scarcely known, except to antiquaries; nor is it one of them that will bear a second perusal," and perhaps poor material for a plagiarist.

Some may find it significant that when Malone came to write the life of William Shakespeare, beginning in 1788, by 1812 when he died he was nowhere near completing it.[68] After 24 years he had only reached the point of William Shakespeare's arrival in London. Perhaps he realized the potential inanity of the exercise. Anyway, he entrusted the completion of it to the younger James Boswell, who duly produced it in 1821. To the critic the life is "in some ways deeply disappointing," and he is scathing on Malone's opinion of "Shakespeare's" relationship to Spenser, which Malone gets dead right, that "Shakespeare" was "duly appreciated by his illustrious and amiable contemporary; who in talents and virtues, more nearly resembled Shakespeare than did any writer of that age; and who, we find, at a very early period of our great poet's dramatic life, had a high and just sense of his transcendent merits."[69] Of the 287 pages Malone completed, 112 were devoted to the Spenser relationship. While he disavowed the obvious connection with *Tears of the Muses*, he agrees that *Aetion in Colin Clout Comes Home Again* (1591, rather early for William Shakespeare to acquire a reputation) is "Shakespeare":

> And there though last not least is Aetion
> Whose muse full of high thoughts invention
> Doth like himself Heroically sound [ll. 444–47].

By 1821, times had changed, and Coleridge, Lamb, Hazlitt and de Quincey had all considered "Shakespeare" as a writer, a poet dramatist rather than just a playwright, and Lamb as early as 1811 extolled the other Elizabethan dramatists.

As to primacy in time, Coleridge[70] was certainly unimpressed with Malone's labors: He is reported by Collier in a diary entry for Sunday, October 13, 1811, in these terms:

> Coleridge was recently asked for his opinion as to the order in which Shakespeare had written his plays. His answer was to this effect, as well as I can remember: that although Malone had collected great many external particulars regarding the age of each play, they were all in Coleridge's mind much less satisfactory than the knowledge to be obtained from the internal evidence. If he were to adopt any theory on the subject, it would rather be physiological and pathological than chronological.

His edited notes for his 1818 series of lectures tell us:

> Various attempts have been made to arrange the plays of Shakespeare each according to its priority in time, the proofs obtained from external documents. How unsuccessful these have been might easily be shown not from the widely differing results arrived at by men, all deeply versed in the black-letter books, old plays, pamphlets, manuscript records and catalogues of that age, but also from the fallacious and unsatisfactory nature of the facts and assumptions on which the evidence rests.

Coleridge tried several times to construct an order, rather than a dating scheme, instancing only the dates of the printings of *Venus and Adonis* (1593), *The Rape of Lucrece* (1594) and *Romeo and Juliet* (1595)—"with no other presumptions than that the poems ... were written many years earlier." He also gives no credit to any influence from Marlowe, Lyly, Greene, Peele or Kidd; he does not even mention them.

Unfortunately there was no contemporary mind to investigate the basic misconception that William Shakespeare of Stratford-upon-Avon wrote the works, and with it the manifest error that the plays must be dated from 1590 on, to fit in with that man's biography.

In James Boswell's completed version of *The Life* he repudiated Malone's stance on the pre–1592 dramatists, the excuse being because Malone had constantly before him the example of "Shakespeare," he undervalued those he would have thought of as his predecessors by date. Malone himself seems to suggest that there were no such predecessors (except apparently those virtually unknown incompetents whose works Shakespeare plagiarized), so to him Marlowe must be a successor in time: after all we have evidence that Malone did know of Marlowe.[71]

So the modern version of the distortion of Shakespeare's biography begins, and with it the defective perception of the development of the English language and culture. To the modern critic there is merely some evolutionary slide from barbarism to Marlowe, and then to William Shakespeare, the devalued version alter ego of Shakespeare. He or she has to dismiss the received critical wisdom of Dryden, Johnson and Coleridge as to the primacy in date of "Shakespeare's" earliest works in return for the fabricated construct of Malone's dating schedule bolted on to William Shakespeare's actual biography.

This distorted "Shakespeare" is made to be in debt to his successors, in particular Marlowe. He has a large portfolio of "sources," who, when the dating of the plays is considered, will be postdated or even eliminated, or who will be shown to have entreated "him fair on a frosty morning," so that, "he will afford ... whole Hamlets, I should say handfuls, of tragical speeches." That critic's confidence that Holinshed, Lodge, Greene, Whetstone, Lyly, Marlowe, Markham, Riche, and so forth may be advanced as those sources, would be impressive were it not misplaced. Nobody of any consequence, in the view of that critic, wrote (or could have written) anything much in any genre worth recording except as examples of the literature of the time period 1575–80—except that summary must be rubbish, because as we have seen Peacham, Mulcaster, Gosson and others tell us something totally different. Elizabethan drama "seems to spring fully formed into existence in the 1580s," writes Wiggins,[72] a statement that is criticizable in logic and in date.

It is possible to illustrate the extreme point of the effect of Malone's distortion from that same critic, the final paragraph of whose book reads:

> Much of this book has been concerned with the defining contents of Shakespeare's plays: they have been shown to be indebted not only to the many ambient literary and theatrical practices of his time but also to specific acts of originality by other playwrights, like Chapman devising the comedy of humors or Marston development of tragic-comedy. The typical effect of such works was to spark off a vogue for commercial imitations of their surface features, like the wave of conqueror plays after Tamburlaine, but also to make fundamental, long-term changes in the kind of drama that could be written. Shakespeare never made that kind of impact on his contemporaries and heirs. He was an enormously successful writer: it is easy to document the commercial popularity and critical acclaim that greeted many of his plays, particularly *Henry IV* Part I, *Hamlet*, *Othello* and *The Winter's Tale* and to show the frequency with which other dramatists drew on his work. But on the whole that work was admired and imitated narrowly, as single plays whose influence is unusually easy to quantify in terms of the specific narrative features which were adopted. Shakespeare did not open new and influential modes of drama in the way that Marlowe and Chapman and Marston had done, enabling later writers to exercise their own creativity with a treasure-house of new source material. In that sense, he was essentially a secondary talent (by which I do not mean a second-rate one): he was a great completer, maximising the potential of other men's inspirations and thereby, perhaps, beautifying himself with their feathers. The plays so adorned, seen in themselves, were among the greatest glories of English drama. Seen as part of the historical process, they were also its curse.[73]

In contrast to this analysis, Schoenbaum credits the historian and critic Henry Hallam with a real perspicacity: "Hallam can only wonder at the unmeasurable chasm separating the indifferent provincial player and the mighty genius who conceived Macbeth and Lear." Hallam laments: "All that insatiable curiosity and unwearied diligence have hitherto detected about [William] Shakespeare serves rather to disappoint and perplex us than to furnish the slightest illustration of his character ... no letter of his writings, no record of his conversation, no character of him drawn with any fullness by a contemporary has been produced."[74]

But Hallam did supply a first glimmer of a way out: "There seems to have been a period in Shakespeare's life when his heart was ill at ease and ill content with the world and his conscience; the memories of hours misspent, the pang of affection misplaced or unrequited, the experience of man's worser nature which intercourse with unworthy associates by choice or circumstance, particularly teaches — these as they sank into the depths of his great mind, seem not only to have inspired in it the conception of Lear and Timon, but of one primary character, the censurer of mankind."[75] Misled by Malone's distortion he misdates the "period of disillusion," and cannot of course link it biographically to William Shakespeare, but it is the study of the plays and their relationship to the later products by lesser writers of the age (and here perhaps Coleridge points the way) which causes the primary undermining doubt of Malone's chronology and with it the identification.

While the distortion is received wisdom in all "orthodox" circles, even recent critics have argued hard to maintain "Shakespeare's" primacy, and to save us from the "modernist"-type mindset. Thus to one,[76] not only is "Shakespeare" a cultural phenomenon, he is "universally judged to be a more adequate representer of the universe of fact than anyone else, before him or since"; Freud "is nothing but belated Shakespeare"; and he denounces the current academic efforts to explain away "Shakespeare's" uniqueness as a white Western cultural conspiracy. Another believes that the moments of major philosophical importance[77] are "the exploration of the ontological status of the imagination in *A Midsummer Night's Dream* and *Antony and Cleopatra* and the analysis of identity and ethical subjectivism in *Troilus and Cressida*. Here indeed Shakespeare, though working with maximum intellectual power, finds no terminus to his thought. He was simply too intelligent to persuade himself that the problems were completely solved, but it would be absurd to conclude that nothing has been achieved; he gets further — much further — than anyone I have ever read. And in his love for the 'just-possible' he scores over and over again, as a dramatist (as distinct from a sage). By this means he joins verisimilitude to wonder."

Here indeed, we find a marvelous perception and review of that wonder-mind Oxford.

Afterword

For valour, is not love a Hercules / Still climbing trees in the Hesperides? / Subtle as sphinx, as sweet and musical, / As bright Apollo's lute, strung with his hair; ... [*Love's Labour's Lost* IV, iii, ll. 316–19].

 I can compare my task to that of a solver of a jigsaw puzzle: the success of my argument depends on whether the life and career of Oxford supply that final piece to complete that puzzle. Its failure will only be demonstrated when a more accurate example is put forward as a candidate for that piece. Particular correlations on which I rely will be criticized and indeed some may be ruled out with new ones added, but the whole picture will need to be discounted along with every piece of evidence and logical conjecture arising from the evidence and accompanying the provision of that alternative candidate backed by superior evidence and superior logic, before the candidature of the Earl of Oxford can be rejected. I am satisfied that this will not be possible: Oxford is the only person with the requisite education, talent, social standing and leisure opportunities, in the right place at the right time.

 Success in completing a jigsaw puzzle depends on method. It is very difficult to do this by taking a piece, however important-looking (and authentic to generations of previous critics), and endeavoring to find its fellows: a better way is to build the frame and select the pieces which can be affixed to the frame. So in Chapters One, Four, and Five I set out the frame for a book on the development of Elizabethan literature with a view to finding more about the relevance of "Shakespeare" to it. The more I read, however, the more it became clear that "Shakespeare's" effect was that of a revolutionary presiding over a revolution. The many pieces identifying Oxford as "Shakespeare" as that leading revolutionary are guaranteed to fit because of the work done to that frame and the other pieces that readily attach to it.

 This book might succeed in convincing some and interesting more: the real measure of any effect will be the extent to which from now on Oxford is considered a serious contender for the pedestal where I place him in relation to the historical framework I have identified. Of course there will be those in this generation of literary critics who will never agree, but the next may well be more sympathetic. Not being a literary critic, how can I do other than stand in awe at (let alone deny) the expertise of our current leaders and their predecessors in that field: my target is the failure of their biographical method. Indeed, frequently I use these critics' own arguments where they lend credibility to Oxford's claim — much more credibility than any which their arguments may be thought to afford to William Shakespeare's alleged authorship.

At the same time the light must be dawning, or the scientific method revealing, that after two hundred years of attempts to find the link between William Shakespeare and the works that bear his name, science should tell them that they never will. "Barring a copy of a business letter to him which may never have been sent, no correspondence, no manuscripts, no record of education, no Church attendance, no diary accounts (his or anyone else's), no record of table talk, and no wonder, then, that the common sense historian Blair Worden is sufficiently bemused by this chronicle of immaculate absenteeism to imagine that, while the relationship between an artist's life and work is always problematic, 'because there is no other writer since the invention of printing for whom we are unable to demonstrate any relationship at all.'"[1] If I demonstrate only the most tenuous relationship between Oxford's life and Shakespeare's work, then I am light-years ahead of anything demonstrated by any of William's admirers.

In putting forward the Earl of Oxford as the chief element of the catalyst for the revolution, I realize that some will reject the argument out of hand. Their problem will arise, not from the exercise of rational criticism, which they may in their own terms exhibit for every page of this book, but in each one's inability to refute the whole basic thesis. The only way to erect a refutation is to provide an alternative better candidate or candidates as the catalyst (or elements for it) for that revolution. Before, therefore, this book reaches the wastepaper basket or vitriol short-circuits the computer keyboard, each critic ought to try to provide the rest of us with such an alternative, or justify his or her attachment to the irrelevant William Shakespeare — which is the same thing.

There can be no doubt that there was a revolution in English literature in the period 1575–80. For many academics perhaps an alien world appears,[2] as they do not recognize Shakespeare/Oxford and that premier position which he occupies, not just in English and world literature and in the process of the triumph of English as the means of communication between peoples on this planet, but in the understanding and revelation of the particular humanity of each one of us. That is the reason the whole question of "Shakespeare's" identity demands a solution, so that we may correctly comprehend and appreciate this marvel of history and the record of his triumph.

I would like this book to be a step in that direction.

APPENDIX A

Tables of Literary References

Contemporary works and references believed to relate to Oxford (in addition to those under the name of "Shakespeare")

A. Plays — Either Anonymous or Otherwise Attributed

Arden of Feversham
Doctor Doddypoll
Edmund Ironside
Edward III
The Famous Victories of Henry V
Harthacanute
Horestes (J. Pykerynge)
No-body and Some-body
Palamon and Arcite 1566 (R. Edwards)
"Palamon and Arsett" 1594
Romeus and Juliet (A. Brooke)
Sir John Oldcastle
Sir Thomas More
Thomas of Woodstock
Three Sisters of Mantua
The Troublesome Reign of King John
The True Tragedy of King Richard III
A Yorkshire Tragedy

B. Other Works

(See note on early Shakespeare poetry, pages 38ff)

An Exposition on the Epistle of St. Paul to the Ephesians
The Fable of Narcissus (T. Hatchett)
Ovid: early translation
Metamorphoses (A. Golding)
A Compendious or Brief Relationship ("W.S")
Theocritus: translation

Excluding references to "Shakespeare" as the pseudonym for Oxford, I list 23 contemporary authors who refer to Oxford covertly in lists C and D below.

C. Pseudonyms or Possible Pseudonymous References of or to Oxford

(In addition to the clear references in 33 Dedications by contemporary authors and the works of Chapman and Southern)

* = derogatory reference

Tables of Literary References 233

Achilles (Harvey)
Adon (T.Edwards)
Apis Lapis (Nashe)
Apollo (Ronsard)
Black Will, George Shakebag (himself)
Boar * (Hatton)
Caesar (Brome, Nashe)
Canaidos (Marston)
Craftie Cuttle (-fish) * (Hall)
Elmond milord of Oxford (Perrucci)
Endymion (Lyly)
English Seneca (Nashe)
English Terence (Davies)
Euphues (Lyly, Nashe)
Labeo * (Hall)
L'autheur de la Lyre (Ronsard)
Lynceus, Lynx (Hall, Jonson, Marston, Nashe)
Maecenas (Nashe)
Melicert (Chettle)
Melicertus — Maximius (Greene)
Mutius (Marston)
Nisus, Laelius, Damides, Archiadas, Musodorus*
  (Harvey: all in one reference)
Pontian (Hall)
Puntarvolo (Jonson)
Roscius (Nashe)
(William) Shakespeare or W.S.
  (many and various)†
Torquato * (Bruno)
Torquatus (Marston)
Vain Delight * (Gascoigne)
Virgil (Jonson), (Lane — as Maro)
Will Monox, William (Nashe)
Willy (Spenser)

† Anon.: *Willobie, His Avisa* (1594) Along with every critic I am totally baffled by the references to "W.S." in it. As it is early in William Shakespeare's career in London, it is unlikely to refer to him. It might well refer to Oxford but I can provide nothing to build up a theory, nor commend any other theory I have read.

D. Anonymous Oxford-Type Characters

Anon — Third Blast: "a noble"; "old ass"
Armin: "my right Honourable, my good Lord, my Master"
Brome: "that English Earl"
Chettle (as Greene): "Johannes fac totum"; "Shake-scene"; "the player magnificently dressed"
Chettle: (the addressee of the apology in *Kind Heart's Dream*)
Gascoigne: "a Noble"
Gosson: "Author"
Hall: (actor-author)
Harvey: (Nashe's) "author," "old ass," "elder friend"
Jonson: "Noble breeder" (of *Two Noble Kinsmen*);
Lyly: "Nobleman"
Riche: (the rider)
Sidney: (author of un-named plays)
Spenser: "sad"; example of a "gentle mind"; "unseemly sorrow"
Vicars: "celebris(em) ille(um) poeta(am) qui a quassatione et hasta nomen habet" ("that famous poet who derives his name from shake and spear")

E. Oxford's Self-Portraits, Caricatures or Role Parallels

Autolycus, Leontes *The Winter's Tale*
Benedick *Much Ado About Nothing*
Berowne *Love's Labours Lost*
Bertram *All's Well That Ends Well*
Black Will and George Shakebag *Arden of Feversham*
Clown *Antony and Cleopatra*

Egeon   *Comedy of Errors*
Hamlet   *Hamlet*
Henry Prince of Wales   *1 Henry IV; Famous Victories*
Jaques and Touchstone   *As You Like It*
Lear   *King Lear*
The lord   *The Taming of the (a) Shrew* (Induction Scenes)
Mercutio   *Romeo and Juliet*
Pericles   *Pericles*
Postumus   *Cymbeline*
Prospero   *The Tempest*
Sir Thomas More and Surrey   *Sir Thomas More*
Timon   *Timon of Athens*
Valentine   *Two Gentlemen of Verona*
Throughout   *Sonnets 1–126*

F. Oxford as Writer Distinguished from William Shakespeare

"Orthodox" opinion tells us that no contemporary of William Shakespeare ever suggested that he was not the author. The following references take it as read (and show the comparison) that Oxford was the author and Shakespeare was not.

	Oxford appears as	*William* appears as
1. Oxford:		
In *Taming of a (the) Shrew*	the Lord	Sly
In *Merry Wives of Windsor*	-	William Page
In *As You Like It*	Jaques/Touchstone	William
In *The Winter's Tale*	Autolycus	Clown
In *Hamlet*	Hamlet	(one of) "many wearing rapiers are afraid of goosequills"
2. Ben Jonson:		
In Everyman Out of His Humour	Puntarvolo	Sogliardo/Sordido
3. In the Parnassus Plays:		
The Return (Part 1)	"Shakespeare"	Gullio
4. Joseph Hall:		
Virgedemarium IV	"crafty cuttle"	"another's name"
5. Michael Drayton:		
Verse letter 1627	The dramatist	(ignored, even though the father-in-law of his doctor)

The caricatures of Oxford could not portray him of a higher rank than a knight: there were so few hereditary peers 1590/1600 that if he had been caricatured as a member of that class, he would have been readily recognized, at the peril of the proponent of the caricature.

APPENDIX B

William Shakespeare: The Irrelevant Life

Any man who believes that William Shakespeare of Stratford wrote Hamlet *or* Lear *is a fool.* — John Bright (d. 1889), radical politician and orator[1]

In a study of Shakespeare's revolution, William Shakespeare (1564–1616) of Stratford-upon-Avon should barely merit a five-line footnote. However, because literary "orthodoxy" persists in giving him pride of somewhat reduced place (compared to that properly due to Oxford/Shakespeare) in the history of English and universal literature, it is necessary to review his role in rather more detail.[2] However comprehensive such review is, he remains devoid of any cultural connection with "Shakespeare,"[3] apart from the use of a version of his name (sometimes hyphenated, sometimes not; when hyphenated, sometimes the second part starts with a capital — Shake-Speare). The proposition that a hyphen in the name denotes the use of it as a pseudonym is sometimes countered by the proffering of examples of other non-pseudonymous hyphenated names. This idea does not refute the original proposition; it merely sets out the battle lines of the contention. Similar debate about the spelling of the name Shakespeare when printed are usually inconclusive, although there are times when the arguments that both the spelling and the hyphenation are just the usual printers' vagaries seem tenuous. Indeed, there are superscript question marks instead of exclamation marks under the portrait in the 1640 edition of the poems (see page 217).

In addition, the comparatively secular attitude of the plays is unlikely to have been mirrored by that of the inhabitants of a small town in the middle of the sixteenth century, all of whom are likely to have been bigots of one sectarian religious persuasion or another. It would be a surprise if any one inhabitant was in accord with the liberal views of the author of "Shakespeare's" plays.

He was baptized on April 26, 1564, at Stratford-upon-Avon.[4] Perhaps because the family was illiterate,[5] nothing is known of his childhood, education or early career. Sometime between late November 1582 and the birth of his daughter Susanna in Mary 1583 he married the child's mother, Anne Hathaway. They had twins in February 1585 named Hamnet and Judith, apparently named after some neighbors, Hamnet and Judith Sadler. Hamnet Shakespeare died in August 1596. Those family details take William Shakespeare up to the age of thirty-two. In addition, his name appears in two sets of local legal proceedings in 1586 and 1587.[6]

A critic writes, "In 1589 (William) Shakespeare was 25 years old, just the right age to apply himself to the stage."[7] So we are to think of him applying himself, say, to *Love's Labour's Lost*, that effete comedy on a dated theme in a style long out of date, and presumably expecting to make a living (see pages 98ff and 123).

By 1596, we are given to understand that William is the leading cultural light of the nation. What is the evidence? There was a grammar school at Stratford, but no evidence exists that William attended. Indeed, with William subsequently failing to ensure any real standard of education for his daughters, one concludes that, along with the vast majority of the population, education was not a primary concern of the Shakespeare family. Great things are claimed for William's unevidenced education at the school. Books have been written extrapolating from generally larger schools what the curriculum might have been for a school serving those who wanted education for their children in a population of, say, fifteen hundred. The proof is in the fruits of that education: only one pupil (not William) went on to either of the universities between the years 1570 and 1610, and that only after attendance at Winchester College, then as now a leading academic establishment for prospective university entrants.[8]

On balance William probably did attend the school, but perhaps only for a short time. The evidence for that opinion is not in the documentation but in the appearances of caricatures of William in contemporary plays. First, in *The Merry Wives of Windsor*, there is William Page in Act IV, scene i, who is tested on his rudimentary Latin skills by his Welsh schoolmaster Sir Hugh Evans. He is reasonably competent with *hic, haec, hoc*, the declension of the Latin pronoun "this," and within the ambit of every second-year child student,[9] but the declension of *qui, quae, quod* (masculine, feminine, "which" or "what" respectively) is beyond him. Evans says, "If you forget your qui's, quaes and your quods [I suspect a vulgarity] you must be preaches [caned]. Go your ways, and play, go" [ll. 71–72]. I believe that this scene should be played by a sub-teenage lout (referred to as a "child")—after all, William is the brother of the juvenile lead Anne Page, and the joke about William's incompetence allied to the interjections by Mistress Quickly must have been hilarious to a frequently caned literate Elizabethan audience, especially when the view of Mrs. Page, William's mother ("He is a better scholar than I thought he was"—l. 75), is taken into account. The point of the scene is that it is dragged in. William plays no part in the development of the plot: he is dragged in to bring to our notice an extraneous element which the playwright wishes us to know: William has culturally not much standing. He is, however, known to the theatrical fraternity, otherwise there would not be much point in lampooning him.

Secondly, we have the appearance of William in the forest in *As You Like It*, Act V, scene i. William's role in the plot is peripheral—he is there to be made a fool of by Touchstone—but although he thinks he is wise and has a pretty wit, he agrees he is not learned, and presumably plays gormless in the light of Touchstone's "You are not ipse, for I am he" speech (see page 188).

The other non-historical Williams in Shakespeare have minimal references, and none of them complimentary: the references in 2 *Henry IV* to William, a law student at Oxford, cousin to Justice Shallow and apparently there at Justice Shallow's expense (III, ii, ll.8-11), and to Will Squele, a Cotswold man, a roisterer cum student lawyer may be enjoyed (*ibid.*, l. 19). William Visor (in a mask?) is an "arrant knave" (*ibid.*, V, i, l. 42).

There are, however, other references in Shakespeare to the clown (i.e., provincial or countryman) type. We will meet the clown and his father in *The Winter's Tale*, and Sly in *The Taming of a* (and *the*) *Shrew*.

The point about these references is that they are mostly extraneous or quite peripheral to the plot; they could most likely be added to the play at any stage. They are all detrimental, mainly to the academic standard reached by the character, showing him and therefore William Shakespeare as totally unequipped to be Shakespeare.[10]

However, by far the most important evidence of William's intellectual attainments is produced by Ben Jonson in his play *Every Man Out of His Humour* (1599). Jonson produces a double caricature in the two brothers Sordido and Sogliardo, a situation reminiscent of the double self-caricature by Oxford of Touchstone and Jaques in *As You Like It*. We will return to this play again and again, but for the moment will concentrate on the educational and cultural sledgehammer hints that these caricatures impart concerning William. Jonson kindly supplies us with program notes in the shape of thumbnail sketches of the characters. Thus Sogliardo:

> an essential clown, brother to Sordido, yet so enamored of the name of gentleman, that he will have it, though he buys it. He comes every term to learn to

> take tobacco, and see new motions [puppet shows]. He is in his kingdom, when in company he may well be laughed at.

And Sordido:

> a wretched hob-nailed chuff, whose recreation is reading of almanacs; and felicity, foul weather. One that never prayed but for a lean dearth, and ever wept in a fat harvest.

On his first appearance in the first scene of the play, Sogliardo refers to himself as "Signor Insulso Sogliardo," "insulso" being the Italian for "gormless."

Commentators accept that the seeking after arms and the rank of gentleman, and the grain speculation are clear digs at William. With an absence of logic they do not take on board the accompanying cultural achievements of the pair as reflecting on William, while Jonson seems to have been very good at being rude intentionally, even if, for the sake of a good picture, his caricatures are soundly based, if heavy-handed. Sogliardo's cultural achievements are limited to an appreciation of puppet shows. His acting reduces the rest of the cast to complete mockery. Sordido can at least read his almanacs — aloud, and probably, a producer might surmise, with the help of his forefinger.

There is a school of commentators that seeks to show that William obtained his education while in the service of a Roman Catholic gentleman in Lancashire, with whom the library of William Campion is deposited, but recent scholarship has shown that the "William Shakeshaft" on which these commentators rely is quite distinct, and that Campion's library was elsewhere.[11]

The question remains: Where did William Shakespeare obtain an education that would make him the playwright of our civilization? Answer: He did not. Equally, there is no evidence that William had access to, let alone possessed any of, that stunning library which the dramatist would need.

One critic believes that William was in fact learned, not in an academic way, but in the way Johnson conjectured for Dryden:

> I rather believe that the knowledge of Dryden was gleaned from accidental intelligence and various conversation, by a quick apprehension, a judicious selection, and a happy memory, a keen appetite of knowledge, and a powerful digestion, by vigilance that permitted nothing to pass without notice, and a habit of reflection that permitted nothing useful to be lost.... I do not suppose that he despised books, or intentionally neglected them; but that he was carried out, by the impetuosity of his genius, to more vivid and speedy instructors; and that his studies were rather desultory and fortuitous than constant and systematical.

This argument might have been even more instructive if this critic had reminded his readers that Dryden spent seven years at university, seven more than William.[12]

There remains a group of critics who think Shakespeare was endowed with such natural genius that he did not need so marvelous an education. Education to a high standard is an absolutely essential element in such a playwright's equipment. Without it he can only aspire to be some "mute, inglorious Milton" lying unworshipped in his graveyard. Where did William, if he were the playwright, obtain Shakespeare's peerless knowledge of law, theology, medicine, astronomy, philosophy, military and naval sciences, history, European geography, botany, literary scholarship, music, classical studies, French, Italian, court life, heraldry, aristocratic pursuits, et cetera?[13] But, as Nicoll wrote, "In the wonder of his genius he was able to grasp in lightning speed what could be obtained only after dull years of work by ordinary minds"; no question of ninety-nine percent perspiration and one percent genius for him.[14]

Before leaving the question of William's academic achievements, we ought to consider the six signatures of his which have come down to us.[15] Compared to his contemporaries', these are astonishingly poor efforts, and they are the only apparent examples (with the exception of the phrase "by me" preceding the last of the six) of his handwriting. Some have supposed that the signatures of a man not quite illiterate, but unfamiliar with the exercise of writing his own name: they even suggest that Aubrey's account (1681) is sufficiently reliable in the matter. Aubrey wrote, "And, if invited to writ, he was in pain"—the classic illiterate's excuse. What Aubrey meant using the past participle as part of the infinitive "to write," we may never know. The modern scholar's penchant for "correcting" Aubrey's grammar by placing the comma between "to" and "writ" seems logical until the context is included: "The more to be admired he was not a company keeper lived in Shoreditch, would not be debauched, and if invited to, writ he was in pain." This seems to indicate that these critics are persuaded that invitations to debauchery in 1600 were in writing on deckled stationery with "RSVP" in the bottom left-hand corner.

All six signatures (especially the last three on the will) date from the period 1612–16, when William may have been ill. Certainly the last one in full, "by me William Shaksper," seems to show that the first three words are written by a more competent hand. In summary the orthodox case for the signatures being those of the playwright, considered in isolation, is very weak, but not quite impossible.

There is a case for saying that the signatory and the writer of Hand D of part of the manuscript of *Sir Thomas More* are the same. On its own the point may be unresolvable, but if one imports the dating and the ambience of the play into the equation, then it is clear that Hand D is merely that of another of Oxford's secretaries taking his dictation (see page 120 and Chapter Six, note 98).[16]

To sum up, if we discount the references in any of the works on the title pages or the dedications to him (which are dealt with in Chapter Five) there is no evidence of William's education, no university, nothing written by, to or about him, let alone anything on cultural matters, and no evidence of books owned or borrowed. Indeed, after 1604, when Oxford died, a number of dubious works, sometimes referred to as Shakespeare's Apocrypha,[17] are attributed to Shakespeare, sometimes using the full name and sometimes by initials: there is no evidence that William ever objected.

For this period, covering the first thirty years or so of William's life, the last word must be that of E.K. Chambers:

> Whatever imprint Shakespeare's Warwickshire contemporaries may have left upon his imagination inevitably eludes us. The main fact is that his early career is still that unexplored hiatus, and who shall say what adventures, material and spiritual, six or eight crowded Elizabethan years [i.e., 1586–94] may have brought him. It is no use guessing. As in so many other historical investigations, after all the careful scrutiny of clues and all the patient balancing of possibilities, the last word of self-respecting scholarship must be that of nescience.

If Chambers had said, "no evidence of relationship, therefore no relationship," it might have been germane. "Self-respecting scholarship" should have decided that there was no link or relevance, however unpalatable that conclusion might be.

In terms of chronological biography we have reached 1592. Two documents are called as evidence of William's progress to cultural stardom, based on a few phrases in them, which under investigation seem to have little relevance: "Upstart crow"; "Supposes he is well able to bombast a blank verse as the best of you"; "The only Shake-scene in a country."

And these, it is contended, refer to William Shakespeare of Stratford-upon-Avon. If (as is the case) they do not, then there is no nexus between him and the works of Shakespeare, and the Stratford biography scenario begins to melt completely. Without the two pieces, called for short *Groatsworth* and *Chettle's Apology*, there are no contemporary complimentary references said to be applicable to William at all, and none of any sort in London before 1594.[18]

On September 3, 1592, the poet and dramatist Robert Greene died. On September 20, a pamphlet entitled Greene's *Groatsworth of Wit Bought with a Million of Repentance* is registered at Stationer's Hall.[19] In outline of the relevant part, it is a plea to three dramatists not to give employment to actors and in particular to an "upstart crow" with a "tiger's heart."

On December 8, 1592, Chettle registered *Kind-Heart's Dream* which contains a fulsome yet elegant apology to one of the three dramatists.

Some contend that Chettle wrote both pamphlets, and they have at least five good reasons for saying so:

1. *Groatsworth* is a prolix diatribe and scarcely reeks of deathbed repentance. It may be contrasted with the genuine article in fact written by Greene[20]:

> Sweet wife, as ever there was any good will or friendship between thee and me, see this bearer (my host) satisfied of his debt: I owe him ten pound, and but for him would have perished in the streets. Forget and forgive my wrongs done unto thee, Almighty God have mercy on my soul. Farewell till we meet in heaven, for on earth, thou shalt never see me more.
>
> This 2nd day of September 1592. Written by thy dying husband, Robert Greene.

2. Over thirty years ago computer tests established that the pamphlets were by the same author, namely Chettle.[21] While these remain quite widely accepted they are under substantial challenge, and it may be that Chettle only made certain amendments and insertions.

3. The reference to Greene's son Fortunatus as the son of his wife and himself is distorted.[22] Fortunatus was another woman's son of whom Greene/Chettle writes, addressing Greene's wife, "in whose face regard not the father so much as thy own perfections," an insult to a childless widow by an ignorant author. Greene's genuine letter to his wife is much more sensitive and does not mention the son who was apparently anyway in the care of his mother.

4. Nashe, almost certainly the second dramatist listed in *Groatsworth*, denounced it as a "scald trivial lying pamphlet," as he clearly agreed with the suggestion that Greene was not the author. I will come to why Nashe might be worried that someone might think that he (Nashe) was.

5. Chettle admits that the printer typeset *Groatsworth* from Chettle's own manuscript,[23] which he implies was only a fair copy of what Greene originally wrote.

So who was Chettle? He was a London-born apprentice stationer who became a partner in a printing firm in 1591. Although he later became a prolific playwright (usually in collaboration with other authors), these two pamphlets were his first literary efforts.[24] This I believe is an important consideration, because if Chettle had had more knowledge and experience, he would not have made the mistakes he did in *Groatsworth*.

The heading of the relevant portion of *Groatsworth* is: "To those gentlemen, his quondam acquaintance, that spend their time in making plays R.G. wisheth a better exercise and wisdom to prevent his extremities." We will come back to the phrase "his quondam acquaintance."

Next, three playwrights are addressed.

First, Marlowe: "Wonder not (for with thee will I first begin), thou famous gracer of tragedians, that Greene, who hath said with thee (like the fool in his heart) 'There is no God,' should now give glory unto his greatness. For penetrating is His power..." and so forth. The address continues at length with a naive and un–Greene-like attempt to warn the atheistic, sophisticated Marlowe.

Secondly, Nashe: "With thee [Marlowe] I join young Juvenal [Nashe], that biting satirist that lastly with me together writ a comedy...." Chettle is probably wrong again here: no trace or reference to a joint work by Greene and Nashe can be found. "Sweet boy, might I advise thee, be advised; and get not many enemies by bitter words..." and so on. Nashe is advised to choose his targets carefully and not to be outspoken.

Thirdly, Oxford the real Shakespeare (as I will show): "And thou, no less deserving than the other two, in some things rarer, in nothing inferior; driven (as myself) to extreme shifts; a little I have to say to thee. And were it not an idolatorous oath, I would swear by sweet Saint George[25] thou art unworthy better hap, sith thou dependest on so mean a stay." The writer appears not to know very much about this dramatist notwithstanding his/Greene's "quondam acquaintance."

"Base-minded men, all three of you, if by my misery, ye be not warned," continues Chettle, but I will stop there to consider what was the nature of the offense committed against the playwrights by these descriptions.

Marlowe's atheism was common knowledge, and attempts to convert him could hardly be offensive. Chettle even has the cheek to suggest that he did edit "Greene's" remarks about Marlowe in *Kind-Heart's Dream* (see below) and should have done the same to the references to the other playwrights, in an attempt to lend verisimilitude to an otherwise unimpressive scenario. Later in the pamphlet, he repeats his claim of defective editing which only draws further attention to his problem.

Of Nashe there is nothing objectionable and nothing to edit.

Of Oxford, apart from a reference to financial insecurity,[26] and an apparent ignorant comparison, there is nothing. The Shakespearean adjective "base-minded"[27] is conditionally applied only if the advice is ignored.

No apology of any substance to any of the dramatists, let alone anything to edit, appears on the face of it to be necessary. Nevertheless Chettle wrote in *Kind-Heart's Dream*:

> About three months since died M. Robert Greene leaving many papers in sundry book sellers hands amongst other his "Groatsworth of Wit," and which a letter is written to divers play-makers, is offensively by one or two of them taken: and because of the dead they cannot be avenged, they willfully forge in their conceit a living author ... [i.e., himself, who has written nothing previously published which survives] and after tossing it to and fro no remedy, but it must light on me. With neither of them that take offence was I acquainted.... [So much for "Greene's" "quondam acquaintance"; this is a confession of ignorance about the complaining playwrights] and with one of them I care not if I never be.

This could be Nashe whose description of Groatsworth (point 4 above) may well have hurt Chettle — and see another possible reason below.

> The other whom at that time I did not so much spare, as since I wish I had for I have moderated the heat of living writers and might have used my own discretion (especially in such a case) the author being dead, that I did not, I am sorry as if the original fault had been my fault.

This approaches an admission and certainly provides internal evidence (because of the absence of the need to edit) that Chettle did write *Groatsworth* and what he wrote in it was offensive to the playwright, even though that offensive bit is not specifically linked to the playwright, as I show above. The playwright was sufficiently important and powerful to have to be apologized to in fulsome terms.

Back to *Groatsworth*; there follows "Greene's" warning about actors:

> ... for unto none of you (like me) sought those burrs to cleave: those puppets (I mean) that spake from our mouths those Antics garnished in our colours: is it not strange that I, to whom they have all been beholding; is it not like that you, to who they have all been beholding shall (were ye in that case as I am now) be both at once of them forsaken? Yes trust them not; ...

Now comes the offensive passage:

> ... for there is an upstart crow, beautified with our feathers, that, with his tiger's heart ...

If an upstart crow really is an upstart crow, he would be flattered to be characterized as having a tiger's heart. As the metaphorical converse is applicable, Oxford might well be mightily offended.

> ... wrapped in a player's hide ...

The famous parody from *Henry VI* Part 3 ("O tiger's heart wrapped in a woman's hide" I, iv, l. 38): it is ludicrous to suggest that a knowing writer (unlike Chettle) would parody the words of the play's author to denounce that same author as an actor who thinks he can write plays.[28] This is further evidence of Chettle's ignorance of the true circumstances.

> ... supposes that he is as well able to bombast out a blank verse as the best of you.

This (and particularly the word "supposes") would be very offensive as the actor is as good (and more) a dramatist as the three addressed in *Groatsworth*. Shakespeare and Marlowe[29] were the only actors at the time who were also writing plays.

> ... and, being an absolute Johannes fac totum, is, in his own conceit, the only Shake-scene in a country.

In other words, he thinks himself not only a class playwright, but able to play all parts and the only first rank actor about — which was of course accurate, but in the way expressed and joined with the earlier suggestions must have been highly obnoxious. "Shake-scene" is clearly a cut at someone called, or known as, Shake-speare, but who is meant? Certainly not William, of whom there is no trace in the period 1586–94 in London, let alone any public record of him as an actor and/or dramatist, to attract such an attack: nevertheless his putative rise to star and impresario is based on that half-word and nothing else. The only other "Shake..." is Oxford, who after his illness (suggested in Chapter Seven) may have only recently returned to the stage.

Groatsworth finishes with a plea to the playwrights not to write anymore and to let the actors act only in old plays which would cut off the playwrights' income at the same time.

What does Chettle in his apology *Kind-Heart's Dream* say to the actor? On the face of it, not a word. Still addressing the playwright, he writes a full, well-mannered and ingratiating apology:

> I am sorry as if the original fault had been my fault, because my self hath seen his demeanour no less civil than he excellent in the quality he professes [i.e., his acting]: besides divers of worship have reported his uprightness of dealing, which argues his honesty and his facetious [urbane or polished, as the Latin] grace in writing that approves his art [i.e., that justifies, puts the seal of approval, on his art].

The skill of the dramatist justifies and puts the seal of approval on the dramatist's own art of acting, a vocation that certainly would not otherwise receive such approval. This slightly concealed reference to acting might be thought sufficient to mollify the actor/writer. The playwright being apologized to in such elegant terms has to be the actor who has been insulted for his acting and for his playwriting. In effect, Chettle is confessing again that when he wrote *Groatsworth* he was not in the know. There is sufficient independent evidence, first for the playwriting, and secondly for the acting. Shakespeare was the only remaining actor (with Marlowe not relevant, having been disposed of earlier) with a playwriting track record at the time; he must be Chettle's third playwright and the actor. There is no contemporary evidence of either activity for William. Before 1593 nothing had been published under the name of William Shakespeare. Had William been the dramatist there would be no reason to omit identification of him, as there was no social or other need to conceal his authorship, and of course, no question of apologizing to a person of his social status in the terms used by Chettle. There is thus no realistic candidate for the identification except Oxford; he alone provides a reason for requiring anonymity/pseudonymity, as we have examined in Chapter Seven, and attracts an apology of such fulsomeness.

Nashe would be seriously concerned that Oxford might think he, Nashe, was the author of *Groatsworth*. At some time he may have been supported by Oxford, and would wish to abjure responsibility for *Groatsworth*.

I note also that, as long ago as 1907, Sir Walter Raleigh (the critic, died 1922) drew attention to an earlier passage in *Groatsworth*. I cannot do better than quote in full his summary:

> Greene, in his Groatsworth of Wit, tells how he was first invited to write for the stage. A player, magnificently dressed, like a gentleman of great living, overheard him repeating some verses, and offered him lodging and employment. The player, by his own account, was both actor and dramatic author. Besides playing the king of the Fairies, he had borne a part in The Twelve Labours of Hercules, and in a piece called The Devil on the Highway to Heaven. His own works were Morality plays, suitable for country audiences; the two that he mentions were entitled The Moral of Man's Wit and The Dialogue of Dives. But these educational plays, he said, had fallen out of esteem and there was room for the newer inventions of a scholar. Greene went along with him.[30]

Of course, in 1907 Raleigh did not have the benefit of the computer; but his apparent lack of interest in "the player magnificently dressed" who also wrote plays ought to be noted, as at least the other remaining Chettle authorship reasons were available to him. Unconsciously Raleigh provides a sixth reason. Either Chettle had learned directly of Greene about this player/author or some third party had fed Chettle with a version of the player/author's modest achievements. Greene (or this third party) was deliberately pulling Chettle's leg. Perhaps Chettle is also apologizing in *Kind-Heart's Dream* for publishing the suggestion that Oxford (for surely the anonymous man is he — he would be in funds at the beginning of Greene's career to be magnificently dressed) acted only in minor parts and his own works were only morality plays suitable for country audiences. Unless Chettle invented the conversation himself (unlikely), the joke must have been on him for buying that version. If Nashe had fed Chettle the story (which would certainly seem to have Nashist symptoms) this would embarrass and antagonize Chettle even further and provide good reason for his wish to deny his original acquaintanceship with Nashe, let alone a desire to acquire it.

This explanation is put forward as it seems to cover all the possible scenarios needed to explain the two passages: it might be instructive to run through all the others, but criticisms of these explanations generally seem too strong for the theses put forward.

Generally critics fail to examine what is actually written. The problem that they cannot resolve is that the original insult in *Groatsworth* is to a Johnny-come-lately actor (Oxford on his return to the stage after his nervous breakdown, suggested in Chapter Seven) and the groveling apology in *Kind-Heart's Dream* is to a well-established playwright who acts as well (and we know who that is). Certainly the language would be over-the-top if addressed to a provincial actor of any standing. Only Chambers realized the basic problem. He stated that Chettle was responsible for some looseness of language. David Kathman, the "orthodox" campaigner,[31] defends Chambers and accuses his opponents of strict literalness — that terrible defect of all Oxfordian arguments. There are no examples in *Kind-Heart's Dream* or for that matter *Groatsworth* where Chettle the professional editor employs loose language. Dr. Kathman also points out that *Groatsworth* goes on to mention two other playwrights (before reverting to the original three) and tries to suggest that *Kind-Heart's Dream* could be addressed to one of them, but this does not cure the basic problem recognized by Chambers.

As "orthodoxy" maintains that Greene wrote *Groatsworth* it is saddled with these tortured arguments, in an attempt to reconcile and make sense of the two pamphlets taken together and to force a reference to William into them. Every word in Elizabethan English is a piece of evidence and thus must have some significance, and the simplest solution to any interpretation difficulties is likely to be the right one. A literal solution taking into consideration all the facts we know about Greene and Chettle and using all the phrases presents much the strongest arguments for Oxford the actor/dramatist as the protagonist in both *Groatsworth* and *Kind-Heart's Dream*. *Groatsworth* is "obscure in the best Elizabethan tradition" and, say the critics, "we cannot but wish it had never been discovered."[32] Not everybody has such problems.

Nobody knows why William Shakespeare came to London or what his family circumstances were back at Stratford.[33] However, he was presumably helping his father in the business of whittawer, stripping rotting flesh off the skins off dead sheep, and then we are assured that "from the very beginning he brought from Stratford a delicate nose, which found the effluvia of London, human or otherwise, highly distasteful."

Sometime in the 1590s he became quite suddenly well-off. The cause is mysterious — some have even suggested the proceeds of crime[34] — but a slightly more innocent explanation comes from Ben Jonson and his caricature Sogliardo in *Every Man Out of His Humour* (1599). Sogliardo's first words in the play are: "Nay, look you, Carlo; this is my humor now! I have lands and money, my friends left me well, and I will be a gentleman whatsoever it cost me." It is worth pointing out that this happy state is not attained through family inheritance, or the sweat of his brow, or business acumen, crime or artifice, but as a result of direct gifts in unrevealed circumstances. By this time William had already purchased New Place back in Stratford.

There is clearly a direct link with the theater, and I think William, either through sheer luck[35] or possibly because he had heard of the successful playwright Shakespeare, came to London at precisely the moment he was needed as a cover for the real Shakespeare, who in 1593 had just published *Venus and Adonis* and *The Rape of Lucrece*. For this service, whatever it was, he seems to have received a substantial payment, and/or a share in Shakespeare's theatrical company. He does not appear to have done any actual acting (see below). The putative arrangement and the reason for being required as a cover are considered in Chapter Seven.

So the first mention of William in London is not directly in a document, but by way of caricature, this time in the play *The Taming of a Shrew*.[36] This play was produced and published in 1594. It was probably written in about 1579, and the 1594 version is probably only a rewrite. The 1623 folio contains the sophisticated final version, *The Taming of the Shrew*. The 1594 folio does, however, incorporate the fuller Induction scenes, whereby Christopher Sly (William's alter ego) is rescued by the Lord (Oxford) and his retainers, and endowed by all the poet's expertise with all the attribute of lordship, including the enjoyment of his treasures (an allegory for the canon). This provides the answer to the critic who wondered "Why does the poet lavish such lyrical beauty on this queer theme?"[37] In the 1594 version, there are interruptions by Sly to the play, one of which gives too much away as to the identity of the real Shakespeare ("Vary" is close to Vere, and probably even closer when spoken aloud in 1594):

> (Bianca wishes characters sent to jail)
> SLY: I say we'll have no sending to prison.
> LORD: My lord, this is but the play. They're but jest.
> SLY: I'll tell thee, Sim, we'll have no sending to prison, that's flat. Why, Sim, am I not Don Christo Vary? Therefore I say they shall not go to prison [Induction C, ll. 3–5].[38]

In the later version this scene and the scene at the end, where Sly is returned to the gutter, are cut. This sounds as if the Oxford was leaned on, but he took a subtle revenge in deleting the last scene, because it leaves the sleeping Sly onstage, in charge of all the Lord's riches, thus giving the answer to the critic's question. In effect William becomes the keeper of the "Shakespeare" treasure.

Perdita presents the same allegory in *A Winter's Tale*, where the Clown and his father the Old Shepherd suffer the playwright's ridicule, but this time they play a fuller role in the plot: they rescue the baby Perdita (Latin for "she who has been lost," i.e., the canon) and bring her up. The Old Shepherd's first speech contains unmistakable family allusions:

> I would there were no age between ten and three and twenty, or that youth would sleep out the rest, for there is nothing (in the between) but getting wenches with child, wronging the ancientry, stealing, fighting [III, iii, ll. 57–61].

This would seem as apt a description of William's career up to the age of twenty-three, in 1587, as any, with its authentication of his alleged problems with Sir Thomas Lucy over poaching. (I say "alleged" as there is considerable scholarly debate over them.[39])

When all is revealed and the sixteen-year-old Perdita is reunited with her parents, the Clown and his father are rewarded and wickedly lampooned in Act V, scene ii. Autolycus is portrayed as a run-down ex-courtier (as Oxford would see himself) living on the fringes of society, who in an earlier scene picks the Clown's pocket — an allegory, I suggest, of the collection by the playwright from William of local Stratford "colour" as required by *A/The Taming of The Shrew* induction scenes and the education scene in *The Merry Wives of Windsor*. The scene runs:

> Here come those who I have done good to against *my will* (now read that again — we are being told something relevant), and already appear in the blossoms of their fortune.
> OLD SHEPHERD: Come boy: I am past more children, but thy sons and daughters will all be gentlemen born.
> CLOWN (to Autolycus): You are well met, sir: you denied to fight with me the other day because I was no gentleman born. See you these clothes? Say you see them not, and think me still no gentleman born. You were be best say these robes were not gentleman born. Give me the lie, do, and try whether I am not now a gentleman born.
> AUTOLYCUS: I know you are now a gentleman born.
> CLOWN: Ay, and have been so anytime these last four hours.
> OLD SHEPHERD: And so have I, boy.
> CLOWN: So you have, but I was a gentleman born before my father, for the King's son took me by the hand and called me brother: and then the two kings called my father brother; then the Prince my brother. and the Princess my sister called my father father; and so we wept; and these were the first gentlemanlike tears that we ever shed.
> OLD SHEPHERD: We may live, son to shed many more.
> CLOWN: Ay, or else 'twere hard luck being in so preposterous estate as we are [ll. 123–146].

The reference to the Old Shepherd would seem to date the rewriting of this scene the play to after 1596 when, at William's insistence, his father, John Shakespeare, applied for, initially unsuccessfully, a coat of arms, and his death in 1601. William would on his father's death inherit the arms, and would therefore be more highly rated than his arriviste father, the original grantee. Very subtly the playwright has incorporated a farcical allusion to the prospective superior status of the son ("gentleman ... before my father").

This leads us naturally to consider the grant, apparently on a second application — the first having failed in 1596 — of the coat of arms itself, with which Diana Price deals fully in her book. The silver falcon crest is taken from the Earl of Southampton, and may be an attempt to link the owner with the Earl of Southampton the dedicatee of *Venus and Adonis*.[40] The falcon[41] is shown before flight, known in falconry as "shaking"; that and the golden spear in its claw give out a punning "shake-spear." Gold is the color of aristocratic and military achievement, neither of which is evidenced in anything known of William's antecedents. It looks as though the herald at first intended to refuse the application, for the first version has the superscription in lowercase, "non, sanz droict" ("No, without right"), written twice and twice crossed out, and then replaced by "NON SANZ DROICT" in capitals without a comma, meaning "Not without right," William's slightly downplayed motto. William (on behalf of his father) tried in 1599 to combine the arms by exemplification with the arms of the Arden, a family of Warwickshire gentry, as Arden was his mother's maiden name. She does not appear (at best) to have been a close relative, and the application appears not to have been pursued. The behavior of Sir William Dethick, garter king of arms, subsequently came under review in respect of some twenty-three "mean persons" to whom he had granted arms. The name "Shakespeare" comes fourth in the list. Although William's only son had died in 1596, there was no reason to believe that in 1600 that the great name would not survive for more generations, as William's three younger brothers were still alive. In point of fact, all three predeceased William, without descendants.

The grant of arms to the Shakespeare family name attracted the attention of young Ben Jonson and comes in for a merciless hammering in *Every Man Out of His Humour* (1599):

> SOGLIARDO [as we have seen, one of the caricatures of William]: By this parchment, gentlemen, I have so toiled among the harrots [rustic for heralds] yonder, you will not believe! they do speak the strangest language, and give a man the hardest terms for his money, that ever you knew [especially if Sir William required something extra, which caused him to re-punctuate his French as shown in the previous paragraph].

CARLO [a man about town]: But have you arms, have you arms?

SOGLIARDO: I 'faith I thank them: I can write myself gentleman now; here's my patent, it cost me thirty pound by this breath.

PUNTARVOLO [a caricature of Oxford as Shakespeare the playwright[42]]: A very fair coat, well charged, and full of armory.

SOGLIARDO: Nay, it has much variety of colors in it, as you have seen a coat have, how like you the crest, sir?

PUNTARVOLO: I understand it not well, what is't?

SOGLIARDO: Marry, sir, it is your boar [in fact the crest of Oxford] without a head rampant. A boar without a head, that's very rare!

CARLO: Ay, and rampant, too! troth, I commend the herald's wit, he hath deciphered him well: a swine without a head, without brain, wit, anything indeed, ramping to gentility.[43] You can blazon the rest, signior, can you not?

SOGLIARDO: Oh, ay, I have it here in writing of purpose, it cost me two shillings the tricking.

CARLO: Let's hear, let's hear.

PUNTARVOLO: It is the most vile, foolish absurd, palpable and ridiculous escutcheon that ever this eye survised.

CARLO: Silence, good Knight: on, on.

SOGLIARDO [reads the heraldic description, which justifies Puntarvolo's critique]

CARLO: Slud, it is a hog's cheek and puddings on a pewter field, this [i.e., pig's cheek and black puddings on a pewter plate].

SOGLIARDO: How like you them, signior?

PUNTARVOLO: Let the word be "Not without mustard"[44]; your crest is very rare, sir.

CARLO: A frying pan to the crest, had had no fellow.

While it may be that after the success of *Every Man in His Humour*, his first play (1598), he may have been put up to writing *Every Man Out of His Humour* by Oxford or his admirers, we must be reminded that Jonson was a young playwright, making vicious fun at the expense of William, the company's allegedly all-important playwright, actor and impresario, who presumably would, if it were so, have power of life or death over at least his career. Jonson took an extraordinary step to preserve his own copyright (again, perhaps encouraged by Oxford). One biography states, "A printer named William Holmes entered *Every Man Out of His Humour* in the Stationers' Register on April 8, 1600. Jonson's sale of his manuscript to Holmes was highly unorthodox. Elizabethan playwrights normally transferred exclusive control over their manuscripts to the acting companies that purchased them."[45] Jonson seems to have retained control, if only to prevent rewriting favorable to William Shakespeare. As for William's interest in the play, "In the third folio of the play (1616, which dates the play to 1599) the players listed are 'R. Burbage, John Hemmings, Aug Phillips, Hen Condell, Will Sly and Tho Pope.' (William) Shakespeare evidently stood aside.'"[46]

Shakespeare's own mockery opens *The Merry Wives of Windsor* (and this passage started life at a cut at the comparatively recently ennobled Dudley family instanced by Leicester and his nephew Sidney):

> SHALLOW: Sir Hugh, persuade me not. I will make a Star Chamber matter of it. If he were twenty Sir John Falstaffs, he shall not abuse Robert Shallow, Esquire.
> SLENDER: In the county of Gloucester, Justice of the Peace and Coram.
> SHALLOW: Ay, cousin Slender, and Custalorum.[47]
> SLENDER: Ay, and Ratalorum, too; and a gentleman born, Master Parson, who writes himself "Armigero" in any bill, warrant, quittance, or obligation: "Armigero."
> SHALLOW: Ay, that I do, and have done any time these last three hundred years.
> SLENDER: All his successors gone before him hath done't, and all his ancestors that come after him may [I, i, ll. 1–13].

So what was William's career in London? There is a record of a loan in 1592 to a farmer in Bedfordshire of seven pounds by "Willelmus Shackspere," and of action taken eight years later to recover it. This seems to relate to another William Shakespeare. William of Stratford would never have delayed so long.[48]

William was not above consorting with low life: in 1596 a writ was issued against him and others to keep the peace.[49]

In 1597 "William Shakspere" was listed as owing taxes for the taxable period 1593–97 subsidy in Bishopsgate, but cannot be traced. In 1598 and 1600 he is listed as delinquent again. These records are backed by Jonson's reference to Sogliardo in *Every Man Out of His Humour*: "He comes up every term to learn to take tobacco, and to see new motions [puppet shows]." In other words William was never a permanent resident in London.[50]

In 1600 John Lane[51] produced a poem of a hundred and twenty-six line stanzas comparing William to Batillus, who claimed to be writing Virgil before he was exposed:

> Like to Batillus, every ballet-maker
> That never climbed unto Parnassus mount
> Will so incroach that he will be partaker,
> To drink with Maro at the Castale fount [Virgil][52]
> Yea more than this to wear a laurel crown
> By penning new gigges for a country clowne.

That is, William Shakespeare the pseudo-poet encroaches to write with Oxford, and, worse, Oxford writes for him the "country clown," so he William can claim "a laurel crown."

In 1602, John Manningham,[53] a barrister, recalls in his diary an incident that perhaps occurred some years earlier:

> Upon a time when Burbage played Richard III there was a citizen who grew so far in liking with him that before she went from the play she appointed him to come that night unto her by the name Richard the Third. Shakespeare, overhearing their conclusion, went before and was entertained, and at his game ere Burbage came. The message being brought that Richard the Third was at the door, Shakespeare caused return to be made that William the Conqueror was before Richard the Third. Shakespeare's name was William.

Earlier indications from the diary indicate that Manningham, who was something of a theater buff, did not connect the plays with "Shakespeare" and had to remind himself that the Christian name of the great actor/dramatist and impresario was "William," and to tell the world that by "Shakespeare" he meant the now absent William, back in Stratford-upon-Avon.

Nothing further is heard of him residing or visiting London until 1604. While Sogliardo may have made him a laughingstock, his brother caricature Sordido may have put him in physical danger. The three previous summers up to 1599 had seen poor harvests, and the government took steps against hoarders and speculators by collecting a list of amounts held.[54] In Stratford, William was the second-largest holder of ten quarters, or two and a half tons, of corn or "malte" (barley). A quarter is usually 28 pounds weight, or a quarter of a hundredweight; but when grain is weighed it is a fraction measurement of a ton. Stratford itself was in uproar, and starving men were complaining in no uncertain terms. One "hoped within a week to lead some of them in a halter, meaning the maltsters," and a local weaver trusted "to see them hanged on gibbets at their own doors."

That, however, is only the half of it. In a scene in Act I of the play, Sordido's servant brings him a government precept:

> Here's a device
> To charge me bring my grain unto the markets;
> Ay, much! when I have neither barn or garner,
> Nor earth to hide it in, I'll bring 't: till then,
> Each corn I send shall be as big as St. Paul's
> O, but (say some) the poor are like to starve.
> Why, let 'em starve, what's that to me? are bees
> Bound to keep life in drones and idle moths? no;
> Why such are these that term themselves the poor,
> Only because they would be pitied,
> But are indeed a sort of lazy beggars,
> Licentious rogues, and sturdy vagabonds,
> Bred by the sloth of a fat plenteous year,
> Like snakes in heat of summer, out of dung;
> And this is all that these cheap times are good for;
> Whereas a wholesome and penurious dearth
> Purges the soil of such vile excrements,
> And kills the vipers up.

SERVANT: O, but master,
    Take heed they hear you not.
SORDIDO: Why so?
SERVANT: They will exclaim against you.
SORDIDO: Ay, their exclaims
    Move me as much, as thy breath moves a mountain
    [a Shakespearean thought![55]]
    Poor worms, they hiss at me while I at home
    Can be contented to applaud myself,
    To sit and clap my hands, and laugh, and leap,
    Knocking my head against my roof, with joy
    To see how plump my bags are, and my barns.
    Sirrah go hie you home, and bid your fellows
    Get all their flails ready again I come.
SERVANT: I will, sir.
SORDIDO: I'll instantly set all my hinds to thrashing
    Of a whole rick of corn, which I will hide
    Under the ground: And with the straw thereof
    I'll stuff the outside of my mows:
    That done, I'll have them empty all my garners,
    And in the friendly earth bury my store,
    That when the searchers come, they may suppose
    All's spent, and that my fortune were belied. [misrepresented]
    And to lend more opinion to my want,
    And stop that many-mouthed vulgar dog,
    Which else would be baying at my door,
    Each market day I will be seen to buy
    Part of the purest wheat for my household;
    Where when it comes, it shall increase my heaps:
    'Twill yield me treble gain at this dear time
    Promised in this dear book: I have cast all. [his almanac]
    Till then I will not sell an ear, I'll hang first.
    O, I shall make my prices as I list;
    My house and I can feed on peas and barley.
    What though a world of wretches starve the while;
    He that will thrive must think no courses vile.

    In the role of chorus, as it were, another character describes Sordido as a "wolf in the commonwealth"[56]; "wolves" is in the phrase used by the Privy Council in considering its order. With this detailed description of the cheating and exploitation that William was thought at least capable of, being or about to be declaimed on the public stage and with the possibility that William might be readily identified, even if only a small part of the allegations were true, he is clearly in peril, so what is he to do? As he is not heard of again in London till 1604, it is reasonable to suppose that he decamped to Stratford, where no one would know of the play and the possibility of being lynched would disappear if the fraud exposed by Jonson remained unexposed there. Then Oxford/Shakespeare seems to note his absence: In *Hamlet*, Rosencrantz tells us:

> But here is sir an eyrie of children little eyases that cry out on the top of question and are most tyrannically clapped for 't. They are now the fashion and so berattle the common stages — so they call them — that many with rapiers [e.g., William the ersatz gentleman] are afraid of goose quills and dare scarce come thither [II, ii, ll. 340–45].

So we must now consider what William did during his stays in London. We note that he is not on the list of actors given license to tour in 1594. The treasury to the court chamber's accounts in 1595 records the payment of twenty pounds to "Will Kempe, Will Shakespeare & Richard Burbage servants to the Lord Chamb(er)lain for two several comedies or interludes shewed by them before her Ma(jesty) ... upon St. Stephens day and Innocents day [December 27 and 28, 1594]." Precisely who is meant by "Will Shakespeare" is not clear. There is another problem with the record. As we have seen, the treasurer to the chamber responsible for the accounts at the time was Sir Thomas Heneage, who died on October 17, 1595, leaving his widow with the accounts in a mess. The queen became involved: she wrote asking for the widow to account for the balance: at death he held £1,314 15s 4d, and she as executrix had paid back £401 6s 10d and £394 9s 11d, leaving a balance unaccounted for of £518 18s 7d. The problem with the record of payment for the putative performance is a false record. The records for December 28, 1594, show that it was the admiral's company that was playing before the queen at Greenwich, while the lord chamberlain's company was performing at Gray's Inn that day. The other point to note is that this payment was the first and only payment stated to have been received by "Will Shakespeare."[57]

The widow of Sir Thomas was the dowager countess of Southampton, the mother of the third earl, the dedicatee of *Venus and Adonis* and *The Rape of Lucrece*: she would have every reason to know who the author was. It might be a sort of defense to her to invoke William's name at her moment of extreme embarrassment, not to say peril. On balance I think "Will Shakespeare" refers to Oxford's pseudonym. The queen and anyone auditing the accounts would know the real identity of the pseudonymous author, whose status would be thought enough (as it apparently proved — no further investigation into the accounts seems to have taken place) to protect her ladyship.

William is also the victim of undergraduate wit in the three Parnassus plays produced at Cambridge in the period 1598–1602.[58] In the first two, Gullio, a rich, conceited and ill-educated man, is the arrogant paymaster of scholars, who fools himself by quotation from Shakespeare and mistranslation of foreign phrases. In the third play the actor playing Kempe the comic actor says:

> Few of the university pen plays well, they smell too much of that writer Ovid, and that writer Metamorphoses, and talk too much of Proserpina and Jupiter. Why here's our fellow Shakespeare puts them all down.

"Kempe" (the real Kempe, who was well connected, would have known better) shows that he and his fellows were so illiterate as not to know that *Metamorphoses* was Ovid's work, yet "Shakespear puts down" (confounds) all the university wits — effectively informing the audience that there were two Shakespeares: Gullio as William and Oxford under the pseudonym.

The performance of *Richard II* at the time of Essex's attempted coup in 1601 did not cause William as its putative author to be hauled before the Privy Council in spite of the dreadful insult implied to the queen: he must have been irrelevant. The company was represented by the actor/shareholder Augustine Phillips. Nothing happened: perhaps Oxford's status saw to that.

While Oxford was indeed an actor, there is virtually no evidence that William was. However, on the misreading of *Groatsworth*, dealt with above, and this payment record, the whole of the case for Shakespeare being an established actor and theatrical luminary is built.

The only reference to William's acting is contained (of course!) in *Every Man Out of His Humour*, this time in Act V, scene ii, where the friends have arranged for the airhead socialite Saviolina to meet on a blind date Sogliardo (whose travels "have changed his complexion"):

> PUNTARVOLO: But that which transcends all, lady; he doth so peerlessly imitate any manner of person for gesture, action, passion, or whatever.
> FASTIDIOUS BRISK (another man about town): Ay, especially a rustic or a clown, madam, that it is not possible for the sharpest-sighted wit to discern any sparks of the gentleman in him, when he does it.

Sogliardo enters and puts on a display of clown playing gentleman nicely mixed up with misunderstood rudery, and totally convinces Saviolina that he is a gentleman playing a clown (perhaps playing a gentleman). The cast, unable to stand any more, gets Sogliardo to show the lady his hand, and Sogliardo confesses the palms became rough with holding the plow. Scales fall, even from Saviolina's eyes, and she departs forthwith in anger. Sogliardo does not realize it: "I did my part in courting," he complains in the next scene. Some might consider the reference in Act II to Sogliardo and his father dancing in his hobbyhorse:

> SOGLIARDO: I have danced in it myself.
> CARLO: Not since the humour of gentility was upon you, did you?
> SOGLIARDO: Yes, once; marry, that was but to show what gentleman might do in a humour.

He then launches into description of the various wheezes of hobbyhorse dancing.

William's competence and technique as an actor is evidenced only by these heavy parodies. It is reasonable to assume that he had and kept a strong regional accent, which might well have been a handicap. His name appears in certain lists of players in the front of Ben Jonson's *Works* which he published in 1616 (with the name hyphenated) and also of the 1623 Folio, but these clearly relate to Oxford, as we have seen from the previous chapter. In the light of the caricatures, the thought of William having to attend rehearsals of, say, *The Merry Wives of Windsor* and *Every Man Out of His Humour* no doubt is well comprehended by "orthodox" critics, if by no one else. Interestingly, the University of Glasgow folio on the preface page that lists the actors has in manuscript "Leass for making" doubly underlined: this suggests that the annotator thought William an actor, and less of a poet or writer: why was William put at the head of the list?[59] This is the quality of the evidence on which "orthodoxy" relies to show William as an actor, and apparently therefore the dramatist.[60]

Apart from the dubious record of the payment in 1594/5 there is no record of William having any financial dealings or shareholding in the lord chamberlain's company until 1599. Certainly on the evidence of *Every Man Out of His Humour*, no one would have entrusted a person of his manifest limitations with anything responsible on the artistic side of the enterprise. However, by 1597 the company was in financial trouble. In 1598 the shareholders had to decamp from the north side of the river to the South Bank, taking on December 28 their theater with them, which in February 1598/9 they re-erected as the Globe.[61] The finances were reconstructed, and a thirty-one-year lease taken on. Under this reconstruction the two Burbage sons took on five-tenths share and the remaining half was allotted, one-tenth share each, to William Shakespeare, Hemmings, Condell, Kempe and Phillips. We do not know the circumstances but Kempe soon left the partnership. Because changes in the particulars of the tenants of a lease did not at that time have to be evidenced in writing we have no direct evidence of any transfers and have to rely on the inevitable litigation that ensues.

Soon after his accession by letters patent dated May 19, 1603, the new King James[62] reconstitutes the lord chamberlain's company as the king's men, authorizing and licensing "these our servants Lawrence Fletcher [apparently the king's favorite Scottish actor], William Shakespeare, Richard Burbage, Augustine Phillips, John Heminges, Henry Condell, William Sly, Robert Armin, Richard Cowley and the rest of their associates freely to use and exercise the art and faculty of playing comedies, tragedies, histories, interludes, morals, pastorals, stage plays and such like." For his official entry into London, March 15, 1604,[63] a vast pageantry was devised, and apparently "skarlet red cloth" allotted for the coronation (the celebrations for which were curtailed because of plague) was reallotted to the "Players," so that the first-named in the list, "William Shakespeare," receives four and a half yards. Whether William personally or Oxford in disguise are intended by these references is not clear. Although the second reference seems to be evidence that William was a player, it may have only been included only because William was a leading shareholder in the Globe and named as one of the king's men.

One of the actors and fellow sharers Augustine Phillips died in 1605. By his will dated May 4, 1605:

> item, I give and bequeath to my fellow William Shakespeare a thirty shilling piece in gold; to my fellow Henry Condell one other thirty shilling piece in gold; to my servant Christopher Beeston thirty shillings in gold; to my fellow Lawrence Fletcher twenty shillings in gold; to my fellow Robert Armin twenty shillings in gold; to my fellow Richard Cowley twenty shillings in gold; to my fellow Alexander Cook twenty shillings in gold; to my fellow Nicholas Tooley twenty shillings in gold.[64]

It is noticeable that the fellow actors are given twenty shillings in gold. The fellow shareholders in the Globe come first and are given thirty shillings in gold. Hemmings was, like Phillips, an actor as well as a shareholder, but it seems a comparatively weak statement to base any kind of acting career for William.

Prior to Phillips' death on February 13, 1604, Pope had also died, and his widow desired to encash his interest. A sale was negotiated before the death of Sly whereby each shareholder sold out a one-third interest to Condell and Sly.[65] It is reasonable to suppose that William at this time came to London to take part in the negotiations and possibly receive his sale proceeds: he appears to have lodged, apparently keeping a low profile, in Silver Street, a back street in the north of the city, with a Mr. Mountjoy, an immigrant hatmaker of dubious reputation, and his family.[66] Here he became involved as a witness in a case involving the daughter's dowry whereby the son-in-law Bellott sued his father-in-law Mountjoy: William remembered nothing of great consequence, and perhaps by design, both in 1604 and at the time of the case, drew the minimum of attention to himself. In his affidavit, he does say "(he) the deponent ... hath known [*not* "resided with"] them [the plaintiff Bellott and the defendant Mountjoy] ... for the space of ten years or thereabouts"— that is, from 1602 or thereabouts. That is scarcely evidence of continuous residence with the Mountjoys in the period.

The discovery of this association has created much speculation, which ignores the prime historico-literary facts of that year, 1604, namely the death of Oxford in June, the publication of the "good" quarto of *Hamlet* with the Royal Arms of approval at the top of page 2, and the production of eight Shakespeare plays out of ten before the new king and the court for the court Christmas revels of 1604/5 by way of memorial for Oxford. William's services were not required, nor did he, notwithstanding the clear signs of his wealth and "gentlemanliness," stay with any of his acting or literary fellows, let alone with the great and good at or near court, and this at the time of what should have been (we are led to believe) the apogee of his career.

One of the other plays performed at this memorial was *Every Man Out of His Humour*— now five years out of date, but no doubt to remind its audience of the total inconsequence of William Shakespeare.

The record of the revels spells the name of the author of some of the plays "Shaxberd," no doubt a subtle clerkly joke (deliberately made — the record is in manuscript) on the attainments of the alleged author: it may be readily linked with the exchange from *Guy of Warwick* (a play thought to have been written after 1593, but not after 1600 as there would be no point in a reference to Stratford-upon-Avon, by which time William would be gone from London):

> SPARROW: I' faith, Sir, I was born in England at Stratford-upon-Avon Warwickshire.
> RAINBORNE: Wer't born in England? What's thy name?
> SPARROW: I have a fine finical name, I can tell ye, for my name is Sparrow, nor no hedge sparrow, nor no peaking Sparrow, nor no sneaking Sparrow, but I am a high-mounting lofty minded Sparrow [V, ii].[67]

In addition, there is a fine piece of "absence" evidence. There was no Shakespeare to write or polish up a comedy at short notice, shown in a letter from the chamberlain of the exchequer to Robert Cecil in January 1605:

> Burbage is come and says there is no new play that the queen [i.e., Anne, wife of James I] hath not seen, but they have revived an old one called *Love's Labour's Lost* which for wit and mirth will please her exceedingly, and this is appointed to be played tomorrow night at my Lord of Southampton's.[68]

To conclude the Globe shareholding interest story, according to a statement made by Hemmings in the claim, *Witter v. Hemmings* (1619), on February 20, 1612, William Witter (Mrs. Phillips' new husband), Pope's Executors, William Shakespeare and Witter himself, each owning a one-sixth share plus Hemmings and Condell owning three-sixths in partnership (having apparently bought out Sly's executors), assigned a one seventh interest to Ostler. In the same statement Hemmings says that thereafter Witter's share was one-sixth.

Chambers remarks, "by a slip as one sixth instead of a one seventh of the moiety." But if Hemmings' "one sixth" was right, then William Shakespeare may have already dropped out.[69] Certainly he takes no step and is not recorded in the calls on shares at the time of the Globe rebuilding after the fire in 1613. Resident in Stratford with Oxford dead, he would have no interest in maintaining a commercial interest a hundred miles away in London. In 1615, Thomasina Ostler sued her father, Hemmings, as the widow of her husband in respect of his share.[70] She makes an interesting error, describing three shareholders in the Globe as "generosis defunctis"—deceased gentlemen: the three are Augustine Phillips, Thomas Pope and William Shakespeare—the last named being of so little consequence that it mattered not whether he was dead or, as he was in fact, still alive.

Biographers make a desperate effort to show William to have connections to the new indoor Blackfriars Theater, both in terms of theater history (discussed on page 138), and in terms of business interest. The one place where we might expect to see his name, if he were interested in that enterprise, is as a defendant in an action called *Keysar v. Burbage* and others,[71] where Keysar, the successor in title to the original nominee shareholder in the Blackfriars lease, sued Richard and Cuthbert Burbage and the three other sharers for a one-sixth share of the profits. William is not one of the defendants, ergo as any lawyer would advise he was not a partner or profit-sharer and so not concerned. The case was heard on February 8–12, 1610/11, and concerned the immediate early profit of the syndicate since the opening of the theater in 1609. A subsequent affidavit of 1615 in that same case (*Ostler v. Hemmings*, referred to in the previous paragraph) named him as a partner in Blackfriars at the commencement of the enterprise in August 1608. This could be an error of the deponent's memory, or William either never had an interest or disposed of his interest before the commencement of the Keysar suit. Even so, if he had received any profit at all he would have been made an additional defendant.

It may be of significance that Cuthbert Burbage's reference in the Sharers' Papers of 1635 mentions the problems of the company when the boy players grew up. The reference does not actually say that shares were transferred to William Shakespeare: "the transfer of Blackfriars placed [i.e., enabled to be placed] men players which were Hemmings, Condell, Shakespeare etc."[72] In addition, William's name is not in a list of actors at Blackfriars in 1608.

William's biographers contend that he was the poet who wrote *Venus and Adonis* (1592) and *The Rape of Lucrece* (1593).[73] The tone of the dedications is discussed in Chapter Seven. Likewise the sonnets. One critic writes:

> What passes for evidence and rational argument in criticism of the sonnets would hardly pass for either in any other department of life. The absurdities

are nearly always found in association with one, or both, of two ideas: the first, that most of the sonnets are written to a "patron," who is almost inevitably thought of as a great nobleman; the second, that some or all of them are purely "literary," having no reference to real people or events. Singly or together, these two notions can only have one effect: to remove the sonnets from the realities of Shakespeare's private life. There can be little doubt that they were invented for that reason, and that they continue to appeal because they can still serve that purpose.

His conclusion is that one should assume the poems mean what they say. They are not literary exercises. They are not merely addressed to a patron, as we have seen in Chapter Seven. His view is, "The social conditions of the time render most improbable that a true intimacy between a man in (William) Shakespeare's position, and such princelings as the earls of Southampton and Pembroke." That is true and the dedications to *Venus and Adonis* and *The Rape of Lucrece* evidence this; likewise the tone of the first 126 sonnets addressed to Southampton. There must be more of a query over the rest as to whether they or some of them (and the evidence is set out on page 185) are exercises rather than autobiographical.

While William's cultural impact on London seems zero, his business impact on Stratford is considerable.[74] In 1597 he was able to purchase New Place at Stratford for some £60, apparently as an investment. In 1598, he received ten pence for a load of stone from the council, as well as being the subject of correspondence over a prospective loan, and in the same year he was cited as a grain hoarder.[75] In 1602 he purchased 107 acres from the Combe family for £320 and a cottage in Chapel Lane. In 1604 he was reported as having substantial dealings in malt; he made and sued on a small loan. A record of his ownership of real estate in Stratford appears in a local survey. In 1605, after the conjectured sale of his interest in the Globe, he invested £440 (which could be some part of that sale price) in tithes, thus becoming a tithe owner and entitled to burial inside the church. In 1608 William apparently still owed £20 on the purchase of the tithes. A debtor for £6 escaped his net, but William sued the guarantor of the debt, and this litigation continued into 1609. In 1610 the Combes transferred further land to him. In 1611 he was involved in litigation against defaulting tenants. In 1614 he was heavily involved in proposed pasture enclosures of common land in the nearby parish of Welcombe.

Those who contend that William continued to be involved with the king's men have a problem. In 1597–98 the acting companies were continuously busy either in London or touring: William would have had to absent himself to deal with his purchase of New Place in early 1597 and his grain hoarding in February 1597/8. In 1604 he was apparently to receive the four and a half yards of scarlet red cloth for the king's official entry into London, but two weeks later he was in Stratford selling malt in commercial quantities to a Philip Rogers, with further transactions recorded on March 27, April 10 and 24, May 3, 16, and 30, and June 25, 1604. He could not possibly have been in London continuously during those months. After the plague ban was lifted, on April 9, the company (King's Men) performed continuously well into the second half of 1604.[76]

In 1613 the Globe burned down.[77] Under the lease, he would have been liable as part owner for the rebuilding costs, so we may assume that William had already parted with his shareholding, as he does not appear to have reinvested in the rebuilding of the Globe, or have been asked to. In that same year with others he bought the Blackfriars Gate House for £140 with the help of a £60 mortgage.[78] These deeds survive: the interesting point is that William signed his name on slips of paper which were then inserted in slits on the deeds: a most unlawyerlike proceeding, but one that evidently proves that he was not in London at the time of the execution of the deeds. There is a record that in the same year he received a commission (with Richard Burbage as painter) to prepare an impresa for the Earl of Rutland. It may be the record is in error because William does not appear to have done anything similar in his career, and the task is perhaps below that which a gentleman might undertake, unless some old scrap of verse was modified and attributed to William Shakespeare: someone may have pocketed a fee to which he was not entitled.

To account for the superlative education that enabled William to be the playwright, as we have seen, some have suggested that as the family were staunch old-style Catholics, he was sent to Lancashire as a servant, but able to study at one of the libraries there (perhaps Campion's, but subsequent research proves this not possible[79]). While Anglican Protestant ascendancy had taken over the commanding heights of the town in the shape of the town's offices and the headmastership of the grammar school, there was a listing in 1592 of the town's non-attenders at church. John Shakespeare absented himself for fear of debt-process, perhaps as a cover for his recusancy (i.e., his loyalty to the pope[80]). Susanna, William's daughter, was listed in 1606, and the inference is that William was involved with the local Roman Catholics, in spite of his right of burial in the church. Certainly, unlike his father in the early part of his career, William never held any public appointments. So it is surmised that William, being a distance from London, was a suitable choice to be a trustee of the Blackfriars Gate House, which is now known to have been a substantial Roman Catholic safe house, on its purchase in 1613.[81]

In 1615 one of the many Rosicrucian manifestos of the period desires its readers to ostracize persons: "Quales aetas nostra plurimos produxit: unum ex iis praecipuum/Amphitheatralem histrionem, hominem ad imponendum satis ingeniosum" ["of the sort of which our age has produced several, principal among them, a man of the stage with sufficient wit to impose himself on you"]. This seems clearly to refer to William Shakespeare.[82]

On March 25, 1616, he made his will,[83] a document totally devoid of literary merit. Some would think, however ill William was, the playwright would have injected some life into the work, which contains rational enough (cold and bloodless, some think) provisions. The will makes no reference to William's books or "his" plays. He seems to have taken no interest or care at any stage of "his" plays nor any thought to their survival.[84] It includes by way of interlineation a bequest of 26s 8d each to buy themselves rings "to my fellows John Hemynge, Richard Burbage and Henry Condell," the interlineation presumably by way of (prompted?) afterthought.

On April 23, he died. His death provoked no reaction in London at all. We may contrast the poetic outpourings on the death of Beaumont the month before, and there is no record of any immediate tribute in Stratford.

We cannot examine the evidence for the impact of the world's "greatest literary figure" on his hometown because there is none. By 1602 the corporation in Stratford succeeded in banning all plays of any type in the town, the official authorizing any performance to be fined ten shillings. Perhaps some were made: anyway, the fine was raised to ten pounds in 1612. In 1622 the corporation actually paid six shillings to the king's players *not* to perform at Stratford Town Hall.[85] No doubt there is an interesting "orthodox" explanation for this treatment of the art of the town's favorite son.

A monument appeared in Stratford Church with a curious inscription to the effect that William was a Nestor in wisdom, a Socrates by nature and a Virgil in art; it is followed a crude set of verses.[86] With it is an effigy of a trader fronting a woolsack: this was modernized probably between 1740 and 1760 to turn the woolsack into a (less than convenient) cushion desk, and the effigy given a goose quill pen.[87] Ben Jonson has some fun in *Every Man Out of His Humour*, Act I, with Sogliardo-type persons who wish to set aside money for their monuments — can their executors be trusted?[88] William's irrelevance to the 1623 folio can be seen from the references on page 214ff.

These persons[89] all knew or must have been in contact with William Shakespeare. Although they all left substantial paperwork, none mentioned William Shakespeare in any cultural capacity whatever:
William Camden, the historian
Michael Drayton, the poet who lived nearby and was a friend of Dr. Hall
Thomas Greene, the solicitor to Stratford corporation and a relative
Fulke Greville, courtier, poet and dramatist living close to Stratford

Dr. John Hall, William's son-in-law and doctor
Philip Henslowe, the impresario
Edward Alleyn, the prominent actor.

These two met his daughter Susanna, but are silent on her father's accomplishments:

James Cooke, the editor of John Hall's papers
Queen Henrietta Maria[90]

Devoid of any evidential or cultural connection to the works, William died as he had lived, a cultural irrelevance. Ipse he was not.[91]

Chapter Notes

Introduction

1. real writer—William Shakespeare of Stratford-upon-Avon (1564–1616) was only twelve in 1576. Along with practically all other "claimants," he is much too young to play any part in the changes mentioned.
2. "drab": Lewis pp. 157–317; also from p. 1: "The mid century is an earnest, heavy-handed, commonplace age. Then in the last quarter of the century, the unpredictable happens. With startling suddenness we ascend."
3. "Sometimes, speaking of English Literature...": Nicoll, p. 15.
4. "Modern critics agree...": Wiggins, pp. 1, 2. With the publication of James Shapiro's *Contested Will: Who Wrote Shakespeare?*, we have entered a new era. The authorship question is now of such direct importance to the study of Shakespeare that even the most rock-ribbed believer in William Shakespeare's authorship may feel it necessary to combat the attacks on that belief and in turn attack any alternative candidate for authorship. Gradually the playing field is leveling out. The latest argument that the authorship question is only the product of a mutation of the intellect and not for serious scholars is advanced by Professor Shapiro, to the effect that Malone was at fault in seeking links in the works to the life of the author, and that this idea taken up by Coleridge and the other romantics causes the author to reveal himself and his emotional life in the works. The professor argues that while the works might reveal shards of the author's experience, he cannot identify them; everything must be down to the writer's imagination and Elizabethan writers used nothing of their own experiences. Factually this is not correct and logically it does not stand up. Even if there was anything in the argument, the sheer volume of autobiography and topicality connections found in the works and related to Oxford's life buries it completely. Coleridge, for one, would have found it unhelpful (see p. 226).
This book is not concerned by the claims for candidates other than Oxford alone, nor with those claims for him which ignore historical evidence and logic. These claims and the "mutation" argument take up 95 percent of Shapiro's book. The balance is refuted by this book.
5. "Juvenilia"—see Chapter Two.
6. Name on the title page—see Chapter Seven.
7. "as early as": Nicoll, p. 67.
8. "the titles are scarcely known": Malone 1790, p. 1, quoted by Schoenbaum 1970, p. 183.
9. Nashe—see p. 169.
10. Ur-Hamlet—see Jolly, "Ur-Hamlet."
11. "No formal life...": Schoenbaum 1970, p. 725.
12. "Rule 7": Schoenbaum 1966, p. 178.
13. "should have been Rule 1": Sams 1996, p. 152.
14. Fraser 2008. Strachey was of the opinion that modern theater owed more to Racine than to Shakespeare—Halliday p. 328.
15. "risk conjecture": Duncan-Jones, p. x.
16. "stronger sense of the man's experience": Honan (London) *Daily Telegraph*, October 10, 1998.
17. "important to use our imagination": Greenblatt, p. 14.

18. "Perhaps we should despair...": Schoenbaum 1970, p. 767.
19. Malone bogged down — see Chapter Eight.
20. whole caricature of Shakespeare — Ben Jonson (1572–1637). *Every Man Out of His Humour* (1599) is his second play.
21. "it would come naturally": Ackroyd, p. 276.
22. "no solemn-faced and aggressive claim": Nicoll, p. 67.
23. "experiences can never be recovered": Shapiro, p. 305.
24. Circumstantial evidence is defined as "evidence from which the desired conclusion may be drawn but which requires the tribunal of fact not only to accept the evidence tendered but also draw an inference from it." Murphy, p. 20.
25. "difficulty of establishing such allusions": Worden: Essay — "school wall" (Honan p. 214).
26. "standards of fair play": Hopkins, pp. 122–23, 147.
27. Perhaps from lack of time, a common affliction of academics.
28. "fervent loyalty": Brown 1949, p. 9.

Chapter One

1. "Seldom...": Jones p. 211. All the quotations in this chapter except as noted are from Jones pp. 13–25.
2. "Standard work": Barber, p. 244.
3. another translation — Justinus, *Epitome of Trogus Pompeius*. See p. 23.
4. Golding's *Ovid* is considered more fully on p. 30.
5. Burghley's *Ten Precepts to His Son*— part one of two — was first published in 1637 and is considered a clear source for *Hamlet* (I, iii, ll.58ff— Polonius' advice to his son Laertes). How this might have been available to William Shakespeare is not revealed.
6. Gosson, quoted by Wiggins, p. 8.
7. Ascham, *The Scholemaster* I, p. 70ff.
8. "very set against Gallicisms": Saintsbury 1922, pp. 30–31.
9. Wyatt and Surrey: Sir Thomas Wyatt (1503–42) and Henry Howard, third Earl of Surrey (1517–47), were the leading poets of the first half of the century. According to Saintsbury, they were "poets of more promise than performance." Saintsbury 1922, p. 42.
10. "draw frequently on Italian story writers": Arthos, p. 44.
11. Italian critic — Borsellino, quoted by Arthos, p. 45.
12. For large parts of this book I place "Shakespeare" in quotation marks, rather than naming Oxford, as I think the latter reference would interfere with the flow of the argument, which I naturally think applies only to Oxford anyway. In particular, Oxford's knowledge of the original Italian is discussed in Chapter Three.
13. Italian plays as Shakespeare's inspiration — see Arthos.
14. "Italianate Englishman": Whibley, *Cambridge University History of English Literature IV* (1907–21) quoted by K. Gilvary in *The Oxfordian* 8, p. 84.
15. "To have no reading knowledge...": Wickham, pp. 77–78.
16. "Mitigated in Stratford-upon-Avon," see p. 235.

Chapter Two

1. Edward de Vere (1550–1604). With the exception of those for William Shakespeare (1564–1616; see Appendix B) the claims of other candidates for the authorship are not examined in this book, partially as they are outside its scope but principally because these candidates were too young at the time of the revolution (1575–80). The claims of William Shakespeare, Francis Bacon (1561–1626), William, Sixth Earl of Derby (1561–1641), Roger, Fifth Earl of Rutland (1576–1642), Henry Neville (1562–1615), Christopher Marlowe (1564–1593 or later, even if he survived his murder in that year) and Mary, countess of Pembroke (1561–1621) and, no doubt, others could therefore be safely discarded without the need for further explanation. Likewise the "Groupist" theory, that Oxford was a member of, or the leader of, a group of playwrights

including Greene, Lyly, Kidd and Marlowe or one or more of them, and Bacon and William Shakespeare, should also be discarded. The "collaborators" were all too young at the time of the revolution. In addition, with the exception of Marlowe and (putatively) William Shakespeare, none of the claimants has the essential element of hands-on acting. For a realistic opponent to Oxford the critic must find one the same age or older, of sufficient education, life experiences and leisure, and then add the social background, talent and genius, to which must be added an even greater volume of topical and autobiographical references. A common "critique" is that Oxford's candidacy appeals only to snobs or those with some psychological defect, as if a defect in a proponent's character or psychology negates the argument. Users of this "critique" know well that an argument is either right or wrong, defensible or indefensible. The sins or orientations of the proponent are irrelevant.

2. Anderson: factual items and documentary quotations are confirmed by Anderson unless otherwise stated.

3. Nelson: His book's inaccuracies, distortions and general unreliability are comprehensively exposed by Nina Greene on her Phaeton website. I endeavored to persuade her to issue a list of the defects, or failing that a list of the page numbers on which they occur. In reply on her website she wrote, "Frankly, given the numbers in Monstrous Adversary not to mention the bizarre spin Alan has put on the facts, which can sometimes be as confusing as the actual errors, I would treat everything in the book as needing to be checked against a reliable source before depending on it. This sounds like a pretty harsh judgment I know, but I don't think it's too far wide of the mark" (May 28, 2009). Moore, p. 289, wittily compared Nelson to Dr. Jekyll the researcher and Mr. Hyde the analyst.

4. Oxford's libelers — see p. 86.

5. Gepp's *Essex Dialect Dictionary* is referred to by G. Goldstein *DVSNL* November 2009. He makes the incontrovertible point that it would be impossible for William Shakespeare speaking the Warwickshire West Midlands dialect to write *Venus and Adonis* (at whatever date you give it) in the received pronunciation of the East Midlands (London and the universities) court dialect used in the poem without once letting his guard slip. Another nice Essex connection (noted by Peter Cousins) is Prince Harry on Falstaff: "That huge bombard of sack, that stuffed cloak-bag of guts, that roasted Manningtree ox with the pudding in his belly" (I *Henry IV*, II, iv, ll. 455–57). Manningtree in Essex was noted for the size of its oxen.

6. Smith's library — see E. Jolly and P. O'Brien, *GO*.

7. Oxford's knowledge of countryside, gardening, etc. — see Spurgeon. Later on Oxford is responsible for the garden at King's House Hackney, where he resided in the late 1590s — see p. 195.

8. Elyot: quoted by Anderson p. 7

9. Fable of Narcissus — Prechter. He produces a compelling argument for inclusion pre–1575 of the anonymous *Nobody and Somebody*, which has a wealth of Shakespearean inferences — *SOSNL* September 2009.

10. *Romeus and Juliet* — N. Green *Oxfordian* 3. There are four instances where *Romeo and Juliet* differs from *Romeus and Juliet*, all of which appear in the original Italian version by Della Porta. There was no contemporary English or French translation — Price p. 249.

11. Topography of Windsor — see p. 112.

12. Burghley's library — see Jolly: *GO*

13. The quotation from *All's Well That Ends Well* and all other quotations from the canon (except where noted) are taken from Stanley Wells and Gary Taylor.

14. Modern critic: J. Bate, 2008. In his introduction he tells us, "Gathering what we can from his plays and poems — that is how we will write a biography that is true to him. But the process has immense perils"— from what and to whom, I inquire, if logical deductions from, and correlations with, references from those plays and poems are made? He quotes a colleague: "If biography is to be found it has to be here, in the plays and poems, but *never literally and never provably* [his italics]." When taxed at the Bath Literary Festival in 2010 with the suggestion that logical deduction from the quotation from *All's Well That Ends Well* points directly to Oxford, he did not provide a logical answer, even making out that Bertram's marriage was similar to William Shakespeare's (see p. 17). His principal point was that although authors now write from their own experiences, autobiographical writing of this type was unknown to the

Elizabethans generally. In his book, he goes on: "That Shakespeare wrote in Sonnet 37 of being made 'lame by Fortune's dearest spite' does not necessarily mean that he had a limp, as more than one biographer has supposed." But if the author was wounded in a brawl (see p. 24), would not that be evidence? Apparently not; we must rely on "an accurate triangulation of the life, the work and the world [which] must be more subtle.... We must by indirections find directions out." He means that in order to avoid Oxford we must go "around the houses," never in through the front door. His attitude differs from that of James Shapiro, who specifically denounced Malone for attempting to show that there were links between aspects of William Shakespeare's biography and specific characters or events in the plays, and castigated *every subsequent biographer* who is misled by Malone into following his critical approach. There might be "shards" (Shapiro's word) of autobiography, but it is impossible to distinguish and identify these from elements produced from the writer's imagination, in his opinion.— Report by Richard Malim and Kevin Gilvary on the conference at the Globe: "Shakespeare: From Rowe to Shapiro," November 28, 2009. This, with Professor Wells' contribution on the sonnets (reported in note 73 of the appendix) kicks away one of the two major props to the identification of William Shakespeare with Shakespeare the writer; the other is Malone's (and Dowden's and Chambers') dating schedules, which William Shakespeare's own "shard-less" actual biography negates.

15. Rigorous programme — Ogburn p. 392.

16. "thighbone"— see also p. 94.

17. Nowell: If, as Nelson suggests (p. 39), Oxford was unteachable, then Nowell would have said so in what was a private letter to his employer.

18. English not a language of culture to foreigners — see Bruno's apparent reference in 1584, in Chapter Three, note 18.

19. For Ronsard see Levi, p. 1ff. Pierre Ronsard was the leading poet of France, indeed of all Europe in the period. I am indebted to Professor Quainton of Lancaster University who supplied me with the Laumonier edition of Ronsard, and to Madame Poullain, who corrected my journeyman translation on p. 20, where very necessary, and agrees my gloss on "par le premier passant" on p. 50.

20. Soothern more fully quoted on p. 79.

21. Cambridge jargon — D. Charlton *SOSNL* Winter 2008. There is extant an account for the preparation of Oxford's accommodation at university. The university jargon might well be beyond the experiences of William Shakespeare.

22. Horestes: E. Showerman *Oxfordian* 7. Robert Anton writing in 1616 puts "Orestes' incest, Cleopatra's crimes" in the same line. It is possible the author of both was in his mind the same person.

23. Geneva Bible underlinings: as revealed by the researches of Dr. Roger Stritmatter.

24. Italian books: While we do not know what these books were, their relevance is clear — see p. 52. One is likely to have been Francesco Guicciardini's *La Historia d'Italia* (1565). Oxford's own copy is in the Folger Shakespeare Library.

25. Those who dispute Shakespeare's authorship of *Edmund Ironside* have a great deal of work to do.

26. Execution of Norfolk, withdrawal of matrimonial relations — Jeremy Crick found a reference from notes on Rocester made by the Reverend John Allen (1769–1778), rector of Tarporley, Cheshire: "Edwd Vere E of Oxford marryd Elizabeth Daughter to Tho Trentham of Roucester Esq she being at one time one of the Maids of Hon' to Q Eliz. This earl's first wife was daughter to the Ld Treasurer Burghley & perceiving that the life of his most dear & entire friend Tho D of Norfolk was in Danger, for his intrigue with Mary Q of Scots, he earnestly interceded with Burghley his wifes Father, for the saving of his life, but not prevailing, he took that Antipathy to Burghley knowing that it was in his Power to save him, that he declard in heat of Passion to ruin his Daughter, & immediately forsook her bed, sold & consumd his great estate." One *Oxfordian* speculation (Green, *Oxford Authorship* site, no. 12, 1991, 13–17 www.oxford-shakespeare.com) suggests that *The First Part of Sir John Oldcastle* was written by Oxford as an effort to remind the queen that clemency could be exercised on a misled "traitor." Equally, *Thomas of Woodstock* could have been written in revenge for Norfolk's judicial murder, since both Woodstock and Norfolk were victims of their respective sovereigns (see p. 25).

27. No title: see Anderson, and N. Green website.

28. Raffish existence — see p. 33.
29. Tournament poetry: see Young, pp. 138ff.
30. As father of the Third Earl of Southampton: There is an unevidenced theory (the Prince Tudor) which commands some support in England and more in the United States that Southampton was the offspring of a liaison between Oxford and the queen herself. She would have been thirty-nine years of age and certainly not in "the lovely April of her prime" (unlike the countess, who was twenty-one). The theory goes on to surmise that Southampton was brought up by either the Southampton family or the Montagus (the countess's side). Both families were rock-ribbed Roman Catholics in the 1570s, and it is ludicrous to believe that the anti-Roman queen would hand over her secret child to either, and make such a present to the pope and every Roman scribbler in Europe, and to the delight of the band of frequently humiliated foreign ambassadors to her court. Furthermore, testimony was given that in 1572 the second earl (the ostensible father of the third earl) while in the Tower told a fellow inmate that "there was a privy stairs where the queen and my lord Leicester did meet" (Skidmore, p. 141).
31. Plans: these were quite advanced in 1573 but aborted, no doubt adding to Oxford's frustrations (N. Green): Calais — perhaps Flushing would be more relevant.
32. Pierce Penniless: Nicholl 1984, p. 112.
33. Triumph as a spy — see p. 86.
34. Gascoigne: quotations are from Arber 1868, pp. 51–52.
35. References to a young noble can only be to Oxford. The nobility of England in 1575 was a very small group anyway, and apparently no other young noble had offended Gascoigne and his patron Hatton.
36. Sir Sidney Lee, prominent Victorian biographer — his view is supported by Bate, in S. Wells, ed., *Shakespeare Studies 41.*
37. Recent scholarship: S. Saunders, *SOSNL* (Fall 2005).
38. Golding's other works: Garnett and Gosse, p. 137.
39. Pound quoted by P. Altrocchi: *SOSNL* Spring 2005. "Is a fine poet ever translated until another his equal invents a new style in a later language? I suspect [the translation] was Shakespeare's."
40. "mot juste": For which (useful) opinions Pound was no doubt thought even madder!
41. Damian and Pithias: K. Chiljan *SOSNL* Spring 1999.
42. Miles Windsor left an account of the production before the queen without mentioning Oxford. This is not so surprising, as the Windsor family were at daggers drawn with Oxford as they questioned his legitimacy.
43. collaboration — see p. 203.
44. Gabriel Harvey quoted by B.M. Ward, p. 83.
45. Sobran, Appendix 4.
46. Sams 1986.
47. Troublesome Reign: R. Jimenez, *SOSNL* (Winter 2006). See also E.A.J. Honigman's essay in P. Holland, ed., *Shakespeare Survey 53*, pp. 176ff, for nine separate scenes that are for the most part replaced in the same order in *King John*. "The author of Troublesome Reign found meaning in the story: he wrote a play that resembles Shakespeare's in its plotting, yet goes off the rails whenever it differs from Shakespeare in its plotting" (Rosalind King quoted by Honigman). The logic is that the mature author Oxford corrected his own original mistakes when he wrote the later *King John*.
48. Sams 1996. For the *Nonpareil* see p. 196 and Mattingley, p. 281.
49. Thomas of Woodstock — M. Egan 2006. In addition the saintly (as portrayed — he was as much a crook as any of his brothers) Thomas of Woodstock's lineal successor was the Duke of Norfolk who was executed by Elizabeth in 1571 (see p. 25). The play could be a comment on that execution (which apparently disgusted Oxford), covertly comparing it to Woodstock's murder by the king. Curiously Elizabeth (arguably England's most successful monarch for three hundred years) identified herself with Richard II when the play of that name was acted at the time of Essex's attempted putsch in 1601.
50. Famous Victories: S. Pitcher 1962.
51. 1536 and 1569 rebellions: see T. McAlindon 1996.
52. "superior poet in the making" — R. Jimenez *SOSNL* (Winter 2008).

53. George Shakebag and Black Will: I think the reference to the use of the pseudonym in Harvey's address in Cambridge is slightly later see p. 78.

54. Leicester's guilt is further investigated by C. Skidmore. Only a sufficiently senior nobleman could keep on repeating the accusation without fear of official retribution. See Gascoigne on p. 29 and Hall, Chapter Six, note 15. Note also the anonymous "epitaph":

> Here lies the valiant soldier
> That never drew his sword
> Here lies the loyal courtier
> That never kept his word
> Here lies the noble lecher
> That used art to provoke
> Here lies the constant husband
> Whose love was firm as smoke.
> Here lies the politician [same word in *A Yorkshire Tragedy*]
> And nut-worm of the state. [A "Shakespearean" thought.]
> Here lies the Earl of Leicester
> That God and man did hate.— Skidmore p. 374.

55. David Roper: see *GO*.
56. "Saturninus"— Clark p. 50.
57. Enrage the king — M. Anderson p. 212. Perhaps the Italian (*a sue spese* in modern Italian) could be translated to read "at *her* expense"— that is, perhaps the queen's financial support to Oxford for such propaganda.
58. "The Spanish Fury": Clark p. 49.
59. The Buik finished up in the royal library in Windsor Castle.
60. Polonius' speech — see also p. 109.
61. Sideswipe — see p. 254.
62. "strong possibility": Nicoll p. 79.
63. "earlier publications were his first versions": Sams 1995, quoted by Jimenez 2008.
64. From "What thing is love...?"— R. Detobel correspondence. Compare:

> Una desiar, ch'in aspettando un giorno
> Ne porta e poi fugge com' ombra,
> Ne lascia altra di sé, che doglia e scorno.— Pietro Bembo (d. 1547), Rime XXV

and:

> C'est un désir, qui, pour attendre une heure,
> Perd beaucoup d'ans, et puis passé comme ombre,
> Et riens de luy fors douleur ne demeure — Mellin de St. Gallais (d. 1558), Hecatomphile 1534

and:

> Love's a desire, which, for to wait a time,
> Doth lose an age of years, and so doth pass
> As doth shadow sever'd from his prime:
> Seeming as though it were, yet never was;
> Leaving naught but repentant thoughts
> Of days ill-spent of that which profit noughts — Oxford, in a free translation of the above.

65. "When wert thou born, Desire?" based on an Italian poem — R. Detobel correspondence.
66. Note that Puttenham is happy to name the apparently dilettante nobleman, but not the playwright, for his "figures," which are taken from the socially unacceptable plays — see pp. 128.
67. Tournament poetry — Young pp. 138ff.
68. Pain of Pleasure: S. Smith: *Oxfordian* 5.
69. Brame and Popova — Nelson p. 159.
70. Holmes pp. 324–325.
71. "Emaricdulfe": D. Charlton 2005.
72. "To His Friend Florio": Sobran p. 198.
73. Other poets: see, for instance, Ignotus on p. 214; the Theocritus translation, Chapter Three, note 12; and the Leicester spoof epitaph, Chapter Two note 54.

Chapter Three

1. Latin. The view that the alleged attendance at Stratford Grammar School in the mid-1570s was sufficient to supply the writer with all the Latin he needed to know at the start of his career is widely held by biographers.

2. "Small Latin and less Greek"—see p. 215.

3. Plautus: see Arthos generally. Plautus (d. 184 B.C.) is the chief comedy writer in Latin.

4. An element in his bones: Nuttall pp. 84, 57.

5. May I read "cepimus": "we captured" instead of "coepimus": "we begin"?

6. Private joke: Professor Nelson (pp. 66–67) makes out that Oxford was no Latin scholar on the strength of one misplaced "e" for "i," in a legal writ—positing incorrectly an active voice use for a passive; and his three other examples do not stand up to examination.

7. Knowledge of Greek: see p. 85 (Orazio Cuoco's examination).

8. "lightly" worn—Werth: *Oxfordian* 5.

9. Greek tragedy: J.A.K. Thompson p. 250. Other quotations appear in Werth.

10. Socrates: another reference is to the description of his death in Plato's *Phaedo*: "The man who gave him the poison ... after a while he pressed his foot hard, and asked him if he could feel; he said, 'No'; and then his leg, and so upwards and upwards, and showed us that he was cold and stiff" (Jowett translation). Compare the death of Falstaff: "So a bade me lay more clothes upon his feet, put my hand into the bed and felt them and they were as cold as any stone. Then I felt to his knees and so up'rd and up'rd and all the way cold as any stone" (*Henry V*, II, iii, ll. 21–25). There were no translations into English of Plato's *Phaedo*. The Italian philosopher Ficino (whose work would subsequently be plagiarized by Giordano Bruno, whom we shall meet again) had translated Plato into Italian earlier, and two Huguenot exiles dedicated their translation into French to the queen in 1578—Hattaway 2007, p. 49.

11. Nearer to the spirit—J.A.K. Thomson, p. 250,

12. "miracle": Martindale p. 12. In 1588 there was published in Oxford a verse translation of Six Idylla out of Theocritus by an unknown author. Lewis states that parts of this version "sound far more like Greek poetry than anything that was to be written in English before the nineteenth century" (p. 521). I think Oxford is the only likely author. What is even more amazing is that Oxford must have been virtually self-taught in advanced competence and appreciation, as the Restoration critics conclude in regard to the theater (see Chapter Eight).

13. Hebrew—See Goldstein: *DVSNL* Feb 2010 for other possible examples of Hebrew. See also S.J. Schönfeld 1980, where if Portia and Bassanio are concealed Jews, the knowledge of Hebrew given them by the playwright makes Bassanio's choice of the lead casket inevitable.

14. Shalach—the father of Eber or EVER (Genesis 10:24), which might have appealed to Oxford. "Shalach-a" might be the Hebrew for "whittawer," the profession of William Shakespeare, which might have appealed again, but at some later stage—see p. 246.

15. Professor Nelson's website (Socrates.berkeley.edu/-ahnelson) suggests that anyway the letter may have been dictated by a tutor, notwithstanding the use of the acute accent (then, I understand, rare). I do not think a tutor would have allowed the delaying excuse to be forwarded to Sir William in the terms set out.

16. Ironside Gallicisms—Sams 1986, pp. 339–340. Of the "orthodox," one may legitimately inquire, from where did the author, whoever he was, acquire his expertise and interest in French? Sams attributes the play to Shakespeare.

17. Interest in Italian. Note *Romeo and Juliet* source. See Chapter Two, note 10.

18. Shaheen 1994, pp. 160–69. The Italian books would hardly be available for William Shakespeare to study. In addition, in Bruno's *La Cena de le Ceneri* (1584), there is a discussion as to how much, if any, English, Teofilo knows. (Teofilo was Bruno's pseudonym for himself in *La Cena*. At the time he was Walsingham's spy while playing the part of resident Catholic priest at the French embassy in London.) Teofilo denies knowing any, as "English is not worth a scholar's knowing." His servant says he is only pretending so he can understand what is being said in English, but the necessity for Oxford to be fluent in Italian before going to Italy is clear. See Bossy 1991, p. 141.

19. John Florio (1553–1625) was the son of an Italian Protestant exile in England and his English wife, with whom Oxford was apparently on good terms.

20. Shaheen discounts the "tedious moralising" expansion in Sir Geoffrey Fenton's translation (1567).
21. Burghley's library — Jolly, *GO*.
22. Familiarity with languages — Nicoll p. 69.
23. Music — E. Imlay, *DVSNL* (July 2006) — and see p. 96.
24. Law — M. Alexander: *Oxfordian* 4, a complete review and demolition of the objections.
25. Letter to Burghley — Calendar of State papers, SP Foreign 33,47 1575–77 p. 32, quoted by Clark, p. 127.
26. Venice as base: the first public theater in Europe had opened in 1565 and was probably of much interest to Oxford. Unfortunately, no descriptions, let alone a picture, survive (N. Magri — correspondence).
27. P. Johnson, *DVSNL* (December 2005).
28. Oxford's faultless geography: he is taxed with thinking that Bohemia in *The Winter's Tale* (Act III, scene iii) has a seashore. This reference appears in the stage directions (put in perhaps by Jonson as editor in 1623) and in the speeches of the Old Shepherd and the Clown (William Shakespeare's father and William himself), pointing up their ignorance. The shore is the littoral of the Danube at a point where there was a particularly dangerous piece of waterway. See Malim, *DVSNL* (June 2008). Oxford and most educated Elizabethans would not have made the error, but while Jonson himself repeats the same error in *The Drummond Conversations* criticizing the author, this might be evidence that he was the 1623 folio editor. Some (W. R. Hess and others — correspondence), however, on other grounds, think the conversations are a work of fiction.
29. Adonis importuned by Venus — see Magri, *GO*. The lines read: "And therefore put his bonnet on/Under whose brim the gaudy sun would peep./The wind would blow it off..."
30. Horse — J. Hamill, *SOSNL* (Summer 2003).
31. "invention": see also p. 186.
32. Achilles — M. Delahoyde, *Oxfordian* IX. Harvey compares Oxford to Achilles at roughly the same time. See Chapter Six, note 6. For later comparison by Oxford himself of Essex to Achilles see p. 183.
33. "Senior junior": Hamill, *SOSNL* (Summer 2003).
34. "Queer theme": Wilson Knight 1932, p. 104.
35. *The Winter's Tale*, maybe *Le Conte d'HiVER*—"the story of de Vere" with Perdita as the allegory for his "lost" oeuvre in the care of William Shakespeare — the Clown.
36. Bertani's restorations — Hamill, *SOSNL* (Summer 2003).
37. For Bruno, see John Arthos. Bruno also refers in his *Cena de le Ceneri* (1584) to one of the participants in his Dialogue IV as Torquato, a description which seems to refer to the twisted ribbon around Oxford's neck in the Ghaeraedts portrait. Torquato is merely insulting to Bruno's alter ego Teofilo. Bruno has given bad press to Torquato/Oxford, and this may be understandable as Bruno appears as an admirer of Sidney in *La Cena*, and Bruno dedicated some of his later works to Sidney. Both Oxford and Bruno were virulent opponents of the Catholic Lord Henry Howard (see p. 84), but Bruno, the secret spy, could well have wished to distance himself from the (by then) revealed spy Oxford. For Bruno, see Bossy p. 124. For Torquatus, see Chapter Seven, note 16.
38. Repertoire in Italy — Perrucci — extract and translation supplied by Magri. Astolf is a comic English knight who has a fantastic journey to the moon in Ariosto's *Orlando Furioso* (1516) — shades of Don Quixote and Puntarvolo. See Chapter Eight, note 42, and Gardner, pp. 26 and 32.
39. Oxford's life saved — see Dedication herein. See also the reference in *Hamlet*, Act IV, scene vi, ll. 15–22.

Chapter Four

1. The quotations in this chapter except as noted are taken from Jones pp. 170–194.
2. Salluste Du Bartas — contemporary French poet (Roman historian Sallust).
3. "When we look back..." Gavin Alexander, p. xxii.
4. Substantial change: in effect, the post-revolution poets "rejected some of [the earlier] metres almost entirely, set a new standard of melody for those they retained, and purged its

vocabulary" [Lewis, p. 323]. But Lewis also makes clear that it is the element of eloquence brought into play by the new dramatists which is the primary cause of the change, in priority to the "new" poetry. See Chapter Five, note 1.

5. Thomas Nashe (d. 1601), satirist, pamphleteer, playwright, novelist, university wit.
6. Head of a fashion — Dover Wilson, p. 54.
7. Greene's *Menaphon*: *Menaphon*'s Eclogue is quite as explicit: compare *Venus and Adonis*, ll. 229-246, with Melicertus' Eclogue in the former. See Chapter Seven, note 15.
8. Stanyhurst quoted by Saintsbury 1903, p. 24.
9. Harvey: for an example of Harvey's own poetry see *Mirror of Tuscanism*, quoted on p. 76, which was attacked by Nashe. See Nelson, p. 227.
10. Sidney and Spenser: that is not to deny that, say, Sidney was an equally or even more accomplished poet than Oxford at the start of the 1580s.
11. Criticism of Spenser as "alien": Phelps, pp. 31-32.
12. Soothern's *Pandora* (1584) *Elegia*, p. 24, and see p. 80ff.
13. Daniel's *Musophilus*; to him also we owe the contemporary "Admirable Defence of Rhyme which finally smashes the fancy for classical metres introduced long before by Harvey" (Saintsbury 1903, p. 35) Daniel wrote in that work, "In respect of our sovereign's happy inclination this way ... I have now given greater body to the same argument" [*English Prose Selections* I, p. 577].
14. Heywood, quoted by Salingar, p. 71. Emphasis added.
15. Camden: *Essay on the Languages*, quoted by Bolton, p. 30. By these later dates the population would be thoroughly steeped in readings in church from the Bible, the 1562 Prayer Book, and so on, as well as sermons.

Chapter Five

1. The most important development — Lewis, pp. 481, 482: "Until the Golden Period [which corresponds to my revolutionary period, 1575-80, and its immediate aftermath] an historian of poetry need take hardly any notice of the stage. But now, no Form was more suddenly charged with gold than the dramatic.... Indeed the old Drab ... died harder among the literary poets than among the dramatists, *who are the pioneers and masters of the Golden lyric*." (My italics.) My point goes a little farther: eloquence on the *fixed* stage was the main influence on the aftermath poetry, as well as on the development of the English language. An older critic offers a slightly different gloss: he might have agreed with Lewis if Lewis had written "who are the pioneers *and become* the masters": "We have hardly left (if we take their counterparts later we have not left) the wooden verse of Gorboduc, the childish rusticity of Like Will to Like, when suddenly we stumble on the bower, 'Seated in hearing of a hundred streams' of George Peele [*David and Bathsheba*, l. 118], on the myriad fancies of Lyly, on the exquisite snatches of Greene, on the verses, to this day the high watermark of poetry, in which Marlowe speaks of the inexpressible beauty which is the object and despair of the poet. This is wonderful enough. But what is more wonderful is that these lightning flashes are as evanescent as lightning. Lyly, Peele, Greene, Marlowe himself, in probably the very next passages, certainly in passages not very remote, tell [i.e., show] us that this is all a matter of chance, that they are all capable of sinking below the level of Sackville [Buckhurst, author of Gorboduc] at his worst, close to the level of Edwards [see p. 31], and the various anonymous or half-anonymous writers of the dramatic miscellanies.... And then beyond these unequal wits arises the figure of Shakespeare; and the greatest work of all literature swims slowly into our ken." — Saintsbury 1903, p. 63.

As however the revolution is in full flood by 1580, Lyly, Spenser, Sidney, Peele, Greene, Kidd and Marlowe cannot be the leaders of that revolution but are its followers (and debtors or beneficiaries, where they reach the standard of Lewis's golden lyric) and, as Saintsbury points out, sometimes backsliders from the call of that revolution.

2. The Bastille moment: the moment (like the fall on July 14, 1789, of the Bastille Royal Prison where the government's opponents might be imprisoned indefinitely without trial in Paris) when there is a public manifestation of the revolution without necessarily much provable connection between the eventual leader(s) of the revolution and the event itself.

3. Plays prior to 1576: Saintsbury 1903, p. 62.

4. The Theatre: Cuthbert Burbage stated much later in the Sharers' Papers (1635): "The father (James Burbage) of us Cuthbert and Richard Burbage was the first builder of playhouses and was himself in his younger years a player. The Theatre he built with many hundreds of pounds taken up at interest."—E.K. Chambers I, p. 383. "Burbage was a man of small means not worth above a hundred marks (£34) and had no credit"—quotation from Wallace, p. 134. They followed Halliwell-Phillips in delving into some of the resulting litigation which shows that James Burbage had borrowed £500 and (as the litigation shows) required £200 to complete. This was confirmed by Cuthbert Burbage (see Schoenbaum 1970, p. 410). There is no evidence as to who provided that first £500, and the absence of any such evidence is a matter of comment. Ostensibly the best bet would appear to be the Earl of Leicester whose players in the 1570s included James Burbage and continued to perform at court up to 1582, but one suspects that the ownership of a troupe of players was the sign of a noble's status and his desire to please the queen, rather than evidence of his cultural and/or acting interests. The social position of actors would militate against any noble financing or taking a hands-on interest in the new public theaters (especially one of relatively recent ennoblement—Leicester's family was ennobled by Henry VIII), unless there were other elements in which a benefactor might wish to be concerned, such as the actual writing and production of the plays, and the political clout required. Oxford's involvement would not be surprising. Burbage and his associates seem to have left at some unknown date the patronage by Leicester and attached themselves to Lord Hunsdon, the lord chancellor and ally of Oxford's friend Lord Sussex. I suggest that this might have been before 1576 but there is no evidence either way. Leicester's own finances at the time were parlous: the previous year he had to borrow £5,000 from the queen (Skidmore, p. 326), and he would be unlikely to raise the first £500 from capital, that is, sale or mortgage of his lands for The Theatre project.

5. "Stage well suited...": Wiggins, p. 10.

6. The Theatre was open for twenty years until replaced by the Globe.

7. "The Curtain": Wiggins, p. 10.

8. "seems to spring fully-formed...": Wiggins, p. 7. G. Taylor (p. 25) points out that there was no pre-existing theatrical repertoire for the two new theaters opened in 1576 and 1577, by which he means he knows of no evidence for such repertoire.

9. Vagabond status: Wiggins, p. 11.

10. Gosson—Arber, p. 34.

11. Lodge on Gosson: Chambers IV, p. 206, quotes from Lodge (untitled): "Whence fet you Catiline's invective? Believe me, I should prefer Wilson's short and sweet if I were judge, a piece worth praise, the practice of a good scholar: would the wiser overlook that they may perhaps cull some wisdom out of a player's toy."

12. Gosson on "Italian books" quoted by Wiggins, p. 8.

13. "the plays that are feigned" quoted by W.C. Hazlitt, p. 188. Apart from Thomas Lodge with whom Gosson fights a running battle, the only other author Gosson refers to is the author of *The Play of Plays*. It is noticeable and surprising that authors are treated much less severely than are actors and their audiences—surprising, because authors would be the principal conduit of the works of the devil denounced by Gosson and his like. The nobility is also treated a good deal more circumspectly (see note 15 below), and this is the reason why Gosson does not name, let alone trust Oxford, whose plays are stuffed with bawdries (Kiernan passim). Because *A Yorkshire Tragedy* (which I believe to be an early "Shakespeare" play) is even in its adapted form (see Chapter Eight, note 11) only 700 lines long, perhaps it could have formed part of *The Play of Plays*.

14. "Gosson's importance": Wiggins, p. 9.

15. The anonymous *A Second Blast of Retrait from Plays* (1580) gives a nod to this argument on the devil's works: "And so, according to the quality [i.e., their social standing, not their competence], superstition doth increase [i.e., because the author is upper class, so superstition is nurtured]." Quoted by W.C. Hazlitt, p. 116; and see Chapter Seven, note 14.

16. *The Jew, School of Abuse*—Arber, p. 40; not Marlowe's anti-Semitic *Jew of Malta*, which is dated some ten years later.

17. "not regarded as literature": Logan Pearsall-Smith, p. 7. Even by 1600 Sir Thomas Bodley, worried that his projected library should suffer scandal if plays were preserved in it, said: "Happily some plays may be worthy of keeping, but hardly one in forty." Quoted by F.C. Boas.

18. Tilney's patent: Chambers IV, p. 285.
19. Tamburlaine: Raleigh, p. 105.
20. Marlowe: Wiggins, p. 34.
21. Gosson the witness of the revolution: Wiggins, p. 9. My italics.
22. Cross-pollinating: see, for instance, J.A. Lavin III, p. 73.
23. Actors' status: see p. 150ff.
24. "Drama the best art": Nicoll, p. 12. My italics.
25. Identifying early plays: Chambers IV, pp. 285–87.
26. Phillips, quoted by Bell, p. 140.
27. *Ibid.*, approved by Schoenbaum 1970, p. 304.

Chapter Six

1. Opinions of contemporaries and praises of Oxford. Several pinches of salt may be required, but to discount the praise entirely can only be perversely unscholarly. Galateo: the title of Della Cassa's treatise on education and Italian etiquette (1560). "Tuscanism"—also attacked by Nashe—see Nelson, p. 227.
2. "Eared like to Midas" refers to the donkeys' ears given to Midas for judging Pan superior to Apollo in a music contest. The ass (derogatory of an ill-advised man?) theme in relation to Oxford reappears. See p. 173.
3. "saturnine paltery"—A character reference.
4. The Courtier—see p. 31.
5. Sturmius—see p. 53.
6. Oxford compared to Achilles, see p. 78; for the later comparison by Oxford of Essex to Achilles, see p. 182.
7. Barroom humor: see, for instance, Dromgoole, p. 159.
8. Black Will: see p. 34.
9. Rich quoted by Ward p. 193.
10. Louanges: cf. Ronsard. See p. 19.
11. "sold a goodly manor for a song": consider also Rosalind to Jaques in *As You Like It*: "A traveller by my faith, you have great reason to be sad. I fear you have sold your own lands to see other men's and to have nothing is to have rich eyes and poor hands" [IV, i, ll. 22–23].
12. Bed trick: Shapiro, p. 245, uses this reference to try to denigrate Stritmatter's researches into the underlinings in Oxford's Geneva Bible (see Chapter Two, note 23) showing that the rather distantly comparable biblical reference at Genesis 29:23 is not underlined. Oxford had certainly enough material to draw on from his own life.
13. Leontes continues to reject the baby: Nelson, pp. 176–177. Nina Green points up the reference in the play.
14. "The prince's jester": see also p. 102 where Oxford is the Clown in *Antony and Cleopatra*.
15. Hall was an implacable enemy of Oxford, although "Pontian" may be a compliment. The Pontiana Academy in Naples was founded by Giovanni Pontano (d. 1603), who is arguably the finest Italian post-classical poet in Latin (Gardner, p. 26). His other comments, however, include: "Let Labeo, or who else list for me,/Go lose his ears and fall to alchemy" [*Virgedemarium* IV, 4, ll. 14–15]. (Ear loss seems to be a critic's regular punishment fear—see Gascoigne on p. 29.) "Labeo reserves a long nail for the nonce/To wound my margents through the leaves at once" [*ibid.*, VI, 1, ll. 1, 2] ("Margents": comments written in the margins of books) "So Labeo weens it my eternal shame/To prove I never earned a poet's name" [*ibid.*, ll. 184–85]. "Perdy, I loath.../Or Labeo's poems" [VI, 2, ll. 5, 8]. Hall's usual standard for literary criticism can be seen from the quotation on page 85, and from this:

> But let no rebel satyr dare traduce
> Th' eternal legends of thy Faerie Muse,
> Renowmed Spencer, whom no earthly wight
> Dares once to emulate, much less dares despight.
> Sallust of France and Tuscan Ariosto,

[du Bartas and Ariosto]
Yield up the laurel garland you have lost
And let all others wear with me
[i.e., including Oxford]
Or let their undeserving temples bared be [*ibid.*, I, 4, ll. 21–28].

16. Cuoco examination: discovered, transcribed and translated by Magri: DVS Paper April 2003.
17. Court choreography: for another example see J.E. Neale, p. 138.
18. Francis and Robert Southwell were the grandson and great-grandson of the 15th Earl of Oxford. Technically they were the 17th earl's first cousins once and twice removed. Correspondence with Alice Crampin. See p. 96.
19. Eight cartloads of goods: Privy Council Order, September 4, 1578.
20. Gilbert Talbot — see Malim: *GO*. Gads Hill incident — see p. 33.
21. Blackfriars: The original theater had been used by companies of choirboys (one being Mulcaster's — see p. 74) which were amalgamated under Lyly's management at the time of his employment by Oxford, c. 1580.
22. Tower of London: Honan, p. 89
23. *A Compendious or Brief Relationship*: see Schoenbaum 1970, p. 316. Some ascribe this to William Smith, the nephew of Sir Thomas Smith, writing of some unrecorded fall from grace of his.
24. Health: for the rest of his life, Oxford's health was a continuing source of worry to him. See Moore, p. 240.
25. Letter to Burghley: Nelson, p. 285.
26. Commander of the horse: This was an elite appointment. The heavy cavalry was the one department in which the English force was superior to the Spanish, as demonstrated at Zutphen later in the year. While *Henry V* shows Oxford amusingly detrimental towards the infantry recruits, it was they who withstood and beat off the veteran Spanish levies earlier in the year. Leicester's military achievements were modest: he showed himself totally incompetent in regard to the commissariat, and totally hopeless diplomatically towards his Dutch allies (where he did not follow the queen's specific orders) and his English veterans. Elizabeth's best soldier, Sir John Norris, returned to England disgusted by him. He ignored the specific warnings he received about the two traitors he appointed, who betrayed Deventer and the sconce at Zutphen. Mattingly, pp. 56–60, and 133.
27. Burghley's letter quoted by R. Detobel, *DVSNL* (February 1999).
28. "lynx": At p. 27.
29. Notes in *Hecatompathia*: Lewis, p. 483.
30. Latin poets — see p. 46.
31. Lyly: Nelson, p. 24.
32. Hamlet and Ophelia: see p. 92.
33. Absence of post–1588 quotations: the logical deduction is that the library was no longer open to Oxford. See Jolly: *GO*.
34. "Shakespeare's gloomy period" Sir Sidney Lee, p. 417, disposes of any biographical nexus to the life and career of William Shakespeare. The alternative proposition that there is no necessity for it is put by G. Wilson Knight 1930, p. 263ff.
35. Edward Ferrys: possibly Puttenham's mistake for George Ferrers, the part author of *A Mirror for Magistrates*. There is a debate as to when Puttenham's *The Arte of English Poesy* was begun; it could have been at any time between 1568 and 1589. These references might represent an early part of the work.
36. Michael Lok: as an insight into Oxford's character, he employs Lok's nephew some 15 years later — see p. 99; Lok has to complain then of not being paid!
37. Patruchius Ubaldinas: Clark, p. 105.
38. *The Moral of Mind and Measure*: Clark, p. 102.
39. *The Taming of a Shrew* a first shot: Bullough I, p. 58, quoted by R. Jimenez, *SOSNL* (Spring 2008).
40. Impressive play structure: R. Hoseley, p. 289, quoted in Jimenez.
41. *The Rape of the Second Helen*: Clark, p. 304.

42. Saint Jacques (as a French speaker would call it): Magri, *DVSNL* (February 2007).
43. The smart set language: G.P. Krapp, p. 43.
44. The Duke of Millayn and the Marquess of Mantua: Clark, p. 298.
45. Topicalities in *Love's Labour's Lost*: Lamb 1986. The impossibility of this play being written by William Shakespeare is dealt with on pp. 123 and 236.
46. Russian mission (1582): Rima Greenhill, *Oxfordian* IX.
47. *The History of Portio and Demorantes*: Clark, p. 331.
48. Michael Lok: One of the more pleasant aspects of Oxford's character was his kindness in employing Lok's destitute nephew Henry, a very minor religious poet. As well as writing sonnet dedications in his *Ecclesiastes* (1597) to almost anybody who was somebody, he wrote one to Oxford, containing the unmemorable lines: "Your passed noble proof doth well assure/ Your blood's, your mind's, your body's excellence" (quotation from Nina Greene's website).
49. Venetian Law: Magri, *DVSNL* (February 2009).
50. Actual knowledge of Venice: Oxford is sometimes ruled out as he does not mention the canals. He takes knowledge of these for granted in his hearers and distinguishes the *traghetto* which crosses the canals from the "common ferry" which runs across the lagoon and up the River Brenta to Belmont.
51. Belmont: Magri, *GO*. The name Belmont comes from an Italian source, Il Pecorone.
52. Zelauto: see Hamilton, SS54.
53. Ptolome: Clark, p. 349.
54. Clown in *Antony and Cleopatra*: R. Whalen, *SOSNL* (Summer 1998). See also Benedick, "the Prince's jester" in *Much Ado About Nothing* on p. 84.
55. Thomas Browne — Clark, p. 388 — contribution by Ruth L. Miller.
56. "Cataian": Clark, p. 371
57. Bells of the church of St. Bennett — Clark, p. 383–86, quoting Admiral H. Holland. The banning of performances on Sunday in 1581 dates *Twelfth Night* precisely.
58. "alarmingly prescient account" A. Barton quoted by Watson, p. 50.
59. "shall": from Clark, pp. 432, 444. The last two lines of the quotation are sometimes taken out of context to show a date for *Coriolanus*, when Sir Hugh Myddleton proposed a new water channel to bring fresh water to London. The context is, however, clear: The House of Lords should not allow Mildmay to divert the flow of its current of deliberation and allow itself to be used as his "channel."
60. G. Lambin reviewed by Jolly, *DVSNL* (June 2003).
61. *Romeo and Juliet* source, see Chapter Two, note 10.
62. *As You Like It* political situation — Clark, p. 508.
63. Siena mosaic — Bate 2008 introduction links the speech to its depiction of the Seven Ages of Man to a German fourteenth-century wood cut (where would William Shakespeare have seen that?) and ignores the more obvious connection to the mosaic in Siena Cathedral.
64. Axiochus — C. Paul, *SOSNL* (Summer 2003).
65. Pigge — Clark, p. 528.
66. *Historie of fferrar* — *ibid.*, p. 529.
67. Ariodante and Genevora — *ibid.*, p. 534. *Much Ado About Nothing* is firmly dated by the Dogberry Verges references — see p. 86.
68. Saggitary — *ibid.*, p. 570 — contribution of B.R. Saunders.
69. Family of Love — *ibid.*, p. 572 — contribution of R.L. Miller.
70. "disquietingly prescient": A. Barton, again quoted by Watson, see note 58 above.
71. Phyllida and Corin: Clark, p. 603.
72. Musk rose: *ibid.*, p. 625.
73. Monsieur: *ibid.*, p. 618.
74. *Agamemnon and Ulysses*: *ibid.*, p. 627. The fact that *Agamemnon and Ulysses* was played by the Children of the Earl of Oxford is noted in Chambers: "The Earl of Oxford was himself a famous dramatist, was indeed considered as the best of his time for comedy, and therefore it is most natural to suppose that Oxford's boys both in January 1584 and on St. John's Day [December 27] following, acted plays by their own patron. I firmly believe that Agamemnon And Ulysses (though I agree it might have been a probable subject for Lyly as it might have been for any other dramatist of the time) is one of Oxford's lost comedies" [II, pp. 471 and 365,

note 19]. Chambers may be confused by the dating problem; because England had not adopted the Gregorian Roman calendar, the period January 1–March 24 (the old-style New Year's Eve) is in this case 1584 as contemporaneously dated in England: 1585 by the "New Style": and 1584/5 by scholars. St. John's Day precedes January 1584/5, when the Children put on Lyly's *Campaspe*, and *Sappho and Phao* in that month before the queen at Blackfriars.

75. Potato — Clark, p. 618.
76. "The best actors...": "It may be doubted whether there is anything more wonderful in Shakespeare in the way in which this Polonian speech, at one slight side blow, impales sixteenth–seventeenth century criticism, with the due pin, on the due piece of cork, for ever." Saintsbury 1922, p. 149n.
77. Mission to Denmark — Clark, p. 633.
78. Horace de Vere — see p. 199.
79. Astronomists — R. Brazil, *SOSNL* (Summer 2002).
80. Rosenkrantz and Guildenstern — L.J. Swank, *SOSNL* (Fall 2003).
81. *The Murder of Gonzago*: J. Hamill, *SOSNL* (Fall 2003), N. Magri *DVSNL* June 2009.
82. Duke of Urbino: J. Hamill, *SOSNL* (Fall 2003), see p. 57.
83. Slender: see p. 251.
84. Raleigh: Clark, pp. 750, 760.
85. Babington's clock: *ibid.*, p. 768.
86. Darnley assassination drawing: *ibid.*
87. *The Buik of the Cronicles of Scotland*: *ibid.*, p. 854.
88. St. Bartholomew's Day: *ibid.*, p. 839.
89. Dating of *King Lear*: Henry III's massacre: *ibid.*, pp. 883, 884. Most "orthodox" critics date *King Lear* to 1606 or so, because of the reference to Cordel or Cordelia, the third daughter of Sir Brian Annesley (d. 1604), and her efforts to counter the action of her elder sisters to have him declared insane. Where did Sir Brian get this name for his after-thought daughter born in 1590 (just after the topicalities in *King Lear*)? The name Cordelia looks like a "Shakespearean" invention just like Innogen/Imogen and Jessica (see p. 48). In the family circumstances in 1606 it would be a gross insult to a well-connected family to use the name in a new stage-play.
90. "Monsieur La Far": the quotation only in Wells and Taylor: The History of *King Lear* (Scene 17, ll. 1–9) and not in The Tragedy of *King Lear*.
91. Skalliger: R. Jimenez, *SOSNL* (Winter 2008).
92. *Arden of Feversham, A Yorkshire Tragedy*: see p. 34.
93. History plays: see my earlier reference to Thomas of Woodstock on p. 33.
94. Glorification of Oxford's ancestors: D. Wright, *SOSNL* (Spring 2008). See also p. 127.
95. "broached" R. Jimenez, *SOSNL* (Fall 2001).
96. "four swords and bucklers": I point out (p. 143) that "orthodox" critics are in an awful tangle: (to them) what could Sidney be referring to as they say none of the Shakespeare plays with their clashes of armies on stage had been written by the time Sidney died? There are a few pre–Sidney non–Oxfordian examples, such as *Cambises* (Preston, c. 1562) and *Horestes* (1568 — but see p. 22), and only these can be the object of Sidney's scorn, if "orthodox" critics had any case.
97. Holinshed: W.G. Boswell-Stone.
98. *Sir Thomas More* references: Fran Gidley: Shakespeare in Composition — *Oxfordian* 4 (October 2001). See also Honigman 1990, where a manuscript life by Harpsfield is found by Topcliffe at More's son's home in 1582.
99. Brownists: see note 55 above.
100. Surrey: he was the first exponent of the "Shakespeare" sonnet. See p. 11.
101. Dr. Doddypoll: J. Rollett in conversation. P. Mc Carthy discusses at length many other pieces which well be "Shakespearean."
102. *Three Sisters of Mantua*: Magri 2005.
103. Stylometrics: see p. 135.
104. *The Spanish Maze*: R. Stritmatter and L. Kositzky following Malim 2002.
105. *Love's Labour's Lost*: E. Garnett and E. Gosse, pp. 197 and 199: they concede too much to the Baconians — those who maintain that Francis Bacon (1567–1626) wrote the plays — but at the time they wrote in 1903, there was no other extant candidate to replace William Shakespeare.

106. Miracles: J.D. Wilson, p. 41.
107. *Commedia dell'arte*: K Gilvary, *GO*.
108. Bruno: J. Arthos, p. 102. Bruno's neoplatonism does not appear on the grammar school curriculum of the period.
109. *Love's Labour's Lost*: The question arising for the "orthodox" critic to answer is how did William Shakespeare come to write, unmiraculously, this play? Why did he choose to waste his energies in writing an effete comedy in a style five or more years out of date and valueless from the point of view of parody? Even more damning, how did this man with no entrée to any circle of power or literary appreciation expect to make a living from it? Nevertheless, Honan can write, "He [William Shakespeare] was dazzled by models of verbal patterning he was slow to outgrow, and one of his handicaps was that he was likely to imitate styles long out of date and not to adapt to a later age that might possibly ask for more matter and less rhetoric" (p. 55). Emma Jolly noted this quotation for me. One might inquire where William Shakespeare learned those "models of verbal patterning" and "styles long out of date" in the first place. I have from time to time pursued the "orthodox" for an answer to my unanswerable question. The only effort in reply came from the blog of Oliver Kamm in *The Times* newspaper, who quoted from Act I, scene iii: "Now here is three studied ere you'll thrice wink: and how easy it is to put years to the word three and study three years in two words, the dancing horse will tell you" [ll. 49–53]. This reference is to a dancing horse exhibited by one Banks about 1593 — a clear later inserted topicality, but to Kamm it is the basis for dating the whole play.
110. I refer to this work here as *Arte*. For authorship of *The Arte of English Poesie* see also Charles M. Willis, p. 1ff. Quotations are from Gavin Alexander's edition, but the following "figures" are quoted by Rushton (who gives no references) and are not mentioned by Alexander: p. 25 Indent; p. 26 Lion and Lamb; p. 27 Singularity.
111. Sir Thomas Wilson criticized: Saintsbury 1922, pp. 33–34. Note Burke's contention that rules come from examples, not examples from rules. See Chapter Eight, note 60.
112. Disguised in "verse": Puttenham, the gentleman scholar, might wish to conceal his dependency on the stage for his examples: while he occasionally names a poet, he never names the playwright as the basis for one of his examples, or quotes directly from a play.
113. "Jets": Thomson, p. 94, quotes from a letter to Walsingham of January 25, 1586/7: "It is a woeful sight to see two hundred actors [mark that number, and wonder at the number of plays and playwrights required to keep so many in work] *jet* in their silks when five hundred poor people starve in the streets."
114. "Patroclus may *jet*" Gosson: Arber edition, pp. 39, 74.
115. Perdita the gardener: quoted by Willis, p. 226. Incidentally Oxford has some reputation as a gardener based on the magnificent garden at Brooke House Hackney in the last ten years or so of his life. Robert Armin, the comic actor in his *Quips upon Questions*, (1600) writes that he would going "[to wait on the right honorable my good lord my master whom I serve] at Hackney." The house was badly damaged in the war, and was finally pulled down in 1946, against the wishes of Oxfordians then.
116. Dating of Dido — consensus of authorities. The quotation is not apparently from Phaer's translation of the *Aeneid* (1560) which is not in iambic pentameter.
117. Fossils of a verse version: quotation from J.D. Wilson by Granville Barker 1970, p. 185.
118. Granville Barker: *ibid.*, and see p. 46.
119. "more polished versions": Jimenez 2008. Nicoll, p. 79: "We cannot be sure that he may not have been the original author merely expanding and refurbishing his own youthful work." The "improvement" on the original plays suggests a much longer time-scale than the short period between the original and the "improvement" suggested by the "orthodox" dating scheme.
120. Thomas of Woodstock: see Bradley 1961, p. 31: "Even in Richard II, not a little knowledge seems to be assumed, and points to the existence of a popular play on the earlier part of Richard's reign. Such a play exists, though it is not clear it is a genuine Shakespearean work."
121. Collaborations: this point is fortified when reconsidered in Chapter Eight.
122. Style development: there is a school of thought which seeks to date the plays by perceived developments in style allied to the eleven or twelve plays listed by Meres in 1598. See Chapter Seven, note 44.
123. Five-act form critics: e.g., Bate 1997, p. 68.

124. Five-act authorship supposition countered: Nicoll 1971, p. 160, supported by Granville Barker 1970, pp. 36–37.
125. Globe: Lavin, pp. 74, 80: "Again if the rebuilt Globe (1599) did not alter Shakespeare as a playwright — neither would Blackfriars in 1608."
126. Role of modern scholarship: contemporary literary criticism was influenced by the standards as perceived of classical theatre. Wiggins, pp. 79–80, reviews these standards and the subsequent developments.
127. Eloquence: W. Clemen pp. 25, 192ff and 290, and see also the opinion of R. Hoseley on p. 96.
128. "graceless stage effects" sent up by Falstaff — I *Henry IV*, II, v, ll. 381–390.
129. Locrine: although registered in 1594, Tucker Brooke dates it possibly as early as 1585. It is not in the same league as the seven plays mentioned on the previous page, and because it has "sub-Shakespearean' touches might be thought imitative of them.
130. Date of *Apology*: Dutton. p. 24.
131. "Follow Sidney, and goodbye to...": Saintsbury 1903, p. 41. See also note 96 above.
132. Sidney quoted by Dutton, p. 141.
133. *Ibid.*, p. 143
134. Clemen, p. 38. This contention giving no credit or identity to any predecessor or external influence I thought so important that I approached my German friends to see if the translation (by T.S. Dorsch) was a hundred percent accurate. They confirm it is. The original reads: "Ein starkes dramatisches Talent wird ganz von selbst diese festlegungen und starren Begrenzungen durchbrechen und die bestehenden Konventionen so handhaben, dass lebendige dramatische Wirkung von ihnen ausgebt."
135. Candidate: if Clemen considered Marlowe as a playwright with the requisite gifts and initiative, he would have surely named him at least as a possibility. He did not.
136. Sidney again quoted by Dutton, p. 146.
137. "Nothing to be quoted...": Saintsbury 1922, p. 58.
138. Sidney again quoted by Dutton, pp. 136–137. In parentheses we may note the *Oxford English Dictionary* attributes to Sidney the first usage of the words: bugbear (*Troilus and Cressida* IV, ii, l. 34); dumb-stricken (strikes ... dumb — *Two Gentlemen of Verona* II, ii, l. 21); far-fetched (far-fet — 2 *Henry VI* III, i, l. 293); milk-white (e.g., *Timon of Athens* I, ii, l. 183); eye-pleasing (pleasing eye — I *Henry IV* II, v, l. 425); hang-worthy (worthy to be hanged — *The Winter's Tale* II, iii, 109). Sydney as a language innovator: see Melvyn Bragg, pp. 134–135. Bragg and the *Oxford English Dictionary* give Sidney credit for "miniature," "honey-flowing," "well-shading" and "long-with-love-acquainted."
139. *Horestes* — see p. 22.
140. Marlowe: Saintsbury 1903, p. 78.
141. Gielgud (as reported to me): the opinion of actors should be treasured; after all, they have to "sell" the play to their audiences.
142. Marlowe's influence: R. Logan, p. 232. For "Shakespeare" as imitator, compare the quotation from J. Middleton Murry, Chapter Eight, note 77.
143. Marlovians: the comparisons selected are mainly taken from Logan and a list of parallelisms from C. Hoffman. The Marlovians' contentions on the identity aspect are roughly handled by Schoenbaum 1970, p. 622ff, without recourse to the point that, like William Shakespeare, he was born ten years too late to be the catalyst of the revolution. For another comparison example see Chapter Eight, note 71.
144. Marlowe an inspiration — Logan p. 232. Perhaps Malone's editor James Boswell jnr gives us the last word on Marlowe when in dissenting from Malone's views on Marlowe's plays which, " had a prolonged life acquainted with *better models* [i.e. Shakespeare — there could be no one else], *gave promise of a high degree of excellence*" (Variorum 1821 III p. 6).
145. No connection with the stage: Bate 1997, p. 67.
146. P. Brook: conversation reported to me. Indeed, his comments rule out all other claimants to authorship, none of whom, including William Shakespeare, could have written the acting critique which follows.
147. Coleridge: Bell edition, p. 9.
148. William Shakespeare's roles are more fully examined in the appendix p. 235ff.

149. 1576: the year The Theatre was opened.
150. Murderous Michael: see p. 34.
151. Flushing, perhaps, rather than Calais as Oxford's initial destination on his way via Bruges to Brussels in July 1574.
152. "roabes": The same description as in Hall, quoted on p. 160.
153. Epilogue to *2 Henry IV*: e.g., Shapiro, pp. 263–265.
154. Writing specific parts: e.g., *ibid.*, pp. 259–262.
155. Barton, p. 64.
156. Original play: i.e., *The Taming of a Shrew*: Barton, p. 94. There seems to be a ladder of social improvement in the caricatures as evidenced from later references. See p. 247.
157. *Sir Thomas More*: According to his son-in-law William Roper, More is known to have acted in interludes while in the household of Cardinal Morton c. 1490 — Alison Weir 2001, p. 90. I suggest that this piece of information would be only available to court litterati. For the argument that Sir Thomas More is wholly a "Shakespeare" play, see p. 120. Quotation is from the Tucker Brooke version.
158. "Up to the elbows": the author knows the Latin "manus" (hand) includes the hand and the forearm.
159. Nashe: see p. 168.
160. The arguments over *Groatsworth* are fully debated on pp. 240ff. For evidence of William Shakespeare's acting career, see p. 255.
161. Hall: "orthodox" critics might quote the first four lines out of full context as evidence that is limited, unlike the target of Hall's attack. The attack was not on Marlowe or Tamberlaine — Marlowe had been dead five years. Hall was referring to Alleyn and not Oxford. Alleyn however did not play comic parts and his writings were not well-thought of.
162. "Huf-cap" seems to be a reference to strong beer (Lewis, p. 304), to which Oxford seems to have been partial. See p. 160.
163. "Side-robes": Compare the similar description for "Adon" on p. 153.
164. Terence as cover for a nobleman: D. Price quotes (p. 63) both Ascham (1570) and Montaigne (1580) as translated by John Florio in 1603 to this effect.
165. Social rank: Ogburn, p. 92.
166. Talking out of turn: ears might be lost — see p. 29 and Chapter Six n.15.
167. Conspiracy theory: while I cannot see how this idea need arise, I suppose it depends on how you define the term. Peter Moore thought the "conspiracy" whereby the identity of Sidney's Stella, a married aristocrat whose subsequent career might reflect badly on the national hero, was concealed is analogous: pp. 312–21. I still think it is a matter of those who knew, knew that it was in everyone's interest to keep quiet.

Chapter Seven

1. "Willy": identified by both Dryden and Rowe as Shakespeare — Schoenbaum 1970, p. 139. Schoenbaum himself (along with Lewis, p. 308) identified Willy "more plausibly" with Richard Wills, Willes or Willy, the learned author of *De Re Poetica* who died in about 1579. As the next quoted stanza reveals, "Willy" is very much alive in his "idle cell."
2. Preface to *Menaphon*: Text from *Prose of the English Renaissance*, pp. 423ff.
3. "Noverint": "Know (all men)" — start of a deed poll in Latin.
4. Dorna Bewley points out that "fair" is close to "Vair," the suggested contemporary pronunciation of Vere.
5. "Blood is a beggar" rewritten: alternatively Oxford may have deleted the sentence once Nashe had drawn attention to it.
6. Plagiarists: Nashe is not above borrowing himself. See p. 172.
7. Churchyard: Clark, p. 931.
8. Nashe: *ibid.*, p. 937, contributed by C.W. Barrell.
9. "Chaucerism": Chaucer was one of the books purchased for Oxford during his 1569 illness.
10. "Orator" — i.e., one who prays to God.

11. "Special enemies": Observe and enjoy these comparisons: "Doth it not show vilely in me to enjoy small beer" [2 *Henry IV*, II, ii, l. 6]; "Belike then my appetite was not princely got: for by my troth, I do remember the poor creature, small beer" [*ibid.*, ll. 9–11]; Jack Cade: "And I will make it a felony to drink small beer" [2 *Henry VI*, II, ii, l. 69]; Iago (contemptuously of women): "To suckle fools and chronicle small beer" [*Othello* II, i, l. 164].

12. Tobin's reviewer: Harriett Hawkins, p. 184.

13. Martin Marprelate pamphlets: a furious exchange of pamphlets, ranging Harvey and the conservative-minded poets (see pp. 66, 73) allied to a Puritan element on one side and Nashe (supported by Oxford) on the other. See R. Detobel and K.C. Ligon on the Harvey-Nashe quarrel (http://www.elizabethanauthors.com/harvey-nasheOO2.htm)

14. "Ass": The author of *The Third Blast of Retrait from Plays and Theatres* (1580; see p. 72) has a take on the attitude of the nobility (emphasis added):

> An objection: But Some perhaps will say, The noble man delighteth in such things, whose humours must be contented, partly *for fear* and partly for commodity: *and if they write matters pleasant*, they are best preferred in court among the cunning heads.
>
> Answer: Cunning heads, whose whole wits are never well exercised, but in the practice of such exploits! But are those things to be suffered and praised, because they please the rich, and content the Noble man, that always lives in ease? not so. A two legged Ass may be clothed in gold, a man of honour may be corrupt of judgment, though by his authority he may seem wiser than Socrates, whom Phoebus for wisdom judged the bel [best] ...
>
> Who meddles with nettles cannot pass unstinged: and he that deals with men of authority otherwise than may like [please] them, cannot scape from his danger without hurt. I may not stay longer on this point [Coward, "*for fear*" no doubt, but understandable! See p. 29 and Chapter Six, note 15]. As I have a saying to *these versifying playmakers*: so must I likewise deal with shameless inactors [Quotation from W.C. Hazlitt, pp. 146–47].

I take these remarks as personal to Oxford the playwright in 1580. "Ass" may not seem quite so stupid-sounding a description as it does now: perhaps it is applied to a person stupidly accepting bad advice or following bad customs or habits. "Shakespeare's" own usages do seem however more like ours. Note that the second paragraph with its plural usages is general, and not particular anymore.

15. "Mutius": Mutius with the medial "aristocratic 'i'" also exemplified by "Maximius" the final name of the gentle Melicertus the rival shepherd in love to Menaphon in Greene's *Menaphon*, which contains descriptions of the lady's anatomy reminiscent (and imitative) of *Venus and Adonis*. Mutus: "silent" or "dumb" may reflect on Oxford's withdrawal from public life. In default of a logical case, "orthodox" critics are apt to treat such references with derision, but without alternative explanation — e.g., Bate 1997, p. 66.

16. Marston: other references in *The Scourge of Villany* are, it is argued, to Oxford, such as Torquatus, which seems to reflect the twisted necklace in the Gheeraerts portrait of Oxford. The name brings to mind Torquato, Bruno's character — see p. 59. In this Marston repeats his criticism in *The Scourge of Villany* I: "Jack [Kemp] room for a vaulting skip,/Room for Torquatus that ne'er op'd his lip." And in his introduction to his *Second Satire*: "Yet when by some scurvy chance it [*The First Satire*] shall come into the late perfumed fist of judicial Torquatus (that, like some rotten stick in a troubled water, hath got a great deal of barmy froth to stick to his sides) I know he will vouchsafe it some of his new minted epithets [as Real, Intrinsecate, Delphic] when in my conscience he understands not the least part of it. But from thence proceeds his judgment." "Real" is found in *All's Well That Ends Well* (V, iii, l. 308) and *Coriolanus* (III, i, 149); "intrinsecate" is found in *Antony and Cleopatra* (V, ii, l. 209); "Delphic" reference is in *The Winter's Tale* to Delphos in Acts II and III; "understands not the least part of it" — i.e., takes on board not one word of the criticism.

17. Trentame acrostic: Anderson, p. 249.

18. Lady Trentham portrait: J. Crick, *DVSNL* (November 2006).

19. Girls men marry: Lewis, p. 503.

20. The sonnets, certainly numbers 1 through 126 are treated as autobiographical: further reference to this aspect is made at p. 260 of the appendix, where William's claim to authorship of them is discussed.

21. Southampton and Elizabeth de Vere: older British readers will recall Lance Percival's spoof calypso: "Shame and Scandal in the Familee."

22. *Clitophon and Leucippe*: correspondence with Mark Anderson.
23. "E-VER": e.g., Bate 1997, p. 66. See also Marston's reference p. 175.
24. "Name receives a brand": G. Blakemore Evans, p. 222.
25. "common grave": not quite what William Shakespeare perhaps had in mind for himself back in Stratford—see p. 262.
26. Financial efforts: these efforts are sent up by Jonson in Act IV of *Every Man out of His Humour*.
27. 1594 payment: Ogburn, p. 56.
28. Essex: this account of his career follows such authorities as Anderson. As "the Rival Poet" see Moore pp. 2–36. Essex and Southampton: these "affections" were certainly homosexual, differentiated from the paternal ones of Oxford.
29. Physical threat: see the danger Gascoigne thought himself in when attacking Oxford, p. 29.
30. Sonnet 94: see also *Edward III* II, i, l. 451.
31. 1583–84 expedition to Ireland: see p. 116.
32. "male whore": V, i, l. 17. Contrast the much earlier comparisons of Oxford with Achilles at p. 60 (by himself) and p. 87 (by Harvey).
33. Dedication cryptogram: Dr. J. Rollett: *GO*
34. Southampton's titles were restored to him on his release from the Tower on April 10, 1603. If the W.H. suggestion is correct, then the first version of the *Oxford Collection of Sonnets* would not have included Sonnet 107ff. See also Rubinstein and James, p. 185. (I arrived independently at the conclusion that W.H. equals H.W., Southampton's initials when he had lost his titles, and the supposition provides an exact date for the use of the "commoner," non-noble title in the dedication.)
35. "canopy": Rollett, *DVSNL* June and October 2007.
36. Watson parody: correspondence with R. Detobel and W.R. Hess.
37. Anacreontic: no doubt, back in Stratford-upon-Avon they thought of nothing else, like the Irish litigant in the Victorian legal story:

> JUDGE: Has your client never heard of Volenti non fit injuria?
>
> THE COMMON SARGEANT (Irish Barrister): My Lord, my client, back home in his hut in the back of County Tipperary, my lord, warmin' both hands in the t'in trail of smoke curlin' up from his little peat fire, my lord, he t'inks of nothin' else.

38. Pseudonym—see the quotation from Hall on p. 174: "First heir of my invention" means that there were other "heirs" of that "invention": that is, between the actual date of composition and the dedication in 1593. This is Coleridge's thesis—see p. 227. In rhetoric, "invention" is the finding out or selection of topics; or, more widely, the exercise of the imagination—G. Blakemore Evans, p. 183.
39. Patronage: "The system of patronage [by a rich man towards an aspiring author] retarded the development of authorship as a profession in two ways: directly, by encouraging publishers to give less money on the plea that the patron would make it up; indirectly, by so lowering the status of authors who tried to live by their pens that no one with any pretension to rank or fashion could take money for his writings. To escape any imputation of doing so, fashionable authors avoided print altogether, and circulated their writings among their friends in manuscript. It was this practice which encouraged piracy more than anything else" (Pollard, p. 28). Therefore, to get a play (that apparently debased form of literature—see p. 69) into print and protect it against piracy, its author would have to be anonymous or adopt a pseudonym. However, Chute wrote (p. 58), "The case for William Shakespeare, who succeeded in getting [the Earl of Southampton] for his patron and then abandoned the relationship, is so exceptional as to stand alone in the history of Elizabethan letters."
40. Shakespeare in London: the evidence is not strong for these contentions, but see Hall quoted on p. 174. Then there is Nicholas Rowe's curious reference: "There is one instance so singular in the magnificence of this Patron of Shakespeare's [Southampton], that if I had not been assured that the story was handed down by Sir William Davenant, who was probably well acquainted with his affairs, I would not ventured to have inserted, that my Lord Southampton, at one time, gave him a thousand pounds to enable him to go through with a purchase he had in mind to." This looks like a conflation of the conjectured arrangements

made for the use of William's name and the queen's enormous annuity (see p. 89) paid to Oxford.

41. Touchstone: metaphorically, the standard for passing judgment (which he then exercises). Other references in the plays seem to chart an apparent progression in wealth and status and are dealt with on p. 153ff. Other references to William in the plays are dealt with in the appendix on p. 255ff.

42. Oxford is talking to William: Schoenbaum 1970, p. 840, note 106, meets the logical explanation by referring the reader to a review of one of the books: "This particular aberration is cited by Giles E. Dawson in a withering review — see *Shakespeare Quarterly* IV 1953 (165–170)." Inspection of this reference reveals a withering blast of invective against the argument without one word by way of reviewer's counterargument to contradict it or suggest an alternative (let alone a better) explanation.

43. Critical explanation: Duncan-Jones, p. 25.

44. Meres: see p. 198 and note. Mere's listing of the plays is used as a dating argument against Oxford's authorship, but not (anymore) on the basis that it is a comprehensive statement of all the plays written before 1599. The argument now is that Mere's list of eleven identified plays has a usage rate of 35 percent feminine and open endings, while the rate for the remaining plays increases to up to 65 percent, in line with the adoption of such endings by other playwrights. The fault in the argument is that Meres is probably using texts that may date to well before 1598: certainly the comedies will be much earlier, as Oxford in his state of mind in the 1590s would be unlikely to give them much reconsideration. Likewise four of the other plays appear in print before 1599, perhaps on the basis that Oxford had nothing much of consequence to add to the versions written much earlier: *Titus Andronicus* in his eyes did not perhaps merit further rewriting. In contrast he was in all probability rewriting his favorites among the remaining plays at any time from 1590 on, and introducing much greater frequency of feminine endings: in this he was in advance of his younger followers. The stylometric bean-counter arguments are thus met and turned into *Oxfordian* arguments when the actual dating parameters are applied. The rewriting styles also play havoc with stylometric studies. See pp. 135ff.

45. "newly corrected and augmented": put in to give or preserve the illusion that a separate author called William Shakespeare was contributing something to an old play.

46. Psychology: this is an area where it is extremely unwise for a nonprofessional to enter and speculate, although some biographers of William Shakespeare are tempted to add to their house of cards. In the plays there are plenty of examples to point to this basic thesis, as well as the absence of completely fresh plays in this final period (except possibly *The Tempest*). All I can do is to show the basic groundwork: a qualified academic psychologist is needed to look at the scenario through *Oxfordian* spectacles, and diagnose the problems afflicting Oxford from, say, 1588 onwards. The change in William Shakespeare is that dated by "orthodox" biographers (without any nexus of extrinsic evidence) to 1601. Here Oxfordians can readily accept their conclusions from the plays (as and when rewritten) and sonnets from 1588 onwards. For Oxford's own knowledge of contemporary medicine, see Kail, passim.

47. Harold Pinter: p. 8.

48. Other "claimant's" troubles in 1601: Francis Bacon's professional career was in 1601 beginning to take off. Well-connected Sir Henry Neville, imprisoned in the Tower for his minimal part in the Essex putsch, knew he was safe once Southampton was not to be executed.

49. Male heirs: see p. 249.

50. "Actors ... corrupt": Barton, p. 153.

51. Equivocation: defined as "the use of words or expressions susceptible of a double signification, in order to mislead."

52. 1596 trial: "We Must Speak by the Card." R. Desper: *Oxfordian* 4 (October 2001).

53. James I: Oxford was seeking favors from the new king, the last person he would wish to offend by producing *Macbeth*.

54. Strachey letter as a source for *The Tempest*: principally and irrefutably rejected by Nina Green. For the tenuous William Shakespeare connections see p. 213.

55. *The Spanish Maze*: Stritmatter and Kositzky 2007.

56. Florio's translation of Montaigne: See Maguin 1996.

57. "heads stood in their breasts"—possibly a reference to the additional material in the Beowulf manuscript, or to the Blemmyes at the edges of Egypt according to Pliny the elder. Did Oxford know of either of these references? See W.R. Hess and A. Tarica, "Beowulf," *DVSNL* (June 2009).

58. Burghley's cloak: Clark, p. 584.

59. William Shakespeare's connection to the 1608 Blackfriars—Nicoll 1971, p. 161. See also Bate 1997, p. 161. The argument is summarized in *GO* pp. 296ff. See p. 138. There is no evidence that any of the plays or poems contain any matter which can be related to post-1604 events. The "orthodox" have to "find" these to keep the Malone-Dowden-Chambers dating in agreement with William Shakespeare's biography.

60. Hackney: Oxford and his second wife lived for some years at Brooke House—see Chapter Five, note 115.

61. However, when Oxford could have adhered to the pope while in Venice without any comeback, he preferred to attend the Greek Orthodox Church there—See p. 94.

Chapter Eight

1. Puttenham, quoted by Willis, p. 257.

2. "Melicert"—R. Detobel, *GO*. For the "orthodox" these references present a serious problem which is generally ignored. See also p. 175 and note on Mutius.

3. Weever—quoted by Wells and Taylor, p. xliii. "None other": why should anyone else be involved?

4. Meres: Emma Jolly, "Meres: His Usefulness and Limitations," *DVSNL* (October 2007), p. 13. To G. Gregory Smith, Meres is "obviously a dullard to the most casual of readers—but he discloses an editorial cunning which does him credit and indeed makes The Comparative Discourse not the least important of [the documents in contemporary literature]. For by having no mind of his own and only a plodding interest in the whims of others, he gives us a digest of contemporary opinion which is of positive value." p. xci. For the attempted matching of dating to evolution of style, see Chapter Seven, note 44.

5. "Shaxberd": P. Thomson, p. 169. This listing is criticised as a Collier forgery, as an effort to link the use of the name "Shaxberd," which is shown as the author's name of some of the plays, to Stratford made long before Oxford was ever heard of as author—Shapiro, p. 259, accepts it as genuine. The problem is that the spelling "Shaxberd" is used *only* in this listing; for its possible significance as a jibe at William Shakespeare, see p. 258. The other matter is the inclusion of *The Spanish Maze* in the listing. The criticism asks the forger to invent an unknown play which just happens to be readily identifiable with *The Tempest*, see p. 193, and generally to evidence, with the production of a large number of "Shakespeare" plays at court in 1604–05, a scenario for Oxford as the playwright.

6. The somewhat scatter-brained aristocrat—See p. 256.

7. James I—Letter to Robert Cecil, *SOSNL* (February 1989). Why "Great Oxford," unless there was very good reason for that title (for a man, by the world's standards, who was a total failure)?

8. Gowry: Chambers II, p. 211.

9. Barksted: from Mirrha, mother of Adonis (ll. 69–72). See D. Price, pp. 137–38.

10. Webster, quoted by Halliday p. 269.

11. *A Yorkshire Tragedy*—see Chapter Five, note 13. This old play was resurrected, as some of the plot details follow the recent murder of his two children and attempted murder of his wife by Walter Calverly in 1605. Under the title is printed "Not so new [i.e., an old play] as Lamentable and true." At the top of the first page of text, its alternative title is shown as *All's One, or, One of Four Plaies in One, called A York-shire Tragedy*. The play is only some 700 lines and this may indicate that it was even shorter, perhaps being expanded after 1605 (a reason for not including it in the 1623 folio), and one of four plays. The titles of the other three have not survived, but some apparently shorter plays were put in groups. Feuillerat lists (series I, Vol. 21, p. xiii): "Twelfth Day [i.e., January 6, 1584/5]: An Invention called five plays in One" and "Shrove Sunday: An Invention called three plays in One." Also, Craik and Leech list in Volume III per-

formances at the Rose (1592): *Four Plays in One*. *A Yorkshire Tragedy* in its original version could well have been any one of these inventions. Nina Green effectively divorces it from the Calverly episode (Edward de Vere Newsletter — November 1990). See also the Cordel/Cordelia connection in *King Lear*, Chapter Six, note 89.

12. "Comedies out of sale": the chance of a reprint, let alone a collected works, was obviously remote if the grand possessors were involved.

13. Cardenio — see p. 203.

14. Perhaps one of the compromises Jonson may have had to make was to pass over Oxford's role as author. We shall see the small extent to which that constraint was bent.

15. Collaborations: see also p. 31. Other plays identified as "collaborative" reflect the "collaboration" between Oxford's apprentice self and his maturity.

16. Asquith, pp. 267ff. I note that she suggests that "Shakespeare" was an expert on the more arcane aspects of Catholic theology and liturgy: perhaps this was part of Oxford's cover as a spy on devotees.

17. *Henry VIII*: Dr. Johnson's summary appeals: "But the genius of Shakespeare comes in and goes out with Catherine. Every other part may be easily conceived and easily written." Raleigh 1908, p. 152.

18. *Cardenio*: it was entered in the Stationers' Register in 1653 but not apparently published as "The History of Cardennio by Mr. Fletcher and Shakespeare."

19. *Two Noble Kinsmen* — it may be that Oxford's part in this play comes from *Palamon and Arsett*, which had four performances by the Admirals Company in 1594, and itself a resurrection of the effort ascribed to Richard Edwards — see p. 31.

20. Continuity error — Shapiro, p. 294.

21. Counterblast to *The Faithful Shepherdess*: Asquith's overall view receives support from Wiggins, p. 114: "It is an overtly literary work, whose appeal lies more with descriptive lyrical passages than in its narrative which crawls slowly through a sludge of rhyming couplets." In contrast *The Drummond Conversations* ascribe a view to Jonson: "Fletcher and Beaumont ten years since have written The Faithful Shepherdess, A Tragicomedy well done." Perhaps this is a further piece of evidence towards the view that the conversations are a work of fiction (see Chapter Three, note 28). On the failure of the first production of *The Faithful Shepherd* (1608/9) Jonson wrote a sympathetic and encouraging verse to Fletcher, but Jonson (a secret Catholic at the time) would have been revolted by Fletcher's introduction in the printed edition of 1610, which contains a virulent commentary on Roman Catholic practices as attacked in the play itself, and so Jonson's change of attitude is accounted for. A court production nearly twenty years later, however, did achieve acclaim.

22. Jonson's loyalty: see also "De Shakespeare Nostrati," an extract taken from one of his notebooks and evidently written after his earlier notebooks were destroyed by fire in 1623: "He was indeed honest, and of an open and free nature: had an excellent fantasy: brave notions and gentle expressions; wherein he flowed with that facility, that it was necessary he should be stopped: Sufflimandus erat [he had to be suppressed] as Augustus said of Haterius. His wit was in his own power; would the rule had been so too. Many times he fell into those things, could not escape laughter; as when he said in the person of Caesar; one speaking to him: 'Caesar, thou dost me wrong.' He replied, 'Caesar never did wrong, but not without just cause' and such like. There was more in him to be praised than to be pardoned." These are the lines from *Julius Caesar*, as we have them: "Know Caesar doth not wrong, nor without cause/Will he be satisfied" (III, i, ll. 47–48).

23. Peacham is not the only quoter and lister of contemporary poets who does not mention William Shakespeare: there is no social reason for the omission of his name if he were the writer. Contrast Oxford. Professor Eagleton seeks to dispose of the *Oxfordian* argument by relying on the omission of the name of William Shakespeare as well from the works of contemporary minor poets. Peter Dickson makes the illuminating point that Peacham's publisher in 1622 had his shop some 70 feet from where the 1623 folio was being set up.

24. Peacham: Both editions were published after the 1623 folio and so a deliberate covert acknowledgment that "Shakespeare," the omitted name, was the pseudonym of one of his listed authors.

25. Sir George Buck: quoted by Nina Green's website. Bate also relies on him for his proposition that William Shakespeare was "known to be a central figure in the London theater" because

he wrote in his copy of *George a Green the Pinner of Wakefield* (printed in 1599) that this play was "written ... by a minister who act(ed) the Pin(n)er's part in it — teste W Shakespea(re)." With the strong probability that William was no longer in London when the note was written, the witness (testis) was probably Oxford himself (Bate 1997, p. 71). The thought that it could be inferred that a minister of the church would write a play and act in it is at least curious — Sir George, who was perhaps a bit thick and dazzled by his acquaintanceship with an earl, could have had his leg pulled not by William Shakespeare, but by Oxford himself.

26. The 1623 folio, and the prefaces and introductory matter refer to Oxford as "Shakespeare" — see pp. 212ff. Jonson slips in "my gentle Shakespeare (i.e., "noble")" in his ode.

27. Spanish marriage: Peter Dickson's researches referred to in *SOSNL* Summer 1998 and Spring 1999 by William Boyle. There is no known connection between William Shakespeare and the earls of Pembroke and Montgomery.

28. Oxford no time: in contrast to the vast amount of time available in Stratford enjoyed by William Shakespeare from 1600 on. Certainly he took no apparent interest in or defended the integrity of the plays. For instance, with Oxford dead, Daniel was in 1607 able to rewrite his *Cleopatra* (1594), a pale version of *Antony and Cleopatra*, incorporating Shakespearean phrases, names, and stage business (J. R. Brown p. 111) without apparent objection or concern from William Shakespeare.

29. "printed worth": one may speculate that Marston's poem, if it be by him, was a rejected preface to the Good Quarto of Hamlet — the memorial production, see p. 199.

30. Dr. Johnson's summary is in point: "No other author gave up his works to fortune and time with so little care; no books could be left in hands so likely to injure them, as plays frequently acted, yet continued in manuscript; no other transcribers were likely to be so little qualified for their task, as those who copied for the stage, at a time when the lower ranks of the people were universally illiterate."— quoted by Pollard, p. 100.

31. "gentle": i.e., noble: no other contemporary playwright, actor or poet can be found with this adjective applied to him/her.

32. Digges: quoted by Wells and Taylor, p. xlvi, who alter "moniment" to "monument"; Spenser's use of "moniment" is noted by Price, p. 189. While the heading is not hyphenated, the three references in the body of the poem are, as are the heading and the first line reference in the poem by I.M. on the same page of the folio.

33. Digges and Russell: R. Whalen, "Digges and Russell," *SOSNL* (Spring 2001).

34. Quotations from Wells and Taylor, p. xlv. Also Jonson seems to refer to Oxford when he writes: "In each of which [i.e., his "well-turned and true filed lines"]/He seems to shake a lance [same as "shake a spear"]/As brandished in the face of ignorance" [Whose ignorance? That of those who accept William Shakespeare as the author].

35. Basse: *ibid.*, p. xliv. Basse's poem was reproduced in the 1640 Benson edition of the poems headed "On the death of William Shakespeare who died in April 1616." I suspect editorial interference as Basse had been dead five years by 1640.

36. Lyly, Kidd, Marlowe: Jonson does not call on any writer flourishing after 1592.

37. "Shakespeare" unlearned: Jonson made his view perfectly clear when he wrote in *The Poetaster* Act V, scene I, where in the guise of Horace he is asked for his opinion of Virgil (i.e., Shakespeare, according to the pre–Victorian critic William Gifford supported by G. Gregory Smith II, pp. 393–95):

> His learning savours not the school-like gloss
> That most consists of echoing words and terms,
> And soonest wins a man an empty name;
> Nor any long or far-fetch'd circumstance
> Wrapp'd in the curious generalties of Arts;
> But in a direct and analytic sum
> Of all the worth and first effects of arts.
> And for his poesy, 'tis so ramm'd with life,
> That it shall gather strength of life, with being,
> And live hereafter more admired than now.

This is an opinion which no doubt appealed to Andrew Nuttall (see p. 229). "Thou hadst" must be in the pluperfect subjunctive tense signifying an impossible condition. It is followed by "I would not seek...," and therefore Jonson is pointing to a theoretical or impossible condition. Had Jonson meant to write in the indicative mood, making the condition one of fact, he would have written, "I will not seek," after indicative use of "hadst" which could in English be indicative or subjunctive.

38. Thomas Vicars: *Cheiragōgia: Manuductio ad Artem Rhetoricam*, second edition 1624, third edition 1628. References uncovered by F. Schurink: "An unnoticed early Reference to Shakespeare"—*Notes and Queries* (March 2006), pp. 72–74. Vicars married Sir Henry Neville's daughter in 1621, and the proponents of Sir Henry's case to be "Shakespeare" do not provide a reason for Vicars' omission of any reference to his father-in-law (d. 1615) in the 1624 first edition, printed after the 1623 folio—prima facie evidence that Sir Henry's case is unsustainable. See Rubinstein and James. Sir Henry also visited Venice in 1579, two years after the destruction of the Sagittary referred to in *Othello*. See note to p. 107.

39. Drayton quotation taken from Springarn, p. 136. This is apparently Drayton's only critical reference to "Shakespeare." Drayton was a patient of Dr. Hall (William Shakespeare's son-in-law) but neither man leaves any mention otherwise of William Shakespeare (see p. 220). The inference is therefore that to Drayton, Shakespeare the poet and William Shakespeare the doctor's father-in-law were two different people. I note that in 1627 Marlowe had been dead 35 years and the 1623 folio was only four years old, so the order mistake as I see it would be understandable.

40. Milton: quoted by Wells and Taylor, p. xlvii. Although Milton's references to Shakespeare are not hyphenated, the reference in the body of the preceding poem is.

41. I.M.S. quoted by Wells and Taylor, xlvii.

42. Brome quoted in H.C. Bartlett, p. 184. He served for a time as Jonson's secretary. The past tense "loved" rules out the Earl of Derby (d. 1642) as an authorship candidate.

43. The question marks are explained away as alternative exclamation marks (used as late as 1640?). See Moore, p. 326. Shake-speare is hyphenated in the title of Benson's book. Note also the opinion of the "learned."

44. Wood: *Atheniae Oxonienses* (1691) quoted by C. Ogburn, p. 411.

45. Walpole I, p. 166.

46. Fuller quoted by Halliday, p. 277.

47. Duchess of Newcastle: *ibid.*

48. Flecknoe quoted by G. Gregory-Smith II, p. 92.

49. Dryden: M.C. Bradbrook, p. 7.

50. *The Tempest*: quoted in Nichol-Smith 1946, p. 22.

51. *Essay on Dramatick Poesie*: *ibid.*, p. 16.

52. *All for Love* was Dryden's version of *Antony and Cleopatra* "without learning." On balance Dryden must have thought that nonsense. In his *Essay on Dramatic Poetry*: "Those who accuse Shakespeare [and he is not including himself] to have wanted learning give him the greater commendation: he was naturally learned: he needed not the spectacles of books to read nature: he looked inward and found her there." Dr. Johnson's opinion of Dryden is analogous. The argument seems to be that if one devotes very many long years to one's books, as did "Shakespeare" and Dryden, one no longer needs "the spectacles of books to read nature." See Burke, note 60, below. Similarly Nahum Tate wrote (in his address to Edward Tayler) in his tragedy *The Loyal General* (1680):

> I confess I cou'd never get a true account of his learning, and am apt to think it more than common report allows him. I am sure he never touches on a Roman Story, but the persons, the passages, the manners, the circumstances, the ceremonies, all are Roman. And what relishes yet of a more exact knowledge, you do not only see a Roman in his hero, but the particular genius of the man, without the least mistake of the character, given him by their best historians.... But however it far'd with our author for book-learning, 'tis evident that no man was better studied in men and things, the most useful knowledge for a dramatic writer. He was a most diligent spy upon Nature, trac'd her through her darkest recesses, pictur'd her in her just proportion and colours [J.R. Brown, p. 26].

53. *Aurung-Zebe* and *Troilus and Cressida* quoted in Nichol-Smith, p. 23.

54. Rowe: Schoenbaum 1970, p. 132. Perhaps Rowe (legitimately) thought there was no such "context" worthy of critical analysis. He wrote: "Immortal Shakespeare wrote/By no quaint

rules or hampering critics taught" (Prologue to *Jane Shore*, 1714). Perhaps we may transpose the adjectives for even better sense.

55. Tarleton woodcut: P. Holden, p. 90, who shows that William Shakespeare had written enough by 1588 for Tarleton to be an actor in his plays.

56. Pope quoted in Nichol-Smith, pp. 43, 42. Pope's own analysis of "Shakespeare's" want of learning make the author a polymath by our debased standards.

57. Pope: Schoenbaum 1970, p. 136.

58. Bacon: J.O. Fuller p. 35 — see H. Gordon, "Alexander Pope: An Oxfordian at Heart?" *Oxfordian* 5 (October 2002).

59. Farmer: Schoenbaum 1970, p. 149.

60. Samuel Johnson: quoted in Raleigh 1908, pp. xxxi, 2, 31, 36, 37, 39 and 40. Boswell records that Johnson declined to comment on Farmer's view of "Shakespeare's" academic achievements, contenting himself with the observation: "As I always said, Shakespeare had Latin enough to grammaticise his English" (i.e., a quite high degree of competence) Vol. III, p. 415. It is noticeable that where Johnson does not applaud Farmer's view, and Coleridge Malone's (see p. 226), they decline to comment directly but wrap up their fairly contrary reactions. See note 70 below. By way of contrast, Edmund Burke (if it were he — and what he meant by "nature"— see note 62 below) wrote: "Does anyone now [1769] enquire whether Shakespeare was learned? ... Learning, in its best sense, is only nature on the rebound; it is only the discovery of what is; and he who looks on nature with a penetrating eye, derives learning from the source. Rules of poetry have been deduced from the examples, not examples from the rules; as a poet therefore Shakespeare did not need books; *and in no instance in which he needed them as a philosopher, or historian, does he appear ignorant of what they teach*" (my italics). Johnson does not instance "Shakespeare" as an exception to this statement.

61. Garrick's celebration: Schoenbaum 1970, p. 154.

62. Garrick's oration: Stochholm pp. 83–86. She quotes from M.W. England for the theory based on Burke's style that Burke wrote the oration. By "nature" Burke means the whole universality of fact and thought, character and psychology.

63. Malone: Schoenbaum 1970, p. 170.

64. Malone no critic: *ibid.*, p. 242.

65. Malone quoted — *ibid.*, p. 183. For Marlowe, see Boswell — Note on Marlowe: Chapter Six, note 143.

66. "*Gorboduc* typical": Bradbrook, p. 11.

67. Malone, quoted by Clark, p. 2.

68. Malone's biography uncompleted: Schoenbaum 1970, p. 240. The disappointment and futility point may be picked up by Schoenbaum, giving three examples: (A) J. Halliwell Phillips: Preface: "No matter what pains a biographer may take to furnish his store, the result will not present a more brilliant appearance than did the needy shop of Romeo's apothecary. He is baffled in every quarter by the want of graphical documents, and little can be accomplished beyond a very imperfect sketch or outline of the material features of the poet's career." Quoted by Schoenbaum 1970, p. 426; The apothecary and his shop feature in Act V, scene I; (B) Henry Hallam — see notes 74 and 75 below; (C) himself — quoted on p. 4 above.

69. Malone quoted by Schoenbaum, p. 242.

70. Coleridge pp. 8–9, 243–44 and 246. I think Coleridge's attitude to Malone, and Johnson's to Farmer (see note 60 above), probably is that skepticism of a superior mind towards the conclusions of an inferior one and does not have the time or the inclination to check those conclusions.

71. Malone's correspondence. *The Gentleman's Magazine* (1841–42), p. 495, records a letter dated December 1787 to Malone recording Farmer's opinion that Marlowe contributed parts of the *Henry IV* plays, which Malone did not take on board. Farmer is also very rude about Capell, usually reckoned to be a competent critic, for suggesting that there was a relationship between: "What — will the aspiring blood of Lancaster/Sink into the ground? I thought it would have mounted" [3 *Henry VI*, V, vi, ll. 61–62] and "Highly scorning that the lowly earth/Should drink his blood, mounts up into the air" [*Edward II*, V, I., ll. 14–15]. Generally in the period 1660–1800 Marlowe was not totally ignored: adapted and debased versions of *Doctor Faustus* were performed from time to time into the eighteenth century, and a new edition of that play

was published in 1663. Dr. Johnson's own Prologue (1747), the first two lines of which are quoted on p. 222, states: "She [Virtue] saw great Faustus lay the ghost of Wit." The point is that commentators give no credit to Marlowe either as forerunner or as exemplar to "Shakespeare."
72. "Elizabethan drama": Wiggins, p. 7.
73. Shakespeare's plays a "curse": *ibid.*, pp. 131–132.
74. Hallam quoted by Schoenbaum 1970, p. 300.
75. *Ibid.*
76. Shakespeare "universally judged": H. Bloom, p. 31.
77. "Moments of major philosophical importance": A.D. Nuttall, pp. 382–383. This view when applied to current biographical scholarship causes trouble: the convolutions of critical argument result in metaphorical convulsions. Consider John Middleton Murry (pp. 28–29):

> many of the problems raised by the most modern criticism of Shakespeare appear to be falsely conceived. They are formulated on the tacit assumption that because Shakespeare was the supreme poet, it follows that his style must from the beginning have been supremely individual.... The probability is that the formative years of a poet of Shakespeare's peculiar kind would have been not much more but much less marked by idiosyncrasy than those of poets of a different kind. We should expect from such a man a peculiar kind of imitation of his slightly senior contemporaries — that imitation that cannot help doing what his contemporaries do a little better than they do it themselves. And this is, in fact, precisely what we find in much of the early work attributed to Shakespeare by the (1623) Folio. Those who have followed, with due care, the investigations of sceptical criticism will know the baffling frequency with which passages of early Shakespeare betray a marked similarity of style, or rather the manner, of Peele or Greene or Marlowe, and yet are notably superior, in that matter, to anything we know of the authors' own. The result is that the sceptic is driven to postulate a curious miracle by which, so soon as Shakespeare began to tinker with their work, the writing of those contemporaries invariably underwent an improvement in its own manner of which they themselves were *incapable*. And that this particular kind of improvement should be due to Shakespeare's revision is, in reality, less credible than the simple hypothesis it is intended to supersede — namely that Shakespeare is in the main himself the author of all the early work in the Folio.

Murry (again having to refer to "a curious miracle" — a marker phrase of readily explicable "orthodox" puzzlement) seems to be saying that "Shakespeare" wrote "better" Peele or Greene or Marlowe than did Peele or Greene or Marlowe. To imply that they improved thanks to "Shakespeare" (even though they were incapable of such improvement) defies analysis. The logical answer to Murry's problem is that "Shakespeare" borrowed from (let alone collaborated with) nobody: he precedes in time those other playwrights, who in their inferior writing were influenced by him. It is noticeable that, while Wiggins sees Chapman and Marston as the innovators and "Shakespeare" as the beneficiary, Murry mentions Chapman only as the putative "rival poet" of the sonnets and Marston not at all, and neither of them take on board the effect of Clemen's vital argument (pp. 133ff). Nuttall might have added that Restoration critics admit that all "Shakespeare's" advanced classical and cultural competence and appreciation must have been largely self-taught.

Afterword

1. Worden: Richard Wilson, p. 11, quoting Worden: *Shakespeare and Politics*: SS 44.
2. Critics' reaction: I conducted a very short correspondence with Peter Holland's editors of the *Oxford Dictionary of National Biography* (2004) over the misrepresentations of the anti-"orthodox" arguments contained in the entry he had written for William Shakespeare, where he puts into the mouths of disbelievers ridiculous arguments, thus: "All these [anti–William Shakespeare] claims surmount the contemporary evidence for William Shakespeare by arguing for an early modern conspiracy and often a late one among academics and others to suppress 'the truth.' Many resolve the inconveniently early death of their candidate by arguing for the posthumous slow release of the plays" [Volume 51, p. 45]. When the fact that people who have studied the authorship question for twenty years or more know no-one (let alone "many") who

subscribes to one or both of these propositions was pointed out to Professor Holland, he could see "no reason to suggest any revision to my entry in the *Oxford Dictionary of National Biography*," without any defense for his contentions.

Appendix B

1. "fool" quoted by Sir E. Durning Lawrence, p. 179, from the *Rochdale Observer* March 27, 1889, and put forward before any serious "counter-orthodox" authorship studies had been made.

2. The principal and best critiques for the life of William Shakespeare as not-the-author are D. Price and the first thirty pages of Rubinstein and James. Tony Pointon and Bernice Cohen have kindly let me see their books (unpublished as of this writing).

3. Devoid of any cultural connection: even part of the "orthodox" establishment recognizes this. At the Globe Conference on the Shakespeare Biography (From Rowe to Shapiro) in November 2009, James Shapiro himself launched a comprehensive attack on those scholars who seek to find autobiographical connection from the life with references in the plays. To Shapiro, these may exist but he cannot identify any. With the obvious defects of the Malone-Dowden-Chambers play chronology, also acknowledged at that same conference, one wonders what these critics rely on to make any connection at all — perhaps just the name — see p. 188 — and with even greater reliance on "Greene's" *Groatsworth of Wit*, which for that reason is examined in depth on p. 244ff.

4. The dates for his baptism, marriage and births of his children are well evidenced from the records of Stratford Church.

5. Illiterate family: both his parents and probably his daughters were unable to read or write. His apparent attitude to his daughters' education makes him an unlikely candidate for Shakespeare the dramatist.

6. Gosson, quoted by W.C. Hazlitt, p. 172.

7. Ready to apply himself to writing: Nicoll, p. 16

8. "Great things are claimed": see any "orthodox" biography. The purported school standard of the curriculum must be jacked up far beyond the possible, and the comprehensive academic level of the canon debased by these critics so as to meet — both are hopeless distortions. Stratford School educational record: Schoenbaum 1987, p. 71.

9. Competence at Latin: my own experience. David Crystal concludes his article, "Playing with Latin" (based on a talk given at the Globe on April 25, 2006, in which he shows the scene as a patchwork of obscenities — see also Kiernan, p. 50). "(William) Shakespeare must have had some very similar experiences to young Master Page. I wonder ... (he) could have called the lad George Page after his father, or Robert, or Fred, or anything. But he called him William." How Oxford might have obtained the background information is revealed on p. 248.

10. William unequipped to be "Shakespeare": for Oxford's view of William Shakespeare's academic achievements and cultural status see pp. 236ff.

11. No Lancashire connection: report of conference at Stratford-upon-Avon — *DVSNL* (October 2008).

12. Learned like Dryden: E.M.W. Tillyard, p. 13.

13. Peerless knowledge: see Chapter Three.

14. Genius: Nicoll, p. 63.

15. The signatures: Price, pp. 125–26. The wonder is that "orthodoxy" holds that William was educated enough to write the Italian plays but his signature is in the secretary hand, as opposed to the more sophisticated Italian hand. Jane Cox of the Public Record Office in 1985 concluded that only the last two signatures on the Will were by the same man. (The first Will signature was too faded for analysis.) — Moore p. 341.

16. *Sir Thomas More*: F. Gidley: "Shakespeare in Composition" *Oxfordian* 4 (October 2001). See also G.E. Dawson, "Thomas More in Same Hand as Signatures," *Shakespeare Studies 42*.

17. Shakespeare's Apocrypha: C.F. Tucker-Brooke.

18. Greene's *Groatsworth*: The full version of this account may be found at www.sourcetext.com/sourcebook/essays/greene/malim.html See also Price, pp. 25ff. The vast William Shakespeare biography industry depends on the first syllable of "Shake-scene" to show that by 1592

William's unevidenced cultural career not only had started but was well advanced by that date. Contrast his absence from the lists of actors in this period: Chambers II, p. 199.

19. Date of Greene's *Groatsworth*: Price, *ibid.*
20. Deathbed repentance: quoted by C. Ogburn, p. 652.
21. Computer tests: Price, p. 29.
22. Fortunatus: P. Moore, p. 220.
23. *Groatsworth* typeset from Chettle's manuscript: D. Price, p. 35.
24. Chettle's first writings: Chambers III p. 263.
25. "Sweet Saint George": supposed by some to be a reference to George Peele and not "Shakespeare" (e.g., D. Price, p. 47). For evidence that Oxford was well known to Greene see note 30 below.
26. Financial insecurity: see Chapter Seven, p. 89.
27. The Shakespearean adjective "base-minded" is not found in the "orthodox" canon. Compare: "Faith, I'll bear no base mind" (2 *Henry IV*, III, ii, l. 238), and "My lord, 'tis but a base ignoble mind" (2 *Henry VI*, II, i, l. 13). I would include: "Why what art thou but a velvet drudge,/A cheating steward, and base-minded peasant" (*Arden of Feversham* I, l. 323–24).
28. The playwright acting: Schoenbaum 1970, p. 52; also Honan, p. 162.
29. Marlowe is not the one meriting an apology — Schoenbaum 1970, p. 51.
30. Raleigh, p. 104. Greene, however, seems to have a good knowledge of Oxford's accomplishments: in 1584 he dedicated his book Gwydonia or *The Card of Fancie* to Oxford.
31. Kathman: the reference seems to have been removed from his website.
32. *Groatsworth* "obscure": Schoenbaum (and his quotation from a fellow critic), pp. 50, 51.
33. Books at Stratford: no doubt the local aristocracy would be delighted to open their libraries so William could handle their valuable books.
34. Crime: A. Robinson: *GO*.
35. If William had not presented himself c. 1593/4, then only sheer luck would have preserved the plays listed on pp. 190. The chance of publication, if only under a pseudonym (but one recognizable by those in the know) arose.
36. *The Taming of the Shrew*: see R. Jimenez in Chapter Five, p. 96.
37. Ditto: Wilson Knight 1932, p. 104.
38. Ditto: Oxford might deliberately be trying to see how far he could go in disclosing his identity. He adds this caricature in the mouth of Sly: "The Slys are no rogues; look in the Chronicles: we came in with Richard Conqueror" (Induction ll. 3,4). This is also a swipe at William's academic and cultural standing.
39. Poaching: Weis.
40. Arms, etc.: Duncan-Jones, p. 92.
41. Falcon: one of my more eccentric acquaintances points out that the Falcon was the nearest public house to Henley Street in Stratford-upon-Avon.
42. Puntarvolo — a piece of Jonsonian wit, possibly: Punt = Punctum = Aichmē, point or SPEAR in Greek; (T)ar, the root of tarassō, (I) SHAKE; Volo, (I) WILL. Note that in Act I, scene I, Puntarvolo is gently sent up as the returning huntsman in a parody of the introduction to *The Taming of A/The Shrew* and immediately afterwards in a parody of the balcony scene in *Romeo and Juliet*.
43. "A swine without a head, without brain, wit...": these deficiencies would rule out William as the author in all but a critic's opinion. See Malim 2005 for a selection of critical efforts to "explain" these references; also Ackroyd, p. 276.
44. "Not without mustard" Honan, p. 440: "The joke relates less explicitly to WS's motto than to Nashe's joke in Pierce Penniless about emending a vow to give up salt cod ('not without Mustard, Good Lord, not without Mustard')." Jonathan Bate points out that mustard was the cheapest of the condiments: "a true gentleman would have spiced the food exotically and expensively" [1998, p. 25]. William and his mustard appear distinctly common to Jonson and his characters.
45. Jonson's printing arrangements: M. Chute, p. 90.
46. Lists of players: Chambers II, pp. 230, 361.
47. Marmalized Latin: "custalorum rotulorum" for custos rotulorum, keeper of the manorial rolls, a comparatively minor post; "armigero": Spanish-sounding ablative case of armiger (arms

bearer) put after the signature on a formal document; "Coram": Slender thinks this is a title, but it is a Latin preposition ("in the presence of" the judge) used in law reports and the like.

48. 1592 loan: D. Price, p. 20.
49. Low life: A. Robinson: *GO*.
50. Tax delinquent: D. Price, pp. 15, 16.
51. John Lane: see M. Anderson (*SOSNL* Winter 2001).
52. Virgil — see Jonson's similar comparison in Chapter Eight, note 37.
53. Manningham: *ibid.*, p. 40. "Upon a time," that is (possibly) before the 1599 performances of *Every Man Out of His Humour* which would have chased William out of London — see p. 254. Bernice Cohen points out to me that other substantial gossip writers such as John Chamberlain (1553–1627) and Sir Henry Wotton (1568–1639) do not mention him at all. Neither does his neighbor Drayton the poet (1563–1631), who was a friend of his son-in-law Dr. John Hall, except for the unengaged reference set out on p. 216.
54. Government's efforts to combat grain hoarding, and local reaction: Honan, p. 241; Duncan-Jones, p. 121. Tony Pointon points out in correspondence that the conversion to weigh grain results in a slightly smaller weight in tonnage in grain, just over 2.3 tons, than the full 2.5 tons one would expect. Contemporary corn prices (in Oxfordshire) for wheat per bushel are shown below. Note that 12d (pennies) equals 1s. (shilling, one-twentieth of a pound):

> March 25–September 29
> 1594 3s 2d 5s 10d (i.e. 16p, 29p.)
> 1595 5s 6d 5s 4d
> 1596 5s 8s
> 1597 9s 7s
> 1598 6s 8d 4s
> 1599 3s 8d 2s (indicating speculators' stocks being unloaded).

Barley commanded roughly one-half to two-thirds these prices. After 1599 prices were stable (2s 10d to 4s 8d) until autumn 1608. W. F. Lloyd, quoted by D. George: SS 53.

55. Low-class breath: *Coriolanus* I, i, l. 61; III, iii, l. 124.
56. "a wolf in the commonwealth": Cordatus about Sordido at end of Act I of *Every Man Out of His Humour*. "Wolves" Honan, p. 242. Later in the play Sordido with the unexpected collapse in the price of grain as happened in Autumn 1598 — see chart above — attempts to hang himself as is rescued repentant in farcical circumstances by some locals. This incident in the writing of the play may well have been preceded by the Porter's speech in *Macbeth*: "Here's a farmer that hanged himself on the expectation of plenty" (I, iii, ll. 4, 5). Also see Hall on p. 193.
57. 1594 payment: D. Price p. 31; C. Ogburn pp. 55–57, and see p. 181.
58. Parnassus plays: D. Price p. 81.
59. "Leass for making": F. Davis (*SOSNL* Spring 2007).
60. Evidence for William's acting: Bate 1997, p. 67. Shapiro, p. 276, prays in aid the marginal manuscript note of a vicar (born 1596 and likely to have been writing at least ten years after William's death) on his copy of Camden's *Britannica* (1590), which states that Stratford is famous for two local worthies, "et Gugliemo Shakespear planè [ostensibly] nostro Roscio" — Roscius being the most famous actor of classical Roman times. This is hardly a persuasive reference for William as actor, let alone as author. William Shakespeare wrote specific parts for specific actors (see p. 159). Just as his 1623 poem cannot be split up, so neither can Jonson's caricatures. Critics are wrong to reject those parts which do not fit their preconceptions.
61. Erection of the Globe: Honan, p. 268.
62. James I: *ibid.*, p. 298.
63. Official entry into London: *ibid.*, p. 303; also Halliday, p. 48. The word "scarlet" is apparently an addition by Halliwell-Phillips; see Schoenbaum 1970, p. 416.
64. Pope Will: quotation supplied by N. Green.
65. Sale by Sly's executors: Chambers II p. 417.
66. Mountjoy "speculation": Nicholl 2007 suggests that Wilkins, the so-called collaborator in our version of *Pericles*, was familiar with William since he lived close by the Mountjoys' home in Silver Street. Nicholl quotes William's affidavit in *Bellott v. Mountjoy*, and on p. 288 the affidavit of Joan Johnson, who remembered, Mountjoy "did send and persuade one M. Shakespear

that *lay* in the house to persuade the Plaintiff to the same marriage" (emphasis added). The verb "lay" connotes a temporary stay.

67. Sparrow: Helen Cooper, the commentator on *Guy of Warwick*, says there is no parallel for this scene in any of the other versions of the story. There is no plot requirement for it: "there is no particular reason within the play why the Sparrow should think himself 'high mounting lofty minded' nor any particular need to name Stratford-upon-Avon, unless there was some immediate allusion intended, and it is hard to imagine what that might be unless (William) Shakespeare were the subject." The reference "seems altogether too pointed ... to be a random formulation." Sparrows in contemporary literature are distinctly noisy, low-class birds — in fact the scene is dragged in to make a point about William.

68. Cecil's letter quoted by Quennell, p. 300.

69. Hemmings' slip: Chambers II, p. 423a.

70. *Ostler v. Hemmings*: Clark, p. 889. Nina Green makes the valuable point that the Globe lessees under their lease would be bound to rebuild: no evidence of any demand to William Shakespeare would mean he was no longer a lessee.

71. *Keysar v. Burbage*: Schoenbaum 1970, p. 648. He fails to point out that William is not named as a defendant.

72. Shareholders' Papers (1635): Chambers, p. 215.

73. *Venus and Adonis*: F.T. Prince, pp. 21–23. See the review of the sonnets, pp. 177ff. In contrast to Prince, Jonathan Bate writes (*The Times* April 20, 2009): "It might be better to read the opposition between the dark lady and the fair youth as a dramatic device: one is 'character' representing desire in its sexual manifestation, the other in its idealising and spiritual one. This is what I always tell my students — and myself— as I sit down to re-read the sonnets. Don't be drawn into the trap of supposing that they are autobiographical: that is an illusion of Shakespeare's art." His attitude was supported by Professor Wells and Paul Edmondson (head of learning at the Shakespeare Birthplace Trust) who denounced any efforts to identify any "Lovely Boy," Rival Poet or Dark Lady (with her they are on stronger ground) with any historic person. "Shakespeare: Rowe to Shapiro," presentation by Richard Malim and Kevin Gilvary at the Conference at The Globe, November 28, 2009. If one strips out the paternalist attitude of the sonnets — see p. 177 — one is left with an ostensible homosexual attraction: this would seem to clash with the biographical evidence of William's clear heterosexuality (pp. 206, 252). There is no extrinsic evidence of any homosexuality on William's part: it would seem impossible for him to be the author. Both sets of commentators are trapped. Prince is right as to the revelatory nature of the poems; Bate et al. are right that there is no intrinsic connection with William Shakespeare. Neither can show any biographical evidence for their contentions.

74. Stratford business dealings: Price, pp. 17–19. William is portrayed as on the breadline in *The Taming of A/The Shrew*; a "so-so rich" forester in *As You Like It* and finally as a newly wealthy (by a fluke) man in *The Winter's Tale*— an interesting progression.

75. Grain hoarder: see p. 252.

76. Not in London: D. Price, pp. 32–33.

77. Globe burns down: Wood, p. 333.

78. Blackfriars Gate House: D. Price, p. 19.

79. Un-Catholic Shakespeare — see Malim: Report on Conference at Stratford-upon-Avon June 28, 2008. At the meeting Professor Alison Shell demonstrated that contemporary Catholic writers were hostile to "Shakespeare."

80. John as a non-attender at church: perhaps he was able to pull a string or pay a bribe to have himself put in the schedule listing the debtors as opposed to the more dangerous one for recusants.

81. As trustee of Blackfriars Gate House: Wood p. 331.

82. Rosicrucian manifesto quoted by M. Anderson *SOSNL* Spring 2008. See p. 222.

83. The will: Ian Wilson pp. 476–479.

84. Lack of interest in survival of plays: Ivor Brown 1970, p. 69. See p. 211.

85. Stratford Corporation's attitude: L. Fox quoted by R. Jimenez 2005.

86. Church monument: Honan, p. 403.

87. Ditto — modernized in 1740: D. Price, p. 154.

88. Financing the monument: contrast Sonnet 81, quoted on p. 181.

89. Acquaintances of William and Susanna: R. Jimenez 2005.

90. Queen Henrietta Maria: she recorded her stay in Stratford. Tradition says she actually stayed two nights at New Place, William's old residence, in 1647, but there is no evidence. She was a theater buff and enjoyed performing at court masques. It is inconceivable that she would have ignored the relatives of the greatest playwright of the age — if he was that writer.

91. "Ipse" he was not: to be fair he appears never to have claimed he was.

Bibliography

Works by "Shakespeare doubters" are preceded by an asterisk, and the following Oxfordian publications are referred to in shortened form. The Shakespeare Oxford Society publishes *The Oxfordian* and a newsletter, noted as *SOSNL*. The De Vere Society also publishes a newsletter, abbreviated here as *DVSNL*. A De Vere Society–authorized book, *Great Oxford: Essays on the Life and Works of Edward De Vere, 17th Earl of Oxford* (Tunbridge Wells: Parapress, 2004), edited by myself, is abbreviated herein as *GO*. For original articles that are difficult to source, the De Vere Society may be approached (www.deveresociety.co.uk).

Ackroyd, P. *Shakespeare: The Biography* (London: Chatto & Windus, 2005).
Alexander, G. *Sidney's The Defence of Poesy and Selected Renaissance Criticism.* (London: Penguin, 2004).
*Alexander, M. A. "Shakespeare's Knowledge of Law: A Journey Through the History of the Argument." *The Oxfordian* 4 (October 2001).
*Altrocchi, P.: "Edward de Vere as Translator of Ovid's Metamorphoses." *SOSNL*, Spring 2005.
*Anderson, M. *"Shakespeare" by Another Name* (New York: Gotham, 2006).
Arthos, J. *Shakespeare: The Early Writings* (London: Bowes & Bowes, 1972).
Ascham, R. *The Schoolmaster 1570.* Ed. Edward Arber. (London: Murray, 1868).
Asquith, C. *Shadowplay* (New York: Public Affairs, 2005).
Atkins, J.W.H. *English Literary Criticism and the Renascence* (London: Methuen, 1951).
Barber, C. "The English Language in the Age of Shakespeare." *The New Pelican Guide to English Literature.* Vol. II. Rev. Ed. (Harmondsworth, UK: Penguin, 1982).
Barton, A. *Shakespeare and the Idea of the Play* (London: Chatto & Windus, 1962).
Bate, J. *The Genius of Shakespeare* (London: Picador, 1997).
_____. "Is This the Story of the Bard's Heart?" *The Times.* (April 20, 1909).
_____. "Ovid and the Mature Tragedies." *SS*, 41.
_____. *The Soul of The Age* (London: Viking, 2008).
Bell, R. *Poems of Robert Greene and Christopher Marlowe* (London: Parker, 1856).
Blakemore Evans, G. *The New Cambridge Shakespeare: The Sonnets.* (Cambridge: Cambridge University Press, 1996).
Bloom, H. *Shakespeare's Invention of the Human* (London: Fourth Estate, 1999).
Boas, F.S. *Queen Elizabeth in English Drama* (Oxford: Oxford University Press, 1950).
Bolton, W.F., ed. *The English Language* (Cambridge: Cambridge University Press, 1966).
Borsellino, N. *Commedie del Cinquecento* (Milan: Feltrinelli, 1962).
Bossy, J. *Giordano Bruno and the Embassy Affair* (New Haven: Yale University Press, 1991).
Boswell, J. *Life of Dr. Johnson.* Ed. Percy Fitzgerald (London: Sands, 1888).
Boswell-Stone, W.G. *Shakespeare's Holinshed.* (London: Chatto & Windus, 1907).
*Boyle, W. "Political Motive for 1623 Folio." *SOSNL* (Summer 1998 and Spring 1999).
Bradbrook, M. *English Stage Conditions* (Cambridge: Cambridge University Press, 1963).
Bradley, A.C. *Shakespearean Tragedy* (London: Macmillan, 1961).

Bragg, M. *The Adventure of English* (London: Sceptre, 1903).
*Brame, H., and Popova, G. *Who's the Monstrous Adversary?* (Seattle: University of Washington Press, 2004).
*Brazil, R. "Hamlet's Astronomy." *SOSNL* (Summer 2002).
Brown, I. *Shakespeare* (London: Collins, 1949).
_____. *Shakespeare and the Actors* (London: Bodley Head, 1970).
Brown, J.R. *Shakespeare's Antony and Cleopatra: A Casebook*. (London: Macmillan, 1991).
Bullough, G. *Narrative and Dramatic Sources of Shakespeare* (London: Routledge & Kegan Paul, 1957–75).
Chambers, E.K. *The English Stage* (Oxford: University Press, 1923).
*Charlton, D. "Cambridge University "Implications" of Polimanteia." *SOSNL* (Spring 2008).
_____. "Emaricdulfe." *SOSNL* (Fall 2005).
_____. "Some Documents in the Case of Shakespeare's Authorship." *DVSNL* (February 1999).
Chute, M. *Ben Jonson of Westminster* (New York: Souvenir Press, 1953).
*Clark, E.T. *Hidden Allusions in Shakespeare's Plays*. Rev. ed. (Port Washington, NY: Kennikat Press, 1974).
Clemen, W.H. *English Tragedy Before Shakespeare* (London: Methuen, 1967).
Coleridge, S.T. *Lectures on Shakespeare* (London: Bell, 1914).
Cooper, H. "Guy of Warwick, Upstart Crows and Mounting Sparrows." In *Shakespeare Marlowe Jonson: New Directions in Biography*. Ed. Takashi Kozuka and J.R. Mulryne (Farnham, Surrey, UK: Ashgate, 2006).
Craik, T.W., and Leech, C. *The Revels History of Drama in English*. Vol. III. (London: Methuen, 1975).
*Crick, J. "Trentham Descent." *DVSNL* (November 2006).
Crystal, D. "Playing with Latin." Lecture at Shakespeare's Globe Theatre, London, April 25, 2006).
*Davis, F. "Leass for Making." *SOSNL* (Spring 2007).
Dawson, G.E. "Thomas More in Same Hand as Signatures." *Shakespeare Studies* 42.
*Desper, R. "We Must Speak by the Card." *Oxfordian* 4 (October 2001).
*Detobel, R. "Melicertus." *GO*
*_____, and Ligon, K.C. The Harvey-Nashe Quarrel. (http//www.elizabethanauthors.com/Harvey-nasheOO2htm).
Dromgoole, D. *Will and Me* (London: Allen Lane, 2006).
Duncan-Jones, K. *Ungentle Shakespeare* (London: Arden Shakespeare, 2001).
*Durning-Lawrence, E. *Bacon and Shakespeare* (London: Gay & Hancock, 1910).
Dutton, R. *Sir Philip Sidney: Selected Writings* (Manchester, UK: Carcenet, 1987).
Egan, M. *The Tragedy of Richard II: Part I*. (New York: Mellen, 2006).
English Prose Selections. Vol. I (London: Macmillan, 1893).
The English Renaissance. (New York: Appleton-Century-Crofts, 1952).
Feuillerat, A. *Materials for the Study of Old English Drama* (Louvain, Belgium: 1902–14).
Fox, L. *The Borough Town of Stratford-upon-Avon* (Stratford-upon-Avon: The Corporation of Stratford-upon-Avon, 1953).
Fraser, A. *Introduction to How to Write Memoir and Biographies* (London: The Guardian News and Media, 2008).
*Fuller, J.O. *Sir Francis Bacon: A Biography* (London: East-West Publications, 1981).
"Funeral Canopy." *DVSNL* (June and October 2007).
Gardner, E.G. *Italian Literature* (London: Benn, 1927).
Garnett, E., and Gosse, E. *English Literature: An Illustrated Record* (New York: Heinemann, 1903).
Gascoigne, G. *Works*. Ed. Edward Arber (London: Murray, 1868).
George, D. "Plutarch, Insurrection and Dearth in Coriolanus." *SS* 53.
Gepp, E. *Essex Dialect Dictionary* (London: Routledge, 1923).
*Gidley, F. "Shakespeare in Composition." *Oxfordian* 4 (October 2001).
*Gilvary, K. "Shakespeare and Italian Comedy." *GO*.
_____. "Two Gentlemen of Verona." *Oxfordian* 8 (October 2005).
*Goldstein, G. "Hebrew." *SOSNL* (October 1990).

_____. "Shakespeare's Little Hebrew." *DVSNL* (February 2010).
_____. "Shakespeare's Native Tongue." *DVSNL* (November 2009).
*Gordon, H. "Alexander Pope: An Oxfordian at Heart?" *Oxfordian* 5 (October 2002).
Gosson, S. *The School of Abuse (August?) 1579*. Ed. Edward Arber (London: Murray, 1868).
Granville-Barker, H. *Preface to Romeo and Juliet, Coriolanus, Hamlet* (London: Batsford, 1970).
*Green, N. "Who Was Arthur Brooke: Author of *The Tragical History of Romeus and Juliett*?" *Oxfordian* 3 (October 2000). www.oxford-shakespeare.com.
Greenblatt, S. *Will in the World* (London: Jonathan Cape, 2004).
*Greenhill, R. "From Russia with Love: A Case of *Love's Labour's Lost*." *Oxfordian* 9 (October 2006).
Gregory Smith, G. *Elizabethan Critical Essays* (Oxford: Oxford University Press, 1904).
Halliday, F.E. *Shakespeare and His Critics* (London: Duckworth, 1949).
Halliwell Phillips, J.O. *Outlines of the Life of William Shakespeare*. 7th ed. (London: Longman Green, 1884).
*Hamill, J. "Horse Painting." *SOSNL* (Summer 2003).
_____. *The Murder of Gonzago*. *SOSNL* (Fall 2003).
Hamilton, D.B. "Anthony Munday and The Merchant of Venice." *SS* 54.
Hattaway, M., ed. *A Companion to English Renaissance Literature and Culture* (Oxford: Blackwell, 2007).
Hawkins, H. "Critical Studies." *SS* 35.
Hazlitt, W.C. *The English Drama and Stage Under the Tudor and Stuart Princes, 1543–1664*. (1832. Reprint, New York: Burt Franklin, 1969).
*Hess, W.R., and Tarica, A. "Beowulf." *DVSNL* (June 2009).
*Hoffman, C. *The Murder of the Man Who Was "Shakespeare."* (New York: J. Messner, 1955).
Holden, A. *William Shakespeare: His Life and Works* (New York: Vintage, 1990).
*Holmes, E. *Discovering Shakespeare*. (Tunbridge Wells: Parapress, 2008).
Honan, P. "Demystifying Shakespeare." *The Daily Telegraph* (October 10, 1998).
_____. *Shakespeare: A Life* (Oxford: Oxford University Press, 2005).
Honigman, E.A.J. "Shakespeare's Self-Repetitions and *King John*." In *Shakespeare Survey 53: Shakespeare and Narrative*. Ed. Peter Holland. Cambridge: Cambridge University Press, 2000.
_____. "The Play of Sir Thomas More and Some Contemporary Events." In *Shakespeare Survey 42: Shakespeare and the Elizabethans*. Ed. Peter Holland. (Cambridge: Cambridge University Press, 1990).
Hopkins, L. *Beginning Shakespeare* (Manchester, UK: Manchester University Press, 2005).
Hoseley, R. "Sources and Analogues in Taming of the Shrew." *Huntingford Library Quarterly* (1963–64).
*Imlay, E. "Edward de Vere and the Music of the Renaissance." *DVSNL* (July 2006).
James I. Letter to Robert Cecil, 1604. *SOSNL* (February 1989).
*Jimenez, R. "Who Was the Author of the Five Plays That Shakespeare Rewrote As His Own?" *SOSNL* (Winter 2008).
_____. "Troublesome Reign." *SOSNL* (Winter 2006).
*Johnson, P. "Oxford in Italy." *DVSNL* (December 2005).
*Jolly, E. "Meres: His Usefulness and Limitations." *DVSNL* (October 2007).
_____. "Ur-Hamlet." *DVSNL* (November 2006).
*Jolly, E., and O'Brien, P. "Sir Thomas Smith's Library." *GO*.
Jones, R.F. *The Triumph of the English Language* (London: Cumberlege, 1953).
Kail, A.C. *The Medical Mind of Shakespeare* (Balgowah, NSW: Williams and Wilkins, 1986).
Kathman, D. www.shakespeareauthorship.com/kathman.html.
Kiernan, P. *Filthy Shakespeare* (London: Quercus, 2004).
Krapp, G.P. "1916." In *Shakespeare's Later Comedies*. Ed. D.J. Palmer (Harmondsworth, UK: Penguin, 1971).
Knight, G. Wilson. *The Wheel of Fire* (Oxford: Oxford University Press, 1930).
_____. *The Shakespearian Tempest* (Oxford: Oxford University Press, 1932).
Lamb, M.E. "The Nature of Topicality in *Love's Labour's Lost*." *Shakespeare Survey 38: Shakespeare in History*. (Cambridge: Cambridge University Press, 1986).
*Lambin, G. *Voyages de Shakespeare en France et en Italie* (Geneva: E. Droz, 1962).

Lavin, J.A. "Shakespeare and the Second Blackfriars." In *Elizabethan Theatre Essays* (London: Macmillan, 1973).
Lee, S. *Life of William Shakespeare* (London: Smith Elder, 1898).
Levi, P. *The Life and Times of William Shakespeare* (London: Macmillan, 1988).
Lewis, C.S. *English Literature in the Sixteenth Century (Excluding Drama)*. (Oxford: Oxford University Press, 1954).
Lloyd, W.F. "Prices of Corn in Oxford." Quoted in Honigman, "Shakespeare's Self Repetitions," *SS* 53.
Logan, R. *Shakespeare's Marlowe* (Farnham, Surrey, UK: Ashgate, 2006).
*Magri, N. "Geographical Exactness in *All's Well That Ends Well*." *DVSNL* (February 2007).
_____. "The Italian Legal System in *The Merchant of Venice*." *DVSNL* (February 2009).
_____. "The Murder of Gonzago," *DVSNL* (June 2009).
_____. "Three Sisters of Mantua." *DVSNL* (December 2005).
_____. "The Venetian Inquisition Inquiry Into Orazio Cuoco." *DVSNL* paper, 2003.
Maguin, Jean-Marie. "The Tempest and Cultural Exchange." In *Shakespeare Studies 48: Shakespeare and Cultural Exchange.* (Cambridge: Cambridge University Press, 1996).
*Malim, R.C.W. "The Coast of Bohemia." *DVSNL* (June 2008).
_____. "The Fallacy of Selectivity." *DVSNL* (December 2005).
_____. "On Greene's *Groatsworth of Wit*." www.sourcetext.com/sourcebook/essays/greene/malim.html.
_____. "Oxford the Actor." *GO*.
_____. Report on Conference at Stratford-upon-Avon, June 28, 2008.
_____. "The Spanish Maze." *DVSNL* (July 2002).
Malim, R., and K. Gilvary. "Shakespeare: Rowe to Shapiro." Presentation at the Conference at the Globe, November 28, 2009.
Malone, E., and J. Boswell, Jr. *The Plays and Poems of William Shakespeare.* (London, 1821).
Martindale, M., and C. Martindale. *Shakespeare and the Uses of Antiquity* (London: Routledge, 1990).
Mattingley, G. *The Defeat of the Spanish Armada* (London: Jonathan Cape, 1959).
McAlindon, T. "Pilgrims of Grace: *Henry IV* Historicized." *Shakespeare Studies 48: Shakespeare and Cultural Exchange.* (Cambridge: Cambridge University Press, 1996).
McCarthy, P. *Pseudonymous Shakespeare* (Farnham, Surrey, UK: Ashgate, 2006).
*Moore, P. *Studies in Shakespeare* (Buchholz: Laugwitz, 2009).
_____. "The Rival Poet." *SOSNL* (Fall 1999).
Murphy, P. *Murphy on Evidence*. 10th ed. (Oxford: Oxford University Press, 2008).
Murry, J.M. *Shakespeare* (London: Jonathan Cape, 1936).
Neale, J.E. *Queen Elizabeth I* (London: Jonathan Cape, 1934).
Nelson, A.H. *Monstrous Adversary* (Liverpool: Liverpool University Press, 2003).
Nichol-Smith, D. *Shakespeare Criticism: A Selection* (Oxford: Oxford University Press, 1946).
Nicholl, C. *A Cup of News* (London: Routledge & Kegan Paul, 1984).
_____. *The Lodger* (London: Allen Lane, 2007).
Nicoll, Allardyce. *Shakespeare* (London: Methuen, 1952).
_____. "Essay." In *Shakespeare's Later Comedies*. Ed. D.J. Palmer (Harmondsworth, UK: Penguin, 1971).
Nuttall, A.D. *Shakespeare The Thinker* (New Haven: Yale University Press, 2007).
*Ogburn, C. *The Mystery of William Shakespeare* (London: Cardinal, 1988).
"Oxford's Finances." *DVSNL* (February 1999).
*Paul, C. "Axiochus." *SOSNL* (Summer 2003).
Pearsall Smith, L. *On Reading Shakespeare* (London: Constable, 1933).
Perucci, A. *Tirate della Giostra* (Milan, 1699).
Phelps, G. *Short History of English Literature* (London: Folio Society, 1962).
Pinter, H. *Various Voices* (London: Faber & Faber, 1999).
Pitcher, S., *The Case for Shakespeare's Authorship of Famous Victories* (London: Redman, 1962).
Pollard, A.W. *Shakespeare's Fight with the Pirates and the Problems of the Transmission of His Text* (London: Moring, 1917).

Prechter, Robert. "Did Oxford Make His Publishing Debut in 1560 as 'T.H.'?" *Oxfordian* 10 (October 2007).
*Price, D. *Shakespeare's Unorthodox Biography* (Westport, CT: Greenwood, 2001).
Prince, F.T. *Shakespeare: The Poems* (London: Longman Green, 1963).
Raleigh, W. *Shakespeare* (London: Macmillan, 1907).
Johnson, S. *Samuel Johnson on Shakespeare* (Oxford: Oxford University Press, 1908).
*Robinson, A. "The Real William Shakespeare." *GO*.
*Rollett, J. "Cryptogram." *GO*.
_____. "Funeral Canopy 1 and 2." *DVSNL* (June, October 2007).
*Roper, D. "Henry Peacham's Chronogram: The Dating of Titus Andronicus." *GO*.
*Rubinstein, W.D., and B. James. *The Truth Will Out* (London: Longman Pearson, 2005).
Rushton, E. *Shakespeare and the Arte of English Poesie* (Liverpool: H. Young, 1909).
Quennell, P. *Shakespeare: The Poet and His Background* (London: Penguin, 1963).
Saintsbury, G. *A History of English Criticism* (Edinburgh: Blackwood, 1922).
_____. *A History of English Literature* (London: Macmillan, 1903).
Salingar, L.G. "The English Literary Renaissance." In *The New Pelican Guide to English Literature*. Vol. II. Ed. Boris Ford (London: Pelican, 1982).
Sams, E. *Edmund Ironside* (Aldershot, UK: Wildwood House, 1986).
_____. *Shakespeare's Edward III* (New Haven: Yale University Press, 1996).
_____. *The Real Shakespeare* ((New Haven: Yale University Press, 1995).
*Saunders, S. "Arthur Golding's First Decade of Translating." *SOSNL* (Fall 2005).
Schoenbaum, S. *Internal Evidence and Elizabethan Dramatic Authorship* (Evanston, IL: Northwestern University Press, 1966).
_____. *Shakespeare's Lives* (New York: Oxford University Press, 1970).
_____. *William Shakespeare: A Compact Documentary Life* (New York: Oxford University Press, 1971).
Schönfeld, S. J. "A Hebrew Source for *The Merchant of Venice*." *SS* 32.
*Showerman, E. "Orestes and Hamlet: From Myth to Masterpiece, Part 1." *Oxfordian* 7 (October 2004).
Shaheen, N. "Shakespeare's Knowledge of Italian." In *Shakespeare Studies 47: Playing Places for Shakespeare*. (Cambridge: Cambridge University Press, 1994).
Shapiro, J. *Contested Will: Who Wrote Shakespeare?* (London: Faber, 2010).
Shurink, F. "An Unnoticed Early Reference to Shakespeare." *Notes and Queries* (March 2006).
Skidmore, C. *Death and the Virgin* (London: Weidenfeld & Nicholson, 2010).
*Smith, S. "Re-attribution of Munday's *Yhe Pains of Pleasure*." *Oxfordian* 5.
*Sobran, J. *Alias Shakespeare* (New York: Free Press, 1997).
Springarn, J.E. *Critical Essays in the Seventeenth Century* (Oxford: Clarendon, 1908).
Spurgeon, C. *Shakespeare's Imagery* (Cambridge: Cambridge University Press, 1935).
Stochholm, J.M. *Garrick's Folly*. (London: Methuen, 1964).
*Stritmatter, R., ed. *Shakespeare Matters: The Shakespeare Fellowship*. Quarterly newsletter.
*Stritmatter, R., and L. Kositzky. "The Spanish Maze and the Date of *The Tempest*." *Oxfordian* 10 (October 2007).
*Swank, L.J. "Rosenkrantz." *SOSNL* (Fall 2003).
Swinburne, A.C. *A Study of Shakespeare* (New York: Heinmann, 1920).
Taylor, Gary. *Reinventing Shakespeare* (London: Hogarth, 1990).
Thomson, J.A.K. *Shakespeare and the Classics* (London: Allen, 1966).
Thomson, P. *Shakespeare's Professional Career* (Cambridge: Cambridge University Press, 1992).
Tillyard, E.M.W. *Shakespeare's History Plays* (London: Penguin, 1944).
Tucker-Brooke, C.F. *The Shakespeare Apocrypha* (Oxford: Clarendon, 1918).
Wallace, C.W., and H.A. Wallace. *The Evolution of the English Drama* ... (Berlin: G. Reimer, 1912).
Walpole, H. *Catalogue of Royal and Noble Authors of England* (London: Dodsley, 1759).
*Ward, B.M. *The Seventeenth Earl of Oxford* (London: Murray, 1928).
Watson, R.N. *Ben Jonson's Periodic Strategy* (Cambridge, MA: Harvard University Press, 1987).
Weir, A. *Henry VIII, King and Court* (London: Jonathan Cape, 2001).
Weis, R. *Shakespeare Revealed* (London: Murray, 2007).

Wells, S., ed. *Shakespeare Studies 41: Shakespearian Stages and Staging* (Cambridge: Cambridge University Press, 1989).
Wells, S., and G. Taylor. *William Shakespeare: The Complete Works* (Oxford: Oxford University Press, 1988).
*Werth, A *"Shakespeare's 'Lesse Greek.'"* Oxfordian* 5 (October 2002).
*Whalen, R. "Digges and Russell." *SOSNL* (Spring 2001).
_____. "Cleopatra's Worm." *SOSNL* (Summer 1998).
Whibley, C., ed. *Cambridge University History of English Literature* (Cambridge: Cambridge University Press, 1907–21).
Wiggins, M. *Shakespeare and the Drama of His Time* (Oxford: Oxford University Press, 2000).
*Willis, C.M. *Shakespeare and the Arte of English Poesie* (St. Leonards-on-Sea: UPSO, 2003).
Wilson, I. *Shakespeare: The Evidence* (London: Headline, 1993).
Wilson, J. Dover. *The Essential Shakespeare* (Cambridge: Cambridge University Press, 1932).
Wilson, R. *Secret Shakespeare* (Manchester: Manchester University Press, 2006).
Wood, A. *Atheniae Oxonienses* (London, 1691).
Wood, M., narrator. *In Search of Shakespeare*. BBC TV, 2003.
Worden, B. "Shakespeare in Art and Life: Biography in *Richard III*." In *Shakespeare, Marlowe, Jonson: New Directions in Biography*. Ed. Takashi Kozuka and J.R. Mulryne, (Farnham, Surrey, UK: Ashgate, 2006).
_____. *Shakespeare Studies 44: Shakespeare and Politics*. Wells, S., ed. (Cambridge: Cambridge University Press, 1991).
*Wright, D. "Ver-y Interesting." *SOSNL* (Spring 2000).
"A Yorkshire Tragedy." *Edward de Vere Newsletter* (November 1990).
Young, A. *Tudor and Jacobean Tournaments* (London: George Philip, 1987).

Index

Similar early and later titles are run together; and only the works of Shakespeare, Jonson and Marlowe and some early works are indexed separately; for other works see under their reputed authors.

Where a critic is quoted but not named in the body of the text, the page number with the endnote number appears below; the reference is not repeated in the endnote unless there is an additional comment in that endnote.

Achilles 56, 57 (illus.), 78, 183, 187, 272*n*32, 275*n*5, 283*n*32
Ackroyd, Peter 5, 266*n*20, 292*n*43
Aeschylus 23, 48, 215
"Aldon" 153
Alexander, Gavin 64, 279*n*110
Alexander, Mark 22, 53
Allen, Revd. J. 268*n*26
Alleyn, Edward 263, 281*n*61
All's Well That Ends Well 17, 24, 25, 26, 60, 82, 83, 97, 128, 161, 202, 267*n*14, 291*n*16
Altrocchi, Paul 272*n*39
Amyot, Jacques 48
Anderson, Mark 13, 27, 90, 91, 261, 267*n*2, 267*n*8, 268*n*27, 269*n*57, 282*n*17, 282*n*21, 283*n*28, 293*n*50, 294*n*82
Anne, Queen (to James I) 258
Annesley family: and King Lear 278*n*89, 285*n*11
Anon — Thrid Blast 282*n*14
anonymous poem: in 1640 edition of Shakespeare's poems 216
Anton, Robert 268*n*22
Antony and Cleopatra 101, 128, 131, 202, 225, 229, 275*n*14, 275*n*54, 282*n*16, 287*n*28
"Apis Lapis" 171
Apollo 20, 21, 28, 174
Arber, Edward 269*n*34, 274*n*10, 274*n* 16, 279*n*114
"Archiadas" 173
Arden of Feversham 33, 34, 35, 42, 71, 78, 87, 114, 115, 117, 119, 133, 136, 152, 189, 202, 278*n*93 281*n*151, 292*n*27
Aretino, Pietro 58, 201, 272*n*38
Ariosto, Ludovico 11, 52, 58, 108, 275*n*15
Armada (Spanish) 33, 92
Armin, Robert 256, 257, 275*n*11, 279*n*15
Arthos, John 11, 46, 216*n*10, 216*n*11, 271*n*3, 269*n*37, 279*n*108

Arundell, Charles 59, 85ff
As You Like It 5, 48, 51, 88, 105, 136, 149, 150, 151, 152, 188, 191, 202, 236, 275*n*11, 294*n*71, 295*n*91
Ascham, Roger 8, 10, 222, 266*n*7, 281*n*164
Asquith, Clare (Countess of Oxford) 203, 205, 286*n*16, 286*n*21
Atchelow, Thomas 170
Aubrey, John 239
Austen, Jane 15
Autolycus 83, 161, 248
Axiochus 105, 277*n*64

Babington plot 112, 278*n*65
Bacon, Sir F.: Baconians 184, 222, 266*c*2*n*1, 278*n*105, 284*n*48, 288*n*48
Bandello, Matteo 52, 58
Barber, Charles 7
Barksted, W. 200, 289*n*59
Barnes, Barnabe 204
Bartholomew Fair 35
Bartlett, Henrietta C. 217, 288*n*42
Barton, Anne 154ff, 192, 277*n*58, 277*n*70, 281*n*156, 281*n*157
Basse, William 214, 284*n*50, 287*n*31
Bate, Jonathan 30, 150, 195, 256, 268*n*14, 269*n*36, 277*n*63, 279*n*123, 280*n*145, 282*n*16, 282*n*23, 285*n*59, 286*n*25, 292*n*44, 293*n*60, 294*n*73
Beaumont, Francis 206, 214; and Fletcher, John 141, 262, 286*n*21
Bedingfield, Thomas 27, 31, 39
Beeston, Christopher 257
Bell, Robert 75, 275*n*26, 275*n*27, 280*n*147
Bellot, Jacques 63
Bellott v Mountjoy 257, 293*n*66
Bembo, Pietro 270*n*64
Benedick 83
Bénézet, Louis 42

303

Benson, John 217, 287n35, 288n43
Beowulf 285n57
Berowne 98
Bertram 17, 24, 26, 82, 83
Bertrani, Giovanni Battista 272n36
Betterton, Thomas P. 219
Bewley, Dorna 281n4
"Black Will" 34, 88, 152
Blackfriars Theatre (first) 71, 79, 87, 153, 276n21
Blackfriars Theatre (second) 138, 138, 195, 259, 280n125
Blakemore Evans, Gwynne 180, 283
Bloom, Harold 229, 290n76
"Boar" 28
Boas, Frederick S. 274n17
Boccaccio, Giovanni 58, 97ff
Bodley, Sir Thomas 274n17
Bolton, W.F. 273n15
Borde, Andrew 7
Borsellino, Nino 11, 266n11, 266n13
Bossy, John 59, 271n18, 272n37
Boswell, James, Jr. 225, 226, 227, 280n144, 289n65
Boswell, James, Sr. 289n60
Boswell-Stone, W.G. 118ff, 278n97
Boyle, William 289n60
Bradbrook, Muriel G. 154, 224, 288n49
Bradley, Andrew C. 279n120
Bragg, Lord (Melvyn) 280n138
Brahe, Tycho, astronomer 111
Brame, Michael, and Popova, Galina 42
Branagh, Kenneth 98
Brazil, Robert 287n79
Breton, Nicholas 208
Bright, John 235, 291n1
Brome, Richard 217, 288n42
Brontë sisters 15
Brook, Peter 151, 159, 280n146
Brooke, Arthur 15
Brown, Ivor 6, 266n28, 294n84
Brown, John R. 287n28
Browne, Sir T.: and Brownists 102, 121, 277n55, 277n99
Bruno, Giordano 59, 86, 123, 268n18, 271n10, 271n18, 272n37, 279n108, 282n16
Buck, Sir George 208, 286n25
Buckhurst, Lord Thomas Sackville 94, 140, 208, 218, 273n1
Bullough, Geoffrey 96, 276n39
Burbage family 70, 181, 183, 250, 251, 256, 256, 259, 261, 262, 274n4
Burghley, Lord William Cecil 10, 17, 18, 23, 24, 25, 27, 33, 49, 50, 53, 71, 80, 82, 89, 92, 94, 102, 108, 110, 113, 158, 164, 171, 178, 188, 188, 195, 196, 250, 258, 259, 266n5, 268n26, 276n25, 276n27
Burke, Edmund 223, 279n111, 288n52, 289n60, 289n62
Burton, William 178
Byrd, William 53, 182

"Caesar" 158, 170, 217
Cambises 139, 143, 278n96
Cambridge University jargon 21
Camden, William 68, 262, 286n18, 293n60
"Canaidos" 201
Capell, Edward 289n71
Cardenio 202, 203, 212, 286n13, 286n18
Castiglione, Baldassare 31, 78, 277n44
Cecci, Giammaria 11
Cecil, Sir Robert 89, 182, 200, 203, 258, 285n7, 294n68
Cecil, Sir William *see* Burghley, Lord William Cecil
Chambers, Edward K. 73, 75, 191, 200 240, 246, 250, 259, 267n14, 274n4, 274n11, 275n18, 275n25, 277n74, 285n59, 285n7, 291n18, 292n24, 262n46, 293n63, 294n69, 294n72
Chapman, George 79, 216, 228, 290n77
Charlton, Derran 44, 268n21, 270n71
Chaucer, Geoffrey 23, 30, 204, 214, 223, 281n9
Cheke, Sir John 222
Chettle, Henry 159, 169, 198, 241ff, 244, 245, 292n24
Chiljan, Katherine 31, 269n41
Churchyard, Thomas 171, 216
Chute, Marchette 283n39, 292n45
Cinthio, Giambattista 11, 52, 58
circumstantial evidence 5, 266n24
Clark, Eva Turner 49, 93, 101, 270n50, 270n58, 272n25, 276n37, 276n38, 276n41, 277n44, 277n47, 277n53, 277n55, 277n56, 277n57, 277n59, 277n62, 277n65, 277n66, 277n67, 277n68, 277n69, 277n71, 277n72, 277n73, 277n74, 278n75, 278n77, 278n84, 278n85, 278n86, 278n87, 278n88, 278n89, 281n7, 285n58, 294n70
Clemen, Wolfgang 139ff, 142, 280n127, 280n134, 280n135, 290n77
Clerk(e), Bartholomew 31, 222
Clown (from *Antony and Cleopatra*) 102
codes and cryptograms 184, 222
Cohen, Bernice 291n2, 293n53
Coleridge, Samuel T. 151, 226, 227, 229, 265n4, 280n47, 283n38, 289n60
collaboration 31, 95, 115, 120, 137, 203ff, 212, 266c2n1, 269n43, 275n15, 276n18, 277n60, 277n70
Collier, John P 226, 285n5
The Comedy of Errors 18, 26, 41, 46, 48, 59, 83, 94, 133, 136, 144, 181, 190, 199, 202
Commedia dell'Arte 59
Commedia Erudita 58
A Compendious or Brief Relation 88, 276n23
Condell, Henry 213, 250, 256, 256, 257, 258, 262
conspiracy theories 159, 163, 281n167, 290n2
Cook, Alexander 257
Cooke, James 263
Cooper, Helen 294n67

Coriolanus 103, 161, 191, 202, 277*n*57, 282*n*16, 293*n*55
court revels and performances 87, 94, 94, 95, 96, 96, 97, 99, 101, 107, 107, 108, 109, 136, 152, 199, 257, 286*n*21
Cousins, Peter 267*n*5
Cowley, Richard 256, 257
Cox, Jane 291*n*15
"Craftie Cuttle(fish)" 174
Craik, T.W., and Leech, Clifford 285*n*11
Crampin, Alice 276*n*18
Crick, Jeremy 268*n*26, 282*n*18
critics, "orthodox": confusion of 4, 5, 33, 57, 88, 103, 108, 123, 123, 140, 171, 173, 188, 189, 191, 198, 200, 220, 226, 228, 247, 260, 262, 272*n*34, 277*n*58, 278*n*104, 279*n*106, 285*n*2, 290*n*77
Crystal, David 291*n*9
Cuoco, Orazio 85, 276*n*6
The Curtain 70, 87
Cymbeline 83, 95, 133, 138, 138, 195, 202, 209, 278*n*89

"Damides" 173
Damon and Pythias see *Two Noble Kinsmen*
Daniel, Samuel 67, 141, 208, 216, 273*n*13, 290*n*78
Darnley, Henry Earl 278*n*86
David, Richard 13
Davies, John 161
Davies, Sir John 162, 216
Davis, Frank H. 293*n*59
Dawson, Giles E. 284*n*42, 291*n*16
Dekker, Thomas 141
Delahoyde, Michael 56, 272*n*32
Della Cassa, Giovanni 76, 275*n*1
Della Porta, Giambattista 267*n*10
De Mauvissiere, Michel de Castelnau 85
De Quincey, Thomas 226
Derby, William, 6th Earl of 82, 266*c*2*n*1, 288*n*42
De Saint Gallais, Mellin 270*n*64
Desper, Richard 272*n*52
Detobel, Robert 270*n*64, 270*n*65, 276*n*27, 282*n*13, 283*n*36, 285*n*2
De Vere, Elizabeth, Countess of Derby 82, 178, 181, 281*n*2
De Vere, Horatio 110, 156, 177, 199
De Vere, Susan, Countess of Montgomery 209
The Devil Is an Ass 205, 278*n*78
dialect words 14
Dickson, Peter W. 286*n*23, 287*n*27
Dido Queen of Carthage 135, 279*n*116
Digges, Lionel 165, 212, 214, 287*n*32, 287*n*33
Doctor Doddypoll 122, 278*n*101
Doctor Faustus 141, 148, 289*n*71
Dorset, 1st Earl of *see* Buckhurst, Lord Thomas Sackville
Dover Wilson, John 34, 65, 91, 123, 273*n*6, 279*n*106, 279*n*117

Dovisi, Bernardo 11
Drake, Francis 103
Drayton, Thomas 216, 262, 288*n*39, 293*n*53
Dromgoole, Dominic 78, 275*n*7
Drummond, William 272*n*28, 286*n*21
Dryden, John 3, 64, 218ff, 224, 227, 238, 281*n*1, 289*n*49, 289*n*50, 289*n*51, 289*n*52, 53, 291*n*11
Du Bartas, Salluste 62, 272*n*2, 275*n*15
Duncan-Jones, Katherine 4, 189, 265*n*15, 284*n*43, 284*n*54, 292*n*40
Durning-Lawrence, Sir Edward 291*n*1
Dutton, Richard 280*n*130, 280*n*132, 280*n*133, 280*n*136, 280*n*138
Dyer, Sir Edward 208

Eagleton, Terry 286*n*23
Edmund Ironside 24, 32, 37, 46, 50, 115, 116, 136, 137, 139, 202, 268*n*25
Edward II 150, 206, 285*n*71
Edward III 32, 33, 48, 115, 116, 136, 137, 139, 190, 202, 283*n*30
Edward VI 8, 14, 31
Edwards, Richard 31, 38, 39, 115, 273*n*1, 286*n*19
Edwards, Thomas 153, 281*n*152
Egan, Michael 33, 269*n*49
Egeon 83
Elderton, William 171
Elizabeth I 17, 19, 23, 25, 28, 35, 85, 89, 923, 99, 109, 182, 184, 196, 198, 203, 269*n*49, 274*n*4, 283*n*40
"Elmond milord of Oxfort" 59
Elyot, Sir Thomas 7, 14, 267*n*8
Emaricdulfe 44, 270*n*71
"Endymion" 91
England, Martha W. 289*n*62
England's Helicon 40
English language 18
"English Seneca" 169
"English Terence" 161
Erasmus 47, 173
Essex, Robert, 2nd Earl of 116, 181, 181ff, 196, 255, 269*n*49, 272*n*32, 283*n*28
"Euphues" 91, 169, 171
Euripides 47, 215
Evans, Henry 91, 109
Everett, Barbara 267*n*14
Every Man in His Humour 108, 200, 250
Every Man Out of His Humour 5, 28, 103, 151, 154, 161, 192, 199, 237, 24 249, 251ff, 255, 256, 258, 262, 266*n*20, 283*n*26, 292*n*42, 293*n*53, 293*n*55
An Exposition on the Epistle of St. Paul to the Ephesians 122

Family of Love 108
The Famous Victories of Henry V 32, 33, 87, 115, 116, 117, 135, 136, 137, 152, 173, 190, 202
Farmer, John 53
Farmer, Richard 222, 289*n*59, 289*n*60, 289*n*71

Ferrys, Edward 276n34
Feuillerat, Albert 285n11
Ficino, Massilio 271n10
1569 rebellion 33, 270n57
Flecknoe, Richard 218, 288n48
Fleming, Abraham 9
Fletcher, John 31, 115, 120, 141, 202, 203ff, 219, 286n18, 286n21
Fletcher, Lawrence 256, 257
Florio, John 51, 194, 271n19, 280n144, 284n56
Ford, John 141
Forman, Simon 138
Fox, Levi 262, 294n85
Fraser, Lady Antonia 4, 265n14
French civil wars, politics 19, 21, 49, 98, 104, 114
Freud, Sigmund 229
Fuller, Jean O. 288n46, 288n58
Fuller, Thomas 218

Gadshill incident 26, 33, 80, 87, 152, 276n20
Gardiner, Stephen (Bishop) 222
Gardner, Edward G. 272n38, 275n15
Garnett, Richard, and Gosse, Edmund 30, 123, 269n38, 278n104
Garrick, David 222, 223, 289n61, 289n62
Gascoigne, George 29ff, 44, 49, 61, 102, 139, 208, 216, 269n33, 270n54
Geneva Bible 23
George, David 293n54
George Shakebag 34, 88, 152
Gepp, Edward 14, 267n5
Gidley, Fran 120, 240, 278n98, 291n16
Gielgud, Sir John 143, 276n41
Gifford, William 287n37
Gilvary, Kevin 123, 266n14, 267n14, 294n73
Gismonde of Salerne 127, 139, 279n107
The Globe 14, 70, 138, 190, 201, 256, 259, 260, 261, 274n6, 280n126, 293n61, 294n70, 294n77
Golding, Arthur 9, 9, 15, 23, 30
Goldstein, Gary 14, 148, 267n5
Googe, Barnabe 61
Gorboduc 51, 94, 127, 139, 143, 208, 223, 224, 273n1, 289n66
Gordon, Helen 289n58
Gosson, Stephen 1, 10, 71ff, 100, 101, 134, 139, 225, 227, 265n6, 274n10, 274n11, 274n12, 274n14, 275n21, 279n114
Gowry 200, 285n8
Grandage, Michael 164
Granthan, Henry 9
Granville-Barker, Harley 135, 279n117, 279n118, 280n124
The Greek Anthology 48
Green, Nina 208, 267n3, 267n10, 268n24, 268n27, 269n31, 275n13, 277n48, 284n54, 285n11, 286n12, 286n25, 293n64, 294n70
Greenblatt, Stephen 4, 265n17
Greene, Robert 3, 40, 65, 72, 96, 140, 150, 158, 159, 168, 169, 198, 224, 225, 227, 227, 240ff, 266c2n1, 273n1, 282n15, 283n53, 290n77, 291n3, 291n18, 292n19, 274n30, 274n32, 293n63, 294n70
Greene, Thomas 262
Greenhill, Rima 277n46
Gregory Smith, G. 285n4, 287n37, 288n48
Greville, Fulke 113, 208, 262
"Groupist" theories 266c2n1
Guicciardini, Francesco 268n24
Gunpowder Plot (1605) 192, 193
Guy of Warwick 258

Hachette, Thomas 15
Haddon, Walton 222
Hall, Dr. John 262, 263, 288n39, 293n53
Hall, Joseph (Bishop) 28, 84, 122, 159, 160, 173, 193, 270n54, 275n15, 281n151, 281n161ff, 283n38, 283n40
Hallam, Henry 228, 289n68, 290n74, 290n75, 293n56
Halliday, Frank E. 201, 265n14, 285n10, 288n46, 293n63
Halliwell Phillipps, James O. 274n4, 289n68, 293n63
Hamill, John 55, 58, 272n30, 272n33, 272n35, 278n81, 278n82
Hamilton, Donna B. 277n52
Hamlet 3, 37, 38, 48, 57, 60, 92, 93, 109, 120, 127, 129, 130, 135, 135, 136 137, 141, 145, 151, 153, 154, 155, 156, 157, 164, 169, 170, 191, 192, 199 (illus.), 204, 225, 228, 254, 257, 265n5, 271n39, 276n32, 284n52, 287n29
Hamlet (character) 60, 92, 156
Harthacanute 122, 137, 202
Harvey, Gabriel 27, 66, 76ff, 90, 91, 102, 164, 171, 173, 173, 270n53, 273n9, 286n13, 287n32
Hattaway, Michael 271n10
Hatton, Sir Christopher 28, 29, 31, 132, 269n33
Hawkins, Harriett 172, 282n11
Hazlitt, William 226
Hazlitt, William C. 72, 274n13, 274n16, 282n14, 291n6
Hedingham Castle 13, 89, 151, 175
Hemmings, John 213, 250, 256, 256, 258, 259, 262, 294n69
Heneage, Sir Thomas 109, 181, 254
Henrietta Maria, Queen 263, 295n90
Henry of Navarre, IV of France 98, 114
Henry, Prince of Wales 33
Henry III of France 53, 101, 114, 123, 278n89
Henry IV 190; 1 *Henry IV* 22, 33, 87, 111, 116, 131, 132, 133, 136, 137, 152, 190, 225, 228, 267n5, 280n128, 280n138; 2 *Henry IV* 33, 111, 116, 136, 137, 148, 154, 190, 225, 236, 267n5, 281n153, 282n11, 292n27
Henry V 33, 48, 111, 116ff, 132, 133, 136, 137, 182, 190, 191, 192, 225, 271n10, 276n26, 278n95, 283n31; 1 *Henry VI* 22, 34, 48, 118,

128, 131, 136, 137, 202, 280*n*138; *2 Henry VI*
  34, 119, 122, 126, 131, 136, 137, 148, 190,
  225, 282*n*11, 292*n*27; *3 Henry VI* 34, 47,
  116, 119, 126, 131, 136, 137, 190, 225, 243,
  289*n*71
Henry VII, First Book of the Preservation of King 66
Henry VIII 120, 136, 137, 138, 202, 203, 224, 212, 286*n*17
Henslowe, Philip 263
Hero and Leander 149, 153
Hess, W. Ron 272*n*28, 283*n*36, 283*n*57
Heywood, Jasper 8
Heywood, Thomas 68, 273*n*14
Hoffman, Calvin 277*n*43
Holden, Anthony 220, 289*n*55
Holinshed, Raphael 26, 63, 114, 118ff, 227, 278*n*97
Holland, H.H. 277*n*57
Holland, Hugh 162, 212
Holland, Peter 232, 290*n*1
Holmes, Edward 42, 270*n*70
Holmes, William 250
Homer 3, 47, 48, 219, 223
Honan, Park 4, 88, 256, 265*n*16, 266*n*25, 276*n*22, 279*n*109, 292*n*27, 292*n*28, 293*n*54, 293*n*56, 293*n*61, 293*n*62, 293*n*63, 294*n*86
Honigman, Ernst A.J. 269*n*47, 278*n*98
Hopkins, Lisa 6, 266*n*26
Horestes 22, 30, 143, 278*n*96, 280*n*139
Hoseley, Richard 96, 276*n*40, 280*n*127
Howard, Henry (later Earl of Nottingham) 59, 85ff
Howell, Thomas 15
Hudson, Thomas 62
Hughes, Thomas 140
A Hundred Sundry Flowers 31, 61
Hunsdon, Lord Henry 274*n*4

I.M. 162, 211, 287*n*32
I.M.S. 216, 288*n*41
Imlay, Elizabeth 53, 273*n*23
Italy 1, 32, 46ff, 106 (illus.)

Jack Straw 139
James VI and I 62, 113, 193, 200, 203, 209, 211 256, 284*n*43, 285*n*7, 293*n*62
Jaques 105, 189
Jew of Malta 100, 150, 274*n*16
Jimenez, Ramon 32, 34, 63, 96, 115, 247, 262, 271*n*52, 271*n*63, 276*n*39, 280*n*140, 292*n*36, 294*n*85, 295*n*89
Johnson, Dr. Samuel 64, 70, 222ff, 224, 227, 238, 266*n*20, 287*n*30, 288*n*52, 288*n*60
Johnson, Philip 54, 272*n*57
Jolly, Emma 265*n*9, 267*n*6, 272*n*21, 276*n*33, 277*n*60, 279*n*109
Jones, Richard F. 7, 266*c*1*n*1, 272*n*1
Jonson, Ben v, 5, 28, 35, 46, 141, 162, 165, 192, 199, 200, 202, 204, 205, 205, 206,
211ff, 216, 219, 220, 224, 237, 246, 249, 250, 251ff, 256, 262, 272*n*28, 283*n*26, 286*n*14, 286*n*21, 286*n*22, 287*n*26, 287*n*34, 287*n*36, 287*n*37, 292*n*44, 292*n*45, 293*n*52, 293*n*60
Jowett, Benjamin, academic 48, 271*n*10
Julius Caesar 108, 128, 129, 136, 157, 192, 202, 225, 288*n*22
Justinus 266*n*3

Kail, Aubrey C. 284*n*46
Kamm, Oliver 279*n*109
Kathman, David 246, 292*n*31
Kemp(e), William 181, 254, 255, 256
Keysar v. Burbage 259, 294*n*71
Kidd (Kyd, Kydd), Thomas 3, 59, 72, 96, 141, 169, 169, 215, 224, 225, 227, 266*c*2*n*1, 274*n*1, 287*n*36
Kiernan, Pamela 274*n*13, 292*n*19
King, Rosalind 269*n*47
King John 32, 96, 116, 122, 135, 136, 137, 137, 139, 146, 155, 189, 190, 202, 225, 270*n*47
King Lear 22, 37, 63, 114, 136, 137, 137, 139, 148, 161, 173, 191, 201, 225, 228, 278*n*89, 278*n*90, 285*n*11
Knyvet, Sir Thomas 88, 179
Krapp, G.P. 97

"Labeo" 84, 173
"Laelius" 173
Lamb, Charles 226
Lamb, Mary E. 277*n*45
Lambin, Georges 277*n*60
Lane, John 251, 293*n*50
"L'autheur de la Lyre" 20
Lavin, J.A. 125, 138, 275*n*22, 280*n*125
Lear 115
Lee, Sir Sidney 30, 93, 276*n*34
Leicester, Robert, 1st Earl of 24, 25, 28, 35, 89, 92, 164, 196, 251, 269*n*30, 269*n*54, 269*n*73, 274*n*4, 276*n*26
Lennox, Matthew, 4th Earl of, and Countess 232, 37, 274*n*4, 276*n*26
Leontes 83, 161, 248
Levi, Peter 18ff
Lewis, Clive S. 1, 65, 70, 177, 265*n*2, 266*n*2, 271*n*2, 272*n*4, Ch 273*n*1, 275*n*1, 281*n*1, 282*n*19
Ligon, Katherine C. 282*n*13
Linacre, Thomas 222
Lloyd, W.F. 293*n*54
Locrine 140, 202, 280*n*129
Lodge, Thomas 65, 72, 140, 227, 273*n*11, 273*n*13
Logan, Robert 146, 280*n*142
Lok, Henry 49, 94, 99, 276*n*36
Lok, Michael 276*n*36, 277*n*48
The London Prodigal 202
A Lover's Complaint 131, 136, 201
Love's Labours Lost 41, 56, 57, 59, 69, 76, 88, 98ff, 123, 127, 129, 130, 130, 133, 144, 157,

190, 190, 200, 231, 236, 258, 276n21, 276n31, 277n49, 277n57, 278n104, 279n109, 287n36
Love's Labours Won 190
Lyly, John 1, 2, 3, 9, 41, 53, 57, 66, 72, 77, 90, 91, 96, 141, 162, 169, 215, 216, 227, 227, 266c2n1, 273n1, 276n21, 276n31, 277n74, 287n36
Lyly, William 222
"Lynceus" 27, 77, 89
"Lynx" 27, 77, 89

Macbeth 32, 37, 48, 90, 96, 113, 137, 149, 150, 161, 191, 192, 193, 195, 202, 228, 284n43, 293n56
Machiavelli, Nicolò 11, 58
"Maecenas" 171
Magri, Noemi 54, 58ff, 85, 101, 111, 122, 272n26, 272n29, 276n16, 276n38, 277n42, 277n49, 277n50, 277n51, 278n81
Maguin, Jean-Marie 284n56
Malim, Richard C.W. 267n14, 272n28, 276n20, 292n43, 294n73, 294n79
Malone, Edmund 2, 3, 5, 5, 146, 191, 224ff, 228, 265n4, 265n8, 267n14, 280n144, 285n59, 289n60, 289n63, 289n64, 289n65, 289n68, 289n69, 289n70, 289n71, 291n3
Manningham, John 251, 293n53
Markham, Gervase 227
Marlowe, Christopher 1, 2, 3, 72, 96, 100, 135, 141, 143, 145ff, 153, 159, 162, 206, 215, 216, 224, 225, 225, 227, 227, 228, 242, 266c2n1, 265n2, 273n1, 274n16, 279n116, 280n135, 280n140, 280n142, 281n161, 288n39, 289n65, 289n71, 290n77, 292n29; as follower of Shakespeare 73, 74, 75, 140, 156, 169
Marston, John 28, 159, 174, 200, 206, 211 228, 282n16, 282n23, 285n9, 290n77
Martindale, Charles, and Michelle 48, 271n12
Mary I 14, 17, 31
Mary, Queen of Scots 85, 90
Mattingly, Garrett 33, 269n48, 276n26
McAlindon, Thomas 33
McCarthy, Penny 278n101
Measure for Measure 59, 57, 83, 104, 122, 161, 191, 192, 199, 202, 225
"Melicert" 197
"Melicertus-Maximus" 198
The Merchant of Venice 49, 52, 57, 58, 59, 71, 72, 89, 99, 132, 146, 146, 148, 190, 199, 200, 225, 271n3
Mercutio 88
Meres, Francis 65, 190, 208, 218, 278n89, 279n122, 284n44, 285n4; his playlist as evidence against Oxford's authorship 198
The Merry Wives of Windsor 5, 15, 25, 37, 91, 110, 111, 117, 127, 129, 136, 149, 191, 191, 199, 236, 248, 251, 256, 292n47
Metamorphoses 9, 15, 30ff, 46, 170, 186, 259

Middleton, Thomas 203, 212
A Midsummer Night's Dream 5, 48, 108, 109, 136, 147, 157, 159, 170, 191, 229
Miller, Ruth 108, 277n55
Milton, John 75, 216, 288n40
Montagu family 269n30
Montaigne, Michel de 14, 194, 281n164, 284n56
Moore, Peter 267n3, 276n24, 281n167, 283n28, 288n43, 291n15, 292n22
More, Sir Thomas 222, 281n157
Mountjoy *see* Bellott v Mountjoy
Much Ado About Nothing 83, 86, 88, 107, 132, 136, 150, 277n54, 277n67
Mulcaster, Robert 1, 2, 63ff, 74, 75, 223, 227, 276n21
Munday, Anthony 41, 101, 277n52
The Murder of Gonzago 111
Murderous Michael see *Arden of Feversham*
Murphy on Evidence 266n24
Murry, John M. 280n142ff, 290n77
"Musodorus" 173
"Mutius" 175

Naseeb Shaheen 51, 271n18, 272n20
Nash(e), Thomas 3, 27, 65, 72, 77, 122, 135, 150, 158, 159, 159, 168ff, 216, 227, 241, 242, 245, 273n5, 273n9, 275n1, 281n2, 281n4, 282n13, 292n44
Neale, John E. 276n17
Nelson, Alan H. 13, 42, 82, 83, 86, 88, 164, 227, 267n3, 268n17, 270n69, 271n6, 271n15, 273n9, 275n1, 275n13, 276n25, 276n31, 281n159
Neville, Alexander 8
Neville, Sir Henry 266c2n1, 284n48
Newcastle, Duchess of 218
Nichol-Smith, D. 288n50, 288n51, 288n52, 288n53, 289n56
Nicholl, Charles 27, 59, 269n32, 293n66
Nicoll, Allardyce 1, 38, 52, 74, 138, 195, 236, 239, 265n3, 265n7, 266n21, 270n62, 272n22, 275n24, 279n119, 280n124, 285n59, 291n7, 293n63
"Nisus" 173
No-body and Some-body 267n9
Norfolk, Thomas, 4th Duke of 25, 31, 268n22, 268n24, 269n49
North, Thomas 48
Nowell, Lawrence 18, 50
Nuttall, Andrew D. 46, 229, 271n4, 287n37, 290n77

O'Brien, H.H. Judge Patrick 267n6
Ogburn, Charles 162, 254, 268n15, 281n166, 283n27, 288n44, 292n20, 293n57
Ostler v Hemmings 258, 259
Othello 48, 52, 107, 132, 136, 161, 191, 199, 201, 201, 209, 228
Ovid 9, 198
Ovid's Fable of Narcissus 15, 30

Oxford, Anne, Countess of 24, 25, 82, 92, 95, 122, 158, 268*n*26, 282*n*11, 289*n*38
Oxford, 9th Earl of 115
Oxford, 11th Earl of 33, 115
Oxford, 12th Earl of 116
Oxford, 13th Earl of 116, 119, 208
Oxford, 15th Earl of 99, 100 (illus.)
Oxford, 16th Earl of 13, 14, 17
Oxford, Edward, 17th Earl of: acting 53, 150ff, 179, 191; alliteration references 17, 174, 179, 184, 283*n*23; anonymous or attributed works see A of Tables of Literary References; appearance 22 (illus.), 177; biographic references 17; birth 13; book purchases 23; burial 198; character 15, 25, 26, 60, 76ff, 152, 163, 275*n*3, 277*n*48, 283*n*28; countryside, gardening, etc. 268*n*27, 279*n*115; court entertainments 87; dating of plays 17, 32, 52; death 195; dedications 23, 23; education 14ff, 32, 48; finances 25, 89, 92, 158, 176, 181, 209, 283*n* 26, 283*n*40, 292*n*26; first marriage and family problems 24, 25, 82ff; geography 18, 54, 58, 97, 272*n*28, 277*n*50; gloomy period 93, 276*n*34; habitual rewriting 37, 38, 93, 137, 144, 279*n*109; health 23, 88, 93, 97, 164, 179, 191, 276*n*24; Italy 32, 46ff, 106 (illus.), 276*n*33; language skills 16 (illus.), 17, 18, 32, 46ff; law 22, 32, 53; letters 14, 16 (illus.), 49, 53, 60, 82, 88, 93, 94, 164; libraries, access to 14, 17, 52, 93, 158, 276*n*33; military experience 23, 89; music 53; Netherlands 89, 281*n*151; poetry 31, 38ff, 58, 209; pseudonyms and other references see C and D in Tables of Literary References; religious views 27, 195, 285*n*61; second marriage 175, 176, 268*n*26; spy 27, 28, 85, 96, 122, 153, 193, 196; word coinage 32
Oxford, Henry, 18th Earl of 176, 209, 210 (illus.)
Oxford Dictionary of English Biography 290*n*2

Paget, Henry, 2nd Lord 208
Pain of Pleasure 41
Painter, William 12, 26
Palamon and Arcite see *Two Noble Kinsmen*
Paradise of Dainty Devices 31, 38, 39
Parnassus plays 254
Parris, Matthew 197
Passionate Pilgrim 184, 190
The Passionate Shepherd to his Love 149
Paul, Christopher 277*n*64
Peacham, Henry, Jr. 206ff, 207 (illus.)
Peacham, Revd Henry, Sr. 35, 36 (illus.), 63, 122, 206, 225, 227, 286*n*23, 286*n*24
Pearsall Smith, Logan 72, 274*n*17
Peele, George 3, 72, 96, 140, 170, 224, 225, 227, 273*n*1, 290*n*77, 292*n*25
Pembroke, Mary Countess of see Sidney, Mary
Pembroke, William, 3rd Earl of 209, 211, 287*n*27

Percival, Lance 282*n*21
Pericles 60, 83, 95, 136, 137, 138, 191, 195, 201, 202, 203, 212
Pericles (character) 60, 83, 95
Perrucci, A. 59, 272*n*38
Pettie, George 63
Phaer, Thomas 61, 279*n*116
Phelps, Gilbert 66, 273*n*11
Phillip II 35, 89, 98, 270*n*57
Phillips, Augustine 183, 250, 255, 256, 257, 259
Phillips, Edward, critic 75, 275, 275*n*26
The Phoenix and the Turtle 191
Phoenix Nest 46
Pilgrimage of Grace 33, 270*n*57
Pinter, Harold 191, 284*n*47
Pitcher, Seymour M. 33
plagiarism 4, 225
Plato 15, 271*n*10
Plautus 46, 271*n*3
The Play of Plays 71, 274*n*13
Plutarch 48
The Poetaster 287*n*37
Pointon, Anthony 291*n*2, 293*n*54
Pole, Cardinal Robert 222
Pollard, Alfred W. 283*n*39, 276*n*30
Pontano, Giovanni 275*n*15
"Pontian" 84
Pope, Alexander 220, 289*n*56, 289*n*57, 289*n*58
Pope, Thomas 250, 257, 258, 259, 293*n*63
Postumus 83, 95
Poullain, Patricia 268*n*19
Pound, Ezra 30
Powell, Enoch 198
Prechter, Robert R. 15, 267*n*9
Preston, Thomas 139, 143, 278*n*96
Price, Diana 200, 235, 241, 249, 251, 251, 254, 254, 260, 261, 266*n*10, 267*n*10, 281*n*164, 286*n*9, 287*n*32, 291*n*2, 291*n*15, 291*n*18, 292*n*21, 292*n*23, 292*n*25, 293*n*48, 293*n*56, 293*n*57, 293*n*58, 294*n*74, 294*n*76, 294*n*87
Prince, Frank T. 260, 294*n*73
"Prince Tudor" theory 269*n*30
Prospero 195
"Puntarvolo" 200
The Puritan Widow 202
Puttenham, George 40, 44, 65, 93, 123ff, 139, 197, 208, 218, 270*n*66, 276*n*34, 279*n*110ff, 285*n*1
Pykeryng, John 22

Quainton, Malcolm 268*n*19
Quennell, Peter 258, 294*n*68

Raleigh, Sir W. 73, 88, 111, 195, 222, 245, 275*n*19, 286*n*17, 289*n*60, 290*n*94, 292*n*30
The Rape of Lucrece 3, 28, 31, 55, 57 (illus.), 159, 170, 177, 186, 187, 198, 198, 209, 227, 247, 254, 259, 260
Recorde, Robert 8

Rich or Riche, Barnabe(y) 10, 78, 163, 227, 275n9
Richard II 33, 34, 38, 115, 136, 137, 148, 155, 183, 190, 190, 225, 255, 269n49, 279n120
Richard III 32, 33, 38, 116, 120, 131, 136, 137, 139, 156, 176, 190, 190, 225
Ridolfi plot 25
Robinson, Alan 292n34, 293n49
Rollett, John 122, 184, 185, 278n101, 283n33, 283n35
Romano, Giulio 56 (illus.), 57 (illus.), 58, 187
Romeo and Juliet 40, 58, 88, 105, 127, 130, 136, 172, 173, 190, 190, 227, 267n10, 271n17, 277n61, 289n68, 292n42
Romeus and Juliet 15, 30, 266n10
Ronsard, Pierre 18ff, 32, 49, 51, 91, 139, 268n19, 275n10
Rookwood, Ambrose 193, 196
Roper, David 35
"Roscius" 170
Rosicrucians 222, 261, 294n82
Rowe, Nicholas 2, 219, 220, 224, 281n1, 283n40, 288n54
Roydon, Michael 170
Rubinstein, William D., and James, Brenda 235, 283n34, 288n38, 291n2
Rushton, William L. 124, 136, 279n110
Russell, Bertrand 2
Russell, Thomas 213, 287n33
Rutland, Roger, 5th Earl of 261, 266c2n1

Sackville *see* Buckhurst, Lord Thomas Sackville
St. Bartholomkew's Day massacre 114, 278n88
St. Paul 215
St. Peter 107
Saintsbury, George 10, 66, 69, 141, 142, 143, 266n8, 266n9, 273n8, 273n13, 273c5n1, 274n3, 278n76, 279n111, 280n131, 280n137, 280n140
Salingar, Leo G. 68, 273n14
Sams, Eric 4, 33, 38, 50, 265n13, 269n48, 270n63, 271n16
Saunders, B.R. 108, 277n68
Saunders, Sam C. 30
Savile, Henry 10
Schoenbaum, Samuel 4, 4, 75, 188, 220, 222, 223, 224, 226, 228, 259, 265n8, 265n11, 265n12, 266n18, 272n4, 273n27, 276n23, 280n143, 281n1, 284n42, 288n54, 289n57, 289n59, 289n63, 289n64, 289n5, 289n68, 289n74, 289n75, 291n8, 292n28, 292n29, 292n32, 293n63, 294n71
Schönfeld, S.J. 271n13
Schurink, Fred 288n38
Scotsman, an unknown i, 60, 272n38
The Second Blast of Retrait from Plays and Theatres 274n15
Sejanus 141
Seneca 8, 215
Shakespeare: as a pseudonym 78

Shakespeare, John 261, 294n80
Shakespeare, Susanna 236, 261, 263
Shakespeare, William 1ff, 55, 181, 183, 188ff, 211, 213, 216, 220, 235ff, 254ff, 261, 262, 263, 266c2n1; as actor 151, 163, 206, 255, 281n160; arms, motto 5, 151, 191, 249ff, 292n40, 292n43, 292n44; attitude to canon 162, 216, 240, 262, 290n84; Blackfriars Gate purchase 261, 294n78; business dealings and career in Stratford 159, 188, 191, 246, 247, 260, 271n14; defaulting ratepayer 188, 251; education 236ff, 271n1, 291n8, 291n9; effigy in Church at Stratford 262, 294n85, 294n86, 294n88; hoarder, speculator 151, 252, 294n75; hyphen in Shakespeare 235, 287n32, 288n40; illiterate family 291n5; impresa 261; Janssen engraving 125 (illus.); Lancashire theory 238, 261, 291n11; literary references *see* literary reference tables; Phillips legacy 257; in London 55, 152, 154, 246ff, 283n40, 292n35, 293n66, 294n76; as plagiarist 225; as poacher 248; signatures 221 (illus.), 239, 291n15; spelling of name 235; will 262, 294n83
Shapiro, James 5, 204, 265n4, 266n22, 267n12, 275n12, 281n153, 281n154, 285n5, 286n20, 291n3, 293n60
Shaw, George Bernard 145
Shell, Dr. Alison 294n79
Showerman, Earl 22, 268n22
Sidney, Mary, Countess of Pembroke 209, 211, 266c2n1
Sidney, Sir Philip 1, 2, 25, 37, 44, 45, 65, 66, 67, 71, 82, 109, 110, 111, 113, 117, 138, 139, 141, 141, 142, 142, 143, 164, 174, 188, 197, 216, 273n10, 280n131, 280n132, 280n133, 280n138, 281n167
The Silent Woman 141
Sir John Oldcastle 139, 202, 268n24
Sir Thomas More 73, 120, 137, 156, 157, 202, 239, 278n98, 281 157, 291n16
Sir Thomas More (character) 121, 156
1623 and later folio 125 (illus.), 162, 166 (illus.), 167 (illus.), 209, 211ff, 216, 292n26, 294n77
1640 edition of poems 217, 235, 292n35, 292n43
Skidmore, Christopher 269n30, 270n54, 274n4
Sly, William 250, 256, 257, 258, 293n63
Smith, Sarah 270n68
Smith, Sir Thomas 14, 15, 17, 18, 19, 20, 49, 61, 77, 222
Smith, William 88, 276n23
Sobran, Joseph 31, 41, 44, 270n72
Socrates 48, 262, 271n10
Somerset, Edward, 1st Duke of 14
Sonnet nos. 1–126 283n33
Sonnet no.1 186
Sonnet no.3 26, 177
Sonnet no.10 177, 178
Sonnet no.20 177, 180

Sonnet no.22 180
Sonnet no.25 180
Sonnet no.29 180
Sonnet no.33 58
Sonnet no.36 178
Sonnet no.37 88, 178
Sonnet no.55 179
Sonnet no.62 82, 180
Sonnet no.66 88
Sonnet no.69 182
Sonnet no.72 179
Sonnet no.73 180
Sonnet no.74 88
Sonnet no.76 179
Sonnet nos. 78–86 181
Sonnet no.81 180
Sonnet no.84 182, 294n88
Sonnet nos. 87–100 181
Sonnet no.87 182
Sonnet no.89 88
Sonnet no.94 182, 283n30
Sonnet no.95 182
Sonnet no.97 22
Sonnet nos. 107–126 283n34
Sonnet no.107 181, 184, 283n34
Sonnet no.110 160, 179
Sonnet no.111 179
Sonnet no.112 160
Sonnet no.121 180
Sonnet no.125 184
Sonnet no.126 179, 185
Sonnet nos. 127–154 185
Sonnet no 130 91, 185, 283n36
Sonnet no.136 42
Sonnet no.138 185
Sonnet no.139 42
Sonnet nos.153 and 154 48, 185, 283n37
sonnets: 31, 58, 109, 122, 202, 217, 235, 259, 261; dedication 183, 282n20, 283n33
Soothern, John 20, 67, 80, 268n20, 273n12
Southampton, Mary, Countess of 26, 32, 109, 177, 181, 254
Southampton, Henry, 2nd Earl of 32, 37, 269n30
Southampton, Henry, 3rd Earl of 26, 27 (illus.), 109, 177ff, 209, 210 (illus.), 249, 254, 258, 260, 269n30, 282n21, 283n28, 283n39, 283n40
Southwell, Francis 85, 86, 276n18
Southwell, Robert 86, 196, 276n18
Spanish marriage crisis 209, 285n7
The Spanish Maze see *The Tempest*
Spencer, Charles 76, 164
Spencer, Edmund 1, 2, 65, 66, 105, 141, 144, 153, 158, 164ff, 170, 171, 197, 198, 208, 214, 214, 216, 223, 226, 270n73, 273n10, 276n18, 287n32
Spingarn, Joel E. 288n39
Spurgeon, Caroline 267n7
Stafford, Sir Edward 49
Stanyhurst, Richard 66
Stratford-upon-Avon 294n85

Stratford-upon-Avon Grammar School 262, 271n1, 291n1
Stritmatter, Robert, and Kositzky, Lynne 268n23, 275n12, 278n104, 284n55
Strype, John 15
Sturmius, Johannes 53, 78, 275n5
Sturtevant 277n49
stylometrics 37ff, 122, 279n103, 279n122
Suckling, Sir John 219
Suffolk, Katherine, Duchess of 83
Surrey (character) 121, 156
Surrey, Henry, Earl of 11, 121, 216, 266n9, 278n100
Sussex, Thomas, 3rd Earl of 23, 87, 274n4
Swank, Lowell J. 278n80
Swinburne, Algernon 152

Talbot, Gilbert 276n20
1 and 2 *Tamberlaine* 3, 73, 144, 146, 147, 147, 148, 149, 275n19, 281n161
The Taming of (a) the Shrew 37, 38, 57, 59, 96, 99, 137, 155, 157, 159, 189, 191, 202, 225, 236, 247, 248, 292n36, 292n37, 292n38, 292n42, 294n74
Tarica, Alan 285n57
Tarleton, Richard 220, 289n55
Tate, Nahum 288n52
Taylor, Gary 274n8
The Tempest 105, 123, 138, 161, 191, 193ff, 200, 202, 209, 284n46, 284n53, 284n54, 285n5
Tennant, David 76
theatres 12, 69ff, 87; suppression of (1642) 218
Theobald, Lewis 203
Theocritus 270n73, 271n12
Third Blast of Retrait from Plays and Theatre 282n14
Thomas Lord Cromwell 212
Thomas of Woodstock 33, 115, 133, 136, 137, 139, 202, 206, 268n24, 278n93, 278n120
Thompson, J.A.K. 48, 48, 271n9, 271n11
Thomson, Peter 119, 279n113, 285n5
Thorpe, Thomas 184
Three Sisters of Mantua 115, 122, 202, 278n102
Throckmorton, Sir Nicholas 19
Throckmorton plot 86
Tillyard, Eustace M.W. 238, 291n11
Tilney, Edward 73, 275n18
Timon (character) 91
Timon of Athens 22, 47, 91, 94, 131, 136, 137, 191, 202, 203, 212, 225, 228
Titian 58, 187 (illus.), 280n138
Titus Andronicus 21, 35, 36 (illus.), 47, 63, 122, 135, 136, 146, 186, 189, 190, 284n44
Tobin, John 172, 282n11
Tooley, Nicholas 257
"Torquato" 272n37
"Torquatus" 282n16
Touchstone 105, 189
tournament poetry 26, 41, 82
Trentham family 173, 176 (illus.), 282n17
Troilus and Cressida 48, 109, 126, 130, 134,

138, 148, 161, 183, 192, 201, 202, 229, 283n32, 285n11
Tucker Brooke, C.F. 280n129, 280n157, 291n17
Turberville, George 208
Twelfth Night 37, 38, 52, 59, 88, 102, 110, 121, 133, 136, 202
Two Gentlemen of Verona 41, 59, 84, 97, 128, 172, 173, 190, 202, 276n38
Two Noble Kinsmen 31, 40, 115, 136, 137, 138, 202, 203ff, 212, 287n19, 287n20
Tyndale, William 61

Ubaldinas, Patruchius 276n37
Underdown, Thomas 23
Urbino, Francesco Maria della Rovere, Duke of 57, 58 (illus.), 111
"Ur-Hamlet" theory 4, 265n10

"Vain Delight" 29
Valentine 84
Vasari, Giorgio 58
Vavasour, Ann 88, 177
Venus and Adonis 3, 31, 58ff, 65, 87, 153, 159, 170, 177, 186, 187, 198, 209, 227, 247, 249, 254, 259, 260, 272n29, 273n7, 282n16, 294n73
Vicars, John 216
Vicars, Thomas 215
Virgil 219, 262, 287n37, 293n52
"Virgil" (as pseudonymous reference) 251, 287n37

Walpole, Horace 218, 288n45
Walsingham, Sir Thomas 85, 86, 89, 196, 268n18, 279n113
War of the Pamphlets 77, 122, 173
Ward, Bernard M. 269n44
Warner, William 216
Warwick, Ambrose, 3rd Earl of 87, 152
Watson, Robert N. 277n58, 277n70
Watson, Thomas 91, 276n29, 283n36
Webbe, Edward 44, 65, 66, 139
Webster, John 141, 201, 285n10
Weever, John 198, 285n3

Weir, Alison 281n157
Weis, Réné 239, 292n39
Wells, Stanley 203, 267n14; and Edmondson, Paul 198, 294n73; and Taylor, Gary 213, 214, 267n13, 278 6n90, 285n3, 287n32, 287n34, 288n40, 288n41
Werth, Alexander 48, 271n8, 271n9
Whalen, Richard 277n54, 287n33
Whetstone, George 227
Whibley, Charles 11, 265n14
Wickham, Glynne 15, 266n15
Wiggins, Martin 3, 70, 71, 73, 227, 228, 265n4, 266n6, 274n5, 274n7, 274n8, 274n11, 274n12, 274n14, 275n20, 275n21, 280n126, 286n21, 290n72, 290n73, 290n77
Wilkins, George 203, 293n66
"Will Monox" 171, 172
Willis, Charles M. 197, 279n110, 279n115, 285n1
Willobie, His Avisa see note at foot of C of the Tables of Literary References
Willoughby d'Eresby, Peregrine, 11th Lord 88, 96, 102, 109
"Willy" 168
Willy, Sir Richard 281n1
Wilson, Ian 262, 294n83
Wilson, Richard 232, 290n1
Wilson, Sir Thomas 11, 124, 279n111
Wilson Knight, George 247, 272n34, 276n34, 292n37
Windsor, Miles 31
The Winter's Tale 58, 83, 111, 128, 134, 136, 138, 138, 161, 191, 195, 202, 228, 236, 248, 272n28, 272n35, 280n138, 282n16, 291n9, 294n74
Witter v. Hemmings 258
Wood, Anthony à 218
Wood, Michael 261, 261
Worden, Blair 5, 232, 290n1
Wright, Dan 278n94
Wyatt, Sir Thomas 11, 216, 266n9

A Yorkshire Tragedy 34, 115, 136, 201, 202, 270n54, 274n13, 278n92, 285n11
Young, Alan 26, 41, 270n67

www.ingramcontent.com/pod-product-compliance
Ingram Content Group UK Ltd.
Pitfield, Milton Keynes, MK11 3LW, UK
UKHW041924140426
5217IPUK00014B/301